DATE DUE

The Catholic Tradition:
Mass and the Sacraments,
Vol. 1

The Catholic Tradition

REV. CHARLES J. DOLLEN
DR. JAMES K. McGOWAN
DR. JAMES J. MEGIVERN
EDITORS

The Catholic Tradition

Mass & the Sacraments

Volume 1

A Consortium Book

Manufactured in the United States of America

Library of Congress Card Catalog Number: 79-1977
ISBN: 0-8434-0738-7
ISBN: 0-8434-0725-5 series

The publisher gratefully acknowledges permission to quote from the following copyrighted sources. In cases where those properties contain scholarly apparatus such as footnotes, such footnotes have been omitted in the interest of the general reader.

ANDREWS AND McMEEL, INC.
Chapters 5, 6 and 7 from *The Spirit of the Liturgy* by Romano Guardini, translated by Ada Lane, 1935.

BURNS OATES AND WASHBOURNE LTD.
"Of the Sacrament of the Eucharist" from the *Summa Theologica* of St. Thomas Aquinas, translated by Fathers of the English Dominican Province, 1923; "Christmas" from *The Liturgical Year* by Prosper Guéranger, translated by Laurence Shepherd, 1927.

CAMBRIDGE UNIVERSITY PRESS
"Eucharistic Prayers" from *The Apostolic Tradition of Hippolytus*, translated by Burton Scott Easton, 1934.

THE CATHOLIC UNIVERSITY OF AMERICA PRESS, INC.
"Catechetical Lectures" from *The Fathers of the Church*, Volume 61, *The Works of St. Cyril of Jerusalem*, Volume I, translated by Leo P. McCauley, S.J. and Anthony A. Stephenson, copyright © 1969; *The Fathers of the Church*, Volume 64, *The Works of St. Cyril of Jerusalem*, Volume II, translated by Leo P. McCauley, S.J. and Anthony A. Stephenson, copyright © 1970; "The Mysteries" from *The Fathers of the Church*, Volume 44, *St. Ambrose: Theological and Domestic Works*, translated by Roy J. Deferrari, Ph.D., copyright ©1965.

M. H. GILL & SONS
On the Priesthood by St. John Chrysostom, translated by Patrick Boyle, C.M., 1910. Reprinted 1943 by The Newman Press.

FRANCIS X. GLIMM
"Didache" from *The Fathers of the Church*, Volume 1, *The Apostolic Fathers*, translated by Francis X. Glimm, Joseph M.-F. Marique, S.J., Gerald G. Walsh, S.J. Copyright 1947, The Catholic University of America Press, Inc. Copyright renewed 1975 by Francis X. Glimm, Joseph M.-F. Marique, S.J., Gerald G. Walsh, S.J. Reprinted by permission of Francis X. Glimm, the Estate of Joseph M.-F. Marique, S.J., and Gerald G. Walsh, S.J.

ESTATE OF JOSEPH M.-F. MARIQUE, S.J.
"Didache" from *The Fathers of the Church*, Volume 1, *The Apostolic Fathers*, translated by Francis X. Glimm, Joseph M.-F. Marique, S.J., Gerald G. Walsh, S.J. Copyright 1947, The Catholic University of America Press, Inc. Copyright renewed 1975 by Francis X. Glimm, Joseph M.-F. Marique, S.J., Gerald G. Walsh, S.J. Reprinted by permission of Francis X. Glimm, the Estate of Joseph M.-F. Marique, S.J., and Gerald G. Walsh, S.J.

THE MISSIONARY SOCIETY OF ST. PAUL THE APOSTLE IN THE STATE OF NEW YORK
Selections from *A Key to the Doctrine of the Eucharist* by Anscar Vonier, O.S.B., The Newman Press, 1925; Chapter 5 from *Mystery of Christian Worship* by Odo Casel, The Newman Press. Copyright 1962 Darton, Longman & Todd.

RICHWOOD PUBLISHING COMPANY
"Sentences" from *Peter Lombard and the Sacramental System* translated by Elizabeth Francis Rogers. 1976 reprint of 1917 edition published as author's thesis by Columbia University.

SOCIETY FOR PROMOTING CHRISTIAN KNOWLEDGE
"The Pilgrimage of Etheria" from *Translations of Christian Literature, Series III, Liturgical Texts* by M. L. McClure and C. L. Feltoe, D.D., 1919; "The Two Liturgical Uses of the Latin West" and "The Roman Mass" from *Christian Worship, Its Origin and Evolution* by Louis Duchesne, translated by M. L. McClure, 1927.

ST. ANTHONY GUILD PRESS
The Breviloquium from *The Works of Bonaventure*, translated by José de Vinck, copyright © 1963. Reprinted by permission of St. Anthony Guild Press.

GERALD G. WALSH, S.J.

"Didache" from *The Fathers of the Church*, Volume 1, *The Apostolic Fathers*, translated by Francis X. Glimm, Joseph M.-F. Marique, S.J., Gerald G. Walsh, S.J. Copyright 1947, The Catholic University of America Press, Inc. Copyright renewed 1975 by Francis X. Glimm, Joseph M.-F. Marique, S.J., Gerald G. Walsh, S.J. Reprinted by permission of Francis X. Glimm, the Estate of Joseph M.-F. Marique, S.J., and Gerald G. Walsh, S.J.

WESTMINSTER PRESS

"First Apology of Justin" from *The Library of Christian Classics*, Volume I, *Early Christian Fathers*, translated and edited by Cyril C. Richardson, Th.D., D.D., 1953; Paschasius Radbertus of Corbie: Selections from "The Lord's Body and Blood" from *The Library of Christian Classics*, Volume IX, *Early Medieval Theology*, translated and edited by George E. McCracken, Ph.D., F.A.A.R., 1957.

Table of Contents

VOLUME 1

Introduction

The Catholic Tradition is a 14 volume anthology of excerpts from the great Catholic writers from antiquity to the present day. *The Catholic Tradition* is intended for the armchair reader who has not studied theology or church history and has not time to struggle unassisted through 198 books. The publisher's intention is to provide such a reader with a compact home library that will permit him to familiarize himself with the great Catholic writers and their works. The works included in *The Catholic Tradition* are all religious in subject. The publisher did not include fiction or nonfiction books on secular subjects written by Catholic authors.

The Catholic Tradition arranges the writings according to religious subjects. There are seven religious subjects, each of which is covered in two volumes: The Church; Mass and the Sacraments; Sacred Scripture; The Saviour; Personal Ethics; Social Thought; and Spirituality. Within each subject, the writings are arranged in chronological order, which permits the reader to follow the development of Catholic thought across 2000 years.

Each excerpt in *The Catholic Tradition* is preceded by a brief biographical and explanatory introduction to help the reader understand the world in which the writer lived and wrote, and the problems with which he was dealing.

The selection of the excerpts and the writing of the introductions has been a long and difficult process. The task of making the final selections was particularly arduous (as such choices always are); the most modern authors, about whose writing there is yet no final judgment provoking the most debate. The selection of authors was made originally in the publisher's offices and then submitted to the three editors of the series who refined the selection. The editors submitted their selection to an unofficial board of scholars who very kindly made constructive comments.

The process of assembling the many hundreds of books from which to make the final selection was in itself a vast task. Many of the books under consideration were very scarce and not available in bookstores or libraries. The work of collecting the books and then making selections among them stretched over a three year period, and many books were selected for inclusion and later rejected after careful scrutiny and reflection.

The editing of *The Catholic Tradition* was a long and difficult job because the literature of Roman Catholicism is a vast and complex body. Of all the Christian denominations, the Roman Catholic Church is by far the oldest and largest. Its ranks include a tremendous number of saints and scholars, writers and thinkers, mystics and preachers: many of whom felt so strongly about their faith that they were willing to die for it. They have left an incomparably rich legacy of art and writing. Selecting from it is not simple.

The selections that we made are representative of the best of mainstream Catholic writing. Generally, they should be intelligible to a thoughtful layman. Some however, may prove more technical than others, and some of the very recent writers may seem controversial. The reader should bear in mind that some theological questions simply do not admit of facile answers, and that some of the earlier writers were considered controversial in their own days. It is also well to remember that the writings gathered here, brilliant and revered as their authors may be, are not necessarily official statements of Church policy. But they are, all of them, solidly part of the Catholic tradition.

The writers are all Catholics, many of them clergymen, some of them converts to Catholicism. They all wrote as loyal servants of the Church and from a Catholic point of view. When they wrote on personal ethics they proceeded from the assumption that man's goal was to imitate Christ, not simply to follow a secular set of ethical rules. When they wrote on social problems they expressed the need to solve social problems because they loved their neighbors, not for the material enrichment of society. Their writings on Christ reflect an intense struggle to bend human language to divine definition. Taken together, their writings form a literary tradition that is Roman Catholic at heart. That tradition has certain ingredients that are not present in the literary traditions of the other Christian denominations. Particularly, the heritage of liturgical ceremony and mystical contemplation have left an incomparable treasure of literature that is here presented in the volumes entitled *Mass and the Sacraments,* and *Spirituality*.

The whole corpus of Catholic thinking and writing, distilled here in *The Catholic Tradition,* is generally considered by scholars to have three important periods: the ancient, or patristic, period; the high middle-ages, which is the era of St. Thomas Aquinas and sometimes called the scholastic period; finally the time in which we live today, the last 100 years. These three epochs are golden ages of Catholic writing. They are separated from each other by the generally unproductive eras of the dark ages and the Reformation.

Through all these epochs the great Catholic writers have preserved and developed the Christian message: love God; love your fellow man. Each writer wrote conscious of the tradition behind him, conscious that he was building on the work of men before him, adapting their work to changed conditions or continuing their work on the outer edges of human speculation.

The present day writers, those of the third great era of Catholic writing, are the most important part of *The Catholic Tradition.* Here for the first time their thinking is presented along with the work of their predecessors; here can be seen the stunning achievement of today's Catholic writing, and how it follows logically from the writing of the patristic and scholastic thinkers.

The present day writers presented in *The Catholic Tradition* number 114, over half of the total number of writers chosen.

Their writing will probably prove more intelligible to the average reader because they write in today's idiom and they address contemporary problems.

Oddly enough, many if not most of the modern writers are not familiar to the average Catholic. St. Augustine, and St. Thomas Aquinas are household names, but only serious Catholic readers today are familiar with the masterful writings of Karl Rahner, Edward Schillebeeckx, Raymond Brown, and Gustavo Gutiérrez. None the less, these men are representative of a great historical flowering of Catholic writing today and their names may well echo down the ages.

THE PUBLISHER

Apostolic Writers
5th to 8th Centuries

The existence in the early Church of a work called The Instructions of the Apostles *is witnessed to by Eusebius of Caesarea in the 4th century. It was valued so highly by some that it nearly made its way into the New Testament. But it disappeared and remained lost until 1883 when an 11th century manuscript of it, discovered in 1875, was published. It became the darling of the critics for the next few decades, receiving such diverse interpretations and evaluations as to be bewildering. More recently, however, the debate about the Didache (Greek for "Teaching" or "Instruction") has settled down, although there are still disagreements over basic points.*

The Didache is the oldest source of church law which we possess. It may not be much later than the canonical Gospels, and its Jewish-Christian tone suggests an eastern origin, probably Egypt or Syria. In any event it is the prototype of all later collections of church law.

The entire work consists of sixteen chapters divided into four parts. The first part (1-6), the doctrine of the Two Ways: the way of life and the way of death, is not reprinted here. Some see this as the earliest part of the Didache which may even have been originally a short instruction for Jewish proselytes that was later revised for Christian use. The second part is the most interesting for our purposes. (chapters 7-10). It presents pre-

scriptions for the liturgy, especially baptism, fasting, prayer, and the Eucharist. Chapter 7 mandates baptism by immersion in running water as the preferred manner of administration, but allows pouring water on the head if immersion could not be done. This is the earliest reference to the modes of baptizing that has survived. In chapter 8 we find the Lord's Prayer with the final verse: "For power and glory are yours forever." This somehow made its way into some New Testament manuscripts as the end of Matthew's version and in this way appeared in the King James Version. It has thus served as a point of difference between English-speaking Protestants and Catholics for three and a half centuries.

The third part (chapters 11-15) is canonical, dealing with church discipline, the respect due the hierarchy, the prophets, and the traveling preachers. And the fourth part is the final chapter (16), an impassioned call for sobriety and vigilance in face of the imminent end. This intense eschatological emphasis argues for an early date and has few parallels. It is easy to see why some felt the work belonged with the others in the inspired collection that became the New Testament. Whatever its precise origin, it is one of the most intriguing of early Christian works, reflecting a Church still in a relatively primitive stage of formation.

DIDACHE

CHAPTER 7

Regarding baptism, baptize thus. After giving the foregoing instructions, 'Baptize in the name of the Father, and of the Son, and of the Holy Spirit' in running water. But if you have no running water, baptize in any other; and, if you cannot in cold water, then in warm. But, if the one is lacking, pour the other three times on the head 'in the name of the Father, and Son, and Holy Spirit.' But, before the baptism, let the one who baptizes and the one to be baptized fast, and any others who are able to do so. And you shall require the person being baptized to fast for one or two days.

CHAPTER 8

But do not let your fasts be with the hypocrites; for they fast on Monday and Thursday; but you shall fast on Wednesday and Friday. And do not pray as the hypocrites, but as the Lord directed in His Gospel, 'Thus shall you pray: "Our Father in heaven, hallowed be Thy name, Thy kingdom come, Thy will be done on earth just as in heaven; give us this day our bread from above, and forgive us our debt as we also forgive our debtors, and lead us not into temptation, but deliver us from evil," ' for Thine is the power and glory forever. Three times in the day pray thus.

CHAPTER 9

In regard to the Eucharist, you shall offer the Eucharist thus: First, in connection with the cup, 'We give Thee thanks, Our Father, for the holy vine of David Thy son, which Thou hast made known to us through Jesus Thy Son; to Thee be glory forever.' And in connection with the breaking of bread, 'We give Thee thanks, Our Father, for the life and knowledge which Thou hast revealed to us through Jesus Thy Son; to Thee be glory forever. As this broken bread was scattered upon the mountain tops and after being harvested was made one, so let Thy Church be gathered together from the ends of the earth into Thy kingdom, for Thine is the glory and the power through Jesus Christ forever.' But let no one eat or drink of the Eucharist with you except for those baptized in the name of the Lord, for it was in reference to this that the Lord said: 'Do not give that which is holy to dogs.'

CHAPTER 10

But, after it has been completed, give thanks in the following way: 'We thank Thee, holy Father, for Thy holy name which Thou hast caused to dwell in our hearts, and for the knowledge and faith and immortality, which Thou hast made known to us through Jesus thy Son; to Thee be glory forever. Thou, Lord Almighty, has created all things for Thy name's sake and hast given food and drink to men for their refreshment, so that they might render thanks to Thee; but upon us Thou hast bestowed spiritual food and drink, and life everlasting through Thy Son. For all things we render Thee thanks, because Thou art mighty; to Thee be glory forever. Remember, O Lord, Thy Church, deliver it from all evil and make it perfect in Thy love and gather it from the four winds, sanctified for Thy kingdom, which Thou hast prepared for it; for Thine is the power and the glory forever. Let grace come, and let this world pass away, "Hosanna to the God of David." If anyone is Holy, let him come; if anyone is not, let him repent. Marantha. Amen.' But allow 'prophets' to render thanks as they desire.

CHAPTER 11

If anyone, therefore, comes to you and teaches all the aforesaid things, receive him. But, if a wicked person comes and teaches another doctrine to contradict this, do not listen to him. But, if one teaches so as to increase justice and the knowledge of the Lord, receive him as the Lord.

In regard to 'apostles' and 'prophets,' act according to the doctrine of the Gospel. Let every apostle who comes to you be received as the Lord. But he shall not remain more than one day. But, if necessary, let him remain a second day. But, if he stays for three, he is a false prophet. And when the apostle departs, let him take only enough bread to last until he reaches shelter; but, if he asks for money, he is a false prophet.

And you shall not tempt any prophet who speaks in the spirit, or judge him; for every sin shall be forgiven, but this sin shall not be forgiven. But not everyone who speaks in the spirit is a prophet, but only if he follows the conduct of the Lord. Accordingly, from their conduct the false prophet and the true prophet will be known. No prophet who in the spirit orders a meal to be prepared eats of it; but, if he does, he is a false prophet. And every prophet who teaches the truth and fails to do what he teaches is a false prophet. Anyone who has been proved to be a true prophet and who does something purporting to be an outward mystery of the Church (so long as he teaches you not to do what he does) is not to be judged by you, for his judgment is with God. For the ancient prophets also acted in this manner. And, whoever says in spirit: 'Give me money,' or anything like it, do not listen to him. But, if he asks that it be given to others in need, let no one judge him.

CHAPTER 12

Let everyone who 'comes to you in the name of the Lord' be received; but, after testing him, you will know him, for you know right and wrong. If the one who comes to you is a traveler, help him as much as you can; but he shall not remain with you more than two or three days, unless there is need. But, if he wishes to settle among you and is a craftsman, let him work and eat. But, if he has no trade, provide according to your conscience, so that no Christian shall live among you idle. But, if he does not agree to do this, he is trading on the name of Christ; beware of such men.

CHAPTER 13

Every true prophet who desires to settle among you is worthy of his food. Likewise, a true teacher is worthy, as a workman, of his food. Accordingly, take all the first-fruits of the winepress and of the harvest, of the cattle and of the sheep, and give them to the prophets, for they are your high priests. But, if you have not a prophet, give it to the poor. If you make bread, take the first share and give according to the commandment. Likewise, when you open a jar of wine or oil, take and give the first share to the prophets. Also of silver and of clothes and every other possession, take the first share as it seems best to you and give according to the commandment.

CHAPTER 14

And on the Lord's Day, after you have come together, break bread and offer the Eucharist, having first confessed your offences, so that your sacrifice may be pure. But let no one who has a quarrel with his neighbor join you until he is reconciled, lest your sacrifice be defiled. For it was said by the Lord: 'In every place and time let there be offered to me a clean sacrifice, because I am the great king'; and also: 'and my name is wonderful among the Gentiles.'

CHAPTER 15

Elect, therefore, for yourselves bishops and deacons worthy of the Lord, humble men and not covetous, and faithful and well tested; for they also serve you in the ministry of the prophets and teachers. Do not, therefore, despise them, for they are the honored men among you, along with the prophets and teachers. And correct one another, not in anger but in peace, as you have it in the Gospel. And let no one speak with anyone who has harmed his neighbor, nor let him be heard until he repents. Offer your prayers and alms and do all things according to the Gospel of our Lord.

CHAPTER 16

'Be vigilant' over your life; 'let your lamps' not be extinguished, or your loins be ungirded, but be prepared, for you know not the hour in which our Lord will come. Come together frequently, and seek what pertains to your souls: for the whole time of your faith will not profit you, unless in the last hour you shall be found perfect. For, in the last days, false prophets and seducers will increase, and sheep will be turned into wolves, and charity will be changed into hate. For, as lawlessness grows, men will hate one another and persecute one another and betray one another, and then will appear the Deceiver of the world, as though he were the Son of God, and will work signs and wonders; and the world will be delivered into his hands, and he will do horrible things, which have not been done since the beginning of the world. Then shall all created men come to the fire of judgment, and 'many will be scandalized' and perish; but those who persevere in their faith will be saved from the curse itself. And then will appear the signs of the Truth: first, the sign of confusion in the heaven; second, the sign of the sound of the trumpet; and third, the resurrection of the dead—not the resurrection of all men, but, as it was said: 'The Lord will come and all His saints with Him.' Then shall the world see the Lord coming on the clouds of heaven.

St. Justin Martyr

100-165

Justin was born in Flavia Neapolis (ancient Shechem, modern Nablus) in Samaria of Greek parents early in the second century. He studied the various philosophies of the day—Stoic, Pythagorean, Peripatetic, Platonic—but found no real satisfaction until he met a Christian in Ephesus who introduced him to the Hebrew prophecies and demonstrated how they were fulfilled in Christ. Around 135 a.d. Justin himself became a Christian teacher and by 150 had moved on to Rome. There he wrote the only books that have survived from among a long list attributed to him in the early Church. They are his Apology, *part of which is given here, and his* Dialogue with Trypho. *He was martyred in Rome around 165 a.d.*

Justin is the most important of the second century apologists for the Christian faith. His nobility of character has always been attractive, even though his style of writing is not especially eloquent. His chief significance lies in the fact that he was the first to undertake a project that has ever since been a perennial challenge to Christian thinkers: he donned the philosopher's cloak and set out with the conviction that the full use of human reason would be a help, not a hindrance, to Christian faith. Thus, instead of fearing and fighting pagan philosophy, he takes Platonism and Stoicism and subjects them to critical evaluation, accepting their truth and correcting their errors. He sees this as a viable enterprise because of his belief that Christ, the divine Logos, is the universal reason in which all rational beings participate, however imperfectly.

His Apology *is addressed to Emperor Antonius and his colleagues. His purpose is to request the emperor to examine seriously the charges made against the Christians by their detractors. It is an appeal to Roman fairness, similar to that of St. Paul, asking Antonius to see for himself that Christians are really decent citizens, obeying the law, and giving no cause for condemnation.*

Justin's major Apology *consists of 68 chapters to which three letters have been appended. But there is also a much shorter* Apology *(15 chapters) that has been handed down too. The precise relationship is disputed: is the "second apology" just a supplement to the "first apology" (as they have come to be called), or was it prepared as a quite independent work? In any event, the following selection is taken from the "first"* Apology. *It reproduces chapters 9 to 29 plus chapters 61 to 67. The first part presents a good sense of how Justin viewed Christian life in contrast to the paganism of his day.*

But it is the second part for which we are most grateful to Justin. These chapters are literally without parallel. They give us all the information we have about how Christian worship was practiced in second-century Rome, when the memoirs of the apostles or the writings of the prophets were read to the congregation as long as time would permit. In fact, he gives us two different descriptions of the central ceremonies: in one (chapter 65) he paints the liturgy of the newly baptized, in the other (chapter 67) he gives the details of the regular Sunday service. Besides the descriptions themselves, however, the more striking fact, it has often been observed, lies in the use that is made of them. Here Justin, a Christian layman defending his faith, points proudly to what goes on every Sunday morning as proof of the dignity and superiority of that faith. That such should be the general experience of Christians of later ages, including our own, is justification enough of trying to recover the spirit of those early Christian assemblies at worship.

THE FIRST APOLOGY

THE FAITH AND LIFE OF CHRISTIANS

Certainly we do not honor with many sacrifices and floral garlands the objects that men have fashioned, and set up in temples, and called gods. We know that they are lifeless and dead and do not represent the form of God—for we do not think of God as having the kind of form which some claim that they imitate to be honored—but rather exhibit the names and shapes of the evil demons who have manifested themselves [to men]. You know well enough without our mentioning it how the craftsmen prepare their material, scraping and cutting and molding and beating. And often they make what they call gods out of vessels used for vile purposes, changing and transforming by art merely their appearance. We consider it not only irrational but an insult to God, whose glory and form are ineffable, to give his name to corruptible things which themselves need care. You are well aware that craftsmen in these [things] are impure and—not to go into details—given to all kinds of vice; they even corrupt their own slave girls who work along with them. What an absurdity, that dissolute men should be spoken of as fashioning or remaking gods for public veneration, and that you should appoint such people as guardians of the temples where they are set up—not considering that it is unlawful to think or speak of men as guardians of gods.

But we have learned [from our tradition] that God has no need of material offerings from men, considering that he is the provider of all. We have been taught and firmly believe that he accepts only those who imitate the good things which are his—temperance and righteousness and love of mankind, and whatever else truly belongs to the God who is called by no given name. We have also been taught that in the beginning he in his goodness formed all things that are for the sake of men out of unformed matter, and if they show themselves by their actions worthy of his plan, we have learned that they will be counted worthy of dwelling with him, reigning together and made free from corruption and suffering. For as he made us in the beginning when we were not, so we hold that those who choose what is pleasing to him will, because of that choice, be counted worthy of incorruption and of fellowship [with him]. We did not bring ourselves into being—but as to following after the things that are dear to God, choosing them by the rational powers which he has given us—this is a matter of conviction and leads us to faith. We hold it to be for the good of all men that they are not prevented from learning these things, but are even urged to [consider] them. For what human laws could not do, that the Word, being divine, would have brought about, if the evil demons had not scattered abroad many false and godless accusations, with the help of the evil desire that is in every man by nature [and expresses itself] in all kinds of ways. None of this, however, matters to us.

When you hear that we look for a kingdom, you rashly suppose that we mean something merely human. But we speak of a Kingdom with God, as is clear from our confessing Christ when you bring us to trial, though we know that death is the penalty for this confession. For if we looked for a human kingdom we would deny it in order to save our lives, and would try to remain in hiding in order to obtain the things we look for. But since we do not place our hopes on the present [order], we are not troubled by being put to death, since we will have to die somehow in any case.

We are in fact of all men your best helpers and allies in securing good order, convinced as we are that no wicked man, no covetous man or conspirator, or virtuous man either, can be hidden from God, and that everyone goes to eternal punishment or salvation in accordance with the character of his actions. If all men knew this, nobody would choose vice even for a little time, knowing that he was on his way to eternal punishment by fire; every man would follow the self-restrained and orderly path of virtue, so as to receive the good things that come from God and avoid his punishments. There are some who merely try to conceal their wrongdoing because of the laws and punishments which you decree, knowing that since you are only men it is possible for wrongdoers to escape you; if they learned and were convinced that our thoughts as well as our actions cannot be hidden from God they would certainly lead orderly lives, if only because of the consequences, as you must agree. But it seems as if you were afraid of having all men well-behaved, and nobody left for you to punish; this would be the conduct of public executioners, not of good rulers. Such things, we are convinced, are brought about by the evil demons, the ones who demand sacrifices and service from men who live irrationally; but we have not learned [to expect] any unreasonable conduct from you, who aim at piety and philosophy. But if like thoughtless men you prefer custom to truth, then go ahead and do what you can. Rulers who respect reputation rather than truth have as much power as brigands in a desert. The Word himself has shown that you will not succeed, and after God who begat him we know of no ruler more royal or more just than he. For just as all men try to avoid inheriting the poverty or sufferings or disgrace of their ancestors, so the sensible man will not choose whatever the Word forbids to be chosen. He foretold that all these things would happen—our Teacher, I mean, who is the Son and Apostle of God the Father and Master of all, that is, Jesus Christ, from whom we have received the name of Christians. We are sure that all the things taught by him are so, since we see that what he predicted is actually coming to pass. This is God's work, to announce something before it happens and then to show it happening as predicted. I might stop here and add no more, having made clear that we ask for what is just and true. But though I know that it is not easy to change over at once a mind which is bound down by ignorance, I am encouraged to add somewhat to persuade the lover of truth, being sure that one can dispel ignorance by putting truth against it.

What sound-minded man will not admit that we are not godless, since we worship the Fashioner of the universe, declaring him, as we have been taught, to have no need of blood and libations and incense, but praising him by the word of prayer and thanksgiving for all that he has given us? We have learned that the only honor worthy of him is, not to consume by fire the things he has made for our nourishment, but to devote them to our use and those in need, in thankfulness to him sending up solemn prayers and hymns for our creation and all the means of health, for the variety of creatures and the changes of the seasons, and sending up our petitions that we may live again in incorruption through our faith in him. It is Jesus Christ who has taught us these things, having been born for this purpose and crucified under Pontius Pilate, who was procurator in Judea in the time of Tiberius Caesar. We will show that we honor him in accordance with reason, having learned that he is the Son of the true God himself, and holding him to be in the second place and the prophetic Spirit in the third rank. It is for this that they charge us with madness, saying that we give the second place after the unchanging and ever-existing God and begetter of all things to a crucified man, not knowing the mystery involved in this, to which we ask you to give your attention as we expound it.

We warn you in advance to be careful, lest the demons whom we have attacked should deceive you and prevent your completely grasping and understanding what we say. For they struggle to have you as their slaves and servants, and now by manifestations in dreams, now by magic tricks, they get hold of all who do not struggle to their utmost for their own salvation—as we do who, after being persuaded by the Word, renounced them and now follow the only unbegotten God through his Son. Those who once rejoiced in fornication now delight in continence alone; those who made use of magic arts have dedicated themselves to the good and unbegotten God; we who once took most pleasure in the means of increasing our wealth and property now bring what we have into a common fund and share with everyone in need; we who hated and killed one another and would not associate with men of different tribes because of [their different] customs, now after the manifestation of Christ live together and pray for our enemies and try to persuade those who unjustly hate us, so that they, living according to the fair commands of Christ, may share with us the good hope of receiving the same things [that we will] from God, the master of all. So that this may not seem to be sophistry, I think fit before giving our demonstration to recall a few of the teachings which have come from Christ himself. It is for you then, as mighty emperors, to examine whether we have been taught and do teach these things truly. His sayings were short and concise, for he was no sophist, but his word was the power of God.

About continence he said this: "Whoever looks on a woman to lust after her has already committed adultery in his heart before God." And: "If your right eye offends you, cut it out; it is better for you to enter into the Kingdom of Heaven with one eye than with two to be sent into eternal fire." And: "Whoever marries a woman who has been put away from another man commits adultery." And: "There are some who were made eunuchs by men, and some who were born eunuchs, and some who have made themselves eunuchs for the Kingdom of Heaven's sake; only not all [are able to] receive this."

And so those who make second marriages according to human law are sinners in the sight of our Teacher, and those who look on a woman to lust after her. For he condemns not only the man who commits the act of adultery, but the man who desires to commit adultery, since not only our actions but our thoughts are manifest to God. Many men and women now in their sixties and seventies who have been disciples of Christ from childhood have preserved their purity; and I am proud that I could point to such people in every nation. Then what shall we say of the uncounted multitude of those who have turned away from incontinence and learned these things? For Christ did not call the righteous or the temperate to repentance, but the ungodly and incontinent and unrighteous. So he said: "I have not come to call the righteous but sinners to repentance." For the Heavenly Father wishes the repentance of a sinner rather than his punishment.

This is what he taught on affection for all men: "If you love those who love you, what new thing do you do? for even the harlots do this. But I say to you, Pray for your enemies and love those who hate you and bless those who curse you and pray for those who treat you despitefully."

That we should share with those in need and do nothing for [our] glory he said these things: "Give to everyone who asks and turn not away him who wishes to borrow. For if you lend to those from whom you hope to receive, what new thing do you do? Even the publicans do this. But as for you, do not lay up treasures for yourselves on earth, where moth and rust corrupt and thieves break in, but lay up for yourselves treasures in heaven, where neither moth nor rust corrupts. For what will it profit a man, if he should gain the whole world, but lose his own soul? Or what will he give in exchange for it? Lay up treasures therefore in the heavens, where neither moth nor rust corrupts." And: "Be kind and merciful, as your Father is kind and merciful, and makes his sun to rise on sinners and righteous and wicked. Do not worry as to what you will eat or what you will wear. Are you not better than the birds and the beasts? and God feeds them. So do not worry as to what you will eat or what you will wear, for your Heavenly Father knows that you need these things. But seek the Kingdom of Heaven, and all these things will be added to you. For where his treasure is, there is the mind of man." And: "Do not do these things to be seen of men, for otherwise you have no reward with your Father who is in heaven."

About being long-suffering and servants to all and free from anger, this is what he said: "To him that smites you on one cheek turn the other also, and to him that takes away your cloak do not deny your tunic either. Whoever is angry is worthy of the fire. And whoever compels you to go one mile, follow him for two. Let your good works shine before men, that they as they see may wonder at your Father who is in heaven."

For we ought not to quarrel; he has not wished us to imitate the wicked, but rather by our patience and meekness to draw all men from shame and evil desires. This we can show in the case of many who were once on your side but have turned from the ways of violence and tyranny, overcome by observing the consistent lives of their neighbors, or noting the strange patience of their injured acquaintances, or experiencing the way they did business with them.

About not swearing at all, but always speaking the truth, this is what he commanded: "Swear not at all; but let your yea be yea and your nay nay. What is more than these is from the evil one."

That God only should be worshiped he showed us when he said: "The greatest commandment is: Thou shalt worship the

Lord thy God and him only shalt thou serve with all thy heart and all thy strength, the Lord who made thee." And: "When one came to him and said, Good Teacher, he answered and said, There is none good, except only God who made all things."

Those who are found not living as he taught should know that they are not really Christians, even if his teachings are on their lips, for he said that not those who merely profess but those who also do the works will be saved. For he said this: "Not everyone who says to me, Lord, Lord, will enter into the Kingdom of Heaven, but he who does the will of my Father who is in heaven. For whoever hears me and does what I say hears him who sent me. Many will say to me, Lord, Lord, did we not eat in your name and drink and do mighty works? And then I will say to them, Depart from me, you workers of iniquity. Then there will be weeping and gnashing of teeth, when the righteous will shine as the sun, but the wicked will be sent into eternal fire. For many will come in my name clothed outwardly in sheep's clothing, but being inwardly ravening wolves; by their works you will know them. Every tree that does not bring forth good fruit is cut down and thrown into the fire."

So we ask that you too should punish those who do not live in accordance with his teachings, but merely say that they are Christians.

More even than others we try to pay the taxes and assessments to those whom you appoint, as we have been taught by him. For once in his time some came to him and asked whether it were right to pay taxes to Caesar. And he answered, "Tell me, whose image is on the coin." They said, "Caesar's." And he answered them again, "Then give what is Caesar's to Caesar and what is God's to God." So we worship God only, but in other matters we gladly serve you, recognizing you as emperors and rulers of men, and praying that along with your imperial power you may also be found to have a sound mind. If you pay no attention to our prayers and our frank statements about everything, it will not injure us, since we believe, or rather are firmly convinced, that every man will suffer in eternal fire in accordance with the quality of his actions, and similarly will be required to give account for the abilities which he has received from God, as Christ told us when he said, "To whom God has given more, from him more will be required."

Look at the end of each of the former emperors, how they died the common death of all; and if this were merely a departure into unconsciousness, that would be a piece of luck for the wicked. But since consciousness continues for all who have lived, and eternal punishment awaits, do not fail to be convinced and believe that these things are true. For the oracles of the dead and the revelations of innocent children, the invoking of [departed] human souls, the dream senders and guardians of the magi, and what is done by those who know about such things—all this should convince you that souls are still conscious after death. Then there are the men who are seized and torn by the spirits of the dead, whom everyone calls demon-possessed and maniacs, and the oracles so well-known among you, of Amphilochus and Dodona and Pytho, and any others of that kind, and the teaching of writers, Empedocles and Pythagoras, Plato and Socrates, and the ditch in Homer and the descent of Odysseus to visit the dead, and other stories like this. Treat us at least like these; we believe in God not less than they do, but rather more, since we look forward to receiving again our own bodies, though they be dead and buried in the earth, declaring that nothing is impossible to God.

Indeed, what would seem more incredible to an observer than if we were not in the body and someone should say that from a single drop of human seed it were possible for the form that we see to come into being, with bones and nerves and flesh? Consider this hypothesis; if you were not such as you are, born of such parents, and someone were to show you the human seed and a picture of a man, and assure you that the one could grow into the other, would you believe it before you saw it happening? No one would dare to deny [that you wouldn't]. In the same way unbelief prevails about the resurrection of the dead because you have never seen an instance of it. But as you at first would not have believed that from a little drop such beings [as men] could develop, yet you see it happening, so consider that it is possible for human bodies, dissolved and scattered in the earth like seeds, to rise again in due time by God's decree and be clothed with incorruption. I cannot imagine how any adequate concept of divine power can be held by those who say that everything returns into that from which it came and that not even God can do anything more than this. But I may remark that they would not have believed it possible for such creatures as they are to have come into being, yet they see themselves as they are, and indeed the whole world [as it is], and what they were made from. We have learned that it is better to believe things impossible to our own nature and to men than to disbelieve like others, since we know that our Teacher Jesus Christ said, "The things that are impossible with men are possible with God." And: "Fear not those who put you to death and after that can do no more, but fear him who after death is able to cast both body and soul into Gehenna." Gehenna is the place where those who live unrighteously will be punished, and those who do not believe that these things will come to pass which God has taught through Christ.

Both Sybil and Hystaspes declared that there will be a destruction of corruptible things by fire. Those who are called Stoic philosophers teach that God himself will be resolved into fire, and the universe come into being again by return. We think that God, the Maker of all, is superior to changeable things. But if on some points we agree with the poets and philosophers whom you honor, and on others [teach] more completely and more worthily of God, and are the only ones who offer proof, why are we above all hated unjustly? When we say that all things have been ordered and made by God we appear to offer the teaching of Plato—in speaking of a coming destruction by fire, that of the Stoics; in declaring that the souls of the unrighteous will be punished after death, still remaining in conscious existence, and those of the virtuous, delivered from punishments, will enjoy happiness, we seem to agree with [various] poets and philosophers; in declaring that men ought not to worship the works of their hands we are saying the same things as the comedian Menander and others who have said this, for they declared that the Fashioner is greater than what he has formed.

SUPERIORITY OF CHRISTIANITY TO PAGANISM

In saying that the Word, who is the first offspring of God, was born for us without sexual union, as Jesus Christ our Teacher, and that he was crucified and died and after rising again ascended into heaven we introduce nothing new beyond [what you say of] those whom you call sons of Zeus. You know how many sons of Zeus the writers whom you honor speak of–Hermes, the hermeneutic Word and teacher of all; Asclepius, who was also a healer and after being struck by lightning ascended into heaven–as did Dionysus who was torn in pieces; Heracles, who to escape his torments threw himself into the fire; the Dioscuri born of Leda and Perseus of Danäe; and Bellerophon who, though of human origin, rode on the [divine] horse Pegasus. Need I mention Ariadne and those who like her are said to have been placed among the stars? and what of your deceased emperors, whom you regularly think worthy of being raised to immortality introducing a witness who swears that he saw the cremated Caesar ascending into heaven from the funeral pyre? Nor is it necessary to remind you what kind of actions are related of each of those who are called sons of Zeus, except [to point out] that they are recorded for the benefit and instruction of students–for all consider it a fine thing to be imitators of the gods. Far be it from every sound mind to entertain such a concept of the deities as that Zeus, whom they call the ruler and begetter of all, should have been a parricide and the son of a parricide, and that moved by desire of evil and shameful pleasures he descended on Ganymede and the many women whom he seduced, and that his sons after him were guilty of similar actions. But, as we said before, it was the wicked demons who did these things. We have been taught that only those who live close to God in holiness and virtue attain to immortality, and we believe that those who live unjustly and do not reform will be punished in eternal fire.

Now if God's Son, who is called Jesus, were only an ordinary man, he would be worthy because of his wisdom to be called Son of God, for all authors call God father of men and gods. When we say, as before, that he was begotten by God as the Word of God in a unique manner beyond ordinary birth, this should be no strange thing for you who speak of Hermes as the announcing word from God. If somebody objects that he was crucified, this is in common with the sons of Zeus, as you call them, who suffered, as previously listed. Since their fatal sufferings are narrated as not similar but different, so his unique passion should not seem to be any worse—indeed I will, as I have undertaken, show, as the argument proceeds, that he was better; for he is shown to be better by his actions. If we declare that he was born of a virgin, you should consider this something in common with Perseus. When we say that he healed the lame, the paralytic, and those born blind, and raised the dead, we seem to be talking about things like those said to have been done by Asclepius.

In order to make this clear to you I will present the evidence that the things we say, as disciples of Christ and of the prophets who came before him, are the only truths and older than all the writers who have lived, and we ask to be accepted, not because we say the same things as they do, but because we are speaking the truth—[second] that Jesus Christ alone was really begotten as Son of God, being his Word and First-begotten and Power, and becoming man by his will he taught us these things for the reconciliation and restoration of the human race—and [third] that before he came among men as man, there were some who, on account of the already mentioned wicked demons, told through the poets as already having occurred the myths they had invented, just as now they are responsible for the slanders and godless deeds alleged against us, of which there is neither witness nor demonstration.

The first point is that though we say the same as do the Greeks, we only are hated, because of the name of Christ. We do no wrong but are put to death as offenders [because of our worship, though] others everywhere worship trees and rivers, mice and cats and crocodiles and many kinds of irrational animals, and the same objects are not honored by all, but different ones in different places, so that all are impious to each other because of not having the same objects of worship. Yet this is the one complaint you have against us, that we do not worship the same gods that you do, and do not bring libations and offerings of fat to the dead, crowns for their statues, and sacrifices. Yet, as you know well, the same beings are gods to some and wild animals to others, while still others think of them as sacred victims.

Secondly, out of every race of men we who once worshiped Dionysus the son of Semele and Apollo the son of Leto, who in their passion for men did things which it is disgraceful even to speak of, or who worshiped Persephone and Aphrodite, who were driven mad by [love of] Adonis and whose mysteries you celebrate, or Asclepius or some other of those who are called gods, now through Jesus Christ despise them, even at the cost of death, and have dedicated ourselves to the unbegotten and impassible God. We do not believe that he ever descended in mad passion on Antiope or others, nor on Ganymede, nor was he, receiving help through Thetis, delivered by that hundred-handed monster, nor was he, because of this, anxious that Thetis' son Achilles should destroy so many Greeks for the sake of his concubine Briseis. We pity those who believe [such stories], for which we know that the demons are responsible.

A third point is that after Christ's ascent into heaven the demons put forward various men who said that they were gods, and you not only did not persecute them, but thought them worthy of honors. One was a certain Simon, a Samaritan from the village of Gitta, who in the time of Claudius Caesar, through the arts of the demons who worked in him, did mighty works of magic in your imperial city of Rome and was thought to be a god. He has been honored among you as a god by a statue, which was set up on the River Tiber, between the two bridges, with this inscription in Latin, SIMONI DEO SANCTO. Almost all the Samaritans, and a few in other nations, confess this man as their first god and worship him as such, and a woman named Helena, who traveled around with him in those days, and had formerly been a public prostitute, they say was the first Concept produced from him. Then we know of a certain Menander, who was also a Samaritan, from the village of Capparetaea, who had been a disciple of Simon's, and was also possessed by the demons. He deceived many at Antioch by magic arts, and even persuaded his followers that he would never die; there are still some who believe this [as they learned] from him. Then there is a certain Marcion of Pontus, who is still teaching his converts that there is another God greater than the Fashioner. By the help of the demons he has made many in every race of men to blaspheme and to deny God the Maker of the universe, professing that there is another who is greater and has done greater things than he. As we said, all who derive [their opinions] from these men are called Christians, just as men who do not share the same teachings with the philosophers still have in common with them the name of philosophy, thus brought into disrepute. Whether they commit the shameful deeds about which stories are told—the upsetting of the lamp, promiscuous intercourse, and the meals of human flesh, we do not know; but we are sure that they are neither persecuted nor killed by you, on account of their teachings anyway. I have compiled and have on hand a treatise against all the heresies which have arisen, which I will give you if you would like to consult it.

That we may avoid all injustice and impiety, we have been taught that to expose the newly born is the work of wicked men—first of all because we observe that almost all [foundlings], boys as well as girls, are brought up for prostitution. As the ancients are said to have raised herds of oxen or goats or sheep or horses in their pastures, so now [you raise children] just for shameful purposes, and so in every nation a crowd of females and hermaphrodites and doers of unspeakable deeds are exposed as public prostitutes. You even collect pay and levies and taxes from these, whom you ought to exterminate from your civilized world. And anyone who makes use of them may in addition to [the guilt of] godless, impious, and intemperate intercourse, by chance be consorting with his own child or relative or brother. Some even prostitute their own children and wives, and others are admittedly mutilated for purposes of sodomy, and treat this as part of the mysteries of the mother of the gods—while beside each of those whom you think of as gods a serpent is depicted as a great symbol and mystery. You charge against us the actions that you commit openly and treat with honor, as if the divine light were overthrown and withdrawn—which of course does no harm to us, who refuse to do any of these things, but rather injures those who do them and then bring false witness [against us].

Among us the chief of the evil demons is called the serpent and Satan and the devil, as you can learn by examining our writings. Christ has foretold that he will be cast into fire with his host and the men who follow him, [all] to be punished for endless ages. God delays doing this for the sake of the human race, for he foreknows that there are some yet to be saved by repentance, even perhaps some not yet born. In the beginning he made the race of men endowed with intelligence, able to choose the truth and do right, so that all men are without excuse before God, for they were made with the powers of reason and observation. Anyone who does not believe that God cares for these things either manages to profess that he does not exist, or makes out that he exists but approves of evil, or remains [unaffected] like a stone, and that virtue and vice are not realities, but that men consider things good or bad by opinion alone; this is the height of impiety and injustice.

And again [we do not expose children] lest some of them, not being picked up, should die and we thus be murderers. But to begin with, we do not marry except in order to bring up children, or else, renouncing marriage, we live in perfect continence. To show you that promiscuous intercourse is not among our mysteries—just recently one of us submitted a petition to the Prefect Felix in Alexandria, asking that a physician be allowed to make him a eunuch, for the physicians there said they were not allowed to do this without the permission of the Prefect. When Felix would by no means agree to endorse [the petition], the young man remained single, satisfied with [the approval of] his own conscience and that of his fellow believers. I think it proper in this connection to remind you of the recent case of Antinoüs, whom everybody, through fear, hastened to worship as a god, though knowing perfectly well who he was and where he came from.

* * * * *

CHRISTIAN WORSHIP

How we dedicated ourselves to God when we were made new through Christ I will explain, since it might seem to be unfair if I left this out from my exposition. Those who are persuaded and believe that the things we teach and say are true, and promise that they can live accordingly, are instructed to pray and beseech God with fasting for the remission of their past sins, while we pray and fast along with them. Then they are brought by us where there is water, and are reborn by the same manner of rebirth by which we ourselves were reborn; for they are then washed in the water in the name of God the Father and Master of all, and of our Saviour Jesus Christ, and of the Holy Spirit. For Christ said, "Unless you are born again you will not enter into the Kingdom of heaven." Now it is clear to all that those who have once come into being cannot enter the wombs of those who bore them. But as I quoted before, it was said through the prophet Isaiah how those who have sinned and repent shall escape from their sins. He said this: "Wash yourselves, be clean, take away wickednesses from your souls, learn to do good, give judgment for the orphan and defend the cause of the widow, and come and let us reason together, says the Lord. And though your sins be as scarlet, I will make them as white as wool, and though they be as crimson, I will make them as white as snow. If you will not listen to me, the sword will devour you; for the mouth of the Lord has spoken these things." And we learned from the apostles this reason for this [rite]. At our first birth we were born of necessity without our knowledge, from moist seed, by the intercourse of our parents with each other, and grew up in bad habits and wicked behavior. So that we should not remain children of necessity and ignorance, but [become sons] of free choice and knowledge, and obtain remission of the sins we have already committed, there is named at the water, over him who has chosen to be born again and has repented of his sinful acts, the name of God the Father and Master of all. Those who lead to the washing the one who is to be washed call on [God by] this term only. For no one may give a proper name to the ineffable God, and if anyone should dare to say that there is one, he is hopelessly insane. This washing is called illumination, since those who learn these things are illumined within. The illuminand is also washed in the name of Jesus Christ, who was crucified under Pontius Pilate, and in the name of the Holy Spirit, who through the prophets foretold everything about Jesus.

When the demons heard this washing proclaimed through the prophets, they arranged that those who go into their temples and are about to approach them to offer libations and burnt offerings should sprinkle themselves—and further they have them wash themselves completely as they pass on into the sanctuaries where they are enshrined. The order given by the priests to devotees to remove their shoes as they enter the temples and approach them [the demons] is an imitation devised by the demons when they learned what happened to Moses, the above-mentioned prophet. For at the time when Moses was ordered to go down to Egypt and bring out the people of the Israelites who were there, as he was pasturing in the land of Arabia the sheep of his maternal uncle, our Christ addressed him in the form of fire out of a bush, and said, "Unloose your sandals and come near and hear." When he had taken them and approached, he heard [that he was] to go down into Egypt, and lead out the people of the Israelites there, and received great power from Christ, who spoke to him in the form of fire. He went down and led out the people after he had done great miracles—if you want to learn about them, you may learn in detail from his writings.

Even now the Jews all teach that the unnamed God himself spoke to Moses. Wherefore the prophetic Spirit said in condemnation of them through Isaiah the above-mentioned prophet, as was quoted before: "The ox knows his owner and the ass his master's crib, but Israel does not know me and my people does not understand." Likewise Jesus the Christ, because the Jews did not know what the Father is and what the Son, himself said in condemnation of them: "No one knows the Father except the Son, nor the Son except the Father and those to whom the Son will reveal it." Now the Word of God is his Son, as I said before. He is also called "Angel" and "Apostle," for [as Angel] he announces what it is necessary to know, and [as Apostle] is sent forth to testify to what is announced, as our Lord himself said, "He that hears me hears him that sent me." This can be made clear from the writings of Moses, in which this is to be found: "And the Angel of God spoke to Moses in a flame of fire out of the bush and said, I am he who is, God of Abraham, God of Isaac, God of Jacob, the God of your fathers; go down to Egypt and bring out my people." Those who wish to can learn what followed from this; for it is not possible to put down everything in these [pages]. But these words were uttered to demonstrate that Jesus Christ is the Son of God and Apostle, who was first the Word, and appeared, now in the form of fire, now in the image of the bodiless creatures. Now, however, having become man by the will of God for the sake of the human race, he has endured whatever sufferings the demons managed to have brought upon him by the senseless Jews. For they have it clearly said in the writings of Moses, "And the Angel of God spoke to Moses in a flame of fire in the bush and said, I am he who is, the God of Abraham, the God of Isaac, and the God of Jacob," yet they say that he who said these things was the Father and Fashioner of the universe. Jesus again, as we cited, when he was with them said, "No one knows the Father except the Son, nor the Son except the Father and those to whom the Son may reveal it." So the Jews, continuing to think that the Father of the universe had spoken to Moses, when it was the Son of God, who is called both Angel and Apostle, who spoke to him, were rightly censured both by the prophetic Spirit and by Christ himself, since they knew neither the Father nor the Son. For those who identify the Son and the Father are condemned, as neither knowing the Father nor recognizing that the Father of the universe has a Son, who being the Word and First-begotten of God is also divine. Formerly he appeared in the form of fire and the image of a bodiless being to Moses and the other prophets. But now in the time of your dominion he was, as I have said, made man of a virgin according to the will of the Father for the salvation of those who believe in him, and endured contempt and suffering so that by dying and rising again he might conquer death. What was said out of the bush to Moses, "I am he who is, the God of Abraham and the God of Isaac and the God of Jacob and the God of your fathers," was an indication that they though dead still existed and were Christ's own men. For they were the first of all men to devote themselves to seeking after God, Abraham being the father of Isaac, and Isaac of Jacob, as Moses also recorded.

From what has been said you can understand why the demons contrived to have the image of the so-called Kore erected at the springs of waters, saying that she was a daughter of Zeus, imitating what was said through Moses. For Moses said, as I have quoted: "In the beginning God made the heaven and the earth. And the earth was invisible and unfurnished, and the Spirit of God was borne over the waters." In imitation of the Spirit of God, spoken of as borne over the water, they spoke of Kore, daughter of Zeus. With similar malice they spoke of Athena as a daughter of Zeus, but not as a result of intercourse—since they knew that God designed the creation of the world by the Word, they spoke of Athena as the first Concept. This we consider very ridiculous, to offer the female form as the image of an intellectual concept. And similarly the other so-called sons of Zeus are condemned by their actions.

We, however, after thus washing the one who has been convinced and signified his assent, lead him to those who are called brethren, where they are assembled. They then earnestly offer common prayers for themselves and the one who has been illuminated and all others everywhere, that we may be made worthy, having learned the truth, to be found in deed good citizens and keepers of what is commanded, so that we may be saved with eternal salvation. On finishing the prayers we greet each other with a kiss. Then bread and a cup of water and mixed wine are brought to the president of the brethren and he, taking them, sends up praise and glory to the Father of the universe through the name of the Son and of the Holy Spirit, and offers thanksgiving at some length that we have been deemed worthy to receive these things from him. When he has finished the prayers and the thanksgiving, the whole congregation present assents, saying, "Amen." "Amen" in the Hebrew language means, "So be it." When the president has given thanks and the whole congregation has assented, those whom we call deacons give to each of those present a portion of the consecrated bread and wine and water, and they take it to the absent.

This food we call Eucharist, of which no one is allowed to partake except one who believes that the things we teach are true, and has received the washing for forgiveness of sins and for rebirth, and who lives as Christ handed down to us. For we do not receive these things as common bread or common drink; but as Jesus Christ our Saviour being incarnate by God's word took flesh and blood for our salvation, so also we have been taught that the food consecrated by the word of prayer which comes from him, from which our flesh and blood are nourished by transformation, is the flesh and blood of that incarnate Jesus. For the apostles in the memoirs composed by them, which are called Gospels, thus handed down what was commanded them: that Jesus, taking bread and having given thanks, said, "Do this for my memorial, this is my body"; and likewise taking the cup and giving thanks he said, "This is my blood"; and gave it to them alone. This also the wicked demons in imitation handed down as something to be done in the mysteries of Mithra; for bread and a cup of water are brought out in their secret rites of initiation, with certain invocations which you either know or can learn.

After these [services] we constantly remind each other of these things. Those who have more come to the aid of those who lack, and we are constantly together. Over all that we receive we bless the Maker of all things through his Son Jesus Christ and through the Holy Spirit. And on the day called Sunday there is a meeting in one place of those who live in cities or the country, and the memoirs of the apostles or the writings of the prophets are read as long as time permits. When the reader has finished, the president in a discourse urges and invites [us] to the imitation of these noble things. Then we all stand up together and offer prayers. And, as said before, when we have finished the prayer, bread is brought, and wine and water, and the president similarly sends up prayers and thanksgivings to the best of his ability, and the congregation assents, saying the Amen; the distribution, and reception of the consecrated [elements] by each one, takes place and they are sent to the absent by the deacons. Those who prosper, and who so wish, contribute, each one as much as he chooses to. What is collected is deposited with the president, and he takes care of orphans and widows, and those who are in want on account of sickness or any other cause, and those who are in bonds, and the strangers who are sojourners among [us], and, briefly, he is the protector of all those in need. We all hold this common gathering on Sunday, since it is the first day, on which God transforming darkness and matter made the universe, and Jesus

Christ our Saviour rose from the dead on the same day. For they crucified him on the day before Saturday, and on the day after Saturday, he appeared to his apostles and disciples and taught them these things which I have passed on to you also for your serious consideration.

St. Hippolytus of Rome
170-235

Hippolytus was born, probably within a few years of the martyrdom of Justin in Rome. A statue of him, which may have been made during his lifetime, was discovered in 1551 and was installed in the Vatican Library by Pope John XXIII in 1959. A list of his writings is inscribed on it, including the Apostolic Tradition.

Hippolytus claimed St. Irenaeus as his teacher, presumably when the latter was in Lyon. He was ordained a presbyter in Rome toward the end of the second century, and was a rigorist who attacked with vehemence those whom he considered too lax, including Pope Zephyrinus and his assistant Callistus. When the latter was chosen to succeed Zephyrinus in 217, Hippolytus protested violently and his followers elected him antipope. This schism lasted until 235 when a reconciliation took place. At that time Hippolytus was exiled by Emperor Maximin to work in the mines of Sardinia. He either died there or was released and died the following year in Rome. He was buried on the road to Tivoli.

Hippolytus was the last major writer in the Western Church to employ the Greek language. He seems to have authored no less than forty works, the majority of which have been lost. His most valuable theological work was his Refutation of All Heresies, *in which he set out to prove the rather surprising proposition that all heretics were atheists. It is an important source, especially for the history of Gnosticism.*

Even though the title of the Apostolic Tradition *was inscribed on the 3rd century statue of Hippolytus, it was considered a lost work until our own century. In 1910 E. Schwarz claimed, and in 1916 R. H. Connolly proved, that the Latin text known as the* Egyptian Church Order *was substantially a translation of the* Apostolic Tradition *of Hippolytus. This document, as Fr. Quasten put it, "provided a new foundation for the history of the Roman liturgy and has given us the richest source of information that we possess in any form for our knowledge of the constitution and life of the Church in the first three centuries."*

Since the very purpose of Hippolytus in writing the Apostolic Tradition *was ultraconservative, we can safely assume that the rites and customs to which he bears witness were, at least in outline and essentials, those practiced in the Roman church of his day. Like Justin a half century before him, Hippolytus gives us two descriptions of the Eucharist, one in connection with the consecration of a bishop, and the other when celebrated with newly-baptized members.*

The Apostolic Tradition, *as a collection of regulations of church order, was translated, enlarged, and adapted in later years, so that there are disagreements about some passages belonging to the original. It consists of 34 sections divided into three parts: the first is concerned with the clergy, the second deals with the reception of converts, and the third gives various prescriptions for living the Christian life. The famous description of baptism by triple immersion is found in chapter 21.*

If it is obvious that more structure is evident in Hippolytus than was true in Justin, that is in part due to the regulatory purpose of the author. But it is also true that such is the natural inclination of institutions, especially in an institution that had reason to want to identify its current practices with the prestigious founding figures, as the very title Apostolic Tradition *reveals. The more surprising fact is that such a document as this did not have more influence than it apparently did, for the liturgy of the Roman Church continued to evolve significantly despite the efforts of Hippolytus to "freeze" it.*

APOSTOLIC TRADITION

We have duly completed what needed to be said about "Gifts", describing those gifts which God by His own counsel has bestowed on men, in offering to Himself His image which had gone astray. But now, moved by His love to all His saints, we pass on to our most important theme, "The Tradition", our teacher. And we address the churches, so that they who have been well trained, may, by our instruction, hold fast that tradition which has continued up to now and, knowing it well, may be strengthened. This is needful, because of that lapse or error which recently occurred through ignorance, and because of ignorant men. And [the] Holy Spirit will supply perfect grace to those who believe aright, that they may know how all things should be transmitted and kept by them who rule the church.

PART I

2. Let the bishop be ordained after he has been chosen by all the people. When he has been named and shall please all, let him, with the presbytery and such bishops as may be present, assemble with the people on a Sunday. While all give their consent, the bishops shall lay their hands upon him, and the presbytery shall stand by in silence. All indeed shall keep silent, praying in their heart for the descent of the Spirit. Then one of the bishops who are present shall, at the request of all, lay his hand on him who is ordained bishop, and shall pray as follows, saying:

3. God and Father of our Lord Jesus Christ, Father of mercies and God of all comfort, who dwellest on high yet hast respect to the lowly, who knowest all things before they come to pass. Thou hast appointed the borders of thy church by the word of thy grace, predestinating from the beginning the righteous race of Abraham. And making them princes and

priests, and leaving not thy sanctuary without a ministry, thou hast from the beginning of the world been well pleased to be glorified among those whom thou has chosen. Pour forth now that power, which is thine, of thy royal Spirit, which thou gavest to thy beloved Servant Jesus Christ, which he bestowed on his holy apostles, who established the church in every place, the church which thou hast sanctified unto unceasing glory and praise of thy name. Thou who knowest the hearts of all, grant to this thy servant, whom thou hast chosen to be bishop, [to feed thy holy flock] and to serve as thy high priest without blame, ministering night and day, to propitiate thy countenance without ceasing and to offer thee the gifts of thy holy church. And by the Spirit of high-priesthood to have authority to remit sins according to thy commandment, to assign the lots according to thy precept, to loose every bond according to the authority which thou gavest to thy apostles, and to please thee in meekness and purity of heart, offering to thee an odour of sweet savour. Through thy Servant Jesus Christ our Lord, through whom be to thee glory, might, honour, with [the] Holy Spirit in [the] holy church, both now and always and world without end. Amen.

4. And when he is made bishop, all shall offer him the kiss of peace, for he has been made worthy. To him then the deacons shall bring the offering, and he, laying his hand upon it, with all the presbytery, shall say as the thanksgiving:

The Lord be with you.

And all shall say

And with thy spirit.

Lift up your hearts.
We lift them up unto the Lord.

Let us give thanks to the Lord.
It is meet and right.

And then he shall proceed immediately:

We give thee thanks, O God, through thy beloved Servant Jesus Christ, whom at the end of time thou didst send to us a Saviour and Redeemer and the Messenger of thy counsel. Who is thy Word, inseparable from thee; through whom thou didst make all things and in whom thou art well pleased. Whom thou didst send from heaven into the womb of the Virgin, and who, dwelling within her, was made flesh, and was manifested as thy Son, being born of [the] Holy Spirit and the Virgin. Who, fulfilling thy will, and winning for himself a holy people, spread out his hands when he came to suffer, that by his death he might set free them who believed on thee. Who, when he was betrayed to his willing death, that he might bring to nought death, and break the bonds of the devil, and tread hell under foot, and give light to the righteous, and set up a boundary post, and manifest his resurrection, taking bread and giving thanks to thee said: Take, eat: this is my body, which is broken for you. And likewise also the cup, saying: This is my blood, which is shed for you. As often as ye perform this, perform my memorial.

Having in memory, therefore, his death and resurrection, we offer to thee the bread and the cup, yielding thee thanks, because thou hast counted us worthy to stand before thee and to minister to thee.

And we pray thee that thou wouldest send thy Holy Spirit upon the offerings of thy holy church; that thou, gathering them into one, wouldest grant to all thy saints who partake to be filled with [the] Holy Spirit, that their faith may be confirmed in truth, that we may praise and glorify thee. Through thy Servant Jesus Christ, through whom be to thee glory and honour, and [the] Holy Spirit in the holy church, both now and always and world without end. Amen.

5. If anyone offers oil, he shall give thanks as at the offering of the bread and wine, though not with the same words but in the same general manner, saying:

That sanctifying this oil, O God, wherewith thou didst anoint kings, priests and prophets, thou wouldest grant health to them who use it and partake of it, so that it may bestow comfort on all who taste it and health on all who use it.

6. Likewise, if anyone offers cheese and olives, let him say thus:

Sanctify this milk that has been united into one mass, and unite us to thy love. Let thy loving kindness ever rest upon this fruit of the olive, which is a type of thy bounty, which thou didst cause to flow from the tree unto life for them who hope on thee.

But at every blessing shall be said:

Glory be to thee, with [the] Holy Spirit in the holy church, both now and always and world without end. [Amen.]

8. But when a presbyter is ordained, the bishop shall lay his hand upon his head, while the presbyters touch him, and he shall say according to those things that were said above, as we have prescribed above concerning the bishop, praying and saying:

God and Father of our Lord Jesus Christ, look upon this thy servant, and grant to him the Spirit of grace and counsel of a presbyter, that he may sustain and govern thy people with a pure heart; as thou didst look upon thy chosen people and didst command Moses that he should choose presbyters, whom thou didst fill with thy Spirit, which thou gavest to thy servant. And now, O Lord, grant that there may be unfailingly preserved amongst us the Spirit of thy grace, and make us worthy that, believing, we may minister to thee in simplicity of heart, praising thee. Through thy servant Jesus Christ, through whom be to thee glory and honour, with [the] Holy Spirit in the holy church, both now and always and world without end. Amen.

9. But the deacon, when he is ordained, is chosen according to those things that were said above, the bishop alone in like manner laying his hands upon him, as we have prescribed. When the deacon is ordained, this is the reason why the bishop alone shall lay his hands upon him: he is not ordained to the priesthood but to serve the bishop and to carry out the bishop's commands. He does not take part in the council of the clergy; he is to attend to his own duties and to make known to the bishop such things as are needful. He does not receive that Spirit that is possessed by the presbytery, in which the presbyters share; he receives only what is confided in him under the bishop's authority.

For this cause the bishop alone shall make a deacon. But on a presbyter, however, the presbyters shall lay their hands because of the common and like Spirit of the clergy. Yet the presbyter has only the power to receive; but he has no power to give. For this reason a presbyter does not ordain the clergy; but at the ordination of a presbyter he seals while the bishop ordains.

Over a deacon, then, he shall say as follows:

O God, who hast created all things and hast ordered them by thy Word, the Father of our Lord Jesus Christ, whom thou didst send to minister thy will and to manifest to us thy desire; grant [the] Holy Spirit of grace and care and diligence to this thy servant, whom thou hast chosen to serve the church and to offer in thy holy sanctuary the gifts that are offered to thee by thine appointed high priests, so that serving without blame and with a pure heart he may be counted worthy of this exalted office, by thy goodwill, praising thee continually. Through thy Servant Jesus Christ, through whom be to thee glory and honour, with [the] Holy Spirit, in the holy church, both now and always and world without end. Amen.

10. On a confessor, if he has been in bonds for the name of the Lord, hands shall not be laid for the diaconate or the presbyterate, for he has the honour of the presbyterate by his confession. But if he is to be ordained bishop, hands shall be laid upon him.

But if he is a confessor who was not brought before the authorities nor was punished with bonds nor was shut up in prison, but was insulted (?) casually or privately for the name of the Lord, even though he confessed, hands are to be laid upon him for every office of which he is worthy.

The bishop shall give thanks [in all ordinations] as we have prescribed. It is not, to be sure, necessary for anyone to recite the exact words that we have prescribed, by learning to say them by heart in his thanksgiving to God; but let each one pray according to his ability. If, indeed, he is able to pray competently with an elevated prayer, it is well. But even if he is only moderately able to pray and give praise, no one may forbid him; only let him pray sound in the faith.

11. When a widow is appointed, she shall not be ordained but she shall be appointed by the name. If her husband has been

long dead, she may be appointed [without delay]. But if her husband has died recently, she shall not be trusted; even if she is aged she must be tested by time, for often the passions grow old in those who yield to them.

The widow shall be appointed by the word alone, and [so] she shall be associated with the other widows; hands shall not be laid upon her because she does not offer the oblation nor has she a sacred ministry. Ordination is for the clergy on account of their ministry, but the widow is appointed for prayer, and prayer is the duty of all.

12. The reader is appointed by the bishop's giving him the book, for he is not ordained.

13. Hands shall not be laid upon a virgin, for it is her purpose alone that makes her a virgin.

14. Hands shall not be laid upon a subdeacon, but his name shall be mentioned that he may serve the deacon.

15. If anyone says, "I have received the gift of healing", hands shall not be laid upon him: the deed shall make manifest if he speaks the truth.

PART II

16. New Converts to the faith, who are to be admitted as hearers of the word, shall first be brought to the teachers before the people assemble. And they shall be examined as to their reason for embracing the faith, and they who bring them shall testify that they are competent to hear the word. Inquiry shall then be made as to the nature of their life; whether a man has a wife or is a slave. If he is the slave of a believer and he has his master's permission, then let him be received; but if his master does not give him a good character, let him be rejected. If his master is a heathen, let the slave be taught to please his master, that the word be not blasphemed. If a man has a wife or a woman a husband, let the man be instructed to content himself with his wife and the woman to content herself with her husband. But if a man is unmarried, let him be instructed to abstain from impurity, either by lawfully marrying a wife or else by remaining as he is. But if any man is possessed with demons, he shall not be admitted as a hearer until he is cleansed.

Inquiry shall likewise be made about the professions and trades of those who are brought to be admitted to the faith. If a man is a pander, he must desist or be rejected. If a man is a sculptor or painter, he must be charged not to make idols; if he does not desist he must be rejected. If a man is an actor or pantomimist, he must desist or be rejected. A teacher of young children had best desist, but if he has no other occupation, he may be permitted to continue. A charioteer, likewise, who races or frequents races, must desist or be rejected. A gladiator or a trainer of gladiators, or a huntsman [in the wild-beast shows], or anyone connected with these shows, or a public official in charge of gladiatorial exhibitions must desist or be rejected. A heathen priest or anyone who tends idols must desist or be rejected. A soldier of the civil authority must be taught not to kill men and to refuse to do so if he is commanded, and to refuse to take an oath; if he is unwilling to comply, he must be rejected. A military commander or civic magistrate that wears the purple must resign or be rejected. If a catechumen or a believer seeks to become a soldier, they must be rejected, for they have despised God. A harlot or licentious man or one who has castrated himself, or any other who does things not to be named, must be rejected, for they are defiled. A magician must not [even] be brought for examination. An enchanter, an astrologer, a diviner, a soothsayer, a user of magic verses, a juggler, a mountebank, an amulet-maker must desist or be rejected. A concubine, who is a slave and has reared her children and has been faithful to her master alone, may become a hearer; but if she has failed in these matters she must be rejected. If a man has a concubine, he must desist and marry legally; if he is unwilling, he must be rejected.

If, now, we have omitted anything (any trade?), the facts [as they occur] will instruct your mind; for we all have the spirit of God.

17. Let catechumens spend three years as hearers of the word. But if a man is zealous and perseveres well in the work, it is not the time but his character that is decisive.

18. When the teacher finishes his instruction, the catechumens shall pray by themselves, apart from the believers. And

[all] women, whether believers or catechumens, shall stand for their prayers by themselves in a separate part of the church.

And when [the catechumens] finish their prayers, they must not give the kiss of peace, for their kiss is not yet pure. Only believers shall salute one another, but men with men and women with women; a man shall not salute a woman.

And let all the women have their heads covered with an opaque cloth, not with a veil of thin linen, for this is not a true covering.

19. At the close of their prayer, when their instructor lays his hand upon the catechumens, he shall pray and dismiss them; whoever gives the instruction is to do this, whether a cleric or a layman.

If a catechumen should be arrested for the name of the Lord, let him not hesitate about bearing his testimony; for if it should happen that they treat him shamefully and kill him, he will be justified, for he has been baptized in his own blood.

20. They who are to be set apart for baptism shall be chosen after their lives have been examined: whether they have lived soberly, whether they have honoured the widows, whether they have visited the sick, whether they have been active in well-doing. When their sponsors have testified that they have done these things, then let them hear the Gospel. Then from the time that they are separated from the other catechumens, hands shall be laid upon them daily in exorcism and, as the day of their baptism draws near, the bishop himself shall exorcise each one of them that he may be personally assured of their purity. Then, if there is any of them who is not good or pure, he shall be put aside as not having heard the word in faith; for it is never possible for the alien to be concealed.

Then those who are set apart for baptism shall be instructed to bathe and free themselves from impurity and wash themselves on Thursday. If a woman is menstrous, she shall be set aside and baptized on some other day.

They who are to be baptized shall fast on Friday, and on Saturday the bishop shall assemble them and command them to kneel in prayer. And, laying his hand upon them, he shall exorcise all evil spirits to flee away and never to return; when he has done this he shall breathe in their faces, seal their foreheads, ears and noses, and then raise them up. They shall spend all that night in vigil, listening to reading and instruction.

They who are to be baptized shall bring with them no other vessels than the one each will bring for the eucharist; for it is fitting that he who is counted worthy of baptism should bring his offering at that time.

21. At cockcrow prayer shall be made over the water. The stream shall flow through the baptismal tank or pour into it from above when there is no scarcity of water; but if there is a scarcity, whether constant or sudden, then use whatever water you can find.

They shall remove their clothing. And first baptize the little ones; if they can speak for themselves, they shall do so; if not, their parents or other relatives shall speak for them. Then baptize the men, and last of all the women; they must first loosen their hair and put aside any gold or silver ornaments that they were wearing: let no one take any alien thing down to the water with them.

At the hour set for the baptism the bishop shall give thanks over oil and put it into a vessel: this is called the "oil of thanksgiving". And he shall take other oil and exorcise it: this is called "the oil of exorcism". [The anointing is performed by a presbyter.] A deacon shall bring the oil of exorcism, and shall stand at the presbyter's left hand; and another deacon shall take the oil of thanksgiving, and shall stand at the presbyter's right hand. Then the presbyter, taking hold of each of those about to be baptized, shall command him to renounce, saying:

I renounce thee, Satan, and all thy servants and all thy works.

And when he has renounced all these, the presbyter shall anoint him with the oil of exorcism, saying:

Let all spirits depart far from thee.

Then, after these things, let him give him over to the presbyter who baptizes, and let the candidates stand in the water, naked, a deacon going with them likewise. And when he who is being baptized goes down into the water, he who baptizes him, putting his hand on him, shall say thus:

Dost thou believe in God, the Father Almighty?

And he who is being baptized shall say:

I believe.

Then

holding his hand placed on his head, he shall baptize him once. And then he shall say:

Dost thou believe in Christ Jesus, the Son of God, who was born of the Holy Ghost of the Virgin Mary, and was crucified under Pontius Pilate, and was dead and buried, and rose again the third day, alive from the dead, and ascended into heaven, and sat at the right hand of the Father, and will come to judge the quick and the dead? And when he says:

I believe,

he is baptized again. And again he shall say:

Dost thou believe in [the] Holy Ghost, and the holy church, and the resurrection of the flesh?

He who is being baptized shall say accordingly:

I believe,

and so he is baptized a third time.

And afterward, when he has come up [out of the water], he is anointed by the presbyter with the oil of thanksgiving, the presbyter saying:

I anoint thee with holy oil in the name of Jesus Christ.

And so each one, after drying himself, is immediately clothed, and then is brought into the church.

22. Then the bishop, laying his hand upon them, shall pray, saying:

O Lord God, who hast made them worthy to obtain remission of sins through the laver of regeneration of [the] Holy Spirit, send into them thy grace, that they may serve thee according to thy will; for thine is the glory, to the Father and the Son, with [the] Holy Spirit in the holy church, both now and world without end. Amen.

Then, pouring the oil of thanksgiving from his hand and putting it on his forehead, he shall say:

I anoint thee with holy oil in the Lord, the Father Almighty and Christ Jesus and [the] Holy Ghost.

And signing them on the forehead he shall say:

The Lord be with thee;

and he who is signed shall say:

And with thy spirit.

And so he shall do to each one.

And immediately thereafter they shall join in prayer with all the people, but they shall not pray with the faithful until all these things are completed. And at the close of their prayer they shall give the kiss of peace.

23. And then the offering is immediately brought by the deacons to the bishop, and by thanksgiving he shall make the bread into an image of the body of Christ, and the cup of wine mixed with water according to the likeness of the blood, which is shed for all who believe in him. And milk and honey mixed together for the fulfilment of the promise to the fathers, which spoke of a land flowing with milk and honey; namely, Christ's flesh which he gave, by which they who believe are nourished like babes, he making sweet the bitter things of the heart by the gentleness of this word. And the water into an offering in a token of the laver, in order that the inner part of man, which is a living soul, may receive the same as the body.

The bishop shall explain the reason of all these things to those who partake. And when he breaks the bread and distributes the fragments he shall say:

The heavenly bread in Christ Jesus.

And the recipient shall say, Amen.

And the presbyters—or if there are not enough presbyters, the deacons—shall hold the cups, and shall stand by with reverence and modesty; first he who holds the water, then the milk, thirdly the wine. And the recipients shall taste of each three times, he who gives the cup saying:

In God the Father Almighty;

and the recipient shall say, Amen. Then:

In the Lord Jesus Christ;

[and he shall say, Amen. Then:

In] [the] Holy Ghost and the holy church;

and he shall say, Amen. So it shall be done to each.

And when these things are completed, let each one hasten to do good works, and to please God and to live aright, devoting himself to the church, practising the things he has learned, advancing in the service of God.

Now we have briefly delivered to you these things concerning the holy baptism and the holy oblation, for you have already been instructed concerning the resurrection of the flesh and all other things as taught in Scripture. Yet if there is any other thing that ought to be told [to converts], let the bishop impart it to them privately after their baptism; let not unbelievers know it, until they are baptized: this is the white stone of which John said: "There is upon it a new name written, which no one knoweth but he that receiveth the stone".

PART III

25. Widows and virgins shall fast frequently and shall pray for the church; presbyters, if they wish, and laymen may fast likewise. But the bishop may fast only when all the people fast.

26. For it constantly happens that some one wishes to make an offering–and such a one must not be denied–and then the bishop, after breaking the bread, must in every case taste and eat it with the other believers. [At such an offering] each shall take from the bishop's hand a piece of [this] bread before breaking his own bread. [This service has a special ceremonial] for it is "a Blessing", not "a Thanksgiving", as is [the service of] the Body of the Lord. But before drinking, each one, as many of you as are present, must take a cup and give thanks over it, and so go to your meal.

But to the catechumens is given exorcised bread, and each of them must offer the cup. No catechumen shall sit at the Lord's Supper.

But at each act of offering, the offerer must remember his host, for he was invited to the latter's home for that very purpose. But when you eat and drink, do so in an orderly manner and not so that anyone may mock, or your host be saddened by your unruliness, but behave so that he may pray to be made worthy that the saints may enter his dwelling: "for ye", it is said, "are the salt of the earth".

If the offering should be one made to all the guests jointly, take your portion from your host [and depart]. But if all are to eat then and there, do not eat to excess, so that your host may likewise send some of what the saints leave to whomsoever he will and [so] may rejoice in the faith.

But while the guests are eating, let them eat silently, not arguing, [attending to] such things as the bishop may teach, but if he should ask any question, let an answer be given him; and when he says anything, everyone in modest praise shall keep silence until he asks again.

And even if the bishop should be absent when the faithful meet at a supper, if a presbyter or a deacon is present they shall eat in a similar orderly fashion, and each shall be careful to take the blessed bread from the presbyter's or deacon's hand; and in the same way the catechumens shall take the same exorcised bread.

But if [only] laymen meet, let them not act presumptuously, for a layman cannot bless the blessed bread.

Let each one eat in the name of the Lord; for this is pleasing to the Lord that we should be jealous [of our good name] even among the heathen, all sober alike.

27. If anyone wishes to give a meal to widows of mature years, let him dismiss them before evening. But if, on account of existing conditions, he cannot [feed them in his house], let him send them away, and they may eat of his food at their homes in any way they please.

28. As soon as first-fruits appear, all shall hasten to offer them to the bishop. And he shall offer them, shall give thanks and shall name him who offered them, saying:

We give thee thanks, O God, and we offer thee the first-fruits; which thou hast given us to enjoy, nourishing them through thy word, commanding the earth to bring forth her fruits for the gladness and the food of men and all beasts. For all these things we praise thee, O God, and for all things wherewith thou hast blessed us, who for us adornest every creature with divers fruits. Through thy Servant Jesus Christ, our Lord, through whom be to thee glory, world without end. Amen.

Only certain fruits may be blessed, namely grapes, the fig, the pomegranate, the olive, the pear, the apple, the mulberry, the peach, the cherry, the almond, the plum. Not the pumpkin, nor the melon, nor the cucumber, nor the onion nor garlic nor anything else having an odour.

But sometimes flowers too are offered; here the rose and the lily may be offered, but no other.

But for everything that is eaten shall they [who eat it] give thanks to the Holy God, eating unto His glory.

29. Let no one at the paschal season eat before the offering is made, otherwise he shall not be credited with the fast. But if any woman is with child, or if anyone is sick and cannot fast for two days, let such a one, on account of his need, [at least] fast on Saturday, contenting himself with bread and water. But if anyone on a voyage or for any other necessary cause should not know the day, when he has learned the truth he shall postpone his fast until after Pentecost. For the ancient type has passed away, and so the [postponed] fast [of Number 2. 11] in the second month has ceased, and each one ought to fast in accord with his knowledge of the truth.

30. Each of the deacons, with the subdeacons, shall be alert on the bishop's behalf, for the bishop must be informed if any are sick so that, if he pleases, he may visit them; for a sick man is greatly comforted when the high priest is mindful of him.

31. The faithful, early in the morning, as soon as they have awakened and arisen, before they undertake their tasks shall pray to God and so may then go to their duties. But if any instruction in the word is held, let each give first place to that, that he may attend and hear the word of God, to his soul's comfort; so let each one hasten to the church, where the Spirit abounds.

32. But let each of the faithful be zealous, before he eats anything else, to receive the eucharist; for if anyone receives it with faith, after such a reception he cannot be harmed even if a deadly poison should be given him. But let each one take care that no unbeliever taste the eucharist, nor a mouse nor any other animal, and that nothing of it fall or be lost; for the body of Christ is to be eaten by believers and must not be despised. The cup, when thou hast given thanks in the name of the Lord, thou hast accepted as the image of the blood of Christ. Therefore, let none of it be spilled, so that no alien spirit may lick it up, as if thou didst despise it; thou shalt be guilty of the blood, as if thou didst scorn the price with which thou hast been bought.

33. Let the deacons and the presbyters assemble daily at the place which the bishop may appoint; let the deacons [in particular] never fail to assemble unless prevented by sickness. When all have met they shall instruct those who are in the church, and then, after prayer, each shall go to his appointed duties.

34. No exorbitant charge shall be made for burial in the cemetery, for it belongs to all the poor; only the hire of the grave-digger and the cost of the tile [for closing the niche in the catacombs] shall be asked. The wages of the caretakers are to be paid by the bishop, lest any of those who go to that place be burdened [with a charge].

St. Cyril of Jerusalem

315-386

Cyril was born probably in Palestine around 312 and was educated in Jerusalem. He became a cleric there and was ordained a presbyter by Bishop Maximus around 342. After Maximus died Cyril became bishop of Jerusalem in 350, an event that was complicated by the Arian controversy that was causing turmoil. It was in this period that he delivered his famous catechetical instructions, but it is impossible to identify the precise years.

Cyril was expelled from his see three times (357, 360, and 367), his third exile lasting eleven years. After his return in 378 he found peace for his remaining years. He attended the second Ecumenical Council, Constantinople I, (381) where there are grounds for thinking he may have chaired the committee that formulated the Creed. Pope Leo XIII proclaimed him a Doctor of the universal Church.

The Catecheses *of Cyril are 24 in number. The first is the* Procatechesis, *or Prologue to the entire series; then come the 18 Lenten lectures, followed by the five Easter lectures. The following selection presents the* Procatechesis *and the Easter lectures (also called the* Mystagogical Catecheses*). Let it be noted that there still remains some question about the authorship of these latter; they may be the work of Cyril's successor, John of Jerusalem. On the other hand, they could be John's revision of Cyril's lectures. Their very nature as an outstanding* *series that could readily and profitably be repeated year after year complicates ascertaining their precise origin. But, for our purposes, this is a minor question. The important point is to see how the Christian liturgy was taught and practiced in Jerusalem, "the mother of all churches," in the mid-fourth century.*

At Easter the catechumens who had been prepared by the above series were baptized, confirmed, and admitted to the Eucharist. Then the five "mystagogical" (leading into the mysteries) catecheses were addressed to these new Christians in the chapel of the Resurrection to give them a deeper appreciation of what these sacraments should mean to them.

Justin and Hippolytus had described the Christian liturgy as celebrated in second and third century Rome, but from Cyril we receive our earliest description of what was being done in the East. One striking difference is the sense conveyed as to how things have grown. A half-century earlier Christianity had been illegal and persecuted. Now it had become the preferred religion of the Roman Empire, large numbers of people were visiting the splendid new basilicas built by Constantine and his successors. Catechetical instruction was a pressing need if these potential converts were to be evangelized. The solid content of these theological lectures shows how seriously Cyril and his colleagues took their ministry.

CATECHETICAL LECTURES

THE PROCATECHESIS

or

PROLOGUE TO THE CATECHETICAL LECTURES

Already, my dear candidates for Enlightenment, scents of paradise are wafted towards you; already you are culling mystic blossoms for the weaving of heavenly garlands; already the fragrance of the Holy Spirit has blown about you. Already you have arrived at the outer court of the palace: may the King lead you in! Now the blossom has appeared on the trees; God grant the fruit be duly harvested! Now you have enlisted; you have been called to the Colors. You have walked in procession with the tapers of brides in your hands and the desire of heavenly citizenship in your hearts; with a holy resolve also, and the confident hope which that brings in its train. For He is no liar who said: "For those who love Him, God makes all things conspire to good." Yes, God is generous and kind; nevertheless He requires in every man a resolve that is true. That is why the Apostle adds: "For those who are called in accordance with a resolve." It is the sincerity of your resolution that makes you "called." It is of no use your body being here if your thoughts and heart are elsewhere.

Why, there was a Simon the Sorcerer once who approached the baptismal waters: he was dipped in the font, but he was not enlightened. While he plunged his body in the water, his heart was not enlightened by the Spirit; physically he went down and came up, but his soul was not buried with Christ, nor did it share in His Resurrection. If I mention these examples of falls, it is to prevent *your* downfall. "Now all these things happened to them as a type, and they were written for the correction" of those who approach the font to this day. Let none of you be found tempting grace, "lest some bitter root spring up to poison" your heart. Let no one enter saying: "I say, let us see what the believers are doing; I'm going in to have a look and find out what's going on." Do you expect to see without being seen? Do you imagine that while you are investigating "what's going on," God is not investigating your heart?

We read in the Gospels of a busybody who one day decided to "investigate" a wedding-feast. Without dressing correctly for the occasion, he entered the dining room and, unchallenged by the bridegroom, took his place at table. Etiquette, of course, demanded that, seeing everybody's white garments, he should conform; but in fact, though fully the match of his fellow-guests as a trencherman, he did not match them in his dress (I mean, his resolve). The bridegroom, for all his large-heartedness, was not undiscerning and, while going the rounds of the company and observing his guests individually (it was not what they ate, but the correctness of their behavior and dress that interested him), he saw a stranger without a wedding garment, and said to him: "Pray, sir, how did you get in? What a color! What effrontery! The doorkeeper did not stop you in view of the liberality of the host? Quite so. You didn't know the correct dress for a festive occasion? Quite. Nevertheless, you came in; you saw the glittering clothes of those at table. Should not your eyes have been your teachers? Should not a timely exit then have been the prelude to a timely return? As it is, your untimely entrance can lead only to your untimely ejection." Turning to his attendants, he ordered: "Bind those feet" which presumptuously intruded; "bind the hands" which had not the wit to put a bright garment on him; and "cast him into the outer darkness"; for he is not worthy of the bridal torches. Ponder, I bid you, the fate of that intruder, and look to your own safety.

For our part, as Christ's ministers we have given a welcome to every man and, in the role of porter, have left the door ajar. You, maybe, have come in with your soul befouled with the mire of sin and with your purpose sullied. You came in; you were accepted; your name was entered in the register. Do you see the majesty of the Church? Do you behold, I ask, its order and discipline, the reading of the Scriptures, the presence of the ecclesiastical orders, the regular sequence of instruction? You are on holy ground; be taught by what you see. Withdraw in a good hour now, and come back in a right good hour tomorrow. If the fashion of your soul was avarice, put on another fashion, and then come in. Put off, I say, lewdness and impurity; put on the bright robe of chastity. I give you timely warning before Jesus, the Bridegroom of souls, comes in and sees the fashions. You cannot plead short notice; forty days are yours for repentance; you have opportunity in plenty for undressing, for laundry-work, for dressing again and returning. If you persist in an evil purpose, the preacher is guiltless, but you must not expect to receive the grace. Though the water will not refuse to receive you, you will get no welcome from the Spirit. If anyone is conscious of a wound in himself, let him have it dressed; if any has fallen, let him rise. Let there be no Simon among you, no hypocrite—and no Paul Pry.

Perhaps you have come with a different motive: perhaps you are courting, and a girl is your reason—or, conversely, a boy. Many a time, too, a slave has wished to please his master, or a friend his friend. I allow the bait, and I welcome you in the trust that, however unsatisfactory the motive that has brought you, your good hope will soon save you. Maybe you did not know where you were going, or what sort of net it was in which you were to be caught. You are a fish caught in the net of the Church. Let yourself be taken alive: don't try to escape. It is Jesus who is playing you on His line, not to kill you, but, by killing you, to make you alive. For you must die and rise again. Did you not hear the Apostle say: "dead to sin, but living to justice"? Die, then to sin, and live to righteousness; from today be alive.

What honor Jesus bestows! You used to be called a catechumen, when the truth was being dinned into you from without: hearing about the Christian hope without understanding it; hearing about the Mysteries without having a spiritual perception of them; hearing the Scriptures but not sounding their depths. No longer in your ears now but in your heart is that ringing; for the indwelling Spirit henceforth makes your soul the house of God. When you hear the tests from Scripture concerning the Mysteries, then you will have a spiritual perception of things once beyond your ken.

Do not suppose that it is a small thing that you are being given. You, a pitiable creature, are receiving the family name of God. Listen to Paul saying: "God is faithful." Listen to another Scripture saying God is "faithful and just." It was because he foresaw this—because men were to bear a name which belongs to God—that the Psalmist, speaking in the person of God, said: "I have said: you are gods, and all of you the sons of the Most High." But take care that you do not, while rejoicing in the name of "faithful," have the resolve of the faithless. You have entered for a race: run the course; you will not get the like chance again. If it were your wedding day that was fixed, would you not, ignoring everything else, be wholly engaged in preparations for the marriage feast? Then, on the eve of consecrating your soul to your heavenly Spouse, will you not put by the things of the body to win those of the spirit?

A man cannot be baptized a second and a third time. Otherwise, he could say: "I failed once; the second time I shall succeed." Fail once, and there is no putting it right. For, "one Lord, one faith, one Baptism." It is only heretics who are rebaptized, and then because the first was no Baptism.

God requires of us only one thing, sincerity. Do not go on saying, "But how are my sins blotted out?" I answer: "By assenting, by believing." Could any answer be more succinct? If, however, not your heart but only your lips proclaim your assent, well, it is the "Reader of hearts" who is your Judge. From today cease from every evil deed; let not your tongue speak unholy words, nor your eye commit evil or rove after vanities.

Let your feet take you swiftly to the catachetical instructions. Submit to the exorcisms devoutly. Whether you are breathed upon or exorcised, the act spells salvation. Imagine virgin gold alloyed with various foreign substances: copper, tin, iron, lead. What we are after is the gold alone; and gold cannot be purified of its dross without fire. Similarly, the soul cannot be purified without exorcisms, exorcisms which, since they are culled from the divine Scriptures, possess divine power. The veiling of your face is to foster recollection, lest a roving eye make your heart also stray. But the veiling of the eyes does not hinder the ears from receiving salvation. Just as goldsmiths with their delicate instruments direct a blast upon the fire and, by agitating the surrounding flame, cause the gold hidden in the crucible to bubble up and so gain their object, in the same way when the exorcists inspire fear by means of the divine Spirit and regenerate the soul by fire in the crucible of the body, our enemy the Devil flees, and we are left with salvation and the sure prospect of eternal life; and henceforth, the soul, purified of its offenses, has salvation. Let us, then, my brethren, persevere in hope; let us commit ourselves in hope: so will the God of all, seeing our resolution, cleanse us from our sins, grant us a good hope of our estate, and bestow on us repentance unto salvation. It is God who has called, and it is you that He has called.

Be faithful in your attendance of the catechizing. Even though we protract our discourse, do not let your mind yield to distraction. You are taking up arms against the enemy. You are taking up arms against heresies, against the Jews, against the Samaritans, against the Gentiles. Your enemies are many: take plenty of ammunition; you have targets in plenty. You must learn how to shoot down the Greek and do battle with heretic, Jew, and Samaritan. Your weapons are sharp, and sharpest of all is "the sword of the Spirit." But your own right hand must strike with a holy resolution, to fight the fight of the Lord, if you would conquer the opposing powers and make yourself proof against every stratagem of heresy.

Let this also be included in your battle orders: study what you are told and guard it forever. Do not confuse the prebaptismal instructions with the ordinary sermons. Excellent and reliable as those are, still, if we neglect their lessons today, we can learn them tomorrow. But the systematic instruction about the layer of regeneration–if that be neglected today, when shall the loss be made good? Imagine it is the season for planting trees: unless we dig, and dig deep, when can the tree be planted aright that has once been planted amiss? Or let me compare the catechizing to a building. Unless we methodically bind and joint the whole structure together, we shall have leaks and dry rot, and all our previous exertions will be wasted. No: stone must be laid upon stone in regular sequence, and corner follow corner, jutting edges must be planed away: and so the perfect structure rises. I bring you as it were the stones of knowledge; you must be instructed in the doctrine of the living God, of the Judgment, of Christ, of the Resurrection. Many things have to be said in order, which are now being touched upon at random but will then be brought together into harmonious system. Unless you achieve this unity of design, holding the beginning and the sequel in your mind together, the builder may do his best, but your house will be a ruin.

If after the class a catechumen asks you what the instructors have said, tell outsiders nothing. For it is a divine secret that we deliver to you, even the hope of the life to come. Keep the secret for the Rewarder. If someone says, "What harm is done if I know about it too?," don't listen to him. So the sick man asks for wine, but, given to him at the wrong time, it only produces brain-fever, and two evils ensue: the effect on the sick man is disastrous, and the doctor is maligned. So with the catechumen, if he is told the Mysteries by one of the faithful: not understanding what he has been told, the catechumen raves, attacking the doctrine and ridiculing the statement, while the believer stands condemned as a traitor.

You are now a man standing at a frontier: so, no careless talk, please. Not that these are not fit subjects for discussion, but that your interlocutor is not fit to hear them. You yourself were once a catechumen; I did not then describe to you the country which lay ahead. When you grasp by experience the sublimity of the doctrines, then you will understand that the catechumens are worthy to hear them.

All you who have been enrolled are the sons and daughters of one Mother. When you come in before the exorcisms are due to begin, let the conversation of each of you be such as to excite devotion. If anyone is absent, make search for him. If it were to a feast that you had been invited, would you not wait for your fellow guest? If you had a brother, would you not seek what is good for your brother?

Finally, do not indulge in idle curiosity—no asking "what the city has done," or the ward, or the Emperor, or the Bishop, or the priest. Lift up your eyes: now, as your hour strikes, you need Him who is above. "Be still, and know that I am God." If you see the believers not recollected when they are ministering, well, they are safe; they know what they have received; they possess the grace. Your fate is still in the balance, to be accepted or not. Instead of copying the carefree, cultivate fear.

During the actual exorcism, while waiting for the others, let men be with men, and women with women. For now I need Noe's ark, that I may have Noe and his sons together, separate from his wife and his sons' wives. For, although the ark was one and the door was closed, yet decorum was observed. So now, though the church doors are barred and you are all inside, let distinctions be kept: men with men, women with women. Let not the principle of salvation be made a pretext for spiritual ruin. Keeping close together is a good rule, provided that passion is kept at a distance.

Furthermore, let the men have some profitable book in their hands while they sit waiting, and let one read from it and another listen. Or, if there is no book available, let one pray and another talk about something useful. Let the virgins likewise form a separate band, singing hymns or reading; silently, however, so that, while their lips speak, no other's ears may hear what they say. For, "I suffer not a woman to speak in church." Let the married woman imitate them: let her pray, and her lips move, but her voice not be heard. So shall Samuel come among us: your barren soul, that is to say, shall bring forth the salvation of "God who has heard your prayers." For that is the meaning of "Samuel."

I shall be watching the earnestness of each man the piety of each woman. Let your heart be fired to piety; let your soul be tempered like steel, as the stubborn metal of unfaith is hammered on the anvil till the dross scales off and the pure iron is left. Let the rust flake away, leaving the authentic metal.

May God one day show you that night whose darkness is daylight, the dark of which it is said: "Darkness shall not be dark to thee, and night shall be light as the day." Then, may the gate of Paradise be opened to every man of you and every woman. Then, may you enjoy the fragrant, Christ-bearing waters. Then, may you receive Christ's name and the power of things divine. Even now, I beseech you, in spirit lift up your eyes; behold the angelic choirs, and the Lord of all, God, on His throne, with the Son, the Only-begotten, sitting on His right hand, and the Spirit, too, and the Thrones and Dominations ministering, and every man of you and every woman receiving salvation. Even now let there ring in your ears that excellent sound which you shall hear when the Angels, celebrating your salvation, chant: "Blessed are they whose iniquities are forgiven," on the day when, like the new stars of the Church, you will enter, your bodies bright, your souls shining.

Great is the prize set before you in Baptism: ransom for captives, remission of sins, death of sin, a new, spiritual birth, a shining garment, a holy seal inviolable, a Heaven-bound chariot, delights of Paradise, a passport to the Kingdom, the grace of adoption of sons. But a dragon lies in ambush for the traveler; take care he does not bite you and inject his poison of unbelief. Seeing this numerous company winning salvation, he selects and stalks his prey. In your journey to the Father of the souls, your way lies past that dragon. How shall you pass him? You must have "your feet stoutly shod with the gospel of peace," so that, even if he does bite you, he may not hurt you.

With Hope invincible for your sandals and with Faith the guest of your heart, you may pass through the enemy's lines and enter into the house of the Lord. Prepare your heart for the reception of teaching and the fellowship in the holy Mysteries. Pray more frequently, that God may count you worthy of the heavenly and eternal Mysteries. Never be idle, day or night, but so soon as sleep falls from your eyes let your mind occupy itself with prayer. If you notice that an evil thought has entered your mind, hold tightly to the saving remembrance of Judgment. Apply your mind to learning, that it may forget low things. If you find someone saying to you: "So you are to go down into the water? What's wrong with the new public baths?," be sure that this is a ruse of "the Dragon that is in the sea." Attend not, then, to the lips of the speaker of guile, but to the Spirit of unbelief and deceit who works in him. Guard your own soul if you would avoid being trapped and would inherit, after standing fast in hope, everlasting salvation.

These, then, are the instructions, these the battle orders, that I (so far as a man may) give to you. To make our house "hay, straw" and chaff is to risk its total loss by fire; no, make the work of "gold, silver, precious stones." For it is mine to speak, yours to translate my words into action, and God's to perfect the work. Let us prepare our hearts, straining every nerve and sinew of soul and mind. The race is for our souls; we have set our hearts on an eternal prize. God, who knows your hearts and discerns who is genuine and who is only acting a part, is able both to keep the sincere safe and to make a believer of the hypocrite. Yes, even of the unbeliever God can make a believer if only he gives his heart. May He "cancel the decree against you"; may He grant you an amnesty for your former sins; may He set you as His sons in His Church and enlist you in His own service, arraying you in the armor of righteousness. May He fill you with the heavenly treasures of the New Covenant and sign you with that seal of the Holy Spirit which no man shall break forever, in Christ Jesus our Lord, to whom be glory forever and ever. Amen.

TO THE READER

These Catechetical Lectures, addressed to candidates for Enlightenment, may be given to those going forward for Baptism and to the already baptized faithful. They may, on no account, be given to catechumens or to other classes of non-Christians. Anyone making a copy is hereby adjured, as in the sight of the Lord, to preface it with this warning.

FIRST LECTURE ON THE MYSTERIES

The First Part of the Baptismal Ceremony
(The Rites of the Outer Chamber:
Renunciation of Satan, Profession of Faith)
With a Lesson from Peter's First Catholic Epistle,
Beginning, "Be sober, be watchful," to the End
By the same Cyril and Bishop John

It has long been my wish, true-born and long-desired children of the Church, to discourse to you upon these spiritual, heavenly mysteries. On the principle, however, that seeing is believing, I delayed until the present occasion, calculating that after what you saw on that night I should find you a readier audience now when I am to be your guide to the brighter and more fragrant meadows of this second Eden. In particular, you are now capable of understanding the diviner mysteries of divine, life-giving baptism. The time being now come to spread for you the board of more perfect instruction, let me explain the significance of what was done for you on that evening of your Baptism.

First you entered on the antechamber of the baptistery and faced towards the west. On the command to stretch out your hand, you renounced Satan as though he were there in person. This moment, you should know, is prefigured in ancient history. When that tyrannous and cruel despot, Pharaoh, was oppressing the noble, free-spirited Hebrew nation, God sent Moses to deliver them from the hard slavery imposed upon them by the Egyptians. The doorposts were anointed with the blood of a lamb that the destroyer might pass over the houses signed with the blood; so the Jews were miraculously liberated. After their liberation the enemy gave chase, and, seeing the sea part miraculously before them, still continued in hot pursuit, only to be instantaneously overwhelmed and engulfed in the Red Sea.

Pass, pray, from the old to the new, from the figure to the reality. There Moses sent by God to Egypt; here Christ sent from the Father into the world. Moses' mission was to lead out from Egypt a persecuted people; Christ's, to rescue all the people of the world who were under the tyranny of sin. There the blood of a lamb was the charm against the destroyer; here, the blood of the unspotted Lamb, Jesus Christ, is appointed your inviolable sanctuary against demons. Pharaoh pursued that people of old right into the sea; this outrageous spirit, the impudent author of all evil, followed you, each one, up to the very verge of the saving streams. That other tyrant is engulfed and drowned in the Red Sea; this one is destroyed in the saving water.

You are told, however, to address him as personally present, and with arm outstretched to say: "I renounce you, Satan." Allow me to explain the reason of your facing west, for you should know it. Because the west is the region of visible darkness, Satan, who is himself darkness, has his empire in darkness—that is the significance of your looking steadily towards the west while you renounce that gloomy Prince of night.

What was it that each of you said, standing there? "I renounce you, Satan, you wicked and cruel tyrant; I no longer" (you said in effect) "fear your power. For Christ broke that power by sharing flesh and blood with me, planning through their assumption to break, by His death, the power of Death, to save me from subjection to perpetual bondage. I renounce you, crafty scoundrel of a serpent; I renounce you, traitor, perpetrator of every crime, who inspired our first parents to revolt. I renounce you, Satan, agent and abettor of all wickedness."

Then in a second phrase you are taught to say, "and all your works." All sin is "the works of Satan"; and sin, too, you must renounce, since he who has escaped from a tyrant has also cast off the tyrant's livery. Sin in all its forms, then, is included in the works of the Devil. Only let me tell you this: all your words, particularly those spoken at that awful hour, are recorded in the book of God. Whenever, therefore, you are caught in conduct contrary to your profession, you will be tried as a renegade. Renounce, then, the works of Satan, that is, every irrational deed and thought.

Next you say, "and all his pomp." The pomp of the Devil is the craze for the theatre, the horse races in the circus, the wild-beast hunts, and all such vanity, from which the saint prays to God to be delivered in the words, "Turn away mine eyes that they may not behold vanity." Avoid an addiction to the theatre, with its spectacle of the licentiousness, the lewd and unseemly antics of actors and the frantic dancing of degenerates. Not for you, either, the folly of those who, to gratify their miserable appetite, expose themselves to wild beasts in the combats in the amphitheatre. They pamper their belly at the cost of becoming themselves, in the event, food for the maw of savage beasts; of these gladiators it is far to say that in the service of the belly which is their God they court death in the arena. Shun also the bedlam of the races, a spectacle in which souls as well as riders come to grief. All these follies are the pomp of the Devil.

The food, also, which is sometimes hung up in pagan temples and at festivals—meat, bread, and so forth—since it is defiled by the invocation of abominable demons, may be included in "the pomp of the Devil." For as the bread and wine of the Eucharist before the holy invocation of the adorable Trinity were ordinary bread and wine, while after the invocation the bread becomes the Body of Christ, and the wine his Blood, so these foods of the pomp of Satan, though of their own nature ordinary food, become profane through the invocation of evil spirits.

After this you say, "and all your service." The service of the Devil is prayer in the temples of idols, the honoring of lifeless images, the lighting of lamps or the burning of incense by springs or streams; there have been cases of persons who, deceived by dreams or by evil spirits, have gone to this length in the hope of being rewarded by the cure of even bodily ailments. Have nothing to do with these practices. The observation of birds, divination, omens, charms and amulets, magic and similar chicanery—all practices are the cult of the Devil. Shun them. For if you should succumb to such practices after renouncing Satan and transferring your allegiance to Christ, you will find the usurper more cruel than ever. For if formerly, treating you as a familiar, he abated the rigors of your slaver, now he will be furiously exasperated against you. So you will lose Christ and taste Satan's tyranny.

Have you not heard the old story which recounts the fate of Lot and his daughters? Was not Lot himself saved together with his daughters after gaining the mountain, while his wife was turned into a pillar of salt, a monumental warning and a memorial of her wicked choice (her looking back)? So be on your guard: do not turn back to "what is behind," first "putting your hand to the plow" and then "turning back" to the bitter savor of the things of this world. No; flee to the mountain, to Jesus Christ, the "stone hewn without hands" that has filled the world.

When you renounce Satan, trampling underfoot every covenant with him, then you annul that ancient "league with Hell," and God's paradise opens before you, that Eden, planted in the east, from which for his transgression our first father was banished. Symbolic of this is your facing about from the west to the east, the place of light. It was at this point that you were told to say: "I believe in the Father, and in the Son, and in the Holy Spirit, and in one Baptism of repentance." But these subjects have been treated at large, as God's grace allowed, in the previous discourses.

In the security, then, of this formula of faith, "be sober." For "our adversary, the devil," in the words just read, "as a roaring lion, goes without seeking whom he may devour." Yet if in former times Death was mighty and devoured, now, in the time of the holy laver of regeneration, "the Lord God hath wiped away all tears from every face." No more shall you mourn, now that you have "put off the old man," but you shall ever keep high festival, clad in Jesus Christ as in a garment of salvation.

That was what was done in the outer chamber. When we enter, God willing, in the succeeding discourses on the mysteries, into the Holy of Holies, we shall receive the key to the rites performed there. Now to God, with the Son and the Holy Spirit, be glory, power and majesty forever and ever. Amen.

PREFATORY REMARK TO THE SECOND AND THIRD LECTURES ON THE MYSTERIES

THE B THEORY AND THE C THEORY

Mystagogical Lectures 2 and 3 are relevant to an important continuing debate about the relative importance of Baptism and Confirmation, and especially about the answer to the question, "In which sacrament is the Holy Spirit given?" For convenience I shall refer to the theory which exalts Baptism (the theory to which I provisionally subscribe) as the B theory, and to the other as the C (Chrism or Confirmation) theory. The B theory holds that the Spirit, being inseparable from other graces incontestably given in Baptism (dying and rising with Christ, regeneration, adoptive sonship, sanctifying grace, new creation), is Himself given in Baptism. Thus (as the Lenten Lectures hold) Baptism is the sacrament of the Death and Resurrection of the Lord and also corresponds to Pentecost, the primal creation of the Church through the Spirit; so Peter after Pentecost says (Acts 2.38): "Be baptized . . . and you will receive the gift of the Holy Spirit"; cf. John 3.5. On this view Confirmation, whether by imposition of hands or by chrismation (anointing), though primitive, is a subsidiary rite; it rounded off the rite (though sometimes it preceded Baptism) and gave a high sacramental grace (of variable interpretation) but was not strictly essential. The bishop's role is safeguarded in this theory by the fact that the whole initiation rite is under his control and direction.

The C theory holds that Pentecost corresponds to Confirmation (Chrism) and that it is in Chrism that the Spirit is given. Among the texts to which it appeals are Acts 8.14-17 (Peter and

John in Samaria), 19.5, and the problematic 1 John 2.20, 27 ("You have an anointing, *chrisma*. . ."). It holds that quite often in the New Testament "baptism" refers not simply to water-baptism but to a larger rite of which this was only a part. It interprets the "born again of water and the Spirit" of John 3.3-5 as referring to two baptisms, water-baptism and baptism of Spirit by chrismation. Similarly in the Gospel narratives of Our Lord's baptism by John it finds two successive events (the exemplars of Baptism and Confirmation) instead of the dualism of a single event in which one element (the Dove and the Voice) is but the visibilization of the spiritual grace conferred in the other (the baptism in Jordan). Emphasizing that "Christ" means "anointed," it holds that Chrism christens.

While in the notes to Mystagogical Lectures 2 and 3 I have occasionally criticized the theological assumptions and implications of the C theory, I nowhere discuss the earlier evidence, on which the answer to the question depends.

SECOND LECTURE ON THE MYSTERIES

BAPTISM: THE RITES OF THE INNER CHAMBER

"Do you not know that all we who have been baptized into Christ Jesus have been baptized into his death? . . . since you are not under law but under grace."

The daily initiatory expositions, with their new teaching telling of new realities, are profitable to you, especially to those of you who have just been renewed from oldness to newness. I shall, therefore, resuming from yesterday, expound the bare essentials of our next topic, explaining the symbolical meaning of what you did in the inner chamber.

Immediately, then, upon entering, you removed your tunics. This was a figure of the "stripping off of the old man with his deeds." Having stripped, you were naked, in this also imitating Christ, who was naked on the cross, by His nakedness "throwing off the cosmic powers and authorities like a garment and publicly upon the cross leading them in his triumphal procession." For as the forces of the enemy made their lair in our members, you may no longer wear the old garment. I do not, of course, refer to this visible garment, but to "the old man which, deluded by its lusts, is sinking towards death." May the soul that has once put off that old self never again put it on, but say with the Bride of Christ in the Canticle of Canticles: "I have put off my garment: how shall I put it on?" Marvelous! You were naked in the sight of all and were not ashamed! Truly you bore the image of the first-formed Adam, who was naked in the garden and "was not ashamed."

Then, when stripped, you were anointed with exorcised olive oil from the topmost hairs of your head to the soles of your feet, and became partakers of the good olive tree, Jesus Christ. Cuttings from the wild olive tree, you were grafted into the good olive tree and became partakers of the fatness of the true olive tree. The exorcised olive oil, therefore, symbolized the partaking of the richness of Christ; its effect is to disperse every concentration of the cosmic forces arrayed against us. For as the breath of the saints upon you, with the invocation of the name of God, burns the devils like fierce fire and expels them, so this exorcised olive oil receives, through prayer and the invocation of God, power so great as not only to burn and purge away the traces of sin but also to put to rout all the invisible forces of the Evil One.

After this you were conducted to the sacred pool of divine Baptism, as Christ passed from the cross to the sepulchre you see before you. You were asked, one by one, whether you believed in the name of the Father and of the Son and of the Holy Spirit; you made that saving confession, and then you dipped thrice under the water and thrice rose up again, therein mystically signifying Christ's three days' burial. For as our Savior passed three days and three nights in the bowels of the earth, so you by your first rising out of the water represented Christ's first day in the earth, and by your descent the night. For as in the night one no longer sees, while by day one is in the light, so you during your immersion, as in a night, saw nothing, but on coming up found yourselves in the day. In the same moment you were dying and being born, and that saving water was at once your grave and your mother. What Solomon said in another context is applicable to you: "A time for giving birth, a time for dying"; although for you, contrariwise, it is a case of "a time for dying and a time for being born." One time brought both, and your death coincided with your birth.

The strange, the extraordinary, thing is that we did not really die, nor were really buried or really crucified; nor did we really rise again: this was figurative and symbolic; yet our salvation was real. Christ's crucifixion was real, His burial was real, and His resurrection was real; and all these He has freely made ours, that by sharing His sufferings in a symbolic enactment we may really and truly gain salvation. Oh, too generous love! Christ received the nails in His immaculate hands and feet; Christ felt the pain: and on me without pain or labor, through the fellowship of His pain, He freely bestows salvation.

Let no one imagine, then, that Baptism wins only the grace of remission of sins plus adoption, as John's baptism conferred only the remission of sins. No; we know full well that Baptism not only washes away our sins and procures for us the gift of the Holy Spirit, but is also the antitype of the Passion of Christ. That is why Paul just now proclaimed: "Do you not know that all we who have been baptized into Christ Jesus have been baptized into His death? For through Baptism we were buried along with Him." Perhaps this was directed against those who supposed that Baptism procures only the remission of sins and the adoption of sons and does not, beyond this, really make us imitatively partakers of the sufferings of Christ.

To teach us, then, that all that Christ endured "for us and for our salvation," He suffered in actual fact and not in mere seeming, and that we have fellowship in His Passion, Paul cries aloud in unequivocal language: "For if we have become one planting with him by the likeness of His death, we shall be one with him by the likeness of His Resurrection also." "One planting" is apt, for since the true Vine was planted here, we, by partaking in the Baptism of His death, have become "one planting" with Him. Mark closely the words of the Apostle: he did not say: "For if we have become one planting by His death," but "by the likeness of His death." For in the case of Christ death was real, His soul being really separated from his Body. His burial, too, was real, for His sacred Body was wrapped in clean linen. In His case it all really happened. But in your case there was only a likeness of death and suffering, whereas of salvation there was no likeness, but the reality.

That should be sufficient instruction on these points. I urge you to keep it in your memory that I too, though unworthy, may be able to say of you: "I love you because at all times you keep me in mind and maintain the tradition I handed on to you." God, "who has presented you as those who have come alive from the dead," is able to grant to you to "walk in newness of life," because His is the glory and the power, now and forever. Amen.

THIRD LECTURE ON THE MYSTERIES

THE HOLY CHRISM

"But you have an anointing from God and you know all things, etc. . . . that we may have confidence and may not shrink ashamed from him at his coming."

"Baptized into Christ" and "clothed with Christ," you have been shaped to the likeness of the Son of God. For God, in "predestining us to be adopted as his sons," has "conformed us to the body of the glory" of Christ. As "partakers of Christ," therefore, you are rightly called "Christs," i.e., "anointed ones": it was of you that God said: "Touch not my Christs." Now, you became Christs by receiving the antitype of the Holy Spirit; everything has been wrought in you "likewise" because you are likenesses of Christ.

He bathed in the river Jordan and, after imparting the fragrance of His Godhead to the waters, came up from them. Him the Holy Spirit visited in essential presence, like resting upon like. Similarly for you, after you had ascended from the sacred streams, there was an anointing with chrism, the antitype of that with which Christ was anointed, that is, of the Holy Spirit. Concerning this Spirit the blessed Isaia, in the prophetical book which bears his name, said, speaking in the person of the Lord: "The Spirit of the Lord is upon me because he hath anointed me. He hath sent me to preach glad tidings to the poor."

For Christ was not anointed by men with material oil or balsam; His Father, appointing Him Savior of the whole world, anointed Him with the Holy Spirit as Peter says: "Jesus of Nazareth, whom God anointed with the Holy Spirit." The prophet David also made proclamation: "Thy throne, O God, is forever and ever: the sceptre of thy kingdom is a sceptre of uprightness. Thou hast loved justice, and hated iniquity: therefore God, thy God hath anointed thee with the oil of gladness above they fellows."

As Christ was really crucified and buried and rose again, and you at Baptism are privileged to be crucified, buried, and raised along with Him in a likeness, so also with the chrism. Christ was anointed with a mystical oil of gladness; that is, with the Holy Spirit, called "oil of gladness" because He is the cause of spiritual gladness; so you, being anointed with ointment, have become partakers and fellows of Christ.

Beware of supposing that this ointment is mere ointment. Just as after the invocation of the Holy Spirit the eucharistic bread is no longer ordinary bread, but the Body of Christ, so this holy oil, in conjunction with the invocation, is no longer simple or common oil, but becomes the gracious gift of Christ and the Holy Spirit, producing the advent [presence?] of His deity. With this ointment your forehead and sense organs are sacramentally anointed, in such wise that while your body is anointed with the visible oil, your soul is sanctified by the holy, quickening Spirit.

You are anointed first upon the forehead to rid you of the shame which the first human transgressor bore about with him everywhere; so you may "reflect as in a glass the splendor of the Lord." Then upon the ears, to receive ears quick to hear the divine mysteries, the ears of which Isaia said: "The Lord gave me also an ear to hear," and the Lord Jesus in the Gospels: "He who has ears to hear, let him hear." Then upon the nostrils, that, scenting the divine oil, you may say: "We are the incense offered by Christ to God, in the case of those who are on the way to salvation." Then on the breast, that "putting on the breastplate of justice you may be able to withstand the wiles of the Devil." For as Christ after His Baptism and the visitation of the Holy Spirit went forth and overthrew the adversary, so must you after holy Baptism and the mystical Chrism, clad in the armor of the Holy Spirit, stand firm against the forces of the Enemy and overthrow them, saying: "I can do all things in the Christ who strengthens me."

Once privileged to receive the holy Chrism, you are called Christians and have a name that bespeaks your new birth. Before admission to Baptism and the grace of the Holy Spirit you were not strictly entitled to this name but were like people on the way towards being Christians.

You must know that this Chrism is prefigured in the Old Testament. When Moses, conferring on his brother the divine appointment, was ordering him high priest, he anointed him after he had bathed in water, and thenceforward he was called "christ" ["anointed"], clearly after the figurative Chrism. Again, the high priest, when installing Solomon as king, anointed him after he had bathed in Gihon. But what was done to them in figure was done to you, not in figure but in truth, because your salvation began from Him who was anointed by the Holy Spirit in truth. Christ is the beginning of your salvation, since He is truly the "first handful" of dough and you "the whole lump": and if the first handful be holy, plainly its holiness will permeate the lump.

Keep this Chrism unsullied; for it shall teach you all things if it abide in you, as you heard the blessed John declaring just now as he expatiated upon the Chrism. For this holy thing is both a heavenly protection of the body and salvation for the soul. It was of this anointing that in ancient times the blessed Isaia prophesied saying: "And the Lord shall make unto all people in this mountain" (elsewhere also he calls the Church a mountain, as when he says: "And in the last days the mountain of the Lord shall be manifest") ". . . and they shall drink wine, they shall drink gladness, they shall anoint themselves with ointment." To alert you to the mystical meaning of "ointment" here, he says: "All this deliver to the nations: for the counsel of the Lord is upon all the nations."

Anointed, then, with this holy oil, keep it in you unsullied, without blame, making progress through good works and becoming well-pleasing to "the trail-blazer of our salvation," Christ Jesus, to whom be glory forever and ever. Amen.

TWO APPENDED NOTES ON BAPTISM AND CHRISM (CONFIRMATION) AT JERUSALEM

APPENDED NOTE A

Myst. 3.3: When is the Holy Spirit Given?

With *Myst.* 3.3. compare Tert., *Bapt.* 7-8: "(After the Bath) we are anointed thoroughly with a blessed unction according to the ancient rule . . . The unction *runs bodily over us, but profits spiritually.* Next the hand is laid upon us, through the blessing calling upon and inviting the Holy Spirit." B. Neunheuser remarks (*Baptism and Confirmation* 89) that if Tertullian really means what he says (cf. ch. 6), that the Holy Spirit is not given in *Baptism*, he stands in opposition to the universal early tradition.

St. Cyprian says several times that it is by the post-baptismal laying on of hands that the Holy Ghost is given. Besides *Ep.* 73 (72).6 and 21, we read (*Ep.* 74 [73].7): "A person is not *born* through the laying on of hands, when he receives the Holy Spirit, but in *Baptism,* that, born, he may *then* receive the Holy Spirit. Compare the case of the first man, Adam; God first formed him, and then breathed into his nostrils the breath of life (Gen. 2.7). For before the spirit can be received there must be something there to receive it." There could hardly be a stronger statement of the C theory, for Cyprian here implies that the New Creation produced by Baptism is not quickened—has no supernatural life—until a further sacrament follows. (Certainly it is the Spirit who quickens, but He does so in Baptism.) Yet in *Ep.* 73 (72).12 Cyprian can say that Baptism confers the remission of sins, that remission of sins entails sanctification, and "if he was sanctified, he was made the temple of God"—without receiving the Holy Spirit? The context excludes the possibility that Cyprian was using the word "Baptism" in the broad sense. When Cyprian reserves the gift of the Spirit to imposition of hands, one often feels that he is accepting, for argument's sake, premisses which are not quite his own (and perhaps not Stephen's either).

Ca. 252 Cornelius of Rome (Eusebius, *Hist. eccl*, 6.43.14) complained that the anti-Pope Fabian had not received the Spirit because, after a clinical Baptism, he had not bothered to receive the ordinary additional ceremonies, especially the sealing by the bishop. Apparently against this position Cyprian (*Ep.* 69[75].13-14) asserts that clinical Baptism *bestows the Holy Spirit in the same fullness* that ordinary Baptism does. And his whole position, asserting against St. Stephen of Rome the invalidity of heretical schismatic Baptism, is based on his emphasis upon the intimate association of the Holy Spirit with Baptism as at least its agent. M.J. Rouët de Journel, *Enchiridion patristicum* (20th ed. Freiburg im B. etc. 1958) 795 (under the thesis "Confirmatio est verum sacramentum"), is, I think, right in his judgment that Cyprian held that Confirmation is a sacrament (a vague word in Cyprian) but did not hold that it is necessary to salvation. This is still the Roman position (Canon 787). The explanation of Cyprian's contradictions is probably that, though misled in such passages as *Ep.* 74(73).7 (above) by the phrase "the gift of the Spirit," which sounds like a greater grace than any of the Spirit's gifts or graces, yet in his deepest thinking he knew that the grace of Baptism was greater than that of Confirmation. So in *Ep.* 74 (73).5, arguing against Pope Stephen, who refused to rebaptize those who came to the Church after receiving heretical Baptism but only imposed hands to bestow the Spirit, he writes (again, incidentally, implying that Baptism makes one a temple of God): "*If* a man born (i.e., baptized) outside the Church can become God's temple, why cannot further the Holy Spirit be poured out upon the temple? For when sanctified . . . and spiritually recreated a new man, a person is fitted for the reception of the Spirit . . . If a person baptized among heretics can put on Christ, *much more* can he receive the Spirit whom Christ sent. Otherwise he who is sent will be greater than he who sends. . . As if it were possible either for Christ to be put on without the Spirit or for the Spirit to be separated from Christ." That is, the position attacked implies an Ebionite Christology.

The *De rebaptismate* (A.D. *ca.* 256) defended the validity of schismatic Baptism "by a very peculiar and unfortunate distinction between Baptism of water and Baptism of the Spirit to be conferred by the bishop's imposition of hands" (Quasten, *Patrology II,* 368).

Let us now return to *Myst.* 3.3, careful to distinguish the questions what is the right answer to this problem and what is the teaching of the *Mystagogiae*. The author to the *Msytagogiae* is forced by his chosen typology here unduly to exalt Chrism against Baptism (see *Myst.* 2 n. 10). Where he ought (I think) to say that Christ's washing in Jordan corresponds to the sacrament of Baptism, that the descent of the Spirit corresponds to the grace of Baptism (forgiveness of sins and Sonship) and that the Voice and the Dove are but the visibilization of this grace, he has chosen to regard the washing in Jordan and the descent of the Spirit as two successive historical events on the same plane. If they are to be correlated with Baptism and Chrism/Confirmation, the only solution seems to be to say that Baptism gives forgiveness of sins, while Chrism gives the Spirit, or (like the *De rebaptismate*) to correlate the two events with Baptism of water and Baptism of the Spirit (and reinterpret John 3.5 accordingly). *Myst.* 3 avoids such a drastic solution. Still it must say that at Chrism the Holy Spirit descends; He "is given." But we saw (*Myst.* 2 n. 16) that at 2.6 *Baptism* bestowed "the gift of the Spirit (=Adoption)." Still perhaps "upon this gift (of Adoption) *by* the Spirit now comes the gift *of* the Spirit in Chrismation"? In a sense. But, first, this distinction is bogus. Whenever the Holy Spirit gives any grace, He does so by descending, by coming; He can do no other. Second, the Spirit is never, strictly, "given" to us; we do not possess Him, but He us; and He possesses us through the grace of Adoption. Third, we need to correct our semantic or lexical values: "the gift of the Spirit" in the New Testament is not, commonly, a stronger phrase than such descriptions of the benefits of Baptism as regeneration, adoption of sons, new creation, etc. On the contrary, the "giving of the Spirit" often denotes such inessential graces as charismata, speaking with tongues, working miracles, ets.: see Acts *passim.* This seems to be the regular usage of Cyril's Lenten Lectures. The Mystagogical Lectures seem to agree. Not only do the *Mystagogiae* (2.6) ascribe to Baptism the supreme gifts of regeneration, the putting on of Christ and Adoption, but in 3.1 they three times sharply distinguish the grace of Chrism from the Spirit's descent *ousiodes* upon Christ, twice by saying that the candidates received only the antitype of the Holy Ghost, and further by the phrase "in likeness" (*eikonikos*).

Similarly there is a sense in which Chrism *does* give "the fullness" of the Spirit; probably *Myst.* 3.3. has in mind the permanent "indwelling" of the Spirit in us (cf. "resting" in 3.1). Naturally (Basil, *Hom. in Ps.* 44. *PG* 29.405A), since Chrism follows Baptism, it must mark some advance upon it. But this is compatible with giving the esential and supreme gift in Baptism. Chrism completes, confirms and tops off what has been done, like a dash of an additive in the fuel tank. To improve Cyprian's regrettable analogy with Adam: you must have a car, and a tank with fuel in it before there is any point in introducing the additive; or we may say that Confirmation gives a (permanent) "overdrive."

But the Chrism of *Myst.* gives rather more than this. Apart from (or included in) the important grace (*Myst.* 3.3) which we have tried to assess, it is almost certainly in Chrism (4.7; cf. 2 Cor. 1.22?) that the Seal is given (contrast *Cat.* 3.4), though the word used in 4.7 is *elaion.* The "Seal," however, is a variable quantity. It may mean that the great eschatological seal, or a writer may mean that the document (covenant) is not valid until the seal has been affixed, or this may be thought of as a desirable but not essential formality, or the Seal may be thought of merely as the securing of the sanctified soul against unlawful entry by the powers of evil.

Again, the Chrism sanctifies the senses (3.4), makes us incontestably Christians, enables us to do battle with the Enemy (3.5), and confers (3.6) "lay ordination," participation in Christ's royal priesthood, so important in Eastern Christendom (N. Zernov, *Eastern Christendom* [New York 1961] 250).

APPENDED NOTE B

THE DOCTRINE OF BAPTISM IN THE LENTEN LECTURES

On the whole, the Lectures on the Mysteries teach the B theory (see above, p. 160). For, while they correlate Chrism certainly with the descent of the Spirit, almost certainly with the Seal, and probably with the indwelling of the Spirit, yet they do not seem to regard any of these as privileged categories and therefore they do not seem to exalt Chrism over against Baptism.

The Seal is mentioned casually only in *Myst.* 4.7. To Baptism they ascribe forgiveness of sins, the putting on of Christ, regeneration 93.5), participation in Christ's Passion, and "the gift of the Spirit" in the sense of adoptive sonship (2.6).

The opening lectures in the Lenten series teach a very decided B theory, but there are a few passages in the later lectures which perhaps require a (drastic?) modification of the impression left by the early lectures. In the opening lectures it is clear that practically everything is mediated by "the water," and if St. Cyril ever here has any other ceremony in mind, he clearly regards it as supplementary and secondary. But while the two series are thus not very far apart in doctrine, they differ markedly in their biblical exegesis and typology or, as we perhaps may here more appropriately call it, christ-iconology.

For the most part the Lenten Lectures know no distinction between the Spirit as gift and His sanctifying, transforming and recreating activity. When in some later passages such a distinction is implied, the gift of the Spirit (objective, defining genitive) seems to be a *weaker* phrase than the gift (=grace) of the Spirit. In *Procat.* 2A and 4E the Spirit acts through the water. "The reception *of* the Holy Ghost" in *Cat.* 3.2B is clearly the same thing as acceptance *by* the Holy Ghost in *Procat.* 4E and the "reception of the grace" in *Cat.* 3.7E. The "grace" or "gift" (usually *charis,* less often *charisma*; in *Cat.* 1.4E *dorea*) is the commonest and apparently all-inclusive term (especially) in these opening lectures. It is normally thought of as the gift or grace of the Spirit as agent but with no hint of a contrast with the Spirit Himself as gift. And it is clear that this gift is mediated by water. Sometimes this is said explicitly or unmistakably implied (e.g., *Procat.* 2A, 15C; *Cat.* 3.3D, 4C), and it is consistently implied by the very frequent references to "the water" or "the laver." Note especially 3.3-5, with the praise of water in 3.5; also the passages about Simon Magus's baptism, invalid from the first through lack of proper intention (*Procat.* 2A, 4E; cf. *Cat.* 3.7D; 17.35-36; in 17.35 the Spirit seals the soul even, apparently, when a deacon baptizes). Again, water is mentioned in the more or less immediate vicinity of all the great gifts of Baptism: adoption, new birth, new life, union with Christ, the Seal etc.

In the Lenten Lectures (contrast *Myst.* 4.7), the Seal is certainly given through the water. *Cat.* 1.2C, 3D; and 3.3B are most naturally read in this sense, and it is actually said twice in 3.4, once equivalently: "As the water purifies the body, so the Spirit seals the soul," where the two actions are clearly parallel and the dualism is that of inner and outer, of sacramental sign and spiritual grace; once explicitly: "the seal (conveyed) by "water." *Cat.* 5.6D, though not strictly explicit, is equally clear. The Lenten Lectures (4.17A) connect the Seal with the credal profession and so with the baptismal contract or covenant.

Another, equally important and significant, difference from the Mystagogical Lectures is the fact that, while the Mystagogical Lectures (3.1CD, cf. 4E) regard the descent of the Spirit upon Our Lord by the Jordan as an event different from and subsequent to His baptism, and as typifying a different sacrament (Chrism), in the parallel passages in the Lenten Lectures the Holy Spirit descends upon Jesus *while* John is baptizing Him. For in *Cat.* 17.9A the Greek has two present participles: "This Holy Ghost came down while the Lord was being baptized, that the dignity of Him who was being baptized might not pass unnoticed"; and the context shows that "baptism" is water-baptism. So also probably 3.14C: "that John, who *was baptizing* Him (*ho baptizon*) might see (the Spirit in the form of a dove)." (Incidentally, such passages as 3.6A, 7A, 11A, 14: 17.9A, establishing a close connection between John's Baptism and Christian Baptism, show that St. Cyril regarded the physical rite in the two baptisms as the same, and therefore prove that "Baptism" in the Lenten Lectures regularly means water-baptism.) Thus, whereas in the *Mystagogiae* (3.4DE) Jesus, and Christians after Him, give battle to Satan, not immediately after Baptism, but only after the descent of the Spirit regarded as a second event (=Chrism), in the Lenten Lectures (3.11-13), cf. *Procat.* 10, 16BE) Jesus overcomes the Dragon and binds "the Strong One" *in the water* and preaches immediately afterwards, while the candidates likewise receive their armour from the pre-baptismal teaching and from Baptism, after which they fight and preach (*Procat.* 10; *Cat.* 1.4; 3.13-14).

Another striking difference between the typology of the Mystagogical and the Lenten Lectures is that, while the *Mysta-*

gogiae are as enigmatically silent about Pentecost as they are about John the Baptist and John 3.3-5, in the Lenten Lectures Pentecost is the fulfillment and realization of the promise implicit in John's baptism and is the Baptism of the Apostles. See *Cat.* 3.9 (cf. 3.15D) and the fine account (17.13-15) where the Pentecostal baptismal flames which enveloped the Apostles are interpreted as "spiritual" (*noetou*) water and are compared with the waters which encompassed and whelmed the candidates when they "submerged" in the font. The fire/water burns away sin and "further" (*eti*) burnishes the soul and imparts to it *charis* (grace, beauty).

A comparable difference between the two series concerns the Aaronic priesthood. In *Myst.* 3.6 Aaron and Solomon together are the prefiguring type of the royal priesthood which is bestowed on the candidates by the chrismation. Both Aaron and Solomon are said to have first bathed and then been anointed respectively priest and king. In the Lenten Lectures, by contrast, Solomon appears only as an example of a penitent (2.13), and "Aaron was first washed, then became high priest" (3.5E)—no anointing. Moreover in the Lenten Lectures Aaron is a type of Christ's high priesthood in which the ordinary faithful do not partake. For in 3.5E the High Priest "prays for the rest" (cf. Our Lord's intercessory priesthood in Hebrews). So in 10.11, the Lord "is called Christ (anointed), because He is a Priest. . . For Christ is a High Priest like Aaron" (cf. Eus., *Hist. eccl.* 1.3). If there is any reference to the New Covenant in 10.11, 14 and 11.1, it is apparently the ordained ministers of the Church who partake, imperfectly, of Christ's priesthood after ordination by anointing. Apart from 18.33, the Lenten Lectures apparently know nothing of a "priesthood of all believers" bestowed by Chrismation; believers are Christians not Christs. Perhaps *Cat.* 10.16 changes this picture. There all believers have the "new name"; i.e., they are called "Christians" after "Christ" meaning priest king. As, however, it is not inferred that Christians share in the priestly rulership of their Lord, this may be a transitional passage. In *Procat.* 6 the divine name bestowed in Baptism is "faithful" (*pistos*).

Finally, John 3.3-5 and Acts 2.38 are always interpreted in the Lenten Lectures in the B sense. And normally the Lenten

Lectures associate together as inseparable all the great graces of Baptism and connect them with the water. For example, in *Cat.* 1.1-2 the cleansing by water seems inseparable from the new birth, adoption, the mystical Seal, the opening of the gates of Paradise and the singing of the bridal song. Similarly in 3.1-3 the washing clean from sin in the laver seems inseparable from "the reception of the Holy Ghost," introduction into the bridal chamber of the King and the bestowal of the Seal.

Now, however, we must consider briefly a few passages of a very different tenor towards the end of the Lenten Lectures. According to *Cat.* 14.25E (after mention of Elia and Eliseus), Christ bestowed the Spirit upon His disciples (the Apostles?) in such fullness as to enable them "by the laying on of their *hands* to impart the fellowship of It to believers." In 17.25 we are told of the visit of Peter and John to Samaria and how they imparted the fellowship of the Holy Ghost "with prayer and the imposition of hands" to Philip's new converts (cf. Acts 8.14-17). Nothing, however, is made of the fact that Philip was a mere deacon, nor is Baptism explicitly mentioned.

But the crucial passage is *Cat.* 16.26E, for in the above passages the candidates are not brought into the picture. After a discussion of the Seventy Elders (with Eldad and Medad) (Num. 11.24-30), a reference to Deut. 34.9 and the statement that Num. 11.29 was "fulfilled" at Pentecost, we read:

> Thou seest the same figure everywhere in the Old and New Testaments. In the time of Moses the Spirit was given by the laying on of hands (*cheirothesia*), and by the laying on of hands Peter also gives the Spirit [Acts 8.17]. Upon thee also, the baptizand, soon shall the grace come. But just how, I am not telling you now, for I won't anticipate "the proper season."

It looks as if the baptizand will receive the Spirit by some form of imposition of hand (chrismation? consignation?). *Cheirothesia* in ApCo 2.32.3 is consignation; in 3.16.3 it confers the royal priesthood as in *Myst.* 3.6; in 7.44.3 it distinguishes Christian from Jewish baptism; but see also Serapion, *Euchologion* 15, title.

Do these texts transform the whole picture sketched above? They would if that picture had relied on silence instead of on positive texts. Is interpolation at 16.26E a possibility? It has apparently occurred in the "consubstantial" insertion in some manuscripts at 16.24C. And note the repetition (16.26C, 27A) of "Abraham, Isaac and Jacob." *Cat.* 16.27 could follow naturally on 16.25. Again, 16.11-12 strongly suggests that the Holy Ghost is given through water, and 16.12C seems to mean that the candidates are prepared by their Lenten repentance for the Holy Spirit whom they will receive in the water.

But probably the Lenten Lectures are "stratified"; i.e., they contain some additions by Cyril, or possibly by another hand. Another example may be the *hieratikos* ("like priests") in 18.33C; 18.33 looks rather like a later doublet of 18.32, the latter representing a period when there was no Easter Week catechizing.

FOURTH LECTURE ON THE MYSTERIES

THE EUCHARIST (I): THE BODY AND BLOOD OF CHRIST

"For I myself received from the Lord the traditions which in turn I passed on to you. . . ."

The teaching of the blessed Paul is of itself sufficient to give you full assurance about the divine mysteries by admission to which you have become one body and blood with Christ. For Paul just now proclaimed "that on the night in which he was betrayed our Lord Jesus Christ took bread and, after giving thanks, broke it and gave it to his disciples saying, 'Take, eat: this is my body'; then, taking the cup, he gave thanks and said, 'Take, drink: this is my blood.' " When the Master himself has explicitly said of the bread, "This is my body," will anyone still dare to doubt? When He is Himself our warranty, saying, "This is my blood," who will ever waver and say it is not His Blood?

Once at Cana in Galilee He changed water into wine by His sovereign will; is it not credible, then, that He changed wine into blood? If as a guest at a physical marriage He performed this stupendous miracle, shall He not far more readily be confessed to have bestowed on "the friends of the bridegroom" the fruition of His own Body and Blood?

With perfect confidence, then, we partake as of the Body and Blood of Christ. For in the figure of bread His Body is given to you, and in the figure of wine His Blood, that by partaking of the Body and Blood of Christ you may become of one body and blood with Him. For when His Body and Blood became the tissue of our members, we become Christ-bearers and as the blessed Peter said, "partakers of the divine nature."

Once, speaking to the Jews, Christ said: "Unless you eat my flesh and drink my blood, you can have no life in you." Not understanding His words spiritually, they "were shocked and drew back," imagining that He was proposing the eating of human flesh.

The Old Covenant had its loaves of proposition, but they, as belonging to the Covenant, have come to an end. The New Covenant has its heavenly bread and cup of salvation, to sanctify both body and soul. For as the bread is for the body, the Word suits the soul.

Do not then think of the elements as bare bread and wine; they are, according to the Lord's declaration, the Body and Blood of Christ. Though sense suggests the contrary, let faith be your stay. Instead of judging the matter by taste, let faith give you an unwavering confidence that you have been privileged to receive the Body and Blood of Christ.

The blessed David is hinting to you the meaning of these rites when he says, "You have prepared a table before me, against those who oppress me." What he means is this: "Before your coming the devils prepared a table for mankind, a table defiled and polluted, impregnated with diabolical power; but since your coming, Lord, you have prepared a table in my presence." When man says to God, "You have prepared a table before me," what else does he refer to but the mystical and spiritual table which God has prepared for us "over against," meaning "arrayed against and opposed to," the evil spirits? And very aptly: for that table gave communion with devils, while this gives communion with God.

"You have anointed my head with oil." He has anointed your head with oil upon your forehead, meaning the seal which you have of God, that you may be made "the engraving of the signet," that is, the sanctuary of God.

"Your chalice, also, which inebriates me, how goodly is it!" You see here spoken of the chalice which Jesus took in His hands and of which, after giving thanks, he said: "This is my blood shed for many for the forgiveness of sins."

For this reason Solomon also, in Ecclesiastes, covertly alluding to this grace, says: "Come hither, eat your bread with joy," that is, the mystical bread. "Come hither," he calls: a saving, beatific call. "And drink your wine with a merry heart": that is, the mystical wine. "And let oil be poured upon your head": you see how he hints also of the mystical chrism. "And at all times let your garments be white, because the Lord approves what you do." It is now that the Lord approves what you do; for before you came to the grace your doings were "vanity of vanities."

Now that you have put off your old garments and put on those which are spiritually white, you must go clad in white all your days. I do not, of course, mean that your ordinary clothes must always be white, but that you must be clad in those true, spiritual garments which are white and shining. Then you will be able to say with the blessed Isaia: "Let my soul rejoice in the Lord; for he has dressed me in the garments of salvation, and with the robe of gladness he has clothed me."

In this knowledge, and in the firm conviction that the bread which is seen is not bread, though it is bread to the taste, but the Body of Christ, and that the visible wine is not wine, though taste will have it so, but the Blood of Christ; and that it was of this that David sang of old: "Bread strengthens the heart of man, soon his face glistens joyously with oil," strengthen your heart, partaking of this Bread as spiritual, and make cheerful the face of your soul. God grant that, your soul's face unveiled with a clear conscience, you may "reflecting as in a glass the glory of the Lord," go "from glory to glory" in Christ Jesus our Lord, whose is the glory forever and ever. Amen.

APPENDED NOTE C

THE DOCTRINE IN THE MYSTAGOGICAL LECTURES ON THE EUCHARISTIC PRESENCE

Two early Reformed theologians, Aubertin and Rivetus, interpreted the Eucharistic teaching of the Mystagogical Lectures in a way which, though inadequate, will reward the attention of the student. I shall therefore first summarize their interpretation as presented by Touttée and then make the necessary adjustments in a Catholic sense. Their interpretation is as follows.

While the Mystagogical Lectures recognize a real, spiritual (but not substantial) presence of Christ in the Eucharistic action, they view this presence dynamically and in terms of the benefit (spiritual effect) of the sacrament: that is, the devout believer's spiritual communion with Christ and, through his continued eating, his ever-deepening mystical union with Him. References to the Bread and Wine being and becoming the Body and Blood of Christ are only symbolic, the language of signs and symbols which is appropriate to sacraments. The Mystagogical Lectures apply to the sacramental signs language strictly appropriate only to the reality (the spiritual benefit) which they signify and convey. In Holy Communion we spiritually partake of the Lord's Body and Blood in the sense that we gain the benefits of His Body broken and His Blood shed for us and are vouchsafed fellowship with God. Thus the consecrated Bread is the symbol or sacrament of the Body of Christ, or is the mystical Body of Christ; it become the efficacious figure of Christ's Body insofar as it mediates the grace of His Passion. Lest the illustration from the miracle at Cana should mislead the audience, they are immediately warned (4.4) that they do not literally eat Christ's flesh (*sarkophagia*) but that the eating spoken of is spiritual, that (4.7) it is a mystical and spiritual Table to which they are invited, and (4.9) that they must "partake thereof as spiritual." In spite of some rhetorical flights the *Mystagogiae* have no serious doctrine of a "res et sacramentum." In all three sacraments the *Mystagogiae* know only two things: the sacramental sign and the grace-effect of the sacrament. It is true that they speak of the bread as being "changed," but not every change is substantial. In 5.7 it is said that "*everything* that the Holy Spirit touches is sanctified and changed." That "changed" is here defined more precisely by "sanctified" is clear from the numerous passages (*Cat.* 3.3-4; *Myst.* 1.7; 3.3) implying that the changes effected by the consecration in the baptismal water, the chrism, and the eucharistic bread and wine are all of the same kind. It is a qualitative, not substantial, change and is compared to the change effected in meat when offered to idols. The illustration from Cana, therefore, is only intended to prove that He who changed the water substantially and sensibly can also change the wine sacramentally. Again, the warning in *Myst.* 4.6 not to regard the consecrated eucharistic elements as "bare" is exactly parallel to the warning in 3.3 not to regard the consecrated ointment as "bare." In no case is the change effected by the consecration substantial or "physical"; the sacramental elements are "changed" only in the sense that the consecration makes them God's instruments and imparts to them a spiritual or mystic power through which they impart to us the precious gifts promised by the Gospel. It is true that 4.9 says that the Bread is not bread, except to the taste; yet six times *Myst.* 4 calls it bread, and, after the statements in 3.3 that it is "not plain bread" or "bare bread," the 4.9 passage is clearly a metaphor or hyperbole. The comparison with the consecrated ointment in 3.3 is clearly the decisive passage, especially when taken in conjunction with the other parallels. The *Mystagogiae* speak indeed (4.3 and 5; 5.15) of the Body of Christ being "distributed through" or "assimilated into" our members and sanctifying not only our soul but our body, but they speak of the baptismal water and the chrism in exactly the same way: in *Cat.* 3.3-4 Cyril speaks of the water as purifying the body and enabling "the body also to partake of the Grace," while *Myst.* 3.4 and 7 describe the chrism as "a spiritual preservative of the body" and use of it language applicable only to the Holy Spirit whom it conveys.

The lectures are, indeed, somewhat inconsistent, but they are consistently inconsistent. To cite a parallel, the *Mystagogiae* (3.2) speak of the chrism as mere material ointment and as being only the "antitype" of the Holy Ghost, with whom Christ was anointed, and yet they go on (3.3, 4, 7) to identify it with the Holy Ghost, or at least to attribute to it sanctifying power, and even say (3.6) that the newly baptized were, after all, "truly anointed by the Holy Ghost." Similarly, *Cat.* 3.3-4 speaks of the baptismal water as a material element affecting only the body and yet also speaks of it as sanctifying and sealing the soul. In just the same way the *Mystagogiae* speak of the eucharistic Bread as the Body of Christ and yet also speak of it (4.5) as a material element affecting only our body: "for as bread answers to the body, so is the Word appropriate to the soul." In each case the material element sacramentally mediates a divine grace which sanctifies the soul. Such "strong" passages, therefore, as 4.3 and 6 about the eucharistic Bread are entirely analogous (1) to what is said in *Cat.* 3.3-4 about the baptismal water: "Regard not the Bath as simple water, but rather regard the spiritual grace that is given with the water. . . . For since man is body and soul . . . the water cleanses the body and the Spirit seals the soul. . . When going down, therefore, into the water, regard not the bare element. . ."; and (2) to what is said in *Myst.* 3.3 about the Chrism: "But beware of supposing this to be plain ointment. For as the bread. . ., (so the ointment after the invocation becomes Christ's divinizing grace)," for "while your body is anointed with visible ointment, your soul is sanctified by the holy, life-giving Spirit." Again, there is the use of the word "antitype." *Myst.* 5.20 speaks of the Bread and Wine as "the antitype of the (or "the antitypical") Body and Blood of Christ." Now, only thrice elsewhere do the Mystagogical Lectures use the word "antitype": in 2.6 and twice in 3.1: and always in contrast with the archetype or original, though with reference to the spiritual grace conveyed through the sacramental symbol. Baptism (2.4-7) is the antitype of Christ's Passion, because our sacramental imitation of His death and resurrection mediates for us the fruits of the Redemption. Then in 3.1 the Chrism is twice called the antitype of the Holy Spirit, and is *contrasted* with Him; and yet in 3.7 it is identified with the Holy Spirit: "It shall teach you all things if It abides in you." Finally, there is the absurdity that if we take *Myst.* 4 literally, then we must, in logic, take literally the statement in 5.10 that in the Eucharist "we offer Christ slain in sacrifice," where the perfect participle suggests that "slain" represents a present state; then Holy Communion would indeed be a gruesome banquet (but seen n. 33 there).

Now let us make the necessary adjustments. It is clear that the *Mystagogiae* conceive the Presence, not as merely virtual or dynamic, but in the traditional Catholic sense. For (a) neither the Lenten nor the Mystagogical Lectures ever say that the baptismal water actually becomes or is "the grace" which it imparts. (b) There is a closer analogy with Chrism. The Holy Spirit does seem to be conceived as actually "arriving" in person in His "antitype." (c) The parallels drawn between the Bread and the water and ointment show (i) an analogy in the mode of consecration (by invocation) and (ii) that in each case the element is changed. But it remains to inquire into the nature of the change in each case. And the *Mystagogiae* speak of the Bread in a way which contrasts with its language about the water and the Chrism; they say repeatedly and with the utmost emphasis that it becomes and is the Body of Christ. Moreover (4.3) "*in* the figure (the Bread) the Body *is given* to thee." (d) Finally the denial (4.6) that the bread is *psilos* (mere, bare bread) both proves the real Presence and shows how the *Mystagogiae* conceive it. The Lenten Lectures provide the key. In *Cat.* 4.9 Cyril says that "Christ is double" (cf. 15.1) and in 12.1; in 13.2, 3, 33 he says that Christ is not a mere (*pilos*) man, since He is also God. Thus the model of the Jerusalem doctrine of the Eucharistic presence is christological. This, while excluding transubstantiation (for the bread is then as real as the sacred Manhood), safeguards the objective and substantial Presence. The emphasis, however, is upon the action and the eating. Finally, Cyril confined both doctrine and theological speculation to a minimum. He had no theory of *how* the divinity and humanity co-existed in Christ, though he may have thought of this co-presence as the *Mystagogiae* thought of the co-presence in the Eucharist (*Myst.* 4.7: "the mystic, intelligible [*noeten*] Table") on the model of the indwelling of a Platonic "sensible" (earthly reality) by a *noeton* (the corresponding spiritual, heavenly reality) or as the soul permeates the body, "tota in toto et tota in qualibet parte" (cf. the Logos-Sarx Christology). Cyril does not tell us how he conceived the "conversion" of the bread into the Body of Christ; probably he would have accepted the other christological analogy, that of the incarnation of the Word; this is the analogy suggested by Theophilus of Alexandria—as the Word became flesh without ceasing to be the Word (*menon ho en*). Other Fathers, however, from *ca.* 380 use language hardly if at all distinguishable from that of transubstantiation: transelement, *metousioun, metastoicheioun, metarrhythmizein* suggesting a change in what we would call the invisible atomic or nuclear structure of the bread—a regrettable concession, one may think, to the literalist piety of of the simpler faithful.

FIFTH LECTURE ON THE MYSTERIES

THE EUCHARIST (II): THE LITURGY

"Laying aside, then, all malice, deceit and slander"etc.

By the mercy of God you have in our former assemblies received sufficient instruction about Baptism, Chrism, and the partaking [communion] of the Body and Blood of Christ. We must now pass on to the next subject, intending today to crown the work of your spiritual edification.

The Hand-Washing

You saw the deacon who offers the water for the washing of hands to the celebrant and to the presbyters who encircle the altar of God. Not that he offered this water on account of any bodily uncleanness: of course not; for we did not originally enter the church unwashed. No; the ablution is a symbolic action, a symbol of our obligation to be clean from all sins and transgressions. The hands symbolize action; so by washing them we signify evidently the purity and blamelessness of our conduct. Did you not hear the blessed David supplying the key to this ceremony in the divine mysteries when he says: "I will wash my hands among the innocent: and will circle thy altar, O Lord"? The hand-washing, then, is a symbol of innocence.

The Kiss

Next the deacon cries: "Welcome one another," and "Let us kiss one another." You must not suppose that this kiss is the kiss customarily exchanged in the streets by ordinary friends. This kiss is different, effecting, as it does, a commingling of souls and mutually pledging unreserved forgiveness. The kiss, then, is a sign of a true union of hearts, banishing every grudge. It was this that Christ had in view when He said: "If, when you are bringing your gift to the altar, you suddenly remember that your brother has a grievance against you, leave your offering by the altar; first go and make your peace with your brother, and then come back and offer your gift." The kiss, then, is a reconciliation and therefore holy, as the blessed Paul said somewhere when he commanded us to "salute one another with a holy kiss"; and Peter: "Salute one another with a kiss of charity."

The Dialogue

Then the celebrant cries: "Lift up your hearts." For truly it is right in that most awful hour to have one's heart on high with God, not below, occupied with earth and the things of earth. In effect, then, the bishop commands everyone to banish worldly thoughts and workaday cares and to have their hearts in heaven with the good God.

Assenting, you answer, "We have them lifted up to the Lord." Let no one present be so disposed that while his lips form the words, "We have them lifted up to the Lord," in his mind his attention is engaged by worldly thoughts. At all times we should commemorate God, but at least, if this is not possible to human weakness, we must aspire to it in that hour.

Then the priest says: "Let us give thanks [make eucharist] to the Lord." Indeed we ought to give thanks to the Lord for calling us, when we were unworthy, to so great a grace, for reconciling us when we were enemies, and for vouchsafing to us the spirit of adoption.

Then you say: "It is meet and just." In giving thanks we do indeed a meet thing and a just; but He did, not a just thing, but one that went beyond justice, in deigning to bestow on us such marvellous blessings.

Memorial of Creation: Sanctus

After that we commemorate the heavens, the earth and the sea; the sun and moon, the stars, the whole rational and irrational creation, both visible and invisible: Angels and Archangels; Virtues, Dominions, Principalities, Powers, Thrones and the many-faced Cherubim: equivalently saying with David, "O magnify ye the Lord with me." We commemorate also the Seraphim whom Isaia in the Holy Spirit saw encircling the throne of God, "with two wings veiling their faces and with twain their feet, while with twain they did fly," as they chanted: "Holy, Holy, Holy, Lord of Hosts." It is to mingle our voices in the hymns of the heavenly armies that we recite this doxology which descends to us from the Seraphim.

Epiclesis (Invocation) and Consecration

Next, after sanctifying ourselves by these spiritual songs, we implore the merciful God to send forth His Holy Spirit upon the offering to make the bread the Body of Christ and the wine the Blood of Christ. For whatever the Holy Spirit touches is hallowed and changed.

The Intercession

Next, when the spiritual sacrifice, the bloodless worship, has been completed, over that sacrifice of propitiation we beseech God for the public peace of the Churches, for the good estate of the world, for the Emperors, for the armed forces and our allies, for those in sickness, for the distressed: for all, in a word, who need help, we all pray and offer this sacrifice.

Then we commemorate also those who have fallen asleep: first of all, the patriarchs, prophets, apostles, and martyrs, that God through their intercessory prayers may accept our supplication. Next we pray also for the holy Fathers and Bishops who have fallen asleep, and generally for all who have gone before us, believing that this will be of the greatest benefit to the souls of those on whose behalf our supplication is offered in the presence of the holy, the most dread Sacrifice.

Let me use an illustration for an argument. For I know that many of you say: "What does it avail a soul departing this world, whether with or without sins, to be remembered at the Sacrifice?" Well, suppose a king banished persons who had offended him, and then their relatives wove a garland and presented it to him on behalf of those undergoing punishment, would he not mitigate their sentence? In the same way, offering our supplications to Him for those who have fallen asleep, even though they be sinners, we, though we weave no garland, offer Christ slain for our sins, propitiating the merciful God on both their and our own behalf.

The Lord's Prayer

Then, after this, we recite that prayer which the Savior delivered to His own disciples, with a clear conscience designating God as our Father, saying: "Our Father who art in heaven."

Oh, the greatness of the mercy of God! To those who had revolted from Him and been reduced to the direst straits He has granted so liberal a pardon for their crimes, He has been so prodigal of His favor, that they may even call Him "Father": "Our Father who art in heaven." They also are a "Heaven" who "bear the likeness of the heavenly man," since God is dwelling in them and mingling with them."

"Hallowed be thy name." God's name is by nature holy, whether we call it so or not. But because it is sometimes profaned among sinners according to the words: "Through you my name is continually blasphemed among the Gentiles," we pray that the name of God may be hallowed in us: not that from not being holy it becomes holy, but because it becomes holy *in us* when we are sanctified [hallowed] and our actions correspond to our holy profession.

"Thy kingdom come." It is the mark of a pure soul to say without reserve: "Thy kingdom come." For it is the man who has listened to Paul saying: "Therefore do not let sin reign in your mortal body" and has purified himself in action, thought and word, who will say to God: "Thy kingdom come."

"Thy will be done on earth as it is in heaven." God's heavenly, blessed angels do the will of God, as David said in the Psalm: "Bless the Lord, all ye his angels: you that are mighty in strength, and execute his word." In effect, then, this is what you mean by this petition: "As in the angels thy will is done, so on earth be it done in me, O Lord."

"Give us this day our superessential bread." Ordinary bread is not "superessential"; but this holy bread is superessential in the sense of being ordained for the essence of the soul. Not of this Bread is it said that it "passes into the stomach and so is discharged into the drain"; no: it is absorbed into your whole system to the benefit of both soul and body. By "this day" he means "daily," as in Paul's "while it is called to-day."

"And forgive us our debts, as we also forgive our debtors." For our sins are many; we err both in word and in thought, and do many a deed which deserves condemnation. Indeed, "if we say that we have no sin, we are liars," as John says. So we make a bargain with God, begging Him to condone our offenses according as we forgive our neighbours. Bearing in mind, then, the disproportion of this *quid pro quo,* let us not delay or put off forgiving one another. The offenses committed against us are small, paltry and easily settled; but the offenses we have committed against God are great—too great for any mercy except His. Beware, then, lest, on account of slight and trifling transgressions against you, you debar yourself from God's forgiveness of your most grievous sins.

"And lead us not into temptation," O Lord. Is it this that the Lord teaches us to pray for: not to be tempted at all? How, then, is it said in another place: "A man untempted is a man unproved"? And again: "Esteem it all joy, my brethren, when you fall into various temptations"? But "entering into temptation" could mean being overwhelmed by temptation. For temptation is like a raging torrent which defies the traveller. Some people in time of temptation manage to cross this torrent without being overwhelmed by the raging waters, their prowess as swimmers saving them from being swept away by the tide. But if others who are not of the same mettle enter, they are engulfed: like Judas, who entered into the temptation of avarice and, failing to swim across, was overwhelmed and drowned—physically and spiritually. Peter entered into the temptation of the denial; but, though he entered, he was not drowned, but manfully swam across and was delivered from the temptation. Listen again, in another passage, to a company of triumphant saints giving thanks for their deliverance from temptation: "For thou, O God, hast proved us; thou hast tried us by fire, as silver is tried. Thou hast brought us into a net: thou hast laid afflictions on our back: thou didst let men ride over our heads. We have passed through fire and through water: and thou didst lead us out into a refreshment." You see them celebrating their escape from the trap. And "thou hast brought us out," he says, "into refreshment": their being "brought into a refreshment" refers to their rescue from temptation.

"But deliver us from the Evil One." If "lead us not into temptation" referred to not being tempted at all, He would not have said: "but *deliver* us from the Evil One." The Evil One from whom we pray to be rescued is our adversary, the Devil.

Then, after completing the prayer, you say "Amen," which means, "So be it," thus setting your seal upon the petitions of the prayer which we owe to the divine teacher.

The Communion

Next the priest says: "Holy things to the holy." Holy are the offerings after they have received the visitation of the Holy Spirit; and you are holy after you have been privileged to receive the Holy Spirit. So things and persons correspond: both are holy. Next you say: "One is holy, one is the Lord, Jesus Christ." For truly One only is holy–holy, that is, by nature; yet we also are holy, not, indeed, by nature, but by participation, training and prayer.

After this you hear the chanter inviting you with a sacred melody to communion in the holy mysteries, in the words: "O taste and see that the Lord is good." Entrust not the judgment to your bodily palate, but to unwavering faith. For in tasting you taste, not bread and wine, but the antitypical Body and Blood of Christ.

Coming up to receive, therefore, do not approach with your wrists extended or your fingers splayed, but making your left hand a throne for the right (for it is about to receive a King) and cupping your palm, so receive the Body of Christ; and answer: "Amen." Carefully hallow your eyes by the touch of the sacred Body, and then partake, taking care to lose no part of It. Such a loss would be like a mutilation of your own body. Why, if you had been given gold-dust, would you not take the utmost care to hold it fast, not letting a grain slip through your fingers, lest you be by so much the poorer? How much more carefully, then, will you guard against losing so much as a crumb of that which is more precious than gold or precious stones!

After partaking of the Body of Christ, approach also the chalice of His Blood. Do not stretch out your hands, but, bowing low in a posture of worship and reverence as you say, "Amen," sanctify yourself by receiving also the Blood of Christ. While It is still warm upon your lips, moisten your fingers with It and so sanctify your eyes, your forehead, and other organs of sense. Then wait for the prayer and give thanks to the God who has deigned to admit you to such high mysteries.

Preserve this traditional teaching untarnished; keep yourselves unsullied by sin. Never cut yourselves off from the fellowship [communion], never through the pollution of sin deprive yourselves of these sacred, spiritual mysteries. "And may the God of peace sanctify you completely, and may your whole spirit, soul and body be preserved blameless at the coming of our Lord Jesus Christ," whose is the glory now and evermore, world without end. Amen.

St. Ambrose of Milan

339-397

Ambrose was born in Trier of a distinguished Roman family. His father held the office of Pretorian Prefect of the Gauls. After his father's death his mother took the family to Rome and there his older sister Marcellina received the veil from Pope Liberius in 353. After receiving an excellent education Ambrose and his brother Satyrus went to Sirmium in 365 as advocates attached to the Court of the Italian Prefecture. By 370 both of them were provincial governors.

373 was the year that changed the life of Ambrose. The Arian Bishop of Milan had died and the two factions could not agree upon a successor, until the name of Ambrose was raised. He resisted the idea but finally yielded. He was still a catechumen at the time, so was in the space of two weeks baptized, ordained a priest, and consecrated bishop. He gave away his share of the family wealth to the poor and took up a semi-monastic lifestyle. He also applied himself diligently to biblical and theological studies.

His election, however, did not mean that the fighting was over. Ambrose was repeatedly involved in grave difficulties provoked by the Arian party. Despite endless political entanglements he managed to demonstrate a truly pastoral spirit. His homilies were such that the young Augustine came to a new understanding of the Scriptures through them. Ambrose baptized Augustine at Easter 387.

Ambrose and the Emperor Theodosius practically personified Church and State in their era. Their relations were generally cordial, although Ambrose attacked severely the social abuses of the day. On the occasion of the Gothic invasions he did not hesitate to sell the sacred vessels in order to redeem captives. He was also one of the most zealous advocates of virginity in the early Church, and one of the chief founders of devotion to Mary in this regard.

Time and again in his writings Ambrose manifests his splendid training in classical Latin and his own originality in coining concise phrases. It is also largely through him that the allegorical method of interpreting Scripture, after the manner of Philo and Origen, is entrenched in the West.

As one of the four great Doctors of the Western Church, Ambrose has always been an attractive leader. His personal holiness and sincerity were never open to dispute. He was an accomplished administrator who redirected all these skills to the exercise of the pastoral office once it was thrust upon him. Yet he would not allow administrative duties to prevent him from continued study of Scripture and theology. His sermons illustrate his constant concern for doctrine as well as morality. Nor should his role in the promotion of Church music be overlooked. He was greatly lamented as an unparalleled leader when he died in 397. His body lay in state throughout the Easter Vigil in the cathedral of Milan, and, with a liturgical appropriateness that must have pleased him, he was laid to rest on the Feast of the Resurrection.

The Mysteries *is a relatively brief work, consisting of addresses given by Ambrose to the newly baptized during Easter week. The nine chapters treat of the meaning of the rites of baptism, confirmation, and the Eucharist. They may have been written in 387, the very year in which Augustine was among the newly baptized. In any event, their simplicity and clarity are the trademark of Ambrose, a pastor who was so well skilled in finding the right word for each occasion.*

THE MYSTERIES

CHAPTER 1

We have given a daily sermon on morals, when the deeds of the Patriarchs or the precepts of the Proverbs were read, in order that, being informed and instructed by them, you might become accustomed to enter upon the ways of our forefathers and to pursue their road, and to obey the divine commands, whereby renewed by baptism you might hold to that manner of life which befits those who are washed.

Now time warns us to speak of the mysteries and to set forth the very purpose of the sacraments. If we had thought that this should have been taught those not yet initiated before baptism, we would be considered to have betrayed rather than to have portrayed the mysteries; then there is the consideration that the light of the mysteries will infuse itself better in the unsuspecting than if some sermon had preceded them.

So open your ears and enjoy the good odor of eternal life which has been breathed upon you by the grace of the sacraments. This we pointed out to you as we celebrated the mystery of the opening and said: ' "Ephpheta," that is, "Be thou opened," ' so that everyone about to come to grace might know what he was asked and might necessarily remember what he responded.

Christ celebrated this mystery in the Gospel, as we have read, when He healed the deaf and dumb man. But He touched the mouth because He was curing both a dumb person and a man, in the one case, that his mouth might open with the sound of the infused voice, in the other, because this touch befitted a man and would not have befitted a woman.

CHAPTER 2

After this Holy of holies was opened to you, you entered the sanctuary of regeneration. Recall what you were asked; recall what you responded! You renounced the Devil and his works, the world with its luxury and pleasures. Your words are kept not in the tomb of the dead, but in the book of the living.

There you saw the Levite, you saw the priest, you saw the highest priest. Do not consider the bodily forms, but the grace of their ministrations. You have spoken in the presence of the angels, as it is written: 'For the lips of the priest guard knowledge, and they seek the law from his mouth, because he is an angel of the Lord Almighty.' There is no deceiving; there is no denying. He is an angel, who announces the kingdom of Christ, who announces life eternal, to be esteemed by you not according to appearance, but according to office. Consider what he has given over; reflect on his experience; recognize his position.

Having entered, therefore, that you might recognize your adversary, whom you think you should renounce to his face, you turn toward the east. For he who renounces the devil, turns toward Christ, recognizes Him by a direct glance.

CHAPTER 3

What have you seen? Water, certainly, but not this alone; the Levites (deacons) ministering there, the highest priest (bishop) questioning and consecrating. First of all, the Apostle taught you that 'we are not to consider the things that are seen, but the things that are not seen, for the things that are seen are temporal, but the things that are not seen are eternal.' For elsewhere you have: 'The invisible things of God from the creation of the world are understood through the things that have been made; His eternal power also and divinity are estimated by His works.' Therefore, too, the Lord Himself says: 'If you do not believe me, at least believe the works.' Believe, therefore, that the presence of Divinity is at hand there. Do you believe the operation? Do you not believe the presence? Whence would the operation follow, unless the presence went before?

Consider, moreover, how old the mystery is and prefigured in the origin of the world itself. In the very beginning, when God made heaven and earth, it says: 'The Spirit moved over the waters.' He who was moving over the waters, was He not working over the waters? Why should I say: 'He was working?' As regards His presence, He was moving. Was He not working who was moving? Recognize that He was working in that making of the world, when the Prophet says to you: 'By the word of the Lord the heavens were made and all their strength by the breath of His mouth.' Each statement relies on the testimony of the Prophet, both that He was moving over and that He was working. That He was moving over, Moses says; that He was working, David testifies.

Accept another testimony. All flesh was corrupted by its iniquities. 'My Spirit,' says God, 'shall not remain in men, for they are flesh.' By this, God shows that spiritual grace is turned aside by carnal impurity and by the stain of more serious sin. Therefore, God in His desire to repair what He had given caused the flood, and ordered Noe the just man to embark on the ark. When, as the flood subsided, he first sent forth a raven which did not return; he afterwards sent forth a dove, which is said to have returned with an olive twig. You see the water; you see the wood; you perceive the dove—and do you doubt the mystery?

The water is that in which the flesh is immersed, that all carnal sin may be washed away. All disgrace is buried there. The wood is that on which the Lord Jesus was fastened, when He suffered for us. The dove is that in whose form the Holy Spirit descended, as you have learned in the New Testament, who inspires peace of soul and tranquility of mind in us. The raven is the figure of sin, which goes out and does not return, if in you also the custody and form of justice be preserved.

There is also a third testimony, as the Apostle teaches you: 'That our fathers were all under the cloud, and all passed through the sea, and all were baptized in Moses in the cloud and in the sea.' And finally Moses himself says in his canticle: 'You sent your wind and the sea covered them.' You notice that in that crossing of the Hebrews the figure of holy baptism even then was prefigured, wherein the Egyptian perished and the Hebrew escaped. For what else are we taught daily in this sacrament but that sin is overwhelmed and error abolished, but piety and innocence continue on entire?

You hear that our fathers were under a cloud, that is, a good cloud which cooled the fires of carnal passions, a good cloud; it overshadows those whom the Holy Spirit visits. Finally it came upon the Virgin Mary, and the power of the Most High overshadowed her, when she conceived the Redemption for the human race. And that miracle was performed in a figure by Moses. If then the Spirit was in a figure, He is now present in truth, when Scripture says to you: 'For the law was given by Moses, but grace and truth came by Jesus Christ.'

Marra was a bitter fountain. Moses cast the wood in it, and it became sweet. For water without the preaching of the cross of the Lord is to no advantage for future salvation; but when it has been consecrated by the mystery of the saving cross, then it is ordered for the use of the spiritual laver and the cup of salvation. So, just as Moses, that is, the Prophet, cast wood into that fountain, also into this fountain the priest casts the message of the cross of the Lord, and the water becomes sweet for grace.

Therefore, you should not trust only in the eyes of your body. Rather is that seen which is not seen, for the one is temporal, the other eternal. Rather is that seen which is not comprehended by the eyes, but is discerned by the spirit and the mind.

Finally, let the reading from Kings which we have just gone over teach you. Naaman was a Syrian and he had leprosy and he could not be cleansed by anyone. Then a maiden from among the captives said that there was a prophet in Israel who could cleanse him of the pollution of leprosy. The account says that having taken gold and silver he went forth to the king of Israel. This one, when he learned the reason for his coming, tore his garments, saying that he rather was being tried, since those things were being demanded of him which were not within the power of a king. Helisaeus, however, made known to the king that he should direct the Syrian to himself, in order that he might learn that there was a God in Israel. And when he had come, he ordered him to dip seven times in the Jordan river.

Then he began to reflect that the rivers of his own country had better waters, in which he had often dipped and he had been cleansed of leprosy, and being induced by this he did not obey the commands of the Prophet. However, on the advice and persuasion of his servants he acquiesced and dipped, and when he was immediately cleansed he understood that one's being cleansed was not connected with the waters, but with grace.

Understand now who that 'maiden of the captives' is! Obviously, the younger congregation of the Gentiles, that is, the Church of the Lord formerly weighed down by the captivity of sin, when it did not yet possess the liberty of grace, by whose counsel that foolish people of the Gentiles heard the word of prophecy which long before it had doubted; afterwards, however, when it believed that it should obey, it was washed of every pollution of sin. And this man doubted before he was healed; you have already been healed and so ought not to doubt.

CHAPTER 4

On this account it was formerly foretold you that you should not believe this alone which you saw, lest perchance you, too, might say: 'Is this that great mystery which the eye has not seen nor the ear heard nor has it entered into the heart of man? I see waters which I used to see daily; are these able to cleanse me, into which I have often descended and have never been cleansed?' From this learn that water cleanses not without the Spirit.

And so you have read that the three witnesses in baptism are one: the water, the blood, and the Spirit, for if you take away one of these, the sacrament of baptism does not stand. For what is water without the cross of Christ except a common element without any sacramental effect? And again without water there is no mystery of regeneration. For 'unless a man be born again of water and the Spirit, he cannot enter into the kingdom of God.' Moreover, even a catechumen believes in the cross of the Lord Jesus, with which he, too, is signed, but, unless he be baptized 'in the name of the Father and of the Son and of the Holy Spirit,' he cannot receive remission of sins nor drink in the benefit of spiritual grace.

Therefore, that Syrian dipped seven times under the law, but you were baptized in the name of the Trinity, you confessed the Father (recall what you did), you confessed the Son, you confessed the Spirit. Retain the order of things. In this faith you died to the world, you arose to God, and, as if buried in that element of the world, dead to sin you were revived to eternal life. Believe, therefore, that these waters are not without power.

Therefore, it is said to you: 'An angel of the Lord used to come down at certain times into the pool and the water was moved, and the first to go down into the pool after the troubling of the water was healed of whatever infirmity he had.' This pool was in Jerusalem, in which one was healed every year. But no one was healed before the angel had descended. So the angel descended, and, that there might be a sign that the angel had descended, the water was moved. The water was moved because of the unbelievers, for them a sign, for you faith; for them an angel came down, for you the Holy Spirit; for them a creature was moved, for you Christ operates, the Lord of the creature.

Then one was cured; now all are healed, or at least one Christian people alone. For there is in some even a 'deceitful water;' the baptism of unbelievers does not heal, does not cleanse, but pollutes. The Jew washes pots and cups, as if insensible things could receive either blame or grace; but do you baptize this insensible cup of yours, in which your good deeds may shine, in which the splendor of your grace may gleam forth. Therefore, that pool also is by way of a figure, that you may believe that the power of God also descends into this fountain.

Finally, the paralytic was awaiting a man. Who was He but the Lord Jesus born of the Virgin, at whose coming no longer would the shadow heal men one by one, but the truth all men together? This, then, was the one whose descent was being waited for, of whom God the Father said to John the Baptist: 'Upon whom thou wilt see the Spirit descending from heaven and abiding upon Him, He it is who baptizes with the Holy Spirit,' of whom John has testified, saying: 'I saw the Spirit descending from heaven as a dove and remaining upon Him.' Why did the Spirit here descend like a dove, except that you might see, except that you might know that the dove, also, which the just Noe sent forth from the ark, was likeness of this dove, that you might recognize the type of the mystery?

Perhaps you may say: 'Since that was a true dove, which was sent forth, and this One descended like a dove, how do we say that it was a likeness in one place, and truth in another, when according to the Greeks it is written that the Spirit descended "in the likeness of a dove"?' But what is so true as the Divinity, which remains always? Moreover, the creature cannot be the truth, but a likeness which is easily destroyed and changed. At the same time the simplicity of those who are baptized should not be in likeness but should be true. Therefore, the Lord also says: 'Be therefore wise as servants, and guileless as doves.' Rightly, then, did He descend like a dove to admonish us that we should have the simplicity of a dove. Moreover, we read that the likeness is to be accepted as the truth both with regard to Christ: 'And was found in likeness as a man,' and with regard to God the Father: 'Nor have you seen His likeness.'

CHAPTER 5

Is there still some reason for you to doubt, when the Father clearly calls out to you in the Gospel, saying: 'This is my Son in whom I am well pleased;' the Son calls out, upon whom the Holy Spirit showed Himself as a dove; the Holy Spirit also calls out, who descended as a dove; David calls out: 'The voice of the Lord is upon the waters, the God of majesty has thundered, the Lord upon many waters;' when Scripture testifies to you that, in response to the prayers of Jerobaal, fire came down from heaven, and, again, when Elias prayed, fire was sent which consecrated the sacrifice.'

You should consider not the merits of persons, but the duties of priests. And if you regard merits, just as you consider Elias, regard, also, the merits of Peter or of Paul, who handed down to us this mystery which they had received from the Lord Jesus. A visible fire was sent to them that they might believe, an invisible one works for us who believe; for them it was as a figure, for us as a warning. Believe, then, that the Lord Jesus is present, invoked by the prayers of priests, who said: 'Where two or three shall be, there am I also.' How much more does He deign to impart His presence there where the Church is, where the mysteries are!

You have descended them [into the water]; remember what you replied [to the questions], that you believe in the Father, you believe in the Son, you believe in the Holy Spirit. You do not have in your response: 'I believe in a greater and a lesser and a lowest [person].' But you are bound by the same guarantee of your own voice to believe in the Son exactly as you believe in the Father, to believe in the Spirit exactly as you believe in the Son, with this only exception, that you confess that you must believe in the cross of the Lord Jesus alone.

CHAPTER 6

After this, of course, you went up to the priest. Consider what followed. Was it not that which David says: 'Like the ointment on the head, that ran down upon the beard, the beard of Aaron.' This is the ointment of which Solomon also says: 'Thy name is as ointment poured out; therefore young maidens have loved thee and drawn thee.' How many souls renewed today have loved Thee Lord Jesus, saying: 'Draw us after thee; let us run to the odor of thy garments,' that they may drink in the odor of the Resurrection.

Understand why this is done: 'For the eyes of a wise man are in his head.' Therefore, it flows upon the beard, that is, upon the grace of youth; therefore, 'upon the beard of Aaron,' that you may become 'a chosen race,' sacerdotal, precious; for we all are anointed unto the kingdom of God and unto the priesthood with spiritual grace.

You went up from the font; remember the lesson of the Gospel. For our Lord Jesus in the Gospel washed the feet of His disciples. When He came to Simon Peter, and Peter said: 'Thou shalt never wash my feet,' he did not notice the mystery, and so refused the ministry, because he believed that the humility of the servant was being overtaxed, if he should patiently permit the ministry of the Lord. And the Lord answered him: "If I do not wash your feet, you will not have a part with me.' On hearing this, Peter said: 'Lord not only my feet, but also my hands and my head.' The Lord replied: 'He who is washed needs only to wash his feet, but is wholly clean.'

Peter was clean, but he should have washed his feet, for he had the sin of the first man by succession, when the serpent overthrew him and persuaded him to error. So his feet are washed, that hereditary sins may be taken away; for our sins are remitted through baptism.

At the same time note that the mystery itself consists in the ministry of humility. For He says: 'If I have washed your feet, I the Lord and Master,' how much more 'ought you also to wash one another's feet.' For since the very Author of salvation has redeemed us through obedience, how much more ought we, His servants, to offer the service of humility and obedience.

CHAPTER 7

After this you received white garments as a sign that you had put off the covering of sins, and had put on the chaste robes of innocence, of which the prophet said: 'Sprinkle me with hyssop and I shall be cleansed, wash me and I shall be whiter than snow.' For he who is baptized is seen to have been cleansed both according to the law and according to the Gospel; according to the law, because Moses sprinkled the blood of a lamb with a bunch of hyssop; according to the Gospel, because the garments of Christ were white as snow, when in the Gospel He showed the glory of His Resurrection. He whose sin is forgiven is made whiter than snow; and so the Lord said through Isaias: 'If your sins be as scarlet, I shall make them white as snow.'

The Church, having assumed these vestments through the laver of regeneration, says in the Canticles: 'I am black but beautiful, O ye daughters of Jerusalem,' black through the frailty of human condition, beautiful through grace; black, because I am made up of sinners, beautiful by the sacrament of faith. Perceiving these vestments, the daughters of Jerusalem in amazement say: 'Who is this that cometh up made white?' She was black; how was she suddenly made white?

For the angels also doubted, when Christ rose again; the powers of heaven when they saw doubted that flesh was coming up into heaven. Finally they said: 'Who is this king of glory?' And when some said: 'Lift up the gates, ye princes, and be ye lifted up, ye everlasting gates, and the king of glory will come in,' others doubted, saying: 'Who is this king of glory?' In Isaias, also, you have it that the powers of the heavens doubted and said: 'Who is this that cometh from Edom, the redness of his garments from Bosra, beautiful in his white robe?'

Christ, moreover, on seeing His Church in white vestments—for whom He himself, as you have it in the book of Zacharias the Prophet, had put on 'filthy garments'—that is, a soul pure and washed by the laver of regeneration, says: 'Behold, thou art fair, my love, behold thou art fair, thy eyes are as a dove's,' in whose likeness the Holy Spirit descended from heaven. Beautiful are the eyes, because, as we said above, He descended as a dove.

And below: 'Thy teeth are as flocks of sheep, that are shorn, which came up from the washing, all with twins, and there is none barren among them; thy lips are as a scarlet lace.' No ordinary praise is this, first by the pleasing comparison with the shorn sheep; for we know that goats feed in high places without danger and securely take food in steep places; then, when they are shorn, are relieved of the superfluous. The Church is compared to a flock of these, having within herself the many virtues of souls, that put aside through the laver superfluous sins, that offer to Christ the mystic faith and the moral grace, that speak of the cross of the Lord Jesus.

In these the Church is beautiful. Therefore, God the Word says to her: 'Thou art all fair, my love, and there is not a spot in thee,' because sin has been washed away; 'Come hither from Libanus, my spouse, come hither from Libanus; from the beginning of faith thou shalt pass over and pass on,' because, renouncing the world, she passed over temporal things and passed on to Christ. And again God the Word says to her: 'Why art thou made beautiful and sweet, O love, in thy delights? Thy stature has become like the palm, and thy breasts as clusters of grapes.'

And the Church answers Him: 'Who shall give thee to me, my brother, sucking the breasts of my mother? I shall find thee without and shall kiss thee, and no one shall despise me. I shall take hold of thee and bring thee into my mother's house, and into the secret place of her who conceived me. You will teach me.' Do you see how, delighted with the gift of grace she desires to attain to the interior mysteries and to consecrate all her affections to Christ? She still seeks, she still rouses His love and asks that it be roused for her by the daughters of Jerusalem, by whose grace, that is, the grace of faithful souls, she desires that her spouse be provoked to a richer love for her.

Therefore, the Lord Jesus himself, invited by the zeal of such great love, by the beauty of elegance and grace, because now no sins of defilement were among the baptized, says to the Church: 'Put me as a seal upon thy heart as a sign upon thy arm,' that is, 'Thou art elegant, my beloved, thou art fair, nothing is lacking to thee. Place me as a seal upon thy heart,' that thy faith may shine with the fulness of the sacrament. Let your works also shine and bring forth the image of God, according to whose image you were made. Let not your love be diminished by any persecution, a love which many waters, cannot shut off, nor rivers overflow.'

So recall that you have received a spiritual seal, 'the spirit of wisdom and of understanding, the spirit of counsel and of fortitude, the spirit of knowledge and of piety, the spirit of holy fear,' and preserve what you have received. God the Father sealed you; Christ the Lord confirmed you, and gave a pledge, the Spirit, in your hearts, as you have learned in the lesson of the Apostle.

CHAPTER 8

The cleansed people, rich in these insignia, hasten to the altar of Christ, saying: 'And I shall go unto the altar of God who gives joy to my youth.' For the people, having put aside the defilements of ancient error, renewed in the youth of an eagle, hasten to approach that heavenly banquet. They come, therefore, and, seeing the sacred altar arranged, exclaim saying: 'Thou hast prepared a table in my sight.' David introduces these people as speaking when he says: 'The Lord feeds me and I shall lack nothing; in a place of good feeding there he placed me; he led me beside the water of refreshment.' And below: 'For though I should walk in the midst of the shadow of death, I shall fear no evil, for thou art with me. Thy rod and thy staff these have comforted me. Thou doest prepare a table in my sight, against those who trouble me. Thou hast anointed my head with oil, and thy cup inebriating me is wonderful.'

Now let us consider this, lest anyone perchance seeing the visible—since the things that are invisible are not seen and cannot be comprehended by human eyes—may by chance say: 'For the Jews God rained manna; He rained quail, but for this His Church well-beloved by Him, there are these things which He has prepared, concerning which it has been said: "That eye has not seen nor ear heard, nor has it entered into the heart of man what things God has prepared for those who love Him." Therefore, lest anyone say this, we wish with the highest zeal to prove that both the sacraments of the Church are more ancient than those of the synagogue and more excellent than manna is.

The lesson from Genesis, which has been read, teaches them to be more ancient. For the synagogue took its beginning from the law of Moses, but Abraham was far earlier. After he had conquered his enemies and had received back his own nephew, when he was enjoying victory, then Melchisedech met him and brought forth those things, which Abraham venerated and received. Abraham did not bring them forth, but Melchisedech, who is introduced 'without father, without mother, having neither beginning of days nor end, but like to the Son of God,' of whom Paul says to the Hebrews: 'He continues a priest for ever,' who in the Latin version is called King of justice, King of peace.

Do you not recognize who this is? Can a man be a king of justice, when he himself is scarcely just; can he be a king of peace, when he can scarcely be peaceable?—'Without a mother' according to Divinity, because He was begotten of God the Father, of one substance with the Father; 'without a father' according to the Incarnation, because He was born of the Virgin, 'having neither beginning nor end,' for He himself is 'the beginning and the end' of all things, 'the first and the last.' Therefore, the sacrament which you have received is not a gift of man but of God, brought forth by Him who blessed Abraham, the father of faith, him whose grace and deeds you admire.

It has been proven that the sacraments of the Church are more ancient; now realize that they are more powerful. In very fact it is a marvelous thing that God rained manna on the fathers, and they were fed by daily nourishment from heaven. Therefore, it is said: 'Man has eaten the bread of angels.' But yet all those who ate that bread died in the desert, but this food which you receive, this 'living bread, which came down from heaven,' furnishes the substance of eternal life, and whoever eats this bread 'will not die forever;' for it is the body of Christ.

Consider now whether the bread of angels is more excellent or the flesh of Christ, which indeed is the body of life. That manna was from heaven, this is above the heavens; that was of heaven, this of the Lord of the heavens; that was subject to corruption, if it were kept for a second day, this is foreign to every corruption, because whosoever shall taste in a holy manner shall not be able to feel corruption. For them water flowed from the rock, for you blood [flowed] from Christ; water satisfied them for the hour, blood satiates you for eternity. The Jew drinks and is thirsty; when you drink, you will not be able to be thirsty; that was in a shadow, this in truth.

If that which you admire is a shadow, how great is that whose shadow you admire? Hear that what came to pass among the fathers is a shadow. It is said: 'For they drank of the rock that followed, and the rock was Christ; but with many of them God was not well pleased; for they were laid low in the desert. Now these things came to pass in a figure for us.' You recognize the more excellent things; for the light is more powerful than the shade, truth than figure, the body of its author than manna from heaven.

CHAPTER 9

Perhaps you may say: 'I see something else; how do you tell me that I receive the Body of Christ?' This still remains for us to prove. Therefore, we make use of examples great enough to prove that this is not what nature formed but what benediction consecrated, and that the power of benediction is greater than that of nature, because even nature itself is changed by benediction.

Moses held a rod; he cast it down and it became a serpent; again, he took hold of the tail of the serpent and it returned to the nature of a rod. You see then that by the grace of the Prophet the nature of the serpent and that of the rod were interchanged twice. The rivers of Egypt were flowing with a pure stream of water; suddenly, from the veins of the springs blood began to burst forth; there was no drinking water in the rivers. Again at the prayer of the Prophet the blood of the rivers ceased; the nature of the waters returned. The people of the Hebrews were hemmed in on all sides, shut off on the one side by the Egyptians, enclosed on the other by the sea. Moses raised his rod, the water divided and hardened like walls, and a way for travel appeared between the waters. The Jordan turning back contrary to nature returned to the source of its stream. Is it not clear that the nature of the waters of the sea and of the curse of the river was changed? The people of the fathers were thirsty; Moses touched the rock; and water flowed forth from the rock. Did not grace work contrary to nature for the rock to throw forth water which its nature did not have: The Mara was a very bitter stream, so that the people, although thirsty, were unable to drink it. Moses threw a piece of wood into the water, and the nature of the waters laid aside its bitterness, which grace then suddenly infused tempered. In the time of Eliseus the Prophet, one of the sons of the prophets lost the head of his axe, and it sank immediately. He who had lost his axe sought the help of Eliseus; Eliseus also threw a piece of wood into the water, and the axe floated. Surely we realize that this also happened contrary to nature, for the substance of iron is heavier than the liquid of waters.

So we notice that grace is capable of accomplishing more than is nature, and yet thus far we have mentioned only the benediction of a prophet. But if the benediction of man had such power as to change nature, what do we say of divine consecration itself, in which the very words of our Lord and Saviour function? For that sacrament, which you receive, is effected by the words of Christ. But if the words of Elias had such power as to call down fire from heaven, will not the words of Christ have power enough to change the nature of the elements? You have read about the works of the world: 'that He spoke and they were done; He commanded and they were created.' So, cannot the words of Christ, which were able to make what was not out of nothing, change those things that are into the things that were not? For it is not of less importance to give things new natures than to change natures.

But why do we use arguments? Let us use His own examples, and by the mysteries of the Incarnation let us establish the truth of the mysteries. Did the process of nature precede when the Lord Jesus was born of Mary? If we seek the usual course, a woman after mingling with a man usually conceives. It is clear then that the Virgin conceived contrary to the course of nature. And this body which we make is from the Virgin. Why do you seek here the course of nature in the body of Christ, when the Lord Jesus himself was born of the Virgin contrary to nature? Surely it is the true flesh of Christ, which was crucified, which was buried; therefore it is truly the sacrament of that flesh.

The Lord Jesus himself declares: 'This is my body.' Before the benediction of the heavenly words another species is mentioned; after the consecration the body is signified. He Himself speaks of His blood. Before the consecration it is mentioned as something else; after the consecration it is called blood. And you say 'Amen,' that is, 'It is true.' What the mouth speaks, let the mind within confess; what words utter, let the heart feel.

Christ then feeds His Church on these sacraments, by which the substance of the soul is made strong, and, seeing the continuous advancement of her grace, rightly says to her: 'How beautiful thy breasts have become, my sister, my spouse, how beautiful they have become from wine, and the odor of thy garments as the odor of Libanus. A garden enclosed is my sister, my spouse, a garden enclosed, a fountain sealed.' By this he signifies that the mystery should remain sealed with you, lest it be violated by the works of an evil life and by the adulteration of chastity; lest it be divulged to whom it is not fitting; lest it be spread abroad among infidels by garrulous conversation. So the custody of your faith should be good, that the integrity of your life and silence may continue undefiled.

Therefore, the Church also, preserving the depth of the heavenly mysteries, hurls back the severe storms of the winds, and invites the sweetness of blooming grace; and knowing that her garden cannot displease Christ, she calls to the Bridegroom, saying: 'Arise, O northwind, and come, O southwind, blow through my garden and let my ointments flow down. Let my brother go down into his garden and eat the fruit of his apple-trees.' For it has good trees and fruitful, which have touched their roots in the water of the sacred fountain and have burst forth into good fruits with a growth of new richness, so as not to be cut now by the axe of the Prophet, but to abound with the fruitfulness of the Gospel.

Finally, the Lord also, delighted with their fertility, replies: 'I have entered into my garden, my sister, my spouse. I have gathered my myrrh with my spices; I have eaten my food with my honey; I have drunk my drink with my milk.' Understand, faithful one, why I have said 'food' and 'drink.' This, however, is not doubtful, that in us He himself eats and drinks, just as in us you read that He says that He is in prison.

Therefore, the Church also, seeing so much grace, urges her sons, urges her neighbors to come together to the sacraments, saying: 'Eat, my neighbors, and drink and be inebriated, my brethren.' What we eat, what we drink, the Holy Spirit expresses to you elsewhere, saying: 'Taste and see that the Lord is sweet: Blessed is the man who trusts in Him.' Christ is in that sacrament, because the body is Christ's. So the food is not corporeal but spiritual. Therefore the Apostle also says of its type: 'Our fathers ate the spiritual food and drank the spiritual drink,' for the body of God is a spiritual body; the body of Christ is the body of the Divine Spirit, for the Spirit is Christ, as we read: 'The Spirit before our face is Christ the Lord.' And in the Epistles of Peter we have: 'And Christ has died for you.' Finally, that food strengthens our heart, and that drink 'rejoices the heart of man,' as the Prophet has recalled.

Thus, then, having obtained everything, let us know that we have been regenerated. Let us not say: 'How were we regenerated? We have not entered into the womb of our mother and been born again? I do not recognize the course of nature?'—But no order of nature is here, where there is the excellence of grace. Finally the course of nature does not always produce generation; we confess that Christ the Lord was conceived of a Virgin and we deny the order of nature. For Mary did not conceive of man, but received of the Holy Spirit in her womb, as Matthew says: 'She was found with the child of the Holy Spirit.' If, then, the Holy Spirit coming upon the Virgin effected conception, and effected the work of generation, surely there must be no doubt that the Spirit, coming upon the Font, or upon those who obtain baptism, effects the truth of regeneration.

St. John Chrysostom

349-407

John was born in Antioch, Syria, around 349. His father, a high-ranking army officer, probably a Latin and a Christian, died soon after John's birth. His mother, a Greek named Anthusa, renounced remarriage and devoted herself to raising John in piety. He studied four years with Meletius, who baptized him in 368. John then studied and prayed for four more years under the direction of a hermit, then for two years lived by himself in a cave, studying Scripture and practicing austerities, which impaired his health. In 381 he was ordained a deacon by Meletius and for five years exercised a pastoral ministry. It was probably toward the end of this period that he wrote his famous On the Priesthood, *which is excerpted here.*

In 386 John was ordained a priest and began a remarkable career as a preacher of great repute over the next twelve years. But in 398 he was lured to Constantinople where he was against his wishes consecrated bishop. The political intrigue he encountered borders on the incredible. His preaching of rigorous morality was offensive to the Empress Eudoxia, and several attempts were made on his life. He went into exile in 404, but not before writing to Pope Innocent I to request a trial. After hearing witnesses on both sides, Innocent found no grounds for Chrysostom's deposition and requested that he be restored to his see. The papal envoys to Constantinople were jailed, mistreated and finally sent back to Rome.

For three years John's place of exile was Cucusus, Armenia, but his enemies wanted him removed even further to Pityus across the Black Sea. The hardships of the journey were too much for his failing health, and John died in Comana in Pontus. Emperor Theodosius II returned his body to Constantinople three decades later, and the Venetians took it to Rome after plundering Constantinople in 1204.

The surname Chrysostom ("golden-mouthed") was first applied to him in the sixth century; he has always been considered the greatest preacher of the Greek Church, and only Origen was a more prolific writer. Of all his writings, On the Priesthood *has always been viewed as his finest. It consists of six books in dialogue form, with the discussion taking place between Chrysostom and his best friend, Basil. It has been said that his life was merely this treatise reduced to practice. First he pointed out the ideal of the pastoral office, then he set about demonstrating its attainment. Cardinal Newman pointed out that there was nothing artificial or affected about his oratory: "He spoke because his head and his heart were brimful of things to speak about . . . His unrivalled charm . . . lies in his singleness of purpose, his fixed grasp of his aim, his noble earnestness."*

The following selection consists of the second and the fourth of his six books. If his emphasis on the "otherness" of the priest contributed to the growth of too great a gap between clergy and laity, his intention in doing so was thoroughly transparent. He himself possessed the affection and confidence of his people, and by setting the highest standards for himself, hoped to draw his people to the same heights.

THE PRIESTHOOD

BOOK II

1. The priesthood is the greatest proof of love for Christ.
2. This ministry excels others.
3. It requires a great and noble soul.
4. The office is full of difficulty and danger.
5. I shrank from it for love of Christ.
6. Proof of Basil's virtue and of his ardent charity.
7. It was not to insult the electors that I fled from ordination.
8. By flight I saved them from blame.

That it is lawful for a good end to have recourse to the power of artifice, or rather that to act thus ought not to be called artifice, but a laudable species of tact, I might have shown at greater length; but as what I have said is enough for my purpose, it is tiresome and disagreeable to prolong the subject further. For the rest it would be your place to show that in this I have not acted for your benefit.

Basil. What advantage, tell me, said Basil, have I derived from your tact or wisdom, or whatever else you like to call it, that I may be convinced that I have not been injured by you?

1. *John.* What greater advantage can there be, said I, than to be engaged in those things which are the greatest proof of love for Christ, as He Himself has declared. For addressing the chief of the apostles, He says: "Peter, lovest thou Me?" On his replying in the affirmative, He added: "If thou lovest Me, feed My sheep." The Master asks the disciple whether he loves Him, not to ascertain this from him—for how could He, since He searches the hearts of all?—but in order to teach us how much He has at heart the government of His flock. As this is evident, it must also be evident how great and unspeakable a reward is laid up for him who labours in those things which Christ prizes so highly. When we ourselves see any one taking care of our domestics or our cattle, we regard their care of them as a proof of love

for ourselves, though we purchased them all with money. What reward then will He give to those who feed His flock, since He purchased it, not with money or the like, but by His death, and gave His blood as the price of His flock? Wherefore when the disciple said, "Thou knowest, Lord, that I love Thee," and when He took him whom He loved to be the witness of His love, the Saviour did not stop here, but added the mark of His love. For His object, then, was not to prove to us how much Peter loved Him (for of this we had many proofs), but to show Peter and us all how much He loves His Church, that we too might exercise great zeal on its behalf. Why did God not spare His only-begotten Son, but delivered Him up? That He might reconcile to Himself those who were His enemies and make them His peculiar people. Why did He shed His blood? To purchase those sheep which He entrusted to Peter and his successors. Justly then did Christ say, "Who, thinkest thou, is a faithful and wise servant, whom his Lord hath appointed over His family?" These words again express doubt, but the speaker who uttered them entertained no doubt. Just as when He asked Peter whether he loved Him, He put the question not to ascertain the love of His disciple, but to show the magnitude of His love; so now, when He says, "Who is a faithful and wise servant?" He speaks not as though He knew not who is a faithful and wise servant, but to show how rare such qualities are, as well as the greatness of this office. See, then, how great also is the reward: "He shall place him over all His goods."

2. Do you still question whether it was not for your advantage that I deceived you, since you are to be set over all the things that belong to God, and are engaged in an office by the fulfilment of which the Lord declared that Peter would far surpass the rest of the apostles? "Peter," says He, "lovest thou Me more than these?" Yet He might have said to him: "If thou lovest Me, fast, lie on the bare ground, watch, protect the oppressed, be a father to the orphan, and as a husband to their mother." But, passing over all these things, what does He say? "Feed My sheep." For the aforesaid works many of the faithful, both men and women, may easily perform. But when there is question of setting a pastor over the Church and confiding to him the care of so many souls, let the whole female sex and the majority of

men withdraw from so great a task. Let such be brought forward as surpass all others, and who are as much, or more, above them in spiritual excellence as Saul surpassed the whole Hebrew nation in stature. And here do not seek for a measure of stature greater from the shoulders and upwards, but let the difference between the pastor and his flock be as great as that which exists between senseless beasts and men endowed with reason; not to say greater, for there is more risk. For he who loses sheep either by reason of ravening wolves, or the attack of robbers, or from pestilence, or some other mishap, may, perchance, be pardoned by the owner of the flock; and if compensation be required, the fine will be only in money. But the man to whom the reasonable flock of Jesus Christ is entrusted is liable, in the first place, to a penalty, not in money only but in his own soul, if the sheep be lost. Moreover, the contest he has to endure is greater and more difficult; for his contest is not against wolves, nor his alarm about robbers, nor his anxiety to ward off pestilence from the flock. Against whom, then, is the contest? Listen to the blessed Paul, who says: "Our wrestling is not against flesh and blood, but against principalities and powers; and the rulers of the darkness of this world, against the spirits of wickedness in high places." Do you perceive then the dreadful number of the enemy and their fierce array, armed not with steel, but by nature tempered to suffice for every kind of armour? Do you wish to behold another fierce and cruel army lying in ambush to attack the flock? This you will perceive from the same vantage ground; for he who described the above-mentioned foes, points out these also in the following terms: "The works of the flesh are manifest, which are fornication, adultery, uncleanness, immodesty, idolatry, witchcraft, enmities, contentions, emulations, wraths, quarrels, detractions, tale-bearing, indignations, dissensions, and many more," for he did not enumerate all, but from these he gave us to infer the rest. In the case of the shepherd of irrational animals, when they who propose to destroy the herd see the shepherd flying, they cease attacking him, and are satisfied with carrying off the sheep; but in our case, even though they have captured the entire flock, they do not desist from their attacks upon the shepherd; but they become more bold, and never cease until they either overcome him or are themselves defeated. Moreover, the infirmities of animals are manifest, be they hunger or contagion or wounds or any other distemper, and this circumstance contributes not a little to the cure of sufferers. There is another feature too of much importance, which expedites the cure of their distempers. What, pray, is that? The shepherds have great power to compel the sheep to undergo treatment, even though they submit with reluctance. For it is easy to bind them, should it be necessary to apply the cautery or the knife, or to keep them shut up in the fold, should that be advisable, or to change one pasture for another, or keep them from water, and everything else they think conducive to the health of the animals they apply with the greatest ease.

3. But in the case of men, first of all it is no easy matter for a man to perceive their infirmities. "For no man knoweth the things of a man, but the spirit of man which is in him." How then is it possible to apply a remedy to a malady when one does not know its nature, and in many cases one cannot see whether the patient is ill? And even when the malady is manifest it occasions great difficulty. For it is not possible to treat men with the same facility as the shepherd treats a sheep. For in this case too it is necessary to bind and keep away from pastures, to use the cautery and the knife; but the power of accepting the treatment rests not with him who applies it, but with the patient, and knowing this that admirable man said to the Corinthians: "We do not exercise dominion over your faith, but are helpers of your joy."

For to Christians lest of all is it allowable to correct the faults of sinners by violence. Secular judges indeed use great authority in dealing with malefactors, when they find them amenable to the laws, and they hinder them even against their will from following their usual course of life; but as for us, it behoves us to correct such persons not by constraint, but by persuasion. For the laws do not confer on us so much power to restrain sinners; and even if they did, we could not use it, since God crowns not those who refrain from evil by necessity, but those who refrain from it by their own choice. Hence it requires much skill to persuade those who are ill to submit to treatment at the hands of priests, and not merely to submit, but to be grateful to them for their care. For if the patient struggles when bound—and he can do so if he pleases—the evil becomes worse. If he rejects words of admonition, which cut like steel, by his contempt, he inflicts on himself an additional wound, and the treatment becomes the occasion of a more dangerous malady. For no man can be cured against his will.

4. What then can be done? For if you treat gently a patient who needs a severe operation, and do not make a deep incision when necessary, you remove a part and leave a part of the wound. But if you make the requisite incision unsparingly, it oftens happens that the patient, distracted by pain, casts away at once both remedy and bandages, and throws himself headlong, breaking the yoke and bursting the bonds. I could mention many instances of persons who were driven to desperation because a satisfaction proportioned to their sins was required of them. For you must not indiscreetly impose satisfaction in proportion to the sins, you must also take into consideration the disposition of the sinner, lest by trying to mend what was torn, you make the rent the greater, and while striving to raise the fallen you make the fall the greater. The weak and languid, and such as are entangled in the pleasures of the world, or are proud of their birth and rank, if quietly and gradually turned away from the things wherein they have sinned, may be delivered in part at least if not entirely from the passions which held them in bondage. But if you apply a severe correction, you deprive them even of this smaller improvement. For once the soul has been driven to cast away shame, it becomes callous, and neither yields to exhortation nor is moved by threats nor influenced by benefits, but it becomes far worse than that city which the prophet reproached, saying: "Thou hast a harlot's forehead; towards all thou hast acted unblushingly." Hence the pastor needs great wisdom and circumspection to examine the state of the soul from every point of view. For as there are many who are driven to arrogance, and fall into despair of salvation by reason of their being unable to endure sharp remedies, so there are some, who through not having made sufficient satisfaction for their sins, are rendered careless and become much worse and are led to fall into greater sins. Therefore, the priest should leave none of these things unexamined, but should enquire into everything carefully,

and do his duty consistently, that his zeal may not be in vain. And this is not his only trouble; he has also great trouble in uniting again to the Church members who had been cut off. A shepherd is followed by his flock wherever he goes, and, if any of them turns aside from the straight road, and browses on sterile and rocky places, it is enough for him to call a little louder to bring back the strayed sheep, and unite it to the herd. But if a man strays from the right faith, the pastor requires great diligence, patience and perseverance. For it is not possible to bring him back by force or to compel him by fear; he must be brought back by persuasion to the truth from which he had fallen away. One must, therefore, have generosity of mind not to lose courage or despair of the salvation of those who have gone astray; and often call to mind these words: "If perchance God may give them repentance to know the truth, that they may recover themselves from the snares of the devil." For this reason the Lord said to his disciples, "Who is the faithful and wise servant?" For he that attends to his own perfection, profits himself only; but the benefit of the pastoral office extends to all the people. He indeed who bestows alms on the poor, or in any other way defends the injured, benefits his neighbour to some extent, but so much less than the priest, as the body is inferior to the soul. With reason, then, did our Lord say that zeal for his flock was a proof of love for himself.

Basil. But do you, said he, not love Christ?

Chrysostom. I do love Him, and I will never cease to love Him, but I am afraid to offend Him whom I love.

Basil. What riddle could be more obscure than this? For Christ enjoined on him who loves Him to feed his sheep; but you say that you do not feed them because you love Him who gave the injunction.

Chrysostom. What I say is no riddle, but very clear and plain. For if I declined the office, though competent to fulfil it as Christ desired, I should be at a loss how to account for what I say; but since my spiritual weakness renders me unfit for that ministry, how does my assertion merit blame? For I am afraid lest, after having received the flock of Christ in an healthy and sound condition, I should harm it by my negligence, and draw upon myself the indignation of Him who so loves it, that He delivered Himself up as the price of its salvation.

Basil. You are speaking in jest. For if you spoke in earnest, I know not how you could better prove that I am justly pained, than by what you have said to dispel my sorrow. For, though I knew already that you had deceived and betrayed me, now that you have attempted to refute the charge, I understand it better, and I clearly see to what a pass you have brought me. If you withdrew from so great a ministry, because you knew that your mind was not equal to so great a task, you ought first to have rescued me from it; even though I eagerly aspired to it; to say nothing of the fact that I left the decision of the whole affair to you. On the contrary, looking only to your own interest, you neglected mine, and would that you had neglected it! If you had, it would be matter for satisfaction. Instead of that, you plotted that I might be easily caught by those who sought me. Nor can you excuse yourself, and say that you were deceived by the opinion of the public, and led to believe that I was possessed of great and extraordinary merit. For I am not distinguished nor conspicuous, and, even if such were the fact, the opinion of the public should not be preferred to truth. If, by our companionship you had never had experience of what I am, you might have some reasonable excuse for giving your vote according to public opinion; but since no one knows me so well as you (for you know my disposition better than my parents who brought me up), what plausible reason can you allege to convince your hearers that you did not deliberately cast me into such danger? But let us pass over all this at present. I do not require you to stand your trial on this point. But tell me, what defence can we make against our accusers?

Chrysostom. By no means, said I, shall I proceed to that, until I clear myself in what concerns yourself, even though you should repeatedly urge me to refute the other charges. You say that ignorance would have secured me pardon, and acquitted me of all blame, if, being unacquainted with you, I had brought you to this pass; but that, as I betrayed you not through ignorance, but with full knowledge, I am therefore deprived of every reasonable excuse and valid justification. Now I maintain the very contrary. Why? Because a matter of such importance requires much consideration; and because he who puts forward a man as qualified for the priestly office should not be satisfied with the voice of the public merely, but in addition he should himself, most of all and before all, examine the qualities of the candidate. For when the Blessed Paul says: "Moreover he must have a good testimony of those that are without," he does not exclude a careful and searching examination, nor does he set down that testimony as the chief test in the examination of so important a matter. For having spoken first of many other tests he placed this last, to show that one ought not to be satisfied with it in such decisions; but that it too should be taken into account along with the rest. For it often happens that the opinion of the public is mistaken; but when a careful investigation has been made, there is no danger to be apprehended from it. Wherefore he places the clause concerning the testimony from those without after the rest. He does not simply say "He must have a good testimony," but he adds, "Moreover from those without," to show that previous to the testimony from those without a careful examination of the candidate should be made. Since then I knew your qualities better than your parents, as you admit, it is therefore right that I should be acquitted of all blame.

Basil. For this very reason, said he, you would not be acquitted if anyone would accuse you. Do you not remember that you often heard me say, what you must also have known from my conduct, how deficient I am in strength of character? Did you not, many a time, laugh at me for my pusillanimity and for my want of courage in ordinary difficulties and troubles?

5. *Chrysostom.* I cannot deny, said I, that I remember having often heard you say so. But if I ever laughed at you, I did it in jest, not in earnest; yet I will not dispute the point with you now, but I ask you to show me the same indulgence while I proceed to mention some of your good qualities. And should you strive to prove that what I say is false, I will not spare you, but I will show that you are minimising rather than telling the truth, and I will bring forward no other witness than your own words and deeds to prove the truth of what I state. Do you understand then the value of charity? For Christ, passing over

all the other miracles which the apostles were to perform, says: "By this shall all men know that you are My disciples, if you have love one for another." Paul declares, that it is the fulfilling of the law, and that if it be wanting the gifts are of no avail. Now I saw that this excellent virtue, the mark of the disciples of Christ, and greater than the gifts, was deeply implanted in your soul, and gave promise of much fruit.

Basil. That I always paid great attention to that point, and made every effort to fulfill that commandment, I myself admit; but that I have not half fulfilled it you yourself could testify, if you would cease to speak from affection and give your verdict according to truth.

6. *Chrysostom.* Well, said I, I will have recourse to proofs, and as I promised, I proceed to show that you minimise rather than speak the truth. And I will mention a fact of recent occurrence, that no one may imagine that by relating an event long past I am attempting to cloak the truth by the remoteness of the date, as truth does not permit us to exaggerate even in what is said for the purpose of gratification. For when one of our friends was in great danger in consequence of an accusation of insolence and arrogance, though unsolicited by any one, unasked even by him who was imperilled, you rushed into the midst of danger. Such was your act. And to convince you by your words I will remind you of what you said. As some did not approve of your conduct, while others praised and admired it, you said to those who blamed you: What was I to do? I know not how to love in any other way than by giving even my life to save any of my friends from danger. In different terms, but in the same sense, you expressed what Christ said to His disciples when He laid down the limits of perfect charity: "Greater love than this no man hath, that a man lay down his life for his friends." If there cannot be greater love than this, then you have already reached its perfection. By your acts and by your words you have already reached its summit. It was for this reason I betrayed you; for this reason I contrived that strategem. Pray, have I convinced you that it was not with evil intent, nor from a desire to cast you into danger, but from the conviction that it would be for your benefit, that I forced you into this position?

Basil. Do you then think that the power of charity is enough for the correction of the neighbour?

Chrysostom. Certainly, said I, it contributes much to that end. But if you wish me to bring forward a proof of your prudence also, I shall proceed to show that you are as prudent as you are charitable.

Basil. On this he blushed deeply, and said: Let alone for the present what concerns me. At the very outset I did not ask you for an explanation on that head. But if you have any valid defence to make in reply to strangers, I should like to hear what you have to say. Therefore, leave off fighting with shadows, and tell me what justification you can give to the public, to those who purposed to promote you, and to those who sympathise with them as being insulted.

7. *Chrysostom.* I, too, said I, am hastening to that point, for as I have concluded my explanation in what regards yourself, I gladly turn to that portion of my defence. What then is their accusation? what are the charges?

They say they have been insulted and badly treated by us, because we did not accept the dignity they wished to confer. In the first place, I maintain that one ought to make no account of insult to men, if by honouring them one is forced to offend God. I do not think that their displeasure is void of danger to themselves, but rather that it is very hurtful to them. For in my opinion they who serve God, and look to Him alone, should be so piously disposed as not to consider it an insult should they be so treated over and over again. That I never ventured deliberately to insult them may be shown as follows: Had I acted as I have done through pride or vanity, in contempt of excellent and good men, who are moreover benefactors, as according to you I am accused of doing, my accusers might justly hold me guilty of the greatest injustice. For if to injure those who have done one no wrong merits punishment, in what honour are they to be held who of their own accord chose to confer honour upon me? For no man can say that they received benefits either great or small from me and are now requiting them. What punishment would I not deserve if I made them a bad return? Now if I never thought of insulting them, but declined the heavy burden for another reason, why, if they will not approve of my action, do they not pardon me, rather than accuse me for having spared their souls? For my part, so far was I from insulting those men, that I venture to assert I have done them honour by declining. And do not be surprised at what I say, as if it were a paradox, for I will explain my meaning presently.

8. For had I accepted ordination, it would have been possible, if not for all, at least for those who love to find fault, to entertain suspicion, to talk about me and about the electors. It might have been said, for instance, that they look to wealth and admire distinction of birth, that they promoted me because I flattered them; and I am not sure whether it would not have been said that they were bribed by me. Or it would have been said: Christ made choice of fishermen, of tent-makers, of publicans for this office, but these electors despise such as live by their daily toil; but if anyone has a smattering of profane learning and lives an idle life, they select and look up to him. Why did they pass over many who had undergone innumerable labours in the service of the Church, and straightway thrust into such a dignity a man who never had the least experience of such toils, but had spent his whole life in vain and worldly learning? People might have said this and much more had I accepted the office; but now they cannot, for every pretext for accusation has been taken away, and they cannot accuse me of flattery, nor the electors of venality, unless they have quite lost their senses. Is it credible that a person who had recourse to flattery and bribery to obtain a dignity, would leave it to others when the time came for him to receive it? This would be to act like a man who should spend much toil on his land in order to reap an abundant harvest, and that his wine-presses might overflow with wine, and when the time of the harvest and the vintage arrived should after all his toil and expense leave the gathering in of the fruits to others. Do you then perceive that even though what might have been said was far from true, yet persons desirous of fault-finding would have had a pretext for saying that the electors made their choice without discretion. But I have rendered it impossible for them to say a word, or even so much as to open their mouth. This and much more would have been said at first. But after I had entered on the office I should never have been able to refute their accusations, though I discharged every duty faultlessly;

and much less, since I must have made many mistakes through inexperience and youth. By acting as I have done, I have delivered the electors from such censures, whereas by acting otherwise I would have exposed them to endless reproaches. For what would people not have said? "They have confided things so sacred and so great to witless boys. They have ruined the flock of God. The interests of Christians have become a toy and a plaything." "But now all iniquity shall stop her mouth." But if they speak of you in this way, you will soon show them by your works that one must not judge of wisdom by age, nor value an old man for his hoary hair, nor reject a young man from so great a ministry, but only a neophyte. And betweeen the two there is a wide difference.

BOOK IV

1. Not only those who are eager to enter the clerical state, but also those who enter it by compulsion, are severely punished if they sin.
2. They who ordain the unworthy are liable to the same punishment as the ordained, even if they act in ignorance.
3. Priests should have great skill in preaching.
4. They must be prepared to meet the attacks of all—of Greeks, Jews and heretics.
5. They require great skill in argument.
6. The excellence of St. Paul in this respect.
7. He was remarkable, not only for his miracles, but also for his eloquence.
8. He desires that we also should excel in this.
9. If a priest does not possess this qualification, the faithful necessarily suffer great loss.

1. On hearing this, Basil paused a little, and said: Had you been eager to obtain this dignity, you might have had reason to entertain such fear. For when a man, by grasping at an office, professes himself fit for it, he cannot excuse himself for his mistakes on the ground of inexperience if he obtains it. He has already deprived himself of that excuse by his eagerness to get hold of the office. And when he freely and of his own accord puts himself forward he can no longer say: It was against my will I failed in this; it was against my will I mismanaged that. He who shall one day be our Judge shall say to him: "Since you knew your inexperience, and your incapacity to practise that

art without making mistakes, why did you make haste, why did you venture to undertake what was beyond your strength? Who compelled you? Who forced you in spite of your resistance and your efforts to escape?" But no such thing will ever be said of you. Nor can you charge yourself with such a fault, for everybody knows that you did not make the least effort to obtain that dignity; the whole project came from others. Hence the point which leaves others no excuse for their faults supplies you with abundant matter for your justification.

Chrysostom. On this I shook my head, and smiling quietly at his simplicity, I said: I should be very glad, my dearest friend, that the case were as you say, not that I might be able to undertake the office, which I have just now declined. For even were I exposed to no chastisement for feeding the flock of Christ in a negligent and unskilful manner, I would regard it as worse than any chastisement to appear to be ungrateful to him who had so trusted me as to confide to me a matter of such importance. For what reason then would I desire that your opinion were not without foundation? That those wretched and unhappy men—for so they deserve to be called, who are incapable of rightly managing this business, though you will say they were compelled by force and erred through ignorance—that those wretched men might be able to escape the fire that is not extinguished, and the outer darkness and the worm that dieth not, and might not be separated, and perish with the hypocrites. But what would you have me to do, this is impossible.

And if you permit me, I shall prove the truth of what I say, first of all by reference to the royal power which is not of so much importance in the eyes of God as is the priesthood.

It was not at his own desire that Saul, the son of Cis, was made king, but he went in quest of the asses, and began to consult the prophet concerning them, and the prophet spoke to him of a kingdom. Yet not even then did he show eagerness, though it was a prophet that spoke to him. But he declined and begged to be excused, saying: "Who am I, and what is my father's house?" What then? When he had made a bad use of the rank to which God had raised him, were these words sufficient to screen him from the wrath of Him who had made him king? Yet he might have said to Samuel when he rebuked him: "Did

I hasten to assume the power of king? Did I intrude myself into this dignity? My desire was to lead the leisured and quiet life of a private individual; you forced me into this dignity. Had I remained in that humble station I should easily have escaped my present troubles. For were I one of the ordinary people, and undistinguished, I should never have been sent to execute the present task, nor would God have entrusted me with the war against the Amalecites. And had I not been entrusted with it, I should never have committed this fault." But all these reasons were insufficient to excuse him, and not merely insufficient, but they made his case worse, for they excited the anger of God still more. For one who has been honoured beyond his deserts ought not to put forward the greatness of his rank as an excuse for his faults, but he should use God's great love as a motive to make greater progress in virtue. To think that one is at liberty to sin because one has obtained higher dignity is nothing else than to try to make the goodness of God a pretext for sin, as the impious and the careless are wont to do. But such should not be our sentiments, nor should we be so foolish; but we should endeavour, as far as in us lies, to speak and think reverently.

But, to pass from the royal power to the priesthood with which we are now concerned, Heli did not make an effort to obtain that dignity. Yet what did that avail him when he sinned? And why do I say he made no effort to obtain the office? He could not have escaped from it, even if he desired, since the law laid it upon him. For he was of the tribe of Levi, and he was obliged to accept the dignity which devolved on him by descent. Yet even he suffered no slight punishment on account of the frowardness of his sons. What shall I say of him who was the first priest of the Jews, and of whom God spoke such great things to Moses? Because he was unable single-handed to resist the folly of so great a multitude, he was on the verge of destruction, had not the intercession of his brother averted the anger of God.

And as I have mentioned Moses, his fate furnishes an excellent proof of what I assert. This same blessed Moses was so far from grasping at the chief place amongst the Jews that he declined it when offered, and though commanded by God he resisted so far as to provoke His anger. And this was his disposition not only on that occasion, but later on, when he held supreme authority, he would gladly have died in order to be relieved of it. For he said, "Kill me if you are to deal with me thus." What then? When he sinned on the occasion of drawing water from the rock, were these objections sufficient to excuse him and to move God to pardon him? For what other reason was he deprived of entering the promised land? For no other reason, as we all know, than for this fault, in consequence of which that admirable man could not obtain what was granted to his subjects. But after many fatigues and labours, after indescribable wanderings and wars and victories, he died outside the land, for sake of which he had undergone so many toils. After suffering the hardships of the voyage he did not enjoy the good things of the harbour. Do you understand then, that not only those who grasp at this dignity, but even those who are promoted to it by the efforts of others, have no excuse left to them if they sin? For if they who resisted, though God called them, were so severely punished, if nothing could exempt from such a calamity an Aaron or a Heli, or that blessed man who was a saint, a prophet, the meekest of men on earth, who spoke to God as to a friend, it will hardly be a sufficient excuse for us who are so far inferior to them in virtue, to say that we are conscious of having made no effort to obtain this dignity. And most of all now when many ordinations have their origin, not in divine grace, but in human efforts.

God made choice of Judas and admitted him to that holy college and conferred the apostolic dignity on him as well as on the others; He even confided to him something more than to the rest, namely, the dispensation of money. What then? When he had fulfilled both offices badly, when he had betrayed Him whom he had undertaken to preach, and had mis-spent the money entrusted to his management, did he escape punishment? For this very reason the chastisement he brought on himself was the greater, and justly so. For the dignities that have been conferred by God should not be used to offend Him, but to please Him the more. Now for a man who has been honoured more than others to claim exemption from the chastisement he deserves, would be the same as if one of the incredulous Jews, on hearing Christ say, "If I had not come and spoken to them, they would not have sin; if I had not done among them works which no other man hath done, they would not have sin," should accuse his Saviour and benefactor, and say: "Why didst Thou come and speak? Why didst Thou perform miracles in order to punish us more severely?" But this is the language of madness and of utter insanity. For the Physician came to heal, not in order that He might condemn with greater severity, but in order to deliver you completely from your malady. But you of your own choice have withdrawn yourself from His care; receive therefore a more severe punishment! For as you would have been delivered from your sins had you submitted to treatment, so you can no longer be purified from them, since you fled when you saw Him approach, and as you cannot, you will suffer punishment for them, as well as for having, as far as in you lay, rendered His solicitude vain. Therefore the punishment we shall endure after having been raised to honour by God is not the same as we would have suffered before promotion, but much more severe; for he who is not improved by benefits justly deserves to be more rigorously chastised. Since then this defence has been shown to be worthless, and since so far from saving, it rather betrays such as rely upon it, we should provide ourselves with some other means of safety.

Basil. Of what kind? For I no longer know where I am, with such fear and terror have your words inspired me.

Chrysostom. I beg and implore you, said I, be not so downcast. For me, as I am weak, my security is never to get into that position; but for you, as you are strong, your security is to place your hope of salvation in nothing else, after God's grace, but in doing nothing unworthy of such a gift and of God who bestowed it. For they deserve the severest punishment who, having by their own efforts obtained that dignity, do not make a good use of it, either from sloth, or malice, or inexperience. And for the same reason even they who obtained it without any efforts of their own merit no indulgence, but they too are deprived of every excuse. In my opinion, then, though called and pressed by many, a man ought to pay no attention to them; but he should first of all examine his own soul, and weigh everything carefully, and only then should he yield to pressure. For no man would venture to undertake to build a house unless he were a builder, nor would any man undertake to heal the sick unless he had a knowledge of medicine. But though pressed by many, he would decline, and would not be ashamed to admit his ignorance. And will a man to whom the care of so many souls is about to be confided neglect to examine himself, and will he undertake the ministry, in spite of his ignorance, because he is urged by one, pressed by a second, and is afraid to offend a third? Does he not of his own choice cast himself into the abyss along with them? And while he might have been saved by himself, he drags others with him to destruction. Whence can he hope for salvation? Whence can he obtain pardon? Who shall then be our advocates? Will it be those who now offer violence and compel us? But who will save themselves on that day? They too shall need intercessors in order to escape the fire. Now to prove that I do not say this to fill you with alarm, but because truth requires it, give ear to what the Blessed Paul says to his disciple Timothy, his true and well-beloved son: "Impose not hands lightly upon any man; neither be a partaker of other men's sins." Do you perceive, then, from what blame and from what chastisement I have as far as in me lay preserved those who wished to promote me to that dignity?

2. For it is not enough for him who is elected to say in his defence, "It was not of my own accord I approached," "It was through ignorance I did not fly"; so it will not avail the electors to say, "I did not know the candidate." But their sin is the greater because they promoted one whom they did not know, and what they took to be their justification increases their responsibility. Is it not absurd that when they want to purchase a slave, men will show him to the physicians and require sureties for the purchase, and make inquiry from the neighbours, and after all this they are by no means confident, but they ask a long period of time for trial; and yet when they desire to promote anyone to so great a ministry they give testimony and vote for any one whatever without any further inquiry, rashly and at random, through partiality to some or enmity towards others. Who will be our intercessor on that day when they who should be our advocates will stand in need of advocates themselves? Hence it behoves the elector to make a full examination

beforehand, and much more is this the duty of him who is to be ordained. For though he may have his electors as partakers of his punishment if he sins, yet he will not himself escape chastisement, but he will be punished more severely, unless perhaps the electors acted contrary to their conscience. For if it is found that they have committed such a fault, and have for some reason or other elected a person whom they knew to be certainly unworthy, both will suffer equal punishment, and perhaps the punishment of those who elected an unworthy person will be more severe. For whoever affords an opportunity to one who has a mind to injure the Church is responsible for his misdeeds. But if the elector is open to none of these charges, and can say that he was deceived by the mistaken opinion of the public, he will not indeed go unpunished on that account, yet he will be punished less severely than the person elected. Why? Because it is natural to suppose that the electors, misled by the erroneous opinion of the public, acted as they did, but the person elected cannot, like them, say, "I did not know myself." Hence, as he is exposed to be more severely punished than the electors, he should examine himself more carefully than they; and if, through ignorance, they constrain him, he should come forward and state the reasons, which may disabuse them of their error, and by thus showing himself to be undeserving of election, free himself from so great a burden. How comes it that when warfare, commerce or other secular business is in question, a farmer will not undertake the management of a ship, nor a soldier of tillage, nor a pilot of warfare, even under the pressure of repeated threats of death. The reason is, that they foresee the risk that would arise from their want of experience. When matters of no great importance are in question we act with such prudence and do not yield to the violence of pressure; and when everlasting punishment awaits those who are unable to fulfil the office of the priesthood, shall we rashly and readily throw ourselves into such danger under pretext that we have been constrained by others? But the judge will not admit such a plea on that day. We ought to look for greater security in spiritual than in carnal things; but now it is evident we do not give them even equal consideration. Tell me, pray, if we employed a man, believing him to be a mason, though not really such, and if he acceeded to our request, but on putting his hand to the material prepared for the building, spoiled both wood and stone, and built in such a way that the house would immediately fall, would it be enough for him to say in his defence that it was not of his own choice he had undertaken the work? By no means. And very justly. For he ought to have resisted, even though others urged him on. There is then no means of escaping punishment, when a man spoils wood and stone; and if a man ruins souls, and has been negligent in their edification, can it be thought sufficient for him to escape punishment, to say that he was constrained by others? Is not this an excess of folly? And I have not yet added, that no man can be compelled against his will. But granting that he suffered great pressure, and that he yielded only when assailed by various stratagems, will this exempt him from punishment? I beg of you, let us not deceive ourselves so much, nor pretend to be ignorant of what is evident even to children. For assuredly on the accounting day this pretence of ignorance will not avail us: you were conscious of your own inability, and you did not ambition this dignity? This was right and proper. You ought then to have declined it with the same resolution, though others called you to it; you were weak and incompetent when no one called you; but when there were found persons to bestow the dignity on you, did you all at once become strong? This is ridiculous and trifling, and merits the severest punishment. For this reason the Lord also exhorts a man who purposes to build a tower not to lay the foundations until he examines his resources, in order that he may not give the passers by great reason to laugh at him. Yet that man's loss goes no further than being laughed at. But in our case the punishment is unquenchable fire, the worm that dieth not, gnashing of teeth, outer darkness, being separated and ranked with the hypocrites. Yet my accusers are unwilling to give heed to any of these things, else they would have ceased to blame me for not wishing to perish to no purpose. For the duty laid upon us regards not the dispensation of wheat or barley, nor the care of oxen and sheep and the like, but the very body of Christ. For the Church of Christ, according to the Blessed Paul, is the body of Christ; and it is meet that he to whom that body is entrusted, should bestow the greatest attention on its welfare and its beauty, and should take great care that neither spot nor wrinkle nor any such stain mar its grace and comeliness. And what is this but to make it, as far as man can do, worthy of its pure and blessed head? If they who strive to acquire the constitution of an athlete require physicians, training masters, a temperate regimen, frequent exercise, and endless attention, and if the least thing be neglected, it upsets and spoils everything; how shall they whose office it is to take care of the body of Christ, which has to contend not against men, but against the invisible powers, how shall they preserve that body in health and vigour unless they are endowed with a virtue more than human, and are skilled in every useful method of healing the soul?

3. Know you not that this body is subject to more diseases and accidents than our carnal body, and is more easily injured, and more slowly healed? The physicians of the body have, at their disposal, a variety of medicines, different sorts of instruments, a regimen adapted to the patient, and the quality of the air is sometimes of itself sufficient to cure the invalid. Sometimes, too, sleep coming on opportunely relieves the physician of all anxiety. Here, however, no such means can be devised, but after good example there is but one instrument and means of healing; that is preaching. This is the instrument, this the regimen, this the salubrious climate, this serves as medicine, as fire, and knife. If it be necessary to burn or to cut, this must be used, and if it fail, all the rest is useless. By means of this, we raise up the soul when prostrate, and cool it when fevered, and cut off what is superfluous, and fill up deficiencies, and do everything else which contributes to the health of the soul. When there is question of leading a virtuous life, the example of another's life may arouse to emulation; but when the soul is sick by reason of false doctrine, then the preaching of the word is very necessary, not only for the security of the members of the household, but also to repel attacks from without. For if one possessed the sword of the spirit and the shield of faith, to such a degree as to be able to work miracles, and by miracles to stop the mouths of the froward, one would have no need of preaching. Nay, even then, so far from being useless it would be very necessary. For the Blessed Paul made use of it though he was everywhere an object of admiration by reason of his

miracles; and a certain other of the same apostolic college exhorts us to cultivate the power of preaching, saying: "Be ye ready to satisfy every one that asketh a reason of you of that hope which is in you." And for no other reason did all the apostles together entrust the care of the widows to Stephen, than that they themselves might have leisure to devote themselves to the ministry of the word. Yet if we possessed the power of working miracles, we would not so much require the power of eloquence, but since not a vestige of the former is left, and many enemies menace us on every side, we must arm ourselves with the latter, to repel their attacks and to strike them in turn.

4. Wherefore we should use great diligence "that the word of Christ may dwell in us abundantly." For we have to prepare not for one kind of combat alone, but the warfare is manifold and waged by various enemies. They do not all use the same weapons, nor the same method of attack. It behoves him who has to engage in conflict with all, to know the arts of all, and to be at once archer and slinger, brigadier and captain, soldier and general, foot-soldier and horseman, skilled in battles by sea and in besieging cities. For in military operations, whatever method one has learned, by that he repels assailants. Not so here, for unless he who hopes to conquer knows all the arts of war, the devil can send in his marauders by even one neglected point and ravage the flock. Not so when he perceives that the pastor is vigilant and acquainted with all his stratagems. Hence it is necessary to be guarded well and on every side. For as long as a city is fortified on all sides, it can despise its besiegers and remain in security; but if the wall be pierced even to a door's breadth, all the rest of the fortification, though intact, is of no avail. So too with the city of God. As long as the prudence and intelligence of the pastor surround it on all sides as with a wall, all the machinations of the enemy turn to their own disgrace and confusion, and they who dwell within remain secure; but as soon as a portion of the wall has been demolished, though it has not been all destroyed, the whole, so to speak, is lost by means of the part. For of what advantage is it to fight nobly against the Gentiles, if the Jews plunder the Church; or that both are conquered if the Manichaeans ravage it; or that all

three are overcome, if the Fatalists slaughter the sheep within the fold? why enumerate all diabolical heresies? Yet if the shepherd is unable to refute them all successfully, the wolf may succeed even by means of one, in devouring the greater portion of the flock. In war, victory or defeat depend only on those who are engaged in the struggle, but here the contrary is the case. Oftentimes the conflict of others has given victory to those who had not even engaged in the struggle, nor made any effort whatever, but who sat at their ease; while he who has not had experience has been transpierced by his own sword, and becomes a laughing-stock to friends and foes. For instance—I shall try to explain what I mean by an example—the followers of Valentinian and of Marcion, and others infected with the same error, expunge from the catalogue of the holy Scriptures the Law given by God to Moses. The Jews, on the other hand, hold it in such honour, notwithstanding the distinction of times and contrary to the ordinance of God, that they earnestly endeavour to observe it in its fulness. But the Church of God, avoiding both extremes, takes a middle course, and neither subjects itself to the yoke of the law, nor permits it to be condemned, but praises it though abrogated because it was useful for a time. Now whoever has to resist both must observe the like moderation. For if, desiring to show that the Jews cling unreasonably to the old Law, he begins to find fault with it unsparingly, he gives no small handle to the heretics who attempt to destroy it. But if in order to refute the latter he extols it beyond measure and praises it as though it were necessary at the present day, he strengthens the arguments of the Jews. They, again, who are infected with the frenzy of Sabellius, or the folly of Arius, have both lapsed from the sound faith, yet both fear the name of Christians. Now if their tenets be examined, it will be found that the former are no better than the Jews, differing from them only about names, and that the latter approach very near the heresy of Paul of Samosata, but that both are far from the truth. Here then there is great peril; the way is strait and rugged and bounded by precipices on either side, and there is no small reason to fear lest, while trying to strike one opponent, you be yourself wounded by the other. For if you say there is one Godhead,

Sabellius will interpret the expression in his own sense. If you distinguish and say that the Father and the Son and the Holy Ghost are distinct, Arius presses on, and interprets the distinction of persons as diversity of nature. It is necessary therefore to avoid at the same time the impious confusion of the one and the foolish diversity of the other, confessing that the Godhead of Father and Son and Holy Ghost is one, but adding that there are three persons. In this way you will be able to repel the attacks of both. I could mention many other conflicts wherein a man will receive innumerable wounds unless he combines accuracy with courage.

5. Who can enumerate the disputes of those within the Church? They are no less numerous than the attacks from without, and they cause greater trouble to the teacher. Some persons from curiosity wish to investigate all manner of questions, rashly and uselessly, though the knowledge of them can be of no profit to the learner, and though in some cases they cannot be solved. Others again ask for an explanation of the judgements of God, and strive to fathom that great deep. "For Thy judgements are a great deep." And you will find few concerned about faith and morals, while many curiously search into those things which cannot be understood, and the examination of which offends God. For when we try to learn what He does not wish us to know, and what we shall never know—how could we against His will?—the only advantage we gain is to incur danger by the inquiry. Yet, though this is the case, when one stops the mouths of the curious, he earns for himself the reputation of being proud and ignorant. Therefore the bishop needs great prudence to withdraw the people from foolish questions, and at the same time to keep himself clear of the aforesaid charges. To meet all these difficulties he has no other means but the preaching of the word; and if he is deficient in talent for that, the minds of the faithful, I mean the weaker and more curious among them, will be no better than vessels tempest-tossed. Hence it behoves a priest to make every effort to acquire this talent.

Basil. Why then, said he, did St. Paul make no effort to acquire this talent? and was not ashamed of his want of eloquence; but openly admitted his ignorance, and that too in a letter to the Corinthians, so celebrated and so proud of their eloquence?

6. *Chrysostom.* This, said I, is what has misled many and made them more negligent about real learning. For being unable to fathom the meaning of the apostle and to understand the sense of his words, they spent their time in somnolence and sloth, holding in esteem not that ignorance of which St. Paul speaks, but from which he was as far removed as any man under heaven. But let us reserve this for another occasion. Meanwhile here is what I hold. Granting that he was unlearned in that respect, as they will have it, what has that to do with the men of the present day? He possessed a power greater than that of preaching and capable of producing greater effects. For when he merely appeared, though he uttered not a word, he was an object of terror to the devils. Now all the men of the present day together could not accomplish by endless prayers and tears as much the garments of Paul once accomplished. By prayer Paul raised the dead to life, and worked wonders so great that by those without he was taken for a god; and before he passed from this life he was deemed worthy to be elevated to the third heaven, and to hear words which it is not permitted to the nature of man to hear. But the men of the present day (and I do not mean to say anything disagreeable or offensive, for I speak not by way of insult, but from a sense of astonishment) how is it they do not tremble to put themselves in comparison with such a man? For if we leave miracles out of the question and come to the life of that blessed man and examine his angelic conduct, we shall see the athlete of Christ excel in this respect even more than in miracles. Why mention his zeal, his modesty, his frequent perils, his constant cares, his incessant solicitude for the churches, his compassion for the poor, his many trials, his repeated persecutions, his daily deaths? For what spot in the world, what continent, what sea was not a witness of the contests of this just man? The desert knew him, for it received him often in his perils. He endured every form of attack and obtained every kind of victory, and never ceased to combat and to conquer. But I know not how I have been led on to insult the man, for his good deeds surpass all expression, and all that I can say, as far as the masters of eloquence surpass

me. But not even thus will I desist (for that blessed man will judge me, not by my success but by my intention) until I have stated what as far surpasses all that has been said as he surpasses all men. After so many good works, after so many victories, he prayed that he might be cast into hell and consigned to everlasting punishment, that the Jews who had frequently stoned him, and, as far as in them lay, put him to death, might be saved and come to Christ. Who loved Christ so much as he, if indeed that must be called love, and not something greater than love? Shall we, then, compare ourselves with him, after the many favours which he received from above and all the virtue he displayed in his daily life? Could there be anything more audacious? That he was not so ignorant as these men imagine it now remains for me to prove. For they call a man ignorant not only when he is unskilled in the artifices of profane literature, but also when he is unable to defend true doctrine. And justly. But Paul does not profess himself ignorant in both these respects, but only in one of the two; and to mark this he said that he "was rude in speech, but not in knowledge." Were I looking for the smoothness of Isocrates, the strength of Demosthenes, the gravity of Thucydides, the sublimity of Plato, this testimony of Paul might be quoted. But I pass over all these qualities together with the exquisite ornament of profane writers, and I make no account of diction and delivery. Let a man be deficient in diction, and let his style be simple and plain, provided he is not ignorant in knowledge and in accuracy of doctrine, and provided, to cover his own sloth, he does not rob that blessed man of his greatest excellence and his chiefest praise.

7. How, I ask, did he confound the Jews that dwelt in Damascus, when as yet he had not commenced to perform miracles? How did he overcome the Hellenists? Why was he sent to Tarsus? Was it not because he excelled in eloquence and pressed them so hard that, being unable to endure defeat, they were provoked to kill him? For as yet he had not begun to work miracles, nor can it be asserted that he was regarded with admiration on account of the fame of his miracles, and that his adversaries were overcome by their veneration for him. So far he overcame by his eloquence alone. How did he contend and dispute at Antioch with those who attempted to introduce

Jewish practices? Was it not by his eloquence alone that he made converts of the Areopagite and his wife, citizens of that most superstitious city? How came Eutychus to fall from the window? Was it not because he was occupied in listening to his discourses until far in the night? How did he act at Thessalonica and Corinth, at Ephesus and at Rome? Did he not spend days and nights in expounding the Scriptures? What shall I say of his discourses against the Epicureans and the Stoics? For if I entered into every detail I should never conclude. Since then before he worked miracles, and while he worked them, he evidently displayed great power of eloquence, how will they still dare to style him ignorant, who by his conversation and his discourses was an object of admiration to all? Why did the Lycaonians take him for Mercury? For the fact that they were taken for gods was due to their miracles, but the fact that he was taken for Mercury was due not to miracles but to his eloquence. In what did that blessed man surpass the other apostles? Why is he spoken of throughout the whole world? Why is he most of all admired not only by us but also by Jews and Greeks? Is it not on account of the excellence of his epistles, by which he benefited not only the faithful who lived at that time, but also those who have lived from that time till now, and those who shall live until the final coming of Christ, and he shall never cease to do so as long as the human race exists? For his writings, like a wall of adamant, protect all the churches throughout the entire world. Even now he stands in our midst like a valiant athlete "bringing into captivity every understanding unto the obedience of Christ, and destroying counsels and every height that exalteth itself against the knowledge of God." All this he does by means of those admirable epistles, full of divine wisdom, which he has left us. And his writings are useful, not only to refute false doctrine and to defend that which is true, but they are also of no small utility to instruct us how to lead a good life. For even now by means of them the prelates of the Church deck and adorn and form the spiritual beauty the chaste Virgin whom he espoused to Christ. By these they ward off the diseases which attack her, and preserve her in health. Such remedies did that ignorant man leave us, possessing a power which they who frequently use them know by experience. And that he devoted much attention to eloquence is evident from what I am about to relate.

8. Give ear to what he says in his epistle to his disciple, "Attend to reading, to exhortation, and to doctrine," and he adds what will be the consequence: "For doing this you will save yourself and them that hear you"; and again, "The servant of the Lord must not wrangle, but be mild towards all men, apt to teach, patient." And further on he says: "But continue thou in those things which thou hast learned, and which have been committed to thee, knowing of whom thou hast learned them, and because from thy infancy thou hast known the holy scriptures, which can instruct thee." And again, "All scripture inspired of God is profitable to teach, to reprove, to correct, to instruct unto justice, that the man of God may be perfect." Listen also to the rule he lays down for Titus when speaking of the appointment of bishops: "For a bishop," he says, "must embrace the faithful word, which is according to doctrine that he may be able to convince the gainsayers." How then could one who is ignorant, as they will have it, convince and silence the gainsayers? What need is there to attend to reading and to the scriptures if we should embrace such ignorance? But this is a pretext and an excuse and a cloak for negligence and sloth.

But some one will say these injunctions regard bishops. But it is of bishops we are now speaking. Now, that you may see that this advice is applicable also to the faithful, hearken to what he says in another epistle: "Let the word of Christ dwell in you abundantly in all wisdom." And again: "Let your speech be always in grace, seasoned with salt, that you may know how you ought to answer every man." What concerns being ready to give an answer is addressed to all. Writing to the Thessalonians, he says: "Edify one another, as you also do." But when he speaks of priests he says: "Let priests that rule well be esteemed worthy of double honour, especially those who labour in the Word and in doctrine." For this is the most perfect end of doctrine, to lead one's disciples by act and by word to the blessed life which Christ has taught us. To teach, works are not enough. This is not my doctrine, but that of the Saviour Himself. "But he," He says, "that shall do and teach, he shall be called great in the kingdom of heaven." Now, if to do were the same as to teach, the second clause would be superfluous; it would have been sufficient to say: "He that shall do." Now, since he distinguishes both, he shows that works and teaching are two distinct things, and that to effect perfect edification each stands in need of the other. Do you not hear what that elect vessel of Christ says to the ancients of the Ephesians? "Therefore, watch, keeping in memory that for three years I ceased not with tears to admonish every one of you." What need was there of words of admonition, or of tears, since his apostolic life was conspicuous? Such a life is a great assistance to us in keeping the commandments, but I should not affirm that of itself it is enough.

9. When a dispute has arisen concerning doctrine, and all use the same scriptures in support of their contention, what help does a good life afford? of what advantage are so many labours, if after so many toils, one falls into heresy through ignorance, and is cut off from the Church, a fate which, to my knowledge, has befallen many? What does an austere life avail him? Nothing. Just as soundness in faith is of no avail, if morals be corrupt. For these reasons it behoves him whose office is to teach to be most of all skilled in argument. For though he himself stands secure and unharmed by the gainsayers, yet when the multitude of the simple faithful, who are subject to him, see their head overcome, and unable to reply to his adversaries, they lay the blame of the defeat, not on his incapacity, but on the doctrine, as though it were unsound; and by the ignorance of one, the whole people are brought to utter ruin. And though they do not all go over to the enemy, they are driven to doubt those doctrines which they held with confidence, and they can now no longer hold with the same firmness those tenets which they before held with unshaken faith. And in consequence of the defeat of their teacher, such a tempest assails their minds that the evil ends in shipwreck. But what destruction, what a fire is heaped on his head on account of each of those who perish, I need not tell you, for you are well aware of it. Was it then arrogance, was it vainglory in me, to be unwilling to be the cause of the ruin of so many, and to draw upon myself a chastisement greater than I already deserved? Who can say so? No

man who does not wish to make groundless accusations, and to philosophize on the calamities of others.

Etheria

Early 5th Century

A Christian noblewoman journeyed through Egypt, Palestine, and Asia Minor in the late 4th or early 5th century and kept a diary of what she saw. A mutilated 11th century manuscript of the text was discovered in 1884 in Arezzo, Italy. For nearly a century scholars have been grappling with the challenge of identifying the author, the date of composition, and the personalities alluded to in the narrative. There is still considerable disagreement on most of these points. She was probably a nun from Gaul or Spain.

Whoever she was, the author wrote a rather slipshod Latin but otherwise had a fairly good education and was familiar with the Scriptures. She was quite intelligent, exercised great powers of observation, and had a keen sense of appreciation of what she saw and heard. She was well received along the way and was well enough endowed to be able to prolong her journey for a couple of years.

The work begins with the pilgrims traveling in the Sinai peninsula, then returning to Jerusalem by way of Gessen (chapters 1-9). Visits are then made to Mount Nebo (chapters 10-12) and Idumea (chapters 13-16), then the group travels to Mesopotamia and Constantinople via Tarsus, Seleucia, and Chalcedon (chapters 17-23).

The second part of the work (chapters 24-49) is concerned with Jerusalem and its liturgy, and is of the greatest interest and importance for the history of the liturgy. It is the earliest account in existence that describes with any detail a regular Office of the early Church, with vigils held before dawn, prayers at the third, sixth, and ninth hours, vespers, and two principal services on Sunday, morning and evening. She gives the rules for fasting, describes the catechetical instructions, and the way the Scriptures were taught. Her narrative tallies in most respects with what is found in St. Cyril of Jerusalem's Catechetical Lectures *which were delivered several years earlier, and presumably were still the model being followed.*

All in all, this is an intriguing glimpse of a slice of Church life at a time when the liturgy had developed to a large degree in the direction that was going to characterize it for the coming centuries. Etheria (Egeria, Aetheria, Eucheria) may be a shadowy figure as far as her personal identity is concerned, but she performed a valuable service in recording for posterity the celebration of a vibrant liturgy in the Church of her day.

THE PILGRIMAGES

I

DAILY OFFICES

1. *Matins*

Now that your affection may know what is the order of service (*operatio*) day by day in the holy places, I must inform you, for I know that you would willingly have this knowledge. Every day before cockcrow all the doors of the Anastasis are opened, and all the monks and virgins, as they call them here, go thither, and not they alone, but lay people also, both men and women, who desire to begin their vigil early. And from that hour to daybreak hymns are said and psalms are sung responsively (*responduntur*), and antiphons in like manner; and prayer is made after each of the hymns. For priests, deacons, and monks in twos or threes take it in turn every day to say prayers after each of the hymns or antiphons. But when day breaks they begin to say the Matin hymns. Thereupon the bishop arrives with the clergy, and immediately enters into the cave, and from within the rails (*cancelli*) he first says a prayer for all, mentioning the names of those whom he wishes to commemorate; he then blesses the catechumens, afterwards he says a prayer and blesses the faithful. And when the bishop comes out from within the rails, every one approaches his hand, and he blesses them one by one as he goes out, and the dismissal takes place, by daylight.

2. *Sext and None*

In like manner at the sixth hour all go again to the Anastasis, and psalms and antiphons are said, while the bishop is being summoned; then he comes as before, not taking his seat, but he enters at once within the rails in the Anastasis, that is in the cave, just as in the early morning, and as then, he again first says a prayer, then he blesses the faithful, and as he comes out from [within] the rails every one approaches his hand. And the same is done at the ninth hour as at the sixth.

3. *Vespers*

Now at the tenth hour, which they call here *licinicon*, or as we say *lucernare*, all the people assemble at the Anastasis in the same manner, and all the candles and tapers are lit, making a very great light. Now the light is not introduced from without, but it is brought forth from within the cave, that is from within the rails, where a lamp is always burning day and night, and the vesper psalms and antiphons are said, lasting for a considerable time. Then the bishop is summoned, and he comes and takes a raised seat, and likewise the priests sit in their proper places, and hymns and antiphons are said. And when all these have been recited according to custom, the bishop rises and stands before the rails, that is, before the cave, and one of the deacons makes the customary commemoration of individuals one by one. And as the deacon pronounces each name the many little boys who are always standing by, answer with countless voices: *Kyrie eleyson*, or as we say *Miserere Domine*. And when the deacon has finished all that he has to say, first the bishop says a prayer and prays for all, then they all pray, both the faithful and catechumens together. Again the deacon raises his voice, bidding each catechumen to bow his head where he stands, and the bishop stands and says the blessing over the catechumens. Again prayer is made, and again the deacon raises his voice and bids the faithful, each where he stands, to bow the head, and the bishop likewise blesses the faithful. Thus the dismissal takes place at the Anastasis, and one by one all draw near to the bishop's hand. Afterwards the bishop is conducted from the Anastasis to the Cross [with] hymns, all the people accompanying him, and when he arrives he first says a prayer, then he blesses the catechumens, then another prayer is said and he blesses the faithful. Thereupon both the bishop and the whole multitude further proceed behind the Cross, where all that was done before the Cross is repeated, and they approach the hand of the bishop behind the Cross as they did at the Anastasis and before the Cross. Moreover, there are hanging everywhere a vast number of great glass chandeliers, and there are also a vast number of *cereofala*, before the Anastasis, before the Cross and behind the Cross, for the whole does not end until darkness has set in. This is the order of daily services (*operatio*) at the Cross and at the Anastasis throughout the six days.

II

SUNDAY OFFICES

I. *Vigil*

But on the seventh day, that is on the Lord's Day, the whole multitude assembles before cockcrow, in as great numbers as the place can hold, as at Easter, in the basilica which is near the Anastasis, but outside the doors, where lights are hanging for the purpose. And for fear that they should not be there at cockcrow they come beforehand and sit down there. Hymns as well as antiphons are said, and prayers are made between the several hymns and antiphons, for at the vigils there are always both priests and deacons ready there for the assembling of the multitude, the custom being that the holy places are not opened before cockcrow. Now as soon as the first cock has crowed, the bishop arrives and enters the cave at the Anastasis; all the doors are opened and the whole multitude enters the Anastasis, where countless lights are already burning. And when the people have entered, one of the priests says a psalm to which all respond, and afterwards prayer is made; then one of the deacons says a psalm and prayer is again made, a third psalm is said by one of the clergy, prayer is made for the third time and there is a commemoration of all. After these three psalms and three prayers are ended, lo! censers are brought into the cave of the Anastasis so that the whole basilica of the Anastasis is filled with odours. And then the bishop, standing within the rails, takes the book of the Gospel, and proceeding to the door, himself reads the (narrative of the) Resurrection of the Lord. And when the reading is begun, there is so great a moaning and groaning among all, with so many tears, that the hardest of heart might be moved to tears for that the Lord had borne such things for us. After the reading of the Gospel the bishop goes out, and is accompanied to the Cross by all the people with hymns, there again a psalm is said and prayer is made, after which he blesses the faithful and the dismissal takes place, and as he comes out all approach to his hand. And forthwith the bishop betakes himself to his house, and from that hour all the monks return to the Anastasis, where psalms and antiphons, with prayer after each psalm or antiphon, are said until daylight; the priests and deacons also keep watch in turn daily at the Anastasis with the people, but of the lay people, whether men or women, those who are so minded, remain in the place until daybreak, and those who are not, return to their houses and betake themselves to sleep.

2. *Morning Services*

Now at daybreak because it is the Lord's Day every one proceeds to the greater church, built by Constantine, which is situated in Golgotha behind the Cross, where all things are done which are customary everywhere on the Lord's Day. But the custom here is that of all the priests who take their seats, as many as are willing, preach, and after them all the bishop preaches, and these sermons are always on the Lord's Day, in order that the people may always be instructed in the Scriptures and in the love of God. The delivery of these sermons greatly delays the dismissal from the church, so that the dismissal does [not] take place before the fourth or perhaps the fifth hour. But when the dismissal from the church is made in the manner that is customary everywhere, the monks accompany the bishop with hymns from the church to the Anastasis, and as he approaches with hymns all the doors of the basilica of the Anastasis are opened, and the people, that is the faithful enter, but not the catechumens. And after the people the bishop enters, and goes at once within the rails of the cave of the martyrium. Thanks are first given to God, then prayer is made for all, after which the deacon bids all bow their heads, where they stand, and the bishop standing within the inner rails blesses them and goes out, each one drawing near to his hand as he makes his exit. Thus the dismissal is delayed until nearly the fifth or sixth hour. And in like manner it is done at *lucernare*, according to daily custom.

This then is the custom observed every day throughout the whole year except on solemn days, to the keeping of which we will refer later on. But among all things it is a special feature that they arrange that suitable psalms and antiphons are said on every occasion, both those said by night, or in the morning, as well as those throughout the day, at the sixth hour, the ninth hour, or at *lucernare*, all being so appropriate and so reasonable as to bear on the matter in hand. And they proceed to the greater church, which was built by Constantine, and which is situated in Golgotha, that is, behind the Cross, on every Lord's Day throughout the year except on the one Sunday of Pentecost, when they proceed to Sion, as you will find mentioned below; but even then they go to Sion before the third hour, the dismissal having been first made in the greater church.

* * * * * * * *

[*A leaf is wanting.*]

III

FESTIVALS AT EPIPHANY

I. *Night Station at Bethlehem.*

* * * * * * * *

Blessed is he that cometh in the Name of the Lord, and the rest which follows. And since, for the sake of the monks who go on foot, it is necessary to walk slowly, the arrival in Jerusalem thus takes place at the hour when one man begins to be able to recognize another, that is, close upon but a little before daybreak. And on arriving there, the bishop and all with him immediately enter the Anastasis, where an exceedingly great number of lights are already burning. There a psalm is said, prayer is made, first the catechumens and then the faithful are blessed by the bishop; then the bishop retires, and every one returns to his lodging to take rest, but the monks remain there until daybreak and recite hymns.

2. *Morning Services at Jerusalem*

But after the people have taken rest, at the beginning of the second hour they all assemble in the greater church, which is in Golgotha.

Now it would be superfluous to describe the adornment either of the church, or of the Anastasis, or of the Cross, or in Bethlehem on that day; you see there nothing but gold and gems and silk. For if you look at the veils, they are made wholly of silk striped with gold, and if you look at the curtains, they too are made wholly of silk striped with gold. The church vessels too, of every kind, gold and jeweled, are brought out on that day, and indeed, who could either reckon or describe the number and weight of the *cereofala*, or of the *cicindelae*, or of the *lucernae*, or of the various vessels? And what shall I say of the decoration of the fabric itself, which Constantine, at his mother's instigation, decorated with gold, mosaic, and costly marbles, as far as the resources of his kingdom allowed him, that is, the greater church as well as the Anastasis, at the Cross, and the other holy places in Jerusalem? But to return to the matter in hand: the dismissal takes place on the first day in the greater church, which is in Golgotha, and when they preach or read the several lessons, or recite hymns, all are appropriate to the day. And afterwards when the dismissal from the church has been made, they repair to the Anastasis with hymns, according to custom, so that the dismissal takes place about the sixth hour. And on this day *lucernare* also takes place according to the daily use.

3. *Octave of the Festival*

On the second day also they proceed in like manner to the church in Golgotha, and also on the third day; thus the feast is celebrated with all this joyfulness for three days up to the sixth hour in the church built by Constantine. On the fourth day it is celebrated in like manner with similar festal array in Eleona, the very beautiful church which stands on the Mount of Olives; on the fifth day in the Lazarium, which is distant about one thousand five hundred paces from Jerusalem; on the sixth day in Sion, on the seventh day in the Anastasis, and on the eighth day at the Cross. Thus, then, is the feast celebrated with all this joyfulness and festal array throughout the eight days in all the holy places which I have mentioned above. And in Bethlehem also throughout the entire eight days the feast is celebrated with similar festal array and joyfulness daily by the priests and by all the clergy there, and by the monks who are appointed in that place. For from the hour when all return by night to Jerusalem with the bishop, the monks of that place keep vigil in the church in Bethlehem, reciting hymns and antiphons, but it is necessary that the bishop should always keep these days in Jerusalem. And immense crowds, not of monks only, but also of the laity, both men and women, flock together to Jerusalem from every quarter for the solemn and joyous observance of that day.

4. *The Presentation. Mass*

The fortieth day after the Epiphany is undoubtedly celebrated here with the very highest honour, for on that day there is a procession, in which all take part, in the Anastasis, and all things are done in their order with the greatest joy, just as at Easter. All the priests, and after them the bishop, preach, always taking for their subject that part of the Gospel where Joseph and Mary brought the Lord into the Temple on the fortieth day, and Symeon and Anna the prophetess, the daughter of Phanuel, saw Him,—treating of the words which they spake when they saw the Lord, and of that offering which His parents made. And when everything that is customary has been done in order, the sacrament is celebrated, and the dismissal takes place.

IV

LENT

And when the Paschal days come they are observed thus: Just as with us forty days are kept before Easter, so here eight weeks are kept before Easter. And eight weeks are kept because there is no fasting on the Lord's Days, nor on the Sabbaths, except on the one Sabbath on which the Vigil of Easter falls, in which case the fast is obligatory. With the exception then of that one day, there is never fasting on any Sabbath here throughout the year. Thus, deducting the eight Lord's Days and the seven Sabbaths (for on the one Sabbath, as I said above, the fast is obligatory) from the eight weeks, there remain forty-one fast days, which they call here *Eortae*, that is *Quadragesimae*.

I. *Services on Sundays*

Now the several days of the several weeks are kept thus:

On the Lord's Day after the first cockcrow the bishop reads in the Anastasis the account of the Lord's Resurrection from the Gospel, as on all Lord's Days throughout the whole year, and everything is done at the Anastasis and at the Cross as on all Lord's Days throughout the year, up to daybreak. Afterwards, in the morning, they proceed to the greater church, called the martyrium, which is in Golgotha behind the Cross, and all things that are customary on the Lord's Days are done there. In like manner also when the dismissal from the church has been made, they go with hymns to the Anastasis, as they always do on the Lord's Days, and while these things are being done the fifth hour is reached. *Lucernare*, however, takes place at its own hour, as usual, at the Anastasis and at the Cross, and in the various holy places; on the Lord's Day the ninth hour is kept.

2. *Weekday Services*

On the second weekday they go at the first cockcrow to the Anastasis, as they do throughout the year, and everything that is usual is done until morning. Then at the third hour they go to the Anastasis, and the things are done that are customary throughout the year at the sixth hour, for this going at the third hour in Quadragesima is additional. At the sixth and ninth hours also, and at *lucernare*, everything is done that is customary throughout the whole year at the holy places. And on the third weekday all things are done as on the second weekday.

3. *Wednesday and Friday*

Again, on the fourth weekday they go by night to the Anastasis, and all the usual things are done until morning, and also at the third and sixth hours. But at the ninth hour they go to Sion, as is customary at that hour on the fourth and sixth weekdays throughout the year, for the reason that the fast is always kept here on the fourth and sixth weekdays even by the catechumens, except a martyrs' day should occur. For if a martyrs' day should chance to occur on the fourth or on the sixth weekday in Quadragesima, they do not go to Sion at the ninth hour. But on the days of Quadragesima, as I said above, they proceed to Sion on the fourth weekday at the ninth hour, according to the custom of the whole year, and all things that are customary at the ninth hour are done, except the oblation, for, in order that the people may always be instructed in the law, both the bishop and the priest preach diligently. But when the dismissal has been made, the people escort the bishop with hymns thence to the Anastasis, so that it is already the hour of *lucernare* when he enters the Anastasis; then hymns and antiphons are said, prayers are made, and the service (*missa*) of *lucernare* takes place in the Anastasis and at the Cross. And the service of *lucernare* is always later on those days in Quadragesima than on other days throughout the year. On the fifth weekday everything is done as on the second and third weekday. On the sixth weekday everything is done as on the fourth, including the going to Sion at the ninth hour, and the escorting of the bishop thence to the Anastasis with hymns.

4. *Saturday*

But on the sixth weekday the vigils are observed in the Anastasis from the hour of their arrival from Sion with hymns, until morning, that is, from the hour of *lucernare*, when they entered, to the morning of the next day, that is, the Sabbath. And the oblation is made in the Anastasis the earlier, that the dismissal may take place before sunrise. Throughout the whole night psalms are said responsively in turn with antiphons and with various lections, the whole lasting until morning, and the dismissal, which takes place on the Sabbath at the Anastasis, is before sunrise, that is, the oblation, so that the dismissal may take place in the Anastasis at the hour when the sun begins to rise. Thus, then, is each week of Quadragesima kept, the dismissal taking place earlier on the Sabbath, *i.e.* before sunrise, as I said, in order that the *hebdomadarii*, as they are called here, may finish their fast earlier. For the custom of the fast in Quadragesima is that the dismissal on the Lord's Day is at the fifth hour in order that they whom they call *hebdomadarii*, that is, they who keep the weeks' fast, may take food. And when these have taken breakfast on the Lord's Day, they do not eat until the Sabbath morning after they have communicated in the Anastasis. It is for their sake, then, that they may finish their fast the sooner, that the dismissal on the Sabbath at the Anastasis is before sunrise. For their sake the dismissal is in the morning, as I said; not that they alone communicate, but all who are so minded communicate on that day in the Anastasis.

5. *The Fast*

This is the custom of the fast in Quadragesima: some, when they have eaten after the dismissal on the Lord's Day, that is, about the fifth or sixth hour, do not eat throughout the whole week until after the dismissal at the Anastasis on the Sabbath; these are they who keep the weeks' fast.

Nor, after having eaten in the morning, do they eat in the evening of the Sabbath, but they take a meal on the next day, that is, on the Lord's Day, after the dismissal from the church at the fifth hour or later, and then they do not breakfast until the Sabbath comes round, as I have said above. For the custom here is that all who are *apotactitae*, as they call them here, whether men or women, eat only once a day on the day when they do eat, not only in Quadragesima, but throughout the whole year. But if any of the *apotactitae* cannot keep the entire week of fasting as described above, they take supper in the middle (of the week), on the fifth day, all through Quadragesima. And if any one cannot do even this, take a meal every evening. For no one exacts from any how much he should do, but each does what he can, nor is he praised who has done much, nor is he blamed who has done less; that is the custom here. For their food during the days of Quadragesima is as follows:—they taste neither bread which cannot be weighed, nor oil, nor anything that grows on trees, but only water and a little gruel made of flour. Quadragesima is kept thus, as we have said. And at the end of the weeks' fast the vigil is kept in the Anastasis from the hour of *lucernare* on the sixth weekday, when the people come with psalms from Sion, to the morning of the Sabbath, when the oblation is made in the Anastasis. And the second, third, fourth, fifth and sixth weeks in Quadragesima are kept as the first.

V

HOLY WEEK AND THE FESTIVALS AT EASTER

I. *Saturday before Palm Sunday.—Station at Bethany*

Now when the seventh week has come, that is, when two weeks, including the seventh, are left before Easter, everything is done on each day as in the weeks that are past, except that the vigils of the sixth weekday, which were kept in the Anastasis during the first six weeks, are, in the seventh week, kept in Sion, and with the same customs that obtained during the six weeks in the Anastasis. For throughout the whole vigil psalms and antiphons are said appropriate both to the place and to the day.

And when the morning of the Sabbath begins to dawn, the bishop offers the oblation. And at the dismissal the archdeacon lifts his voice and says: "Let us all be ready to-day at the seventh hour in the Lazarium." And so, as the seventh hour approaches, all go to the Lazarium, that is, Bethany, situated at about the second milestone from the city. And as they go from Jerusalem to the Lazarium, there is about five hundred paces from the latter place, a church in the street on that spot where Mary the sister of Lazarus met with the Lord. Here, when the bishop arrives, all the monks meet him, and the people enter the church, and one hymn and one antiphon are said, and that passage is read in the Gospel where the sister of Lazarus meets the Lord. Then, after prayer has been made, and when all have been blessed, they go thence with hymns to the Lazarium. And on arriving at the Lazarium, so great a multitude assembles that not only the place itself, but also the fields around, are full of people. Hymns and antiphons suitable to the day and to the place are said, and likewise all the lessons are read. Then, before the dismissal, notice is given of Easter, that is, the priest ascends to a higher place and reads the passage that is written in the Gospel: *When Jesus six days before the Passover had come to Bethany*, and the rest. So, that passage having been read and notice given of Easter, the dismissal is made. This is done on that day because, as it is written in the Gospel, these events took place in Bethany six days before the Passover; there being six days from the Sabbath to the fifth weekday on which, after supper, the Lord was taken by night. Then all return to the city direct to the Anastasis, and *lucernare* takes place according to custom.

2. *Palm Sunday—(a) Services in the Churches*

On the next day, that is, the Lord's Day, which begins the Paschal week, and which they call here the Great Week, when all the customary services from cockcrow until morning have taken place in the Anastasis and at the Cross, they proceed on the morning of the Lord's Day according to custom to the greater church, which is called the martyrium. It is called the martyrium because it is in Golgotha behind the Cross, where the Lord suffered. When all that is customary has been observed in the great church, and before the dismissal is made, the archdeacon lifts his voice and says first: "Throughout the whole week, beginning from to-morrow, let us all assemble in the martyrium, that is, in the great church, at the ninth hour." Then he lifts his voice again, saying: "Let us all be ready to-day in Eleona at the seventh hour." So when the dismissal has been made in the great church, that is, the martyrium, the bishop is escorted with hymns to the Anastasis, and after all things that are customary on the Lord's Day have been done there, after the dismissal from the martyrium, every one hastens home to eat, that all may be ready at the beginning of the seventh hour in the church in Eleona, on the Mount of Olives, where is the cave in which the Lord was wont to teach.

(b) Procession with Palms on the Mount of Olives

Accordingly at the seventh hour all the people go up to the Mount of Olives, that is, to Eleona, and the bishop with them, to the church, where hymns and antiphons suitable to the day and to the place are said, and lessons in like manner. And when the ninth hour approaches they go up with hymns to the Imbomon, that is, to the place whence the Lord ascended into heaven, and there they sit down, for all the people are always bidden to sit when the bishop is present; the deacons alone always stand. Hymns and antiphons suitable to the day and to the place are said, interspersed with lections and prayers. And as the eleventh hour approaches, the passage from the Gospel is read, where the children, carrying branches and palms, met the Lord, saying; *Blessed is He that cometh in the name of the Lord*, and the bishop immediately rises, and all the people with him, and they all go on foot from the top of the Mount of Olives, all the people going before him with hymns and antiphons, answering one to another: *Blessed is He that cometh in the Name of the Lord.* And all the children in the neighbourhood, even those who are too young to walk, are carried by their parents on their shoulders, all of them bearing branches, some of palms and some of olives, and thus the bishop is escorted in the same manner as the Lord was of old. For all, even those of rank, both matrons and men, accompany the bishop all the way on foot in this manner, making these responses, from the top of the mount to the city, and thence through the whole city to the Anastasis, going very slowly lest the people should be wearied; and thus they arrive at the Anastasis at a late hour. And on arriving, although it is late, *lucernare* takes place, with prayer at the Cross; after which the people are dismissed.

3. *Monday in Holy Week*

On the next day, the second weekday, everything that is customary is done from the first cockcrow until morning in the Anastasis; also at the third and sixth hours everything is done that is customary throughout the whole of Quadragesima. But at the ninth hour all assemble in the great church, that is the martyrium, where hymns and antiphons are said continuously until the first hour of the night and lessons suitable to the day and the place are read, interspersed always with prayers. *Lucernare* takes place when its hour approaches, that is, so that it is already night when the dismissal at the martyrium is made. When the dismissal has been made, the bishop is escorted thence with hymns to the Anastasis, where, when he has entered, one hymn is said, followed by a prayer; the catechumens and then the faithful are blessed, and the dismissal is made.

4. *Tuesday in Holy Week*

On the third weekday everything is done as on the second, with this one thing added—that late at night, after the dismissal of the martyrium, and after the going to the Anastasis and after the dismissal there, all proceed at that hour by night to the church, which is on the mount Eleona. And when they have arrived at that church, the bishop enters the cave where the Lord was wont to teach His disciples, and after receiving the book of the Gospel, he stands and himself reads the words of the Lord which are written in the Gospel according to Matthew, where He says: *Take heed that no man deceive you.* And the bishop reads through the whole of that discourse, and when he has read it, prayer is made, the catechumens and the faithful are blessed, the dismissal is made, and every one returns from the mount to his house, it being already very late at night.

5. *Wednesday in Holy Week*

On the fourth weekday everything is done as on the second and third weekdays throughout the whole day from the first cockcrow onwards, but after the dismissal has taken place at the martyrium by night, and the bishop has been escorted with hymns to the Anastasis, he at once enters the cave which is in the Anastasis, and stands within the rails; but the priest stands before the rails and receives the Gospel, and reads the passage where Judas Iscariot went to the Jews and stated what they should give him that he should betray the Lord. And when the passage has been read, there is such a moaning and groaning of all the people that no one can help being moved to tears at that hour. Afterwards prayer follows, then the blessing, first of the catechumens, and then of the faithful, and the dismissal is made.

6. *Maundy Thursday—(a) Mass celebrated twice*

On the fifth weekday everything that is customary is done from the first cockcrow until morning at the Anastasis, and also at the third and at the sixth hours. But at the eighth hour all the people gather together at the martyrium according to custom, only earlier than on other days, because the dismissal must be made sooner. Then, when the people are gathered together, all that should be done is done, and the oblation is made on that day at the martyrium, the dismissal taking place about the tenth hour. But before the dismissal is made there, the archdeacon raises his voice and says: "Let us all assemble at the first hour of the night in the church which is in Eleona, for great toil awaits us to-day, in this very night." Then, after the dismissal at the martyrium, they arrive behind the Cross, where only one hymn is said and prayer is made, and the bishop offers the oblation there, and all communicate. Nor is the oblation ever offered behind the Cross on any day throughout the year, except on this one day. And after the dismissal there they go to the Anastasis, where prayer is made, the catechumens and the faithful are blessed according to custom, and the dismissal is made.

(b) Night Station on the Mount of Olives

And so every one hastens back to his house to eat, because immediately after they have eaten, all go to Eleona to the church wherein is the cave where the Lord was with His Apostles on this very day. There then, until about the fifth hour of the night, hymns and antiphons suitable to the day and to the place are said, lessons, too, are read in like manner, with prayers interspersed, and the passages from the Gospel are read where the Lord addressed His disciples on that same day as He sat in the same cave which is in that church. And they go thence at about the sixth hour of the night with hymns up to the Imbomon, the place whence the Lord ascended into heaven, where again lessons are read, hymns and antiphons suitable to the day are said, and all the prayers which are made by the bishop are also suitable both to the day and to the place.

(c) Stations at Gethsemane

And at the first cockcrow they come down from the Imbomon with hymns, and arrive at the place where the Lord prayed, as it is written in the Gospel: *and He was withdrawn (from them) about a stone's cast, and prayed*, and the rest. There is in that place a graceful church. The bishop and all the people enter, a prayer suitable to the place and to the day is said, with one suitable hymn, and the passage from the Gospel is read where He said to His disciples: *Watch, that ye enter not into temptation*; the whole passage is read through and prayer is made. And then all, even to the smallest child, go down with the Bishop, on foot, with hymns to Gethsemane; where, on account of the great number of people in the crowd, who are wearied owing to the vigils and weak through the daily fasts, and because they have so great a hill to descend, they come very slowly with hymns to Gethsemane. And over two hundred church candles are made ready to give light to all the people. On their arrival at Gethsemane, first a suitable prayer is made, then a hymn is said, then the passage of the Gospel is read where the Lord was taken. And when this passage has been read there is so great a moaning and groaning of all the people, together with weeping, that their lamentation may be heard perhaps as far as the city.

(d) Return to Jerusalem

From that hour they go with hymns to the city on foot, reaching the gate about the time when one man begins to be able to recognize another, and thence right on through the midst of the city; all, to a man, both great and small, rich and poor, all are ready there, for on that special day not a soul withdraws from the vigils until morning. Thus the bishop is escorted from Gethsemane to the gate, and thence through the whole of the city to the Cross.

7. *Good Friday—(a) Service at Daybreak*

And when they arrive before the Cross the daylight is already growing bright. There the passage from the Gospel is read where the Lord is brought before Pilate, with everything that is written concerning that which Pilate spake to the Lord or to the Jews; the whole is read. And afterwards the bishop addresses the people, comforting them for that they have toiled all night and are about to toil during that same day, (bidding) them not be weary, but to have hope in God, Who will for that toil give them a greater reward. And encouraging them as he is able, he addresses them thus: "Go now, each one of you, to your houses, and sit down awhile, and all of you be ready here just before the second hour of the day, that from that hour to the sixth you may be able to behold the holy wood of the Cross, each one of us believing that it will be profitable to his salvation; then from the sixth hour we must all assemble again in this place, that is, before the Cross, that we may apply ourselves to lections and to prayers until night."

(b) The Column of the Flagellation

After this, when the dismissal at the Cross has been made, that is, before the sun rises, they all go at once with fervour to Sion, to pray at the column at which the Lord was scourged. And returning thence they sit for awhile in their houses, and presently all are ready.

(c) Veneration of the Cross

Then a chair is placed for the bishop in Golgotha behind the Cross, which is now standing; the bishop duly takes his seat in the chair, and a table covered with a linen cloth is placed before him; the deacons stand round the table, and a silver-gilt casket is brought in which is the holy wood of the Cross. The casket is opened and (the wood) is taken out, and both the wood of the Cross and the title are placed upon the table. Now, when it has been put upon the table, the bishop, as he sits, holds the extremities of the sacred wood firmly in his hands, while the deacons who stand around guard it. It is guarded thus because the custom is that the people, both faithful and catechumens, come one by one and, bowing down at the table, kiss the sacred wood and pass through. And because, I know not when, some one is said to have bitten off and stolen a portion of the sacred wood, it is thus guarded by the deacons who stand around, lest any one approaching should venture to do so again. And as all the people pass by one by one, all bowing themselves, they touch the Cross and the title, first with their foreheads and then with their eyes; then they kiss the Cross and pass through, but none lays his hand upon it to touch it. When they have kissed the Cross and have passed through, a deacon stands holding the ring of Solomon and the horn from which the kings were anointed; they kiss the horn also and gaze at the ring . . . all the people are passing through up to the sixth hour, entering by one door and going out by another; for this is done in the same place where, on the preceding day, that is, on the fifth weekday, the oblation was offered.

(d) Station before the Cross. The Three Hours

And when the sixth hour has come, they go before the Cross, whether it be in rain or in heat, the place being open to the air, as it were, a court of great size and of some beauty between the Cross and the Anastasis; here all the people assemble in such great numbers that there is no thoroughfare. The chair is placed for the bishop before the Cross, and from the sixth to the ninth hour nothing else is done, but the reading of lessons, which are read thus: first from the psalms wherever the Passion is spoken of, then from the Apostle, either from the epistles of the Apostles or from their Acts, wherever they have spoken of the Lord's Passion; then the passages from the Gospels, where He suffered, are read. Then the readings from the prophets where they foretold that the Lord should suffer, then from the Gospels where He mentions His Passion. Thus from the sixth to the ninth hours the lessons are so read and the hymns said, that it may be shown to all the people that whatsoever the prophets foretold of the Lord's Passion is proved from the Gospels and from the writings of the Apostles to have been fulfilled. And so through all those three hours the people are taught that nothing was done which had not been foretold, and that nothing was foretold which was not wholly fulfilled. Prayers also suitable to the day are interspersed throughout. The emotion shown and the mourning by all the people at every lesson and prayer is wonderful; for there is none, either great or small, who, on that day during those three hours, does not lament more than can be conceived, that the Lord had suffered those things for us.

Afterwards, at the beginning of the ninth hour, there is read that passage from the Gospel according to John where He gave up the ghost. This read, prayer and the dismissal follow.

(e) Evening Offices

And when the dismissal before the Cross has been made, all things are done in the greater church, at the martyrium, which are customary during this week from the ninth hour—when the assembly takes place in the martyrium—until late. And after the dismissal at the martyrium, they go to the Anastasis, where, when they arrive, the passage from the Gospel is read where Joseph begged the Body of the Lord from Pilate and laid it in a new sepulchre. And this reading ended, a prayer is said, the catechumens are blessed, and the dismissal is made.

But on that day no announcement is made of a vigil at the Anastasis, because it is known that the people are tired; nevertheless, it is the custom to watch there. So all of the people who are willing, or rather, who are able, keep watch, and they who are unable do not watch there until the morning. Those of the clergy, however, who are strong or young keep vigil there, and hymns and antiphons are said throughout the whole night until morning; a very great crowd also keep night-long watch, some from the late hour and some from midnight, as they are able.

8. *Vigil of Easter*

Now, on the next day, the Sabbath, everything that is customary is done at the third hour and also at the sixth; the service at the ninth hour, however, is not held on the Sabbath, but the Paschal vigils are prepared in the great church, the martyrium. The Paschal vigils are kept as with us, with this one addition, that the children when they have been baptised and clothed, and when they issue from the font, are led with the bishop first to the Anastasis; the bishop enters the rails of the Anastasis, and one hymn is said, then the bishop says a prayer for them, and then he goes with them to the greater church, where, according to custom, all the people are keeping watch. Everything is done there that is customary with us also, and after the oblation has been made, the dismissal takes place. After the dismissal of the vigils has been made in the greater church, they go at once with hymns to the Anastasis, where the passage from the Gospel about the Resurrection is read. Prayer is made, and the bishop again makes the oblation. But everything is done quickly on account of the people, that they should not be delayed any longer, and so the people are dismissed. The dismissal of the vigils takes place on that day at the same hour as with us.

9. *Services in the Easter Octave*

Moreover, the Paschal days are kept up to a late hour as with us, and the dismissals take place in their order throughout the eight Paschal days, as is the custom everywhere at Easter throughout the Octave. But the adornment (of the churches) and order (of the services) here are the same throughout the Octave of Easter as they are during Epiphany, in the greater church, in the Anastasis, at the Cross, in Eleona, in Bethlehem, as well as in the Lazarium, in fact, everywhere, because these are the Paschal days. On the first Lord's Day they proceed to the great church, that is, the martyrium, as well as on the second and third weekdays, but always so that after the dismissal has been made at the martyrium, they go to the Anastasis with hymns. On the fourth weekday they proceed to Eleona, on the fifth to the Anastasis, on the sixth to Sion, on the Sabbath before the Cross, but on the Lord's Day, that is, on the Octave, (they proceed) to the great church again, that is, to the martyrium.

Moreover, on the eight Paschal days the bishop goes every day after breakfast up to Eleona with all the clergy, and with all the children who have been baptised, and with all who are *apotactitae*, both men and women, and likewise with all the people who are willing. Hymns are said and prayers are made, both in the church which is on Eleona, wherein is the cave where Jesus was wont to teach His disciples, and also in the Imbomon, that is, in the place whence the Lord ascended into heaven. And when the psalms have been said and prayer has been made, they come down thence with hymns to the Anastasis at the hour of *lucernare*. This is done throughout all the eight days.

10. *Vesper Station at Sion on Easter Sunday*

Now, on the Lord's Day at Easter, after the dismissal of *lucernare*, that is, at the Anastasis, all the people escort the bishop with hymns to Sion. And, on arriving, hymns suitable to the day and place are said, prayer is made, and the passage from the Gospel is read where the Lord, on the same day, and in the same place where the church now stands in Sion, came in to His disciples when the doors were shut. That is, when one of His disciples, Thomas, was absent, and when he returned and the other Apostles told him that they had seen the Lord, he said: "*Except I shall see, I will not believe.*" When this has been read, prayer is again made, the catechumens and the faithful are blessed, and every one returns to his house late, about the second hour of the night.

11. *Sunday after Easter*

Again, on the Octave of Easter, that is, on the Lord's Day, all the people go up to Eleona with the bishop immediately after the sixth hour. First they sit for awhile in the church which is there, and hymns and antiphons suitable to the day and to the place are said; prayers suitable to the day and to the place are likewise made. Then they go up to the Imbomon with hymns, and the same things are done there as in the former place. And when the time comes, all the people and all the *apotactitae* escort the bishop with hymns down to the Anastasis, arriving there at the usual hour for *lucernare*. So *lucernare* takes place at the Anastasis and at the Cross, and all the people to a man escort the bishop thence with hymns to Sion. And when they have arrived, hymns suitable to the day and to the place are said there also, and lastly that passage from the Gospel is read where, on the Octave of Easter, the Lord came in where the disciples were, and reproved Thomas because he had been unbelieving. The whole of that lesson is read, with prayer afterwards; both the catechumens and the faithful are blessed, and every one returns to his house as usual, just as on the Lord's Day of Easter, at the second hour of the night.

12. *Easter to Whitsuntide*

Now, from Easter to the fiftieth day, that is, to Pentecost, no one fasts here, not even those who are *apotactitae*. During these days, as throughout the whole year, the customary things are done at the Anastasis from the first cockcrow until morning, and at the sixth hour and at *lucernare* likewise. But on the Lord's Days the procession is always to the martyrium, that is, to the great church, according to custom, and they go thence with hymns to the Anastasis. On the fourth and sixth weekdays, as no one fasts during those days, the procession is to Sion, but in the morning; the dismissal is made in its due order.

13. *The Ascension–Festival at Bethlehem*

On the fortieth day after Easter, that is, on the fifth weekday–(for all go on the previous day, that is, on the fourth weekday, after the sixth hour to Bethlehem to celebrate the vigils, for the vigils are kept in Bethlehem, in the church wherein is the cave where the Lord was born)–On this fifth weekday, the fortieth day after Easter, the dismissal is celebrated in its due order, so that the priests and the bishop preach, treating of the things suitable to the day and the place, and afterwards every one returns to Jerusalem late.

VI

FESTIVALS OF WHITSUNTIDE

1. *Whitsunday–(a) Morning Station*

But on the fiftieth day, that is, the Lord's Day, when the people have a very great deal to go through, everything that is customary is done from the first cockcrow onwards; vigil is kept in the Anastasis, and the bishop reads the passage from the Gospel that is always read on the Lord's Day, namely, the account of the Lord's Resurrection, and afterwards everything customary is done in the Anastasis, just as throughout the whole year. But when morning is come, all the people proceed to the great church, that is, to the martyrium, and all things usual are done there; the priests preach and then the bishop, and all things that are prescribed are done, the oblation being made, as is customary on the Lord's Day, only the same dismissal in the martyrium is hastened, in order that it may be made before the third hour.

(b) Station at Sion

And when the dismissal has been made at the martyrium, all the people, to a man, escort the bishop with hymns to Sion, [so that] they are in Sion when the third hour is fully come. And on their arrival there the passage from the Acts of the Apostles is read where the Spirit came down so that all tongues [were heard and all men] understood the things that were being spoken, and the dismissal takes place afterwards in due course. For the priests read there from the Acts of the Apostles concerning the selfsame thing, because that is the place in Sion—there is another church there now—where once, after the Lord's Passion, the multitude was gathered together with the Apostles, and where this was done, as we have said above. Afterwards the dismissal takes place in due course, and the oblation is made there. Then, that the people may be dismissed, the archdeacon raises his voice, and says: "Let us all be ready to-day in Eleona, in the Imbomon, directly after the sixth hour."

(c) Station at the Mount of Olives

So all the people return, each to his house, to rest themselves, and immediately after breakfast they ascend the Mount of Olives, that is, to Eleona, each as he can, so that there is no Christian left in the city who does not go. When, therefore, they have gone up the Mount of Olives, that is, to Eleona, they first enter the Imbomon, that is, the place whence the Lord ascended into heaven, and the bishops and the priests take their seat there, and likewise all the people. Lessons are read there with hymns interspersed, antiphons too are said suitable to the day and the place, also the prayers which are interspersed have likewise similar references. The passage from the Gospel is also read where it speaks of the Lord's Ascension, also that from the Acts of the Apostles which tells of the Ascension of the Lord into Heaven after His Resurrection. And when this is over, the catechumens and then the faithful are blessed, and they come down thence, it being already the ninth hour, and go with hymns to that church which is in Eleona, wherein is the cave where the Lord was wont to sit and teach His Apostles. And as it is already past the tenth hour when they arrive, *lucernare* takes place there; prayer is made, and the catechumens and likewise the faithful are blessed.

(d) Night Procession

And then all the people to a man descend thence with the bishop, saying hymns and antiphons suitable to that day, and so come very slowly to the martyrium. It is already night when they reach the gate of the city, and about two hundred church candles are provided for the use of the people. And as it is a good distance from the gate to the great church, that is, the martyrium, they arrive about the second hour of the night, for they go the whole way very slowly lest the people should be weary from being afoot. And when the great gates are opened, which face towards the market-place, all the people enter the martyrium with hymns and with the bishop. And when they have entered the church, hymns are said, prayer is made, the catechumens and also the faithful are blesssed; after which they go again with hymns to the Anastasis, where on their arrival hymns and antiphons are said, prayer is made, the catechumens and also the faithful are blessed; this is likewise done at the Cross. Lastly, all the Christian people to a man escort the bishop with hymns to Sion, and when they are come there, suitable lessons are read, psalms and antiphons are said, prayer is made, the catechumens and the faithful are blessed, and the dismissal takes place. And after the dismissal all approach the bishop's hand, and then every one returns to his house about midnight.

Thus very great fatigue is endured on that day, for vigil is kept at the Anastasis from the first cockcrow, and there is no pause from that time onward throughout the whole day, but the whole celebration (of the Feast) lasts so long that it is midnight when every one returns home after the dismissal has taken place at Sion.

2. *Resumption of the Ordinary Services*

Now, from the day after the fiftieth day all fast as is customary throughout the whole year, each one as he is able, except on the Sabbath and on the Lord's Day, which are never kept as fasts in this place. On the ensuing days everything is done as during the whole year, that is, vigil is kept in the Anastasis from the first cockcrow. And if it be the Lord's Day, at the earliest cockcrow the bishop first reads in the Anastasis, as is customary, the passage from the Gospel concerning the Resurrection, which is always read on the Lord's Day, and then afterwards hymns and antiphons are said in the Anastasis until daylight. But if it be not the Lord's Day, only hymns and antiphons are said in like manner in the Anastasis from the first cockcrow until daylight. All the *apotactitae*, and of the people those who are able, attend; the clergy go by turns, daily. The clergy go there at first cockcrow, but the bishop always as it begins to dawn, that the morning dismissal may be made with all the clergy present except on the Lord's Day, when (the bishop) has to go at the first cockcrow, that he may read the Gospel in the Anastasis. Afterwards everything is done as usual in the Anastasis until the sixth hour, and at the ninth, as well as at *lucernare*, according to the custom of the whole year. But on the fourth and sixth weekdays, the ninth hour is kept in Sion as is customary.

VII

BAPTISM

1. *The Inscribing of the Competents*

Moreover, I must write how they are taught who are baptised at Easter. Now he who gives in his name, gives it in on the day before Quadragesima, and the priest writes down the names of all; this is before the eight weeks which I have said are kept here at Quadragesima. And when the priest has written down the names of all, after the next day of Quadragesima, that is, on the day when the eight weeks begin, the chair is set for the bishop in the midst of the great church, that is, at the martyrium, and the priests sit in chairs on either side of him, while all the clergy stand. Then one by one the competents are brought up, coming, if they are males (*viri*) with their fathers, and if females (*feminae*), with their mothers. Then the bishop asks the neighbours of every one who has entered concerning each individual, saying: "Does this person lead a good life, is he obedient to his parents, is he not given to wine, nor deceitful?" making also inquiry about the several vices which are more serious in man. And if he has proved him in the presence of witnesses to be blameless in all these matters concerning which he has made inquiry, he writes down his name with his own hand. But if he is accused in any matter, he orders him to go out, saying: "Let him amend, and when he has amended then let him come to the font (*lavacrum*)." And as he makes inquiry concerning the men, so also does he concerning the women. But if any be a stranger, he comes not so easily to Baptism, unless he has testimonials from those who know him.

2. *Preparation for Baptism—Catechisings*

This also I must write, reverend sisters, lest you should think that these things are done without good reason. The custom here is that they who come to Baptism through those forty days, which are kept as fast days, are first exorcised by the clergy early in the day, as soon as the morning dismissal has been made in the Anastasis. Immediately afterwards the chair is placed for the bishop at the martyrium in the great church, and all who are to be baptised sit around, near the bishop, both men and women, their fathers and mothers standing there also. Besides these, all the people who wish to hear come in and sit down—the faithful however only, for no catechumen enters there when the bishop teaches the others the Law. Beginning from Genesis he goes through all the Scriptures during those forty days, explaining them, first literally, and then unfolding them spiritually. They are also taught about the Resurrection, and likewise all things concerning the Faith during those days. And this is called the catechising.

3. *"Traditio" of the Creed*

Then when five weeks are completed from the time when their teaching began, (the Competents) are then taught the Creed. And as he explained the meaning of all the Scriptures, so does he explain the meaning of the Creed; each article first literally and then spiritually. By this means all the faithful in these parts follow the Scriptures when they are read in church, inasmuch as they are all taught during those forty days from the first to the third hour, for the catechising lasts for three hours. And God knows, reverend sisters, that the voices of the faithful who come in to hear the catechising are louder (in approval) of the things spoken and explained by the bishop than they are when he sits and preaches in church. Then, after the dismissal of the catechising is made, it being already the third hour, the bishop is at once escorted with hymns to the Anastasis. So the dismissal takes place at the third hour. Thus are they taught for three hours a day for seven weeks, but in the eighth week of Quadragesima, which is called the Great Week, there is no time for them to be taught, because the things that are [described] above must be carried out.

4. *"Redditio" [Recitation] of the Creed*

And when the seven weeks are past, [and] the Paschal week is left, which they call here the Great Week, then the bishop comes in the morning into the great church at the martyrium, and the chair is placed for him in the apse behind the altar, where they come one by one, a man with his father and a woman with her mother, and recite the Creed to the bishop. And when they have recited the Creed to the bishop, he addresses them all, and says: "During these seven weeks you have been taught all the law of the Scriptures, you have also heard concerning the Faith, and concerning the resurrection of the flesh, and the whole meaning of the Creed, as far as you were able, being yet catechumens. But the teachings of the deeper mystery, that is, of Baptism itself, you cannot hear, being as yet catechumens. But, lest you should think that anything is done without good reason, these, when you have been baptised in the Name of God, you shall hear in the Anastasis, during the eight Paschal days, after the dismissal from the church has been made. You, being as yet catechumens, cannot be told the more secret mysteries of God."

5. *Mystic Catechisings*

But when the days of Easter have come, during those eight days, that is, from Easter to the Octave, when the dismissal from the church has been made, they go with hymns to the Anastasis. Prayer is said anon, the faithful are blessed, and the bishop stands, leaning against the inner rails which are in the cave of the Anastasis, and explains all things that are done in Baptism. In that hour no catechumen approaches the Anastasis, but only the neophytes and the faithful, who wish to hear concerning the mysteries, enter there, and the doors are shut lest any catechumen should draw near. And while the bishop discusses and sets forth each point, the voices of those who applaud are so loud that they can be heard outside the church. And truly the mysteries are so unfolded that there is no one unmoved at the things that he hears to be so explained.

Now, forasmuch as in that province some of the people know both Greek and Syriac, while some know Greek alone and others only Syriac; and because the bishop, although he knows Syriac, yet always speaks Greek, and never Syriac, there is always a priest standing by who, when the bishop speaks Greek, interprets into Syriac, that all may understand what is being taught. And because all the lessons that are read in the church must be read in Greek, he always stands by and interprets them into Syriac, for the people's sake, that they may always be edified. Moreover, the Latins here, who understand neither Syriac nor Greek, in order that they be not disappointed, have (all things) explained to them, for there are other brothers and sisters knowing both Greek and Latin, who translate into Latin for them. But what is above all things very pleasant and admirable here, is that the hymns, the antiphons, and the lessons, as well as the prayers which the bishop says, always have suitable and fitting references, both to the day that is being celebrated and also to the place where the celebration is taking place.

St. Paschasius Radbertus

785-860

Paschasius was born in Soissons around 785 and entered the Benedictine abbey of Corbie sometime between 814 and 821. Although he was only a deacon, he was elected abbot around 843 but resigned sometime before 853 because of opposition to his plans for reform. He was well read in the Scriptures, in the Fathers, and in the pagan classics, and spent much time teaching, studying, and writing.

Paschasius is, however, principally remembered as the author of the first extant work devoted entirely to the Eucharist, part of which is given in the following selection. Written in 831 and revised in 844, the work came under severe criticism from Ratramnus, a colleague of Paschasius who found his presentation too crude and materialistic. But by the eleventh century numerous passages from this work were being circulated under the name of St. Augustine. This gave them an authority that they might not otherwise have enjoyed.

There is no escaping the fact that Paschasius represents a trend in ultra-realism that was destined to be intensified first by the eleventh century controversy with Berengar of Tours, then by the sixteenth century controversies with Martin Luther, Ulrich Zwingli, and John Calvin. The characteristics of that trend were that the Eucharist came to be more and more viewed as an object rather than an action, static rather than dynamic in meaning, and its sacramental nature was further obscured. The transformation of the bread and wine was soon regarded as so complete that they could no longer properly be spoken of as "signs."

Paschasius is significant as an exponent of changing times. He drew upon the Bible and the Fathers but lived in a different world from theirs. The problems of an overly monastic liturgy were not yet as acute as they would later become, but tendencies were discernible that would have unfortunate consequences. The chief reason for noting these is to appreciate why it was both necessary and desirable in our day to renew the Catholic liturgy by recovering lost dimensions and eliminating historical distortions.

Contemporary renewal has brought the emphasis back to the sign-nature of the liturgy. Instead of viewing symbol and reality as two radically different things, the appreciation today is in noting their intimate connection. "Real presence" must not be set over against "symbolic presence," as if they were diametrically opposed understandings. The very notion of sacrament in the best of Catholic tradition is that of a reality present in and through signs, not in spite of them. Insofar as Paschasius reflects a trend toward forgetting this fact, his work is less than satisfactory. But insofar as he demonstrates his true piety and concern to express the importance of the Eucharist and the union with God through Christ which is its goal, his approach is still worth pondering. Certain correctives were called for, but in time they were provided.

THE LORD'S BODY AND BLOOD

It is . . . clear that nothing is possible outside the will of God or contrary to it, but all things wholly yield to him. Therefore, let no man be moved from this body and blood since the Creator so willed it: "For all things whatsoever he willed he did in heaven and on earth," and because he willed, he may remain in the figure of bread and wine. Yet these must be believed to be fully, after the consecration, nothing but Christ's flesh and blood. As the Truth himself said to his disciples: "This is my flesh for the life of the world," and, to put it in more miraculous terms, nothing different, of course, from what was born of Mary, suffered on the cross, and rose again from the tomb. . . . If our words seem unbelievable to anyone, let him note all the miracles of the Old and New Testaments which, through firm faith, were accomplished by God contrary to natural order, and he will see clearer than day that for God nothing is impossible, since all things that God wills to be, and whatsoever he wills, actually take place. . . .

4. . . . For the will in no respect acts without power, nor is the power without wisdom, because God's will is power and wisdom. Therefore, whatever he wills comes to be as he wills, and in no respect is faulty. Because he wills all things in his wisdom, his very wisdom is his will, and for this reason he wills no evil, nothing impossible for himself. Thus, because he so willed that his flesh and blood be this mystery, never doubt it, if you believe God, but with true faith always remember that this is that true flesh which was offered for the life of the world. Whoever eats of it in worthy fashion will never see death through all eternity. For Christ left to his church in a mystery nothing greater than this sacrament and that of Baptism, as well as the Holy Scriptures in all of which the Holy Spirit, who is the pledge of the whole church, inwardly works the mysteries of our salvation unto immortality. But in them nothing miraculous is offered unbelievers, nothing better to believers, nothing more

miraculous and nothing richer in this life, not that they may appear visible to the sight of the eyes but that in faith and understanding they may smell sweetly in the divine mysteries and that in them eternity and participation in Christ may be granted to men in the unity of his body.

5. For this reason therefore this mystery is far different from all those miracles which have occurred in this life, because they all occurred so that this one may be believed, that Christ is truth, yet truth is God, and if God is truth, whatever Christ has promised in this mystery is in the same way truth. Therefore the true flesh and blood of Christ, which anyone worthily eats and drinks, have eternal life abiding in them, but in corporeal appearance and taste they are not on this account changed, as long as faith is exercised for righteousness. And because of faith's desert the reward of righteousness is achieved in it. For the other miracles of Christ confirm this one of his Passion, and so the elements are not outwardly changed in appearance on account of the miracle but inwardly, that faith may be proved in spirit. Most truly we confess that because "the just man lives from faith" he should have the righteousness of faith in the mystery, and through faith receive the life abiding in it, by which, the more securely mortal man has fed on immortality, the faster he speeds to the immortal, where he arrives, not on his feet, but through faith with good works.

6. In every way it is clear that as in paradise there was the tree of life from which the state of man might have continued forever, had he kept the commandments, and immortality, so in the church this mystery of salvation is provided; not that it is like that tree in nature, but an invisible power works inwardly through something visible. So in that visible sacrament of Communion, the divine virtue sustains us into immortality by its invisible power, as if from the fruit of the tree in paradise, both by the taste of wisdom and by virtue, and through it we are immortal in spirit providing we take it worthily, and at last we are carried for the better to immortality. For this then "the Word was made flesh and dwelt among us," and that, through God the Word made flesh, the flesh might progress to God the Word, the Word's flesh, of course, becomes food in this mystery. And the food of the faithful, while it is believed to be the flesh

for the life of the world and nothing else than the flesh of Christ's body from which Christ remains in us, and that we through it might be transformed into Him who was made nothing else than God's flesh deigning to dwell in us. If, then, it dwells in us so that we might remain members of his body in it, it is right that we are in it so that from it we might live and thus feed upon the flesh of the Word and drink his blood. This is, I say, the strengthening of our faith, this, its unity and sharing of life, where if the order of nature is sought, reason fails, and yet the truth of the fact remains outside human reason, so that in the reasoning of faith the force and power of the Godhead is believed in every way effective, because the doubting mind, though he who has the doubt be of good life, excludes it, so as not to reach an understanding of this sacrament.

II, 1. Of the sacrament of the Lord's body and blood daily celebrated in the church, no one of the faithful ought to be ignorant or unaware what in it pertains to faith and what to knowledge, because faith in the mystery is not rightly defended without knowledge, nor is knowledge nurtured without faith which it does not yet receive, yet sometime may perceive. For this reason the power of so great a sacrament must be examined, and Christ's teaching must be learned by faith, so that we may not be thought therefore unworthy, at least if we do not sufficiently discern this and do not understand how very worthy is the mystical body and blood of Christ, and how mighty in power, and how distinct from what may be corporeally tasted that it transcends every sacrifice of the Old Testament.

2. Whoever does not know this is undiscerning and should fear that from ignorance what has been provided us for our cure should end in ruin for those who receive it. Thence the Lord says in Leviticus: "If a man eats of a holy thing unwittingly, let him add a fifth part with what he ate and he will give it to the priest for the sanctuary. You will not profane the holy things of the Children of Israel which they offer to the Lord lest possibly they bear the iniquity of their crime when they have eaten holy things." And he added: "I am the Lord who sanctify them." Then "they are the holy of holies." There, surely, the mystery of Christ's body and blood is meant, of which no one has the power to eat—not only no foreigner, sojourner, or hireling, but

not even one who is blinded by ignorance of so great a mystery. Through ignorance, however, he who is completely ignorant of its power and value and the nature of the sacrament iself, perceives this. He does not truly know what the Lord's body and blood may be according to the truth, though in the sacrament it is received through faith. Indeed, he receives the mystery but does not know the power of the mystery, whence Solomon—no, through him, rather, the divine Spirit—commands us: "When you sit down at the table of a powerful man, to eat with a prince, pay careful attention to what are placed before you, since you know that you ought to prepare such things," that is, to preach the death of Christ in the body that daily must be carried about. Carefully understanding and worthily perceiving the spiritual sacraments by the soul's palate and the taste of faith is like adding the fifth part to what one had earlier eaten through ignorance, when our inner man through Christ's grace receives the divine with understanding and by that power of faith is embodied in Christ. In some other manner the law would order that a fifth part be added to what any man had unwittingly eaten, although now no longer was anything in existence to which something could be further added. For something is not added to what does not exist but to what already exists. The Seventy rightly order the fifth part to be added in addition to itself. For its fifth part is then rightly added to what was formerly unwittingly received, if the five senses of the body are inwardly converted to what are spiritually intelligible, because we know aright or perceive aright, the divine spirit which is in us is also enhanced by that same grace and teaches and increases those senses of ours to perceive them. So also, of course, to entice inwardly to the mystical reality not only taste but also sight and hearing, as well as smell and touch, in some manner it reveals that nothing is felt in them save the divine, nothing save the heavenly elements, and that something very terrifying is communicated. Thus how well is it put: "Let him add a fifth part on top of it," or, as other manuscripts have it, "with it and will give it to the priest." And because we should know that every sanctification of the mystical sacrifice is in some way efficacious, a thing capable of intelligible perception through the senses is divinely transformed by God's power through the Word of Christ into his flesh and blood, and those who communicate in it through these are spiritually nourished. Everything should be universally attributed to Christ, indeed, who is the true and high priest, and everything marked with his virtue and his power. Because, of course, he frees us from all ignorance and removes us from the carnal attractions of this life, and he permits nothing earthly or vile to be seen there, but to know spiritual and mystical things in them, so that our bodily senses may be more eagerly transferred to sanctifying them, if in any way the human element can be called more preeminent. "My heart and my flesh have cried out to the living God."

3. Rightly then does every man cry out to the living God because everyone may daily eat the flesh and blood of Christ, yet the Lamb himself remains alive and whole, for he does not die: "Death has no further dominion over him." He is truly, however, sacrificed each day in the mystery, is consumed for the washing away of sins. Thus the statement in the law is brought to bear: "I am the Lord who sanctify them." He sanctifies, however, those who through these elements properly approach the sanctifying God and prayerfully receive them in the manner they ought. Because of sanctification and not contamination, he has proposed to the reborn in Christ: in some other way "he will bear the iniquity of their sin." As the law says, "Whoever shall contaminate what is holy, unwittingly eating or seeking it in unworthy fashion out of contempt," hence they who receive the sacraments of life ought to be taught that if any man by chance is through sloth unaware of the salutary teachings of faith, he himself may be completely pardoned by the Lord.

III, 1. A sacrament is anything handed down to us in any divine celebration as a pledge of salvation, when what is visibly done accomplishes inwardly something far different, to be taken in a holy sense. They are called sacraments either because they are secret in that in the visible act divinity inwardly accomplishes something secretly through the corporeal appearance, or from the sanctifying consecration, because the Holy Spirit, remaining in the body of Christ, latently accomplishes for the salvation of the faithful all these mystical sacraments under the cover of things visible. By this divine power he teaches the souls of believers about things invisible more than if he visibly revealed what inwardly is effective for salvation: "For we walk by faith and not by sight."

2. Christ's sacraments in the church are Baptism and anointing, and the Lord's body and blood, which are called sacraments because under their visible appearance the divine flesh is secretly hallowed through power, so that they are inwardly in truth what they are outwardly believed to be by the power of faith. There is a legal sense of the word "sacrament," that is, an oath, in which after choosing sides each person takes an oath concerning what he has determined by his agreement. This is called a sacrament because secretly invisible faith, through consecration by prayer to God or through something sacred, is grasped, because outwardly by sight or hearing the voice of the one swearing is heard. The birth of Christ, therefore, and all that dispensation of humanity, becomes, as it were, a great sacrament, because in the visible man the divine majesty inwardly for the sake of our consecration worked invisibly those things which came into being secretly by his power. Thus the mystery or sacrament, which is God made man, is rightly so called, but the word "*mysterion*" is Greek for what has in it a hidden and secret character. It is a sacrament in the divine Scriptures wherever the sacred Spirit accomplishes something in them inwardly by speaking. But instructed by the sacrament of the Scriptures, we are divinely fed from within, and, being fed, we are instructed to fulfillment of Christ's teaching. In the sacrament of his birth and humanity, however, we are also redeemed unto pardon, and the Scriptures are revealed unto understanding, and through it a way is shown to us and power is bestowed on us that we may pass from the condition of servants into that of adopted children. Furthermore, in the sacrament of Baptism a door for entering into adoption is opened for believers, that thenceforth in Christ's members, through that same rebirth freed from evil, we may be made one body. In this baptism, of course, and afterward, the Holy Spirit is poured forth upon the soul of the one being reborn, so that the whole church of Christ may be quickened when a single spirit has been received, and it may be made one body. Because as all members of our body are

animated and guided by one soul, so that from the union of the parts one body results, so the parts of the whole church are guided and animated by one Holy Spirit that they be made one body of Christ. "Because if any man have not the Spirit of Christ, he is not his."

3. No one therefore doubts that each of us, still in his mother's womb, receives a soul secretly, that is, to the end that he be made man with a living soul. So, meanwhile, the mother does not know when, through her, before birth, he enters life. In the same way, of course, no one ought to doubt that in the womb of Baptism, before the babe rises from the fount, the Holy Spirit enters into one reborn, although not seen; that the divine power is no less provident and efficacious for the regeneration of holy adoption than it was previously in the birth by flesh, to quicken the sown members of a man, though conceived in sin. Wherefore, we have no doubt that God, who surveys all things and is powerful over them, always grants grace that is capable of preventing what he has ordained from being changed. If within the father's lust and the sin of the mother the seed of passion becomes the members of a living man, so in times and places when the Holy Spirit is present, because he fills the whole earth, he offers himself rather to everyone reborn through faith, so that through him the members of Christ may feel themselves one, and that all of them may become one body.

4. But on the journey through this life we only feed upon and drink the sacrament of the body and blood so that nourished from it we may be made one in Christ, that being invigorated by tasting him we may be prepared for things immortal and eternal. While we are now fed on angelic grace we may be quickened spiritually. For us, however, in all these sacraments the divine Spirit works. If, indeed, in the Holy Scriptures he illumines our hearts, because "neither he who plants nor he who waters is anything but it is God who gives the increase." Of this Ezekiel says: "For the Spirit of life was in the wheels," and John says: "Let him who has ears for hearing hear what the Spirit says to the churches." But in Christ the same Spirit is at work because Christ is believed to have been conceived from Him and the Virgin Mary. In like manner, in the baptism through the water

we are from him all regenerated, and afterward we daily feed upon Christ's body and drink his blood by his power. No wonder that the Spirit which without seed created the man Christ in the womb of the Virgin, from the substance of bread and wine daily creates the flesh and blood of Christ by invisible power through the sanctification of his sacrament, though outwardly understood by neither sight nor taste. But because they are spiritual things, they are fully received as certainties by faith and understanding, as the Truth foretold.

IV, 1. That in truth the body and blood are created by the consecration of the mystery, no one doubts who believes the divine words when the Truth says: "For my flesh is truly food, and my blood is truly drink." And that when his disciples did not rightly understand, he clearly identified what flesh he meant, what blood: "He who eats my flesh and drinks my blood, abides in me and I in him." Therefore, if it is truly food, it is true flesh, and if it is truly drink, it is true blood. How else will what he says be true: "The bread which I shall give, my flesh, is for the life of the world," unless it be true flesh? and the "bread which came down from heaven," true bread? But because it is not right to devour Christ with the teeth, he willed in the mystery that this bread and wine be created truly his flesh and blood through consecration by the power of the Holy Spirit, by daily creating it so that it might be mystically sacrificed for the life of the world; so that as from the Virgin through the Spirit true flesh is created without union of sex, so through the same, out of the substance of bread and wine, the same body and blood of Christ may be mystically consecrated. It is plainly of this flesh and blood that he says: "Verily, verily, I say to you, except you eat of the flesh of the Son of Man and drink his blood, you will not have eternal life in you." There, certainly, he is speaking about no other flesh than the true flesh and the true blood, that is, in a mystical sense. And because the sacrament is mystical, we cannot deny the figure, but if it is a figure, one must ask how it can be truth. For every figure is the figure of something, and always has reference to it in order that it might be a true thing of which it is the figure. That the figures of the Old Testament were shadows, no one who reads the sacred literature is in doubt, but this mystery is either truth or a figure and in the latter case a shadow. One should certainly inquire whether all this can be called truth without a shadow of falsity, though a mystery of this sort must be called a reality. But it seems to be a figure when it is "broken," when something is understood in visible appearance other than what is sensed by the sight and taste of the flesh, and when the blood in the cup is at the same time mixed with water. Furthermore, that sacrament of faith is rightly called truth; truth, therefore, when the body and blood of Christ is created by the power of the Spirit in his word out of the substance of bread and wine; but a figure when, through the agency of the priest at the altar, outwardly performing another thing, in memory of his sacred Passion, the Lamb is daily sacrificed as he was once for all.

2. If we truthfully examine the matter, it is rightly called both the truth and a figure, so that it is a figure or character of truth, because it is outwardly sensed. Truth, however, is anything rightly understood or believed inwardly concerning this mystery. Not every figure is a shadow or falsity, whence Paul, speaking to the Hebrews about God's only Son, says, "Since he is the splendor of glory and the figure of his substance, bearing all things by the word of his power, making purification of sins." In these words, certainly, he declares that there are two substances in Christ, each of them true. For when he says, "Since He is the splendor of the glory," of divinity, he proclaims him as consubstantial. But since the figure or character of his substance marks the human nature, where the fullness of divinity dwells corporeally, nevertheless, the one and true Christ is universally represented as God. For this reason he takes one thing for the demonstration of two substances and calls it the figure or character of substance, because as through characters or the figures of letters we as small children first progressed gradually to reading, later to the spiritual senses and understanding of the Scriptures, so also there is a progression from the humanity of Christ to the divinity of the Father, and therefore it is rightly called the figure or character of his substance. What else are the figures of letters than their characters, that through them force and power and utterance of spirit are demonstrated to the eyes? So also the Word is formed flesh that through flesh we as small children may be nourished to the

understanding of divinity. Yet the characters of the letters are not falsity, nor are they anything but letters. Neither can the man Christ be called false nor anything but God, with the result, of course, that the figure may rightly be called the character of the divinity's substance. Because he advances us small children through himself to things spiritual, which must be understood inwardly and by our senses, he shows himself in visible form while we receive what is in it. But because he, after the flesh had to penetrate to heavens, so that, through faith, those reborn in him might with greater boldness seek, he has left us this sacrament, a visible figure and character of flesh and blood, so that through them our soul and our flesh are richly nourished for grasping things invisible and spiritual by faith. This which is outwardly sensed is, however, the figure or character but wholly truth and no shadow, because intrinsically perceived, and for this reason nothing else henceforth than truth and the sacrament of his flesh is apparent.

3. As it is the true flesh of Christ which was crucified and buried, truly is it the sacrament of his flesh, which is divinely consecrated through the Holy Spirit on the altar by the agency of the priest in Christ's word. The Lord himself proclaims, "This is my body." Do not be surprised, O man, and do not ask about the order of nature here; but if you truly believe that that flesh was without seed created from the Virgin Mary in her womb by the power of the Holy Spirit, so that the Word might be made flesh, truly believe also that what is constructed in Christ's word through the Holy Spirit is his body from the Virgin. If you ask the method, who can explain or express it in words? Be assured, please, that the method resides in Christ's virtue, the knowledge in faith, the cause in power, but the effect in will, because the power of divinity over nature effectively works beyond the capacity of our reason. Therefore, let knowledge be held in the teaching of salvation, let faith be preserved in the mystery of truth, since in all these "we walk by faith and not by sight."

V, 1. That that sacrifice of the lamb was a figure of Christ's Passion and of our participation in it, no one of the faithful is rightly unaware. But the difference between the two sacraments should, I think, be investigated: whether between the food which came down from heaven, and the water which flowed from the rock, or between that spiritual and divine exchange, especially since the blessed apostle proclaims that "all our fathers ate the same spiritual food and all drank the same spiritual drink." If they received the same food and the same drink, why was it necessary for what it was to be changed and to be given under a different guise, if it were nothing more? From this it must be admitted that that food and that drink was the same that we now receive, and that rock from which the waters flowed was what is now preached, in the apostle's words, as Christ. Of course it was the same food, because to those who spiritually received it the manna was the type of the food of Christ's body, and that water which had flowed from the rock was drink and the figure of blood. If, indeed, in the prefiguration the shadow of the body and its original were the same, but not the same in the fulfillment of truth, because what was then foreshadowed in the symbol of things to come was the image of truth, now, however, the mystery of truth fulfilled and the Eucharist, the flesh of Christ, has been created out of the resurrection. The flesh of Christ was at an earlier time through the lamb or through that same heavenly food prefigured to believers. Of this bread David sang in the proverbs, "Man has eaten the bread of angels." Otherwise that bread, that one which came down from heaven, and the drink, because it was corporeal, was not fitting for angels, but undoubtedly that bread and drink by which Christ was foreshadowed is the food of angels, and this sacrament is his true flesh and blood which man spiritually eats and drinks. And therefore man lives on what the angels live on because everything is spiritual and divine in what man receives.

2. It is clear, then, that both that lamb of the law and the manna, and everything of this kind which bore the figure of the flesh and blood of Christ, because he once suffered in the Passion, and each day on the altar is sacrificed in the morning and the evening, possessed nothing except the figure of that mystery; and if any power to be hallowed lay hidden in these, it has shown forth completely from the faith we enjoy. This they shared, to be sure, sighing, as it were, for the promise, through faith, and they understood from the figures the sacrament of truth. We, however, have now long received this grace promised

to the fathers, and having received it we venerate it, and venerating it we are fed and watered from it. In the mystery we take the true flesh and blood of Christ, not foreshadowed, indeed, by figures drawn from puzzles in the law, but when these are solved and removed, we enjoy truth alone. Thus the Saviour says: "My flesh is truly food and my blood is truly drink. He who eats this flesh and he who drinks this blood has life eternal." But the Lord says to the Jews, "Your fathers ate manna in the desert and died." Shall we not also, who eat these things, die in this life even as they? We shall die but not, however, as they did, in the soul, because, eating carnally, they died eternally. We, however, know nothing carnal in it, but, understanding everything spiritual, shall spiritually remain in Christ. Therefore, concerning those who rightly perceive, he himself proclaims, "He who eats this bread shall live forever." We do not spiritually take the flesh and blood for the sake of this life so that we may not die temporally, but for the sake of life eternal, upon which life, of course, they did not embark who formerly perceived these things worthily in a figure until the promised grace should come to us and to them in like fashion.

3. It is clear, therefore, that there is a great deal of difference, although the same food and the same drink are preached by the apostle, yet they are not actually the same but in appearance and in a figure in which the promise of truth was inherent. From this the spiritual understanding and the sacrament of faith which were to come were shared by them, so that they lacked nothing in the spirit which now they drank in hope, nor do we, remembering them, lack what is profitable for strengthening of faith and laying hold on life. Both we and they, however, being spiritual, are quickened by receiving, because they drank from the spiritual rock that followed them, meaning that after them Christ would come. Likewise, we also spiritually drink and eat the spiritual flesh of Christ, in which eternal life is believed to be. To know otherwise is death after the flesh, but spiritually to receive the true flesh of Christ is life eternal.

VI, 1. This, of course, Christ explains: "Who eats my flesh and drinks my blood remains in me and I in him." This it is to eat that flesh and to drink that blood, if he remains in Christ and Christ can remain in him who receives it worthily. He therefore remains in Christ who, reborn from water and Spirit, is held guilty of no mortal offense, and in him [remains] Christ who opened to him the door of faith through consecration by the Holy Spirit, so that he might be a member in his body, and he is a temple of the Holy Spirit. Because "if any man does not have the spirit of Christ, he is not his." He who is not his, however, cannot truly be in him nor in his body, and he who does not remain in him, nor the life of the spirit live in his body, neither is Christ in him nor can he be in Christ, because in every way Christ is life. He, however, who is guilty of a mortal sin is far separated from life. This is the reason why He says, "Who eats my flesh and drinks my blood remains in me and I in him"; otherwise unless he first remains in me and I in him, he cannot eat my flesh or drink my blood.

2. And what is it that men eat? They all eat, without distinction, what they often receive as sacraments of the altar. They receive them, of course, but one man spiritually eats the flesh of Christ and drinks his blood; another man, however, does not, although he may seem to receive the wafer from the hand of the priest. And what does he take, when there is a consecration, if he does not take the body and blood of Christ? Truly, because a wicked man takes it unworthily, as the apostle Paul says: "He eats and drinks judgment for himself, not first testing himself nor discerning the Lord's body." See what a sinner eats and what he drinks—not flesh and blood of value to himself, but judgment. He may, of course, seem to take the sacrament of the altar with the others. Why? Because he does not test himself nor discern the Lord's body. Let the man without faith consider that, unworthy as he is, he can receive worthy and sacred things, not, indeed, expecting anything except what he sees, nor understanding anything other than he feels with his lip. Vainly, then, does he believe or understand what or how great is the judgment he incurs, because, of course, he visibly sees them all eating together from one substance, and if there is any further power in it he does not sufficiently taste it by faith. On this account the power of the sacrament is withdrawn from him and in the same he is doubly condemned because of his presumption. Of this the apostle speaks: "Let a man test himself first and so eat of that bread and drink from the cup." Having

observed these two rules, he may see whether he can take it worthily, namely, that he discerns the Lord's body, what the sacrament is, or how great it is, what sort of power it has, because it is divine and spiritual. Then let him test himself whether he is in Christ's body, or if Christ remains in him. Otherwise, except he discerns that spiritually and tests whether he is fit to receive it, he eats judgment for himself, because he makes a bad use of something good. In that case he does not take it for life, but in it condemnation to punishment.

3. And to confirm our statements by more certain proofs, let us tell what happened afterward to a certain man without faith who, not discerning the Lord's body nor testing himself according to the apostle, presumed to take this mystery unworthily. When the blessed Syrus, first bishop of Pavia, was celebrating Mass in the church of the martyrs Gervasius and Protasius, which he had himself dedicated, there were present a great number of his children whom he had begotten for God, to use the words of the apostle. Into these devoutly holy mysteries there boldly entered a certain Jew, who was put up by an evil spirit to try to take the Lord's body and to spit it out on a dunghill. In the throng of the faithful receiving the holy Eucharist from the hand of the bishop he approached the hands of the man of God with wicked daring, and with unclean lip took the Lord's body, and opened his mouth to spit it out. Struck with fitting punishment, he began loudly to cry out, but his words were unintelligible, in the sight and hearing of everyone. He attempted to shut his lips but could not; he tried to speak but his tongue would not function properly and, as if he were carrying a burning dart in his mouth, he was tortured with mighty pain. The whole church rang with the clamor of his bawling, and the company of the faithful rejoiced at the power of so extraordinary a miracle of Christ, and the saying, "He himself scoffs at the scoffers" was fulfilled; also what the apostle says, writing to the Galatians: "Do not make a mistake. God is not mocked for whatever a man sows, that he will also reap"; also, what the Truth himself proclaims in the Gospel when he says: "With what measure you measure it shall be measured out to you again." This unbelieving Jew must have neither heard nor read these preachings of the Scriptures if he

thought he could play a trick on Christ and the Holy Spirit. The man of God directed him to be brought into his presence and, when he had come, said to him: "Soul who are without faith and full of perfidy, why have you fulfilled the plan of the wicked adversary to make you think the body of Christ very cheap? Look, what secret enticer has seduced you, poor man, to make you do this has been shown to all his faithful by divine power." The Jew, however, worsted by the great pain, never ceased uttering cries that could not be understood, so long as he had in his throat the pain of his evil, because, according to the prophecy of most holy Simeon, as to the faithless the Word of God is danger and destruction, so to his faithful he is life and exaltation. To those who looked carefully, the Lord's body seemed to hang in the Jew's mouth, neither settling down beneath the tongue nor from above clinging to the palate. When all the faithful begged mercy for him, the Lord's man Syrus stretched forth his hand and withdrew the mystery of the holy Eucharist from the sacrilegious mouth and said: "Look now, unbeliever, you have been freed. From now on take care not to do anything similar or to repeat this, lest something worse happen to you." The Jew, having thrown himself at his feet, said that he would believe in the Lord Christ if the water of sacred Baptism should pour upon him, and he would unite with the pious throng, and he confessed what he had intended to do when rashly presuming to take the Lord's body, also the sin of his former unbelief, and lastly, said that he would hold to the firmness of true faith. "O God the Omnipotent Father," said the blessed bishop Syrus, "to thee I give thanks, who hast not disdained to correct Jewish treachery but convertest it to faith in thy only-begotten Son in full piety." When the man was baptized, many of the Jews, also believing on Christ, were reborn with him in sacred Baptism and were joined to Christ's faithful and the spiritual assembly. We have inserted this story of divine punishment into this little book of ours so that no unbeliever, before he discerns what the Lord's body is, or anyone guilty of a mortal crime, before he reconciles himself to Christ in peace, testing himself through penitence, should presume to eat of this bread or drink of this cup rashly and carelessly.

Peter Lombard
1095-1160

Peter Lombard was born of a poor family near Novara around the year 1100. He found a patron in the bishop of Lucca, who sent him to study at Bologna. His success there made him want to go to France, and his patron again helped by writing a letter of recommendation to Bernard, Abbot of Clairvaux. Bernard in turn provided for him to study at Rheims, then recommended him to the abbot of St. Victor in Paris.

Peter arrived in Paris, probably in 1139, just as Peter Abelard was resuming his career as a teacher there. Lombard soon gained the chair of theology at the Cathedral School of Notre-Dame and quickly established his reputation as an able theologian. He was involved in a fair amount of controversy but personally had few axes to grind. He preferred to report the various "sentences" (opinions) of others rather than to advocate particular ones of his own. It was his students who appreciated the merits of his lectures and urged him to publish them. He could not have realized at the time that they were to become, due to future events, the "textbook of the Middle Ages." In 1159 he was elected bishop of Paris, but was succeeded in July, 1160, by Maurice de Sully, who built the famous Notre-Dame Cathedral. Whether Peter died that year or a couple of years later is disputed.

In the prologue to the "Four Books of Sentences" Peter makes clear that he has no intention of doing anything original. The student was best served by being presented with the time-honored thoughts of the tradition. What was needed was a collection of the opinions of the "Fathers." This was the spirit of the 12th century, with Gratian providing the service in canon law and Peter Lombard in theology. There is hardly a line in the four books that cannot be identified as coming from earlier works.

Joachim of Fiore attacked Lombard's teaching on the Trinity and efforts were made to have the Sentences *condemned at the Fourth Lateran Council in 1215. This backfired, however, as the Council condemned the teachings of Joachim and pronounced the* Sentences *orthodox. This helped to entrench them as the standard textbook for theology from the 13th to the 17th century, when they gave way to the* Summa *of Thomas Aquinas.*

Peter Lombard played a major role in defining the number of sacraments as seven. Earlier there were "major" and "minor" sacraments of various numbers, but as the definition grew more precise, its application naturally became more limited. The following selection is taken from the Fourth Book of Sentences, *which divides the treatment of the sacraments into 26 "distinctions."*

SENTENCES

APPENDIX

DISTINCTION I

PART I

I. *Of Sacraments.*

The Samaritan who tended the wounded man, applied for his relief the dressings of the sacraments, just as God instituted the remedies of the sacraments against the wounds of original and actual sin. Concerning the sacraments, four questions first present themselves for consideration: what a sacrament is, why it was instituted; wherein it consists, and how it is performed; and what the difference is between the sacraments of the old and the new covenants.

II. *What a Sacrament is.*

"A sacrament is the sign of a sacred thing (res)." However, a *sacred mystery* is also called a sacrament, as the sacrament of divinity, so that a sacrament may be the *sign of something sacred,* and the *sacred thing signified;* but now we are considering a sacrament as a *sign.*—So, "A sacrament is the visible form of an invisible grace."

III. *What a sign is.*

"But a sign, is the thing (res) behind the form which it wears to the senses, which brings by means of itself something else to our minds."

IV. *How a sign and a Sacrament differ.*

"Furthermore, some signs are *natural,* as smoke which signifies fire; others *conventional;*" and of those which are *conventional,* some are sacraments, some not. For every sacrament is a sign, but the converse is not true. A sacrament bears a resemblance to the thing, of which it is a sign. "For if sacraments did not bear a resemblance to the things of which they are the sacraments, they could not *properly* be called sacraments." For a sacrament is properly so called, because it is a sign of the grace of God and the expression of invisible grace, so that it bears its image and is its cause. Sacraments, therefore, were not instituted merely in order to signify something, but also as a means of sanctification. For things which were instituted only to signify are signs only, and not sacraments; such as the sacrifices of flesh, and the ceremonial observances of the old law, which could never justify those who offered them; because, as the apostle says, "The blood of goats and of oxen and the ashes of an heifer, being sprinkled, sanctify such as are defiled, to the cleansing of the flesh," but not of the spirit. Now this uncleanness was the touching of a dead body. Wherefore Augustine: "By that defilement which the law cleanses I understand merely the touching of a dead body, since anyone who had touched one, *was unclean seven days;* but he was purified according to the law on the third day and on the seventh, and was cleansed," so that he might enter the temple. These legal observances also cleansed sometimes from bodily leprosy; but no one was ever justified by the *works of the Law,* as says the apostle, even if he performed them in faith and charity. Why? because God has ordained them unto servitude, not unto justification, so that they might be *types of something to come,* wishing that these offerings should be made to him rather than to idols. They therefore were *signs,* yet also sacraments, although they are often called so incorrectly in the Scriptures, because they were rather signs of a sacred thing than availing anything themselves. These moreover the apostle calls *works of the Law,* which were instituted only to signify something, or as a yoke.

V. *Why the Sacraments were instituted.*

The sacraments were instituted for a three-fold reason: for *humility, instruction,* and *exercise.* For *humility,* so that while man, by order of the Creator, abases himself in worship before insensible things, which by nature are beneath him, through this humility and obedience, he may become more pleasing to

God, and more meritorious in his sight, at whose command he seeks salvation in things beneath him, yet not from them, but through them from God. For *instruction* also were the sacraments instituted, so that the mind might be taught by what it sees outside in visible form, to recognize the invisible virtue which is within. For man, who before sin saw God without a mediator, through sin has became so dulled that he is in no wise able to comprehend divine things, unless trained thereto by human things.—Likewise, the sacraments were instituted for exercise, because since man cannot be idle, there is offered him in the sacraments a useful and safe exercise by which he may avoid vain and harmful occupation. For he who devotes himself to good exercise is not easily caught by the tempter; wherefore Jerome warns us: "Always do some sort of work, that the devil may find you occupied." "There are, moreover, three kinds of *exercises:* one aims at the *edification of the soul,* another aims at the *nourishment of the body,* another at the *destruction of both.*"—And inasmuch as without a sacrament, to which God has not limited his power, he could have given grace to man, he has for the aforesaid reasons instituted the sacraments. "There are two parts of which a sacrament consists, namely *words* and *things: words,* as the invocation of the Trinity; *things,* as water, oil, and the like."

VI. *Of the difference between the old and the new Sacraments.*

Now it remains to note the difference between the old and the new sacraments; as we call sacraments what anciently they called sacred things, such as sacrifices and oblations and the like. The difference between these Augustine indicated briefly when he said, "because the former only promised and signified salvation, while the latter give it."

PART II

VII. *Of Circumcision.*

However there was among these sacraments one sacrament, namely that of circumcision, which conferred the remedy against sin which baptism now provides. Wherefore Augustine: "From the time circumcision was instituted among the people of God, which was then a *sign of the justification of faith,* it had power to cleanse old and young from original and previous sin; just as baptism from the time it was instituted, began to have power to renew a man." So Bede: "Under the Law circumcision brought the same aid, a health-bringing cure for the wound of original sin, which baptism has given during the time of revealed grace, except that the men of old were not yet able to enter the door of the heavenly kingdom; however being comforted after death by blessed rest in the bosom of Abraham, they awaited with happy hope their entrance into celestial peace."—By these passages we are clearly taught that circumcision, from the time it was instituted, was ordained by God for the remission of original and actual sin in children and adults, just as now remission is given by baptism.

VIII. *What remedy those had who lived before circumcision.*

We ask now of the men who lived before circumcision, and of the women who lived before and after, what remedy they had against sin. Some say, that sacrifices and oblations were efficacious for them for the remission of their sin. But it is better to say that the men who sprang from Abraham were justified by circumcision, and the women by faith and good works, either their own, if they were adults, or their parents, if children. As for those who lived before circumcision, the children were justified by the faith of their parents; parents on the other hand were justified by the efficacy of sacrifices, that is, by that which they apprehended spiritually in these sacrifices. Wherefore Gregory: "That which is accomplished in our time by the water of baptism, was effected in the time of the ancients by faith alone for children, or by the efficacy of sacrifice for their elders, or by the mystery of circumcision for those who sprang from the stock of Abraham."

IX. *Of the institution and purpose of circumcision.*

Here we must tell *when* circumcision was instituted; and *why;* and *why it was changed* into baptism.—Abraham first received the command for circumcision as a test of obedience; nor of him alone was circumcision required but of his seed, that is, of all the Hebrews; which circumcision was performed according to the Law on the eighth day with a stone knife in the flesh of the foreskin. Moreover circumcision was ordained for many reasons, namely, that Abraham by his obedience to the command might please God, whom Adam had displeased by untruthfulness. Also it was ordained as a sign of the great faith of Abraham, who believed that he would have a son in whom all should be blessed. Next, it was instituted, that by this sign, this people might be distinguished from other nations. In the flesh of the foreskin also circumcision was commanded to be performed, because it was instituted as a remedy for original sin, which we inherit from our parents through concupiscence, which displays itself especially in this part. And because in this part the first man knew the guilt of disobedience, it is proper that there he should receive the sign of obedience.

It was performed on the eighth day with a stone knife, because both in the general resurrection in the eighth age to come, all corruption will be removed from the elect by the rock Christ, and by the resurrection of Christ which took place on the eighth day, the soul of whomsoever believeth on him is circumcised from sins: "There are therefore two parts (res) of this sacrament."

DISTINCTION II

I. *Of the sacraments of the new law.*

Let us now come to the sacraments of the new covenant; which are baptism, confirmation, the blessing of bread, that is the eucharist, penance, extreme unction, ordination, marriage. Of these some offer a remedy for sin, and confer helping grace, as baptism, others are merely a remedy, as marriage; others strengthen us with grace and virtue, as the eucharist and ordination.

If indeed we are asked why these sacraments were not instituted immediately after the fall of man, since in them are justification and salvation; we say that before the advent of Christ, who brought grace, the sacraments of grace could not be granted, for they have derived their virtue from his death and passion. Now Christ was unwilling to come before man was convinced that he could find help in neither natural nor written law.

Marriage, however was instituted before sin, "not at all as a remedy, but as a sacrament and a duty"; after sin indeed it became a remedy against the corruption of carnal concupiscence; of which we will treat in its place.

II. *Of baptism.*

Now let us consider the sacrament of baptism, "which is first among the sacraments of the new grace. The baptism of Christ, John foretold by his own baptism, and he is said to have been the first to perform baptism, but in water, not in the Spirit, as he himself says: 'I baptize you in water unto penance.' He purified indeed only the bodies, he did not cleanse from sins."

III. *Of the difference between the baptism of John and that of Christ.*

The baptism of John was unto penance, not unto remission; whereas the baptism of Christ was unto remission; for John baptizing men called to penance, and those whom he baptized he taught to do penance, according to this passage: "They came to John in the Jordan, confessing their sins." But in the baptism of John sins were not remitted, as they are in the baptism of Christ.

IV. *Of what avail was the baptism of John?*

"What avail therefore had the baptism of John? By the practice of baptism, it prepared men for the baptism of Christ." —But we ask, why is it called the baptism of John, as the Truth says: "The baptism of John, whence is it?" Because the work of John there was only the visible one of washing the outside, not the invisible grace of God working within. Nevertheless this work of John was also from God and his baptism was from God. not from man; but it was called of *man,* because nothing was there done that man did not perform.

V. *If his baptism was a sacrament.*

If indeed we are asked whether it was a sacrament; we may grant that it was, in the sense in which *legal symbols* are called sacraments. For the baptism of John signified a sacred thing, namely the baptism of Christ, which was not only to penance, but also to the remission of sins.

VI. *Of the form of the baptism of John.*

Here we must consider whether those baptized by John were again baptized with the baptism of Christ, and what form of words John used.—Those who were baptized by John, ignorant that the holy Spirit existed, and putting their hope in his baptism, were afterwards baptized with the baptism of Christ.—Also the baptism of John was performed *in the name of the Coming One.* So Jerome on Joel: "He who says that he believes on Christ, and does not believe on the holy Spirit, has not yet clear eyes. Wherefore those baptized by John *in the name of the Coming One,* that is, of the Lord Jesus, because they said: 'But we have not heard if there be a holy Spirit', were baptized a second time, or rather they received the true baptism." But they who had not placed hope in the baptism of John, and believed on the Father and Son and holy Spirit, were not baptized afterwards, but received the holy Spirit by the laying-on of hands upon them by the apostles. Others again who did not so believe were baptized with the baptism of Christ, as we have said before. Hence Jerome: "Those who did not know the holy Spirit, when they received the baptism of John were baptized again," lest any one of the Jews or of the Gentiles should think that water without the holy Spirit could suffice for salvation. On this point also, Ambrose in the first book on the holy Spirit: "Some denied that they knew the holy Spirit, since they said they were baptized with the baptism of John, who baptized in the name of the coming Jesus, not in his own name. These therefore, because they were not baptized in the name of Christ nor with faith in the holy Spirit, could not have received the sacrament of baptism; they were therefore baptized in the name of Christ, nor was baptism repeated for them, but renewed."

DISTINCTION III

PART I

I. *What baptism is.*

In the next place we must consider what baptism is, and what its form is, and when it was instituted, and the cause of its institution.—By baptism we mean an immersion, that is, an exterior cleansing of the body administered under a prescribed form of words. For if the cleansing takes place without the word, there is no sacrament, but with the addition of the word to the element, it becomes a sacrament; not that the *element* itself becomes the sacrament, but the *cleansing* performed in the element. Wherefore Augustine: "Baptism is consecrated by the word; take away the word, and what is water, except water? the word is added to the element, and it becomes a sacrament. Whence is this great virtue of water, that it should touch the body and cleanse the heart, unless it be by the word working? not because the word is said, but because it is believed. For in the word itself the passing sound is one thing, the virtue remaining is another." Therefore the sacrament of baptism consists of two parts, namely the word and the element. So that even if other things are lacking which were instituted for the beautifying of the sacrament, it is none the less a true sacrament and sacred, provided there be present the word and the element. For both in this sacrament and in others some things are customarily done for the beautifying and honoring of the sacrament, some things for the substance and purpose of the sacrament. The word and the element are of the substance of this sacrament, the other things heighten its solemnity.

II. *Of the form of baptism.*

But what is this word, the addition of which to the element, makes the sacrament? The Truth teaches you, what is the form of this sacrament when he says to the disciples: "Go ye, teach all nations, baptizing them in the name of the Father, and of the Son, and of the holy Spirit." Therefore the invocation of the Trinity is given as the *word,* by which baptism is consecrated; and this is the form of words with which baptism is administered. Wherefore Pope Zacharias says to Bishop Boniface: "It was most positively declared in the Synod of the Angles, that whoever was immersed without the invocation of the Trinity, did not have the sacrament of regeneration; a statement which is entirely true, because if anyone is immersed in the font of baptism without the invocation of the Trinity, he is not a complete Christian, unless he is baptized in the name of the Father and of the Son and of the holy Spirit."

III. *That the Apostles baptized in the name of Christ.*

Nevertheless we read in the Acts of the Apostles, that the Apostles baptized *in the name of Christ;* but in this name, as Ambrose explains, the whole Trinity is understood: "For when you say Christ, the Father is understood, by whom he was anointed, and he himself who was anointed, and the holy Spirit through whom he was anointed." Wherefore Pope Nicholas to the inquiries of the Bulgars: "You assert that many were baptized by a certain Jew; and you ask what is to be done in that case. They certainly have been baptized, if they were baptized in the name of the holy Trinity or in the name of Christ, as we read in the Acts of the Apostles; for it is one and the same thing, as Saint Ambrose explains."

IV. *If baptism can be administered in the name of the Father, or of the holy Spirit.*

Here we are asked whether Baptism would be valid, if it were administered in the name of the Father only, or of the holy Spirit, as when it is administered *in the name of* Christ. Ambrose seems to say, that if the mystery of the Trinity is accepted in faith, and but one person is named, the sacrament is complete; and conversely, if three are named, and faith is not right concerning some one of them, the mystery is made void. For he says thus: "Where there is not the complete sacrament of baptism, it is accounted neither a beginning nor any form of baptism. Now it is complete, if you confess the Father and Son and holy Spirit. If you deny one, you destroy the whole. Just as if you mention one in the (baptismal) formula, either Father, or Son, or holy Spirit, and in faith deny neither the Father nor the Son nor the holy Spirit, it is a complete sacrament of faith; so also, although you say Father and Son and holy Spirit, and restrict the power of the Father and of the Son and of the holy Spirit, the whole mystery is void." "For when you say *in the name of Christ,* through the unity of the name the mystery is complete; nor is the Spirit absent from the Baptism of Christ, because Christ baptized in the Spirit."

"Now let us consider, whether, as we read that the sacrament of baptism is complete *in the name of Christ,* so also if we name only the holy Spirit, nothing is lacking to fulfil the mystery. Let us follow the reasoning: whoever has named one, has signified the Trinity; if you say Christ, you designate also the Father, by whom the Son was anointed, and him who was anointed, that is, the Son, and the Spirit with whom he was anointed. For it is written: 'This Jesus of Nazareth, whom God anointed with the holy Spirit.' And if you name the Father, you indicate equally his Son and the Spirit of his mouth, provided that you include them also in your heart. And if you say the holy Spirit, you speak of God the Father from whom he proceeds and his Son, whose the Spirit is. Also, that authority may be added to reason, the Lord says: 'Moreover ye shall be baptized in the holy Spirit.'" By these words he shows that we can rightfully be baptized in the holy Spirit.

From the above you have understood clearly that baptism can be administered in the name of Christ; whence it seems no less to be implied that true baptism can be administered in the name of the Father alone, or of the holy Spirit alone, provided he who baptized holds the faith of the Trinity, which Trinity is signified by any of these names. But if anyone believing wrongly and intending to lead into error, mentions one only of the three, he does not fulfill the mystery. As for what Ambrose says, that the mystery is void even though the three are named, if he who baptized lessens the power of the Father or of the Son or of the holy Spirit, that is if he thinks wrongly of the power of any one of these, not believing the power of the three is one; this must be understood of one who *does not intend* to baptize *nor believe* in baptizing, who not only lacks faith, but also has not the intention of baptizing.—Whoever therefore baptized in the name of Christ, baptized in the name of the Trinity, which is thereby understood. Nevertheless it is safer to name the three, so that we say: in the name of the Father and of the Son and of the holy Spirit; not *in the names,* but *in the name,* that is in invocation or in confession of the Father and of the Son and of the holy Spirit; for thereby the whole Trinity is invoked, that it may work invisibly through itself, just as outside visibly through the ministry. If however we say in *the names,* then it is not a sacrament, because the form of baptism is not preserved.

PART II

V. *Of the institution of baptism.*

As for the institution of baptism, when it began, there are various opinions. Some say baptism was instituted, when Christ told Nicodemus: "Unless a man be born again of water and of the holy Spirit," etc. Others say baptism was instituted when he said to the Apostles: "Go ye, teach all nations, baptizing them in the name of the Father and of the Son and of the holy Spirit." But this he said to them after the resurrection, in his instructions for the calling of the Gentiles, while before his passion he had sent them two by two to preach in Judea, and to baptize, with the words: "Go not aside into the way of the Gentiles." At that time therefore was baptism instituted, because they then both preached and baptized.

If now we are asked, under what form the apostles then baptized; we can surely reply: in the name of the Trinity, that is, under the form which they baptized the Gentiles afterwards; for we can understand that it was given them before the passion, although it is not so recorded. Christ did not therefore first give them this form, when he sent them to evangelize the Gentiles; but rather the form which he had given before when he sent them into Judea, he afterward repeated when he sent them to the Gentiles.–Accordingly it is more fitting to say that the institution was established, when Christ was baptized by John in the Jordan; which he arranged, not because he wished to be cleansed, since he was without sin, but because "by the contact of his pure flesh he bestowed regenerating power on the waters," so that whoever was afterwards immersed, with the invocation of the name of the Trinity, might be cleansed from sin. At that time therefore the baptism of Christ was instituted, by which the Trinity, whose mystery therein was made known, baptized a man within.

VI. *Why it is performed in water only.*

Moreover this sacrament is celebrated only in water, not in any other liquid, as Christ says: "Unless a man be born again of water," etc. And therefore we are directed to perform it uniformly in water, that we may understand that "just as water washes away uncleanness from the body and the garments, so baptism by purifying removes the stains of the soul and the uncleanness of vices." Or for this reason, that poverty may excuse no one, as might happen if baptism were performed in wine or in oil, and in order that the common material for baptizing may be found everywhere; this is what the water, which flowed from the side of Christ, signified, just as blood was the sign of the other sacrament. Therefore baptism cannot be consecrated in any other liquid than water.

VII. *Of immersion, how many times it should be performed.*

If then we are asked how the immersion should be performed; we reply briefly, either once, or thrice, according to the varying custom of the Church. So Gregory: "Concerning the trine immersion of baptism, no truer answer can be given than what you yourselves have already thought; that in the one faith of the holy Church diverse custom does no harm. For since in the three personalities there is one substance, there can be nothing reprehensible in immersing a child in baptism thrice or once, because in three immersions the Trinity of persons may be symbolized and in one the Unity of the Godhead. We indeed, who immerse thrice, also signify the sacrament of the three days' entombment."—According to this, it is allowable to immerse not only thrice, but also only once. However it is only allowable to immerse once, where such is the custom of the Church. If anyone should begin to do it where such was not the custom, or should assert that there should be but one immersion, he would make himself reprehensible. Wherefore Haymo: "Cyprian abounded in his understanding when he immersed children once in baptism, because what he understood, he carried out zealously, abounding in good works, although he ignorantly did wrong in this respect: But because he abounded in good works, afterwards, when he had been rebuked by God, he abounded in a higher understanding, immersing children thrice." —Here you have it that he did wrong, who immersed once; but this was because the custom of his Church held otherwise, or because he asserted that only one immersion was allowable. As for the trine immersion Augustine says: "After we professed to believe, we thrice plunged our heads into the sacred font, and this order of baptism is celebrated so as doubly to symbolize the mystery. Rightly were you immersed thrice, who received baptism in the name of the Trinity. Rightly immersed thrice because you received baptism in the name of Christ, who rose from the dead on the third day. For immersion thrice repeated is a type of the Lord's sepulture."—Therefore it is settled, that those who are to be baptized should be immersed thrice; and yet if they are immersed only once, they receive a true baptism. And he who immerses only once does not sin, unless the custom of his Church is different, or unless he asserts that it should be done only in this way.

VIII. *When circumcision lost its power.*

Also we are frequently asked if circumcision lost its power immediately on the institution of baptism.—To this we reply that all commands of the law were terminated by the death of Christ. From that time therefore circumcision lost its power so that thereafter it did not help; it rather hindered those who performed it; but until the oblation of the true host it was able to help. For if before the passion the commands of the law had come to an end, Christ would not, when the passion was imminent, have eaten the Passover with his disciples.

IX. *Of the cause of the institution of baptism.*

The purpose of the institution of baptism is the renewing of the mind, so that man who had been *old* through sin, might be *renewed* through the grace of baptism, which is accomplished by the putting off of sins and by the taking on of virtues. For by this means anyone is made a *new man,* by effacing his sins and adorning himself with virtues. The effacement of sins drives out uncleanness, the acquisition of virtues conveys beauty, and this is the *object* (res) of this sacrament, namely inward cleanness.

If we are asked, whether baptism has opened heaven, which circumcision did not open; we declare that neither baptism nor circumcision opened to us an entrance to the kingdom, but the sacrifice of the Saviour, and if that had been offered during the time of circumcision, the men of that time would have entered the kingdom. Therefore the object of this sacrament is justification.

DISTINCTION VII

I. *Of the Sacrament of Confirmation.*

Now we must next discuss the sacrament of confirmation, for we are often questioned concerning its virtue. For the form is clear, that is, the words which the bishop says, when he signs the baptized on the forehead with the sacred chrism.

II. *That it can only be performed by the chief priests.*

This sacrament cannot be performed by any except the chief priests, for we read that in the time of the apostles it was not performed by others than the apostles themselves, nor can, nor ought it be performed by others than those who hold the place of the apostles. For if it be undertaken by others, it is held to be null and void, nor will it be counted among the sacraments of the church. But it is lawful for presbyters to touch the baptized on the breast but not to sign them with the chrism on the forehead.

III. *What the virtue of this sacrament is.*

The virtue moreover of the sacrament is the gift of the holy Spirit for strength, who is given in baptism for remission. Wherefore Rabanus: "By the chief priest through the laying on of hands the Paraclete is given to one baptized, that he may be strengthened through the holy Spirit, to proclaim to others that which he has attained in baptism." Also: "All the faithful ought after baptism to receive the holy Spirit by the laying on of hands by the bishops so that they may be found to be complete Christians."

IV. *Whether this sacrament is more worthy than baptism.*

"Know that both are great sacraments, but one must be held in greater veneration, as it is administered by those who are greater."—See he calls the sacrament of confirmation the greater; but perhaps not on account of the greater virtue and utility which it confers, but because it is administered by those who are worthier, and is performed on a worthier part of the body, that is on the forehead; or perhaps because it offers a greater increase of virtue, although baptism has more power for remission. Rabanus seems to mean this when he says that "in the anointing of baptism the holy Spirit descends to consecrate his habitation to God. But in this sacrament his sevenfold grace, with all fullness of sanctity and virtue comes upon man."—This sacrament ought only to be received by persons fasting, and be administered by fasting, just as baptism, unless necessity compels otherwise.

V. *Whether it can be repeated.*

Nor ought it be repeated, as baptism ought not, nor ordination. For injury must not be done to any sacrament; and it would be thought an injury, were we to repeat what must not be repeated.—But whether some can be repeated or none is a question. For that baptism and ordination ought not be repeated. Augustine clearly says: "Each is a sacrament, and is administered with a certain consecration, the one when a person is baptized; but the other when he is ordained. Therefore in the Catholic Church it is not permitted to repeat either," because injury must not be done to either. And without doubt we must hold that this is true also of confirmation; but whether others can or ought to be repeated, we shall discuss later.

Note. Gregory writes to Bishop Januarius thus: "It has come to our ears, that some have been offended, because we restrained presbyters from touching with the chrism those who had been baptized; and we certainly did this according to the old use of our church. But if some are much distressed by this; we concede that where bishops are absent, presbyters may touch the baptized with chrism even on the forehead." "But that concession seems to me to have been made at one particular time for checking a scandal."

DISTINCTION VIII

PART I

I. *Of the sacrament of the altar.*

"After the sacrament of baptism and of confirmation, follows the sacrament of the Eucharist. Through baptism we are cleansed, through the Eucharist, we are perfected in what is good." Baptism extinguishes the fire of sins, the Eucharist restores us spiritually. Wherefore it is well called the Eucharist, that is, good grace, because in this sacrament not only is there increase of virtue and grace, but he who is the fount and source of all grace is received entire.

II. *That in the Old Testament there was a type of this sacrament, just as of baptism.*

"There was a previous type of it, when God rained manna on the Fathers in the wilderness, and fed them with heavenly food; wherefore: 'Man has eaten the bread of angels.' But those who ate that bread then died. But this is the living bread, which 'came down from heaven,' and gave life to the world." That manna was from heaven, this *above* heaven; that when reserved to another day was full of worms; this is free from all corruption; whoever has tasted it religiously shall not see corruption. That was given to the ancients after the crossing of the Red Sea, where the Hebrews were freed by the drowning of the Egyptians; so this heavenly manna ought only be given to those re-born. That bread for the body led the ancient people through the desert to the land of promise; this heavenly food sustains the faithful going through the desert of this world to heaven. Wherefore it is rightly called the 'viaticum,' because it restores us on the way, and leads us unto the fatherland. Therefore just as in the Red Sea we find baptism typified, so in the manna is the Lord's body signified. These two sacraments were indicated when the blood and water flowed from the side of Christ; because Christ came to redeem us from the devil and sin by the blood of redemption, and the water of cleansing, just as he freed the Israelites from the destroyer by the blood of the paschal lamb, and from the Egyptians by the water of the sea.—

Melchisedech also prefigured the rite of this sacrament, when he offered bread and wine to Abraham. Wherefore, as Ambrose says, it is clear, "that the sacraments of the Christians came before those of the Jews."

III. *Of the institution of this sacrament.*

Here four other things present themselves for consideration, that is, the *institution,* the *form,* the *sacrament,* and the *thing* (res). The Lord *instituted* the sacrament, when after the type of the lamb he offered his body and blood to the disciples at supper. Wherefore Eusebius Emisenus: "Because he was about to withdraw from their eyes the body he had assumed, and bear it to the heavens, it was necessary that on the day of the Feast he should consecrate the sacrament of the body and blood for us, so that what was once offered as a ransom, might be perpetually worshipped through a mystery."

PART II

IV. *Of the form.*

But the form is that which he himself taught when he said: "This is my body"; and afterward: "This is my blood." For when these words are uttered, a change of the blood and wine into the substance of the body and blood of Christ takes place. All other words are said to the praise of God. Wherefore Ambrose: "This sacrament is accomplished by the words of Christ, because the words of Christ change the creature; and thus the bread becomes the body of Christ, and the wine with water poured into the chalice becomes the blood by the consecration of the heavenly word. By what words is the consecration made? Hear what the words are: 'Take ye and eat ye all of this; this is my body,' and again: 'Take ye and drink ye all of this, this is my blood.' All the rest that is uttered renders praise to God, offers prayer for the people and for the kings." Also, Augustine: "We must believe that in these words of Christ the sacraments are accomplished; all the rest are merely praises, or the earnest supplications and petitions of the faithful."—See now what is the institution and form of this sacrament.

V. *Why Christ gave this sacrament to his disciples after other food.*

Here it is worthy of consideration why he gave this sacrament to the disciples after supper. The Lord Jesus being about to depart to the invisible majesty of his Father's glory, and having celebrated the symbolical passover with the disciples, wished to commend to them some memorial, and gave them his body and blood under the figure of bread and wine, in order to show that the sacraments of the old law, among which the sacrifice of the paschal lamb was chief, were terminated at his death, and the sacraments of the new law substituted, and among these the mystery of the Eucharist is preeminent. Therefore he ordained the Eucharist after the other sacraments that this sacrament might be more deeply impressed on the memory of the disciples, and thenceforth be repeated frequently by the Church. But he did not on that account appoint it for discipline in the future, that it should be received after other food, but rather it ought to be received fasting, as the Apostle teaches, so that it may be marked by exceptional reverence, that is, set apart from other food; and this the Lord left to the Apostles to arrange. Wherefore Augustine: "It appears, that when the disciples first received the Eucharist, they did not receive it fasting. But we should not therefore scorn the universal Church, because its members always received the Eucharist fasting. For it pleased the holy Spirit, that in honor of so great a sacrament, the body of the Lord should enter into the mouth of a Christian before other food; therefore this custom is observed everywhere. For not because the Lord gave the Eucharist after other food, ought we to receive it after breakfast or dinner, as did those whom the Apostle reproved. For the Saviour that he might the more strongly commend the loftiness of this mystery, wished to impress it last on the hearts and memory of his disciples, from whom he was about to go to his passion. But in what order it was thereafter to be received he left to be taught by the apostles, through whom he would organize his churches."

VI. *Of the sacrament and the thing (res).*

Now let us see what is the sacrament and what the thing (res). "The sacrament is the visible form of invisible grace"; the form therefore of the bread and wine which appears here is the sacrament, that is, "the sign of a sacred thing, because it calls something to mind beyond the appearance which it presents to the senses." Therefore the appearances "keep the names of the things which they were before, namely, bread and wine."

VII. *That the thing (res) of this sacrament is two-fold.*

"Moreover the thing (res) of this sacrament is two-fold: one, what is contained and signified, the other what is signified but not contained. The thing contained and signified is the flesh of Christ which he received from the Virgin, and the blood which he shed for us. The thing signified and not contained is the unity of the Church in those who are predestined, called, justified and glorified." This is the two-fold flesh and blood of Christ. Wherefore Jerome: "In two ways," he says, "are the flesh of Christ and his blood understood: either the flesh which was crucified and buried, and the blood which was shed by the lance of the soldier; or that spiritual and divine body of which he himself says: 'My flesh is food indeed, and my blood is drink indeed'; and : 'Unless ye eat my flesh and drink my blood, ye have not life in you.'" Therefore three things are to be distinguished here: the first which is the sacrament only; the second which is the sacrament and the thing (res); and the third which is the thing and not the sacrament. The sacrament and not the thing is the visible form of bread and wine; the sacrament and the thing is the very flesh and blood of Christ; the thing and not the sacrament, is his mystical flesh.—Furthermore that visible form is the sacrament of something two-fold; because it signifies two things and bears the express likeness of two things. For just as bread more than other foods restores and sustains the body and wine gladdens and inebriates man, so the flesh of Christ spiritually restores and sustains the inward man more than other graces; wherefore: 'My chalice which inebriateth me, how goodly is it!' The visible form bears also a resemblance to a mystical thing, which is the unity of the faithful, because just as one loaf is made from many grains, and wine from many grapes flows together, so ecclesiastical unity is composed of the many persons of the faithful." Wherefore the Apostle: "We being many are one bread and one body." Wherefore Augustine: "The Church is called one bread and one body, because just as one loaf is composed of many grains, and one body of many members, so the Church of many faithful is bound together by uniting charity." "This mystery of our peace and unity Christ consecrated at his table. He who receives this mystery of unity and does not keep the bond of peace, receives this mystery not for himself, but against himself." "And of this unity also Christ's own body received from the Virgin is the sacrament; because as the body of Christ was composed of many very pure and immaculate members, so the society of the Church is composed of many persons freed from the stain of sin. As a type of this unity, the ark of the Lord was made of setim-wood, which does not decay, but is like white thorn."

DISTINCTION X

PART I

I. *Of the heresy of others who say that the body of Christ is not on the altar save in sign.*

There are also others who exceed the madness of the above described, who, measuring the virtue of God by the measure of natural things, deny the truth more audaciously and dangerously, asserting that on the altar there is neither the body of Christ nor the blood, nor is the substance of bread or of wine converted into the substance of flesh and blood but that Christ said: "This is my body," just as the Apostle said: "And the rock was Christ." For they say that the body of Christ is there only in the sacrament, that is, in symbol, and merely in symbol is it eaten by us. These find the occasion of their error in the words of the Truth, from which the first heresy arose among the disciples of Christ. For when he said: "Except a man eat my flesh, and drink my blood, he shall not have eternal life"; they not understanding said: "This saying is hard, who can understand it? and they went back." When they had departed, he taught the twelve who remained: "It is the Spirit," he said, "who giveth life; the flesh profiteth nothing. The words which I have spoken to you, are spirit and life." Have you understood them spiritually? They are spirit and life. Have you understood them carnally? Even so they are spirit and life, but they are not so for you. Understand spiritually that which I have said. It is not this body which you see that you shall eat, nor drink this blood which they who crucify me shall shed. I have commended a certain sacrament to you, which if it be spiritually understood, will give you life; but the flesh profiteth nothing."—There are also other passages which add fuel to the madness of these people. For Augustine says: "Until this age shall be ended, the Lord is on high; but nevertheless there is here also with us the Truth, the Lord. For the body in which he rose again must be in one place; but his truth is diffused everywhere." Also: One person is God and man, inasmuch as Christ is God, he is everywhere, inasmuch as he is man he is in heaven." Christ also says: "The poor ye have always with you, but me ye have not always." The aforesaid heretics use these and other sayings to maintain their error.—All these passages are to be interpreted in the same manner. For these words do not deny that the true body of Christ is received by the faithful or that it is on the altar, but by these words the Truth instructed the Apostles and through them us, that he was giving us his body, not divided into parts, as those disciples thought, who went back, but entire; and not visibly, in human form, but invisible under the form of bread and wine, did he give us his body and blood. Augustine confirms this meaning when he says: "It is his body itself, and not his body which was seen, that is eaten; his body indeed, invisibly; not his body visibly." Also: "And if it is necessary that it should be celebrated visibly, it is necessary that it be understood invisibly." So also the body of Christ must be understood to be in one place, that is, visibly in human form; but his Truth, that is, his Divinity, is everywhere; his truth also, that is, his true body is on every altar, wherever it is celebrated. So also is this to be understood: "The poor ye have always with you, but me ye have not always," that is, with reference to his corporal presence, in which he was conversing with them. Similarly, inasmuch as he is *man,* he is in heaven, that is, visibly; but he is on the altar invisibly, because he does not appear in human form, but is hidden under the form of bread and wine. Wherefore also his flesh, which is truly on the altar, is said to be invisible; but because it does not appear in its own form, it is said to be invisible. For Augustine says: "This is what we say, what we strive in every way to prove: that the sacrifice of the Church is consummated by two things and consists of two things; the visible form of the elements, and the invisible flesh and blood of our Lord Jesus Christ; the sacrament and in that which the sacrament symbolizes, that is, the body of Christ; just as the person of Christ consists and is composed of God and man, since Christ is very God and man, because everything contains in itself the nature and truth of those things, of which it consists. Now the sacrifice of the Church consists of two parts: the sacrament, and the thing of the sacrament, that is, the body of Christ. There is therefore the sacrament and the thing of the sacrament (res sacramenti), that is the body of Christ." See, he said the *invisible* flesh of Christ, because, it is received and given, hidden under the form of bread. Likewise, he said that the body of Christ is the sacrament and the thing; and this confirms what we said above. Then he adds what moves the reader more: "That is his flesh," he says, "which hidden under the form of bread, we receive in the sacrament; and his blood, which we drink under the form and taste of wine. That is, flesh is the sacrament of flesh and blood of blood; and in the flesh and blood, both of which are invisible, intelligible and spiritual, is signified the visible and palpable body of Christ, full of grace and divine majesty."

Pay careful attention to these things, because Augustine here uses a certain figure of speech in which things which signify other things often receive the names of the things which they signify. For here the visible form of bread is called by the name of flesh and the visible form of wine by the name of blood. But the flesh of Christ is said to be invisible and intelligible, because in that form the flesh is not seen, but is known; so also the blood. The invisible flesh therefore is said to be the sacrament of the visible flesh because the form of bread, under which that flesh is not visible, is the sacrament of the visible flesh, for by the invisible flesh, that is, by the form, in which the flesh of Christ does not appear as flesh, is signified the body of Christ, which is visible and palpable, when it appears in its own form. So also should we understand in the case of the blood. Augustine also confirms this sense, showing how the preceding statements are to be understood,–because he had spoken obscurely–saying accordingly that the bread is called the body of Christ when really it is the sacrament of the body of Christ which was crucified; just as that sacrifice which is performed by the hands of the priest is called the passion of Christ, not in the actuality of the fact, but in the mystery of the symbol; and as "Faith is called the sacrament of faith."

PART II

This is a sufficient reply to heretics and the objections of those who deny that the true body of Christ is on the altar, and that the bread is changed into the body or the wine into blood by the mystical consecration, saying: "Who would dare to eat his Lord? Who also would dare to say that the body of Christ is daily formed of matter or substance, which were not the flesh of the Virgin?"

II. *Of the testimonies of the Saints by which he proves that the true body of Christ is on the altar.*

These and similar objections are made by those who seek eagerly the natural law in the divine mystery; whose perfidy the following testimonies reveal. For the Truth says: "Take ye, this is my body." Also, Ambrose: "If the prayer of Elijah had such power that it could bring down fire from heaven; will not the prayer of Christ be of sufficient power to change substances? Of the creation of the whole world we read: 'That he spoke, and they were made,' etc. Therefore the Word that is, the Son, who could create out of nothing that which was not, can not he change those things which are, into those which they were not? For it is not less to create than to change things into a new character." Also: "If we are looking for the regular order, a woman is wont to bring forth offspring from union with a man. Therefore it is evident that the Virgin brought forth outside the order of nature; and this body which we produce is from the Virgin. Why therefore do you seek the order of nature in the body of Christ since he himself was born of the Virgin, outside the order of nature?"—Also: "Before the benediction, another form is mentioned, after consecration the body is signified. Before consecration another thing is mentioned, after consecration, blood is named. You say 'Amen,' that is, 'it is true.' What the words say, let the emotions feel." Also, Augustine: "In the forms of bread and wine which we see, we honor invisible things, that is, flesh and blood; nor do we regard these two forms, as we regarded them before consecration, when we confess faithfully that before consecration they were bread and wine which nature formed; but after consecration, the flesh and blood of Christ which the benediction consecrated." Also, Ambrose: "Bread is used on the altar, before the sacred words, when the consecration takes place, the bread becomes the flesh of Christ. But how can that which is bread, be the body of Christ? By the consecration, which is performed in the words of Christ." The same: "If there is such power in the words of the Lord, that things should begin to be, which before were not; how much more can they bring it about that things which were should continue to be, and be changed into something else? And so that which was bread before the consecration, now after the consecration is the body of Christ, because the words of Christ change the creature; and so bread becomes the body of Christ, and wine mixed with water in the chalice becomes the blood by the consecration of the heavenly words." Likewise, Augustine: "Just as the true flesh of Christ was created by the holy Spirit without sexual intercourse, so by the same Spirit the same body and blood of Christ are consecrated from the substance of bread and wine. The body of Christ is both the truth and the figure: the truth, inasmuch as the body and blood of Christ are made from the substances of bread and wine by the virtue of the holy Spirit; while the figure is that which is outwardly perceived." Likewise, Eusebius Emissenus: "The invisible priest by his word and secret power changes the visible creatures into the substance of his body and blood."—From these and from many other statements, it is plain that the true body and blood of Christ are on the altar; nay rather the entire Christ is there under both forms, and the substance of the bread is changed into his body, and the substance of the wine into his blood.

* * * * *

PART II

V. *Whether Christ be sacrificed on the altar daily, and whether what is done by the priests is a sacrifice.*

After these considerations we are asked if what the priest does is properly called a sacrifice or an immolation, and if Christ is daily sacrificed, or was only sacrificed once.–To this question we can reply briefly, that that which is offered and consecrated by the priest is called a sacrifice and oblation, because it is a memorial and a representation of the true sacrifice and of the holy immolation made on the altar of the cross. And Christ died once on the cross, where he was sacrificed in his own person; but daily he is sacrificed in the sacrament, because in the sacrament a remembrance is made of that which was done once. Wherefore Augustine: "We are certain that Christ rising again from the dead, dieth now no more,' etc.; yet, lest we forget what was once done, it is done again every year in our memory, that is, as often as Easter is celebrated. How often, do you suppose, does Christ die? But the anniversary remembrance only represents what was done aforetime, and moves us, as if we should see the Lord on the cross." The same: "Christ was once sacrificed in his own person, and yet daily is he sacrificed in the sacrament; which is to be understood thus, that in the manifestation of his body and in the distinction of his members once only he hung on the cross, offering himself to God the Father as an efficient victim of redemption, for those, that is, whom he had predestined." Likewise Ambrose: "In Christ the victim sufficient unto salvation was once offered. What therefore do we do? Do we not offer every day? Even if we offer daily, we do it as a remembrance of his death; and the victim is one, not many. How one, and not many? Because Christ was sacrificed only once. But our sacrifice is a copy of his; the same and always the same is offered, therefore this is the same sacrifice; otherwise it would be said, because it is offered in many places: 'Are there many Christs?' No, but one Christ is everywhere, existing here complete and there complete: just as that which is everywhere offered is one body, so also is it one sacrifice. Christ offered the victim; and we offer the same now, but what we do is a remembrance of his sacrifice." "Nor is it repeated because of a weakness in itself, for it makes man perfect, but because of our weakness, because we sin daily."—From these quotations we gather that what is done on the altar is also called a sacrifice; and Christ was offered once long ago, and is offered daily, but in one way then, in another now; and also we are shown what is the virtue of this sacrament, remission, that is, of venial sins, and the perfecting of virtue.

VI. *Of the cause of its institution.*

For this sacrament was instituted for two reasons; for the increase of virtue, that is, of charity, and as a medicine for daily infirmity. Wherefore Ambrose: "If as often as the blood of Christ is shed, it is shed for the remission of sins; I ought always to receive it; I who continually sin, ought continually to have the medicine." Also Augustine: "This oblation is repeated daily, although Christ suffered once, because daily we commit sins, without which mortal infirmity cannot live. And because we fall daily, daily is Christ sacrificed mystically for us." "For he gave us this sacrament of salvation, so that, because we sin daily, and he cannot die again, we might obtain remission through this sacrament. Daily he is truly eaten and drunk, but he remains whole and alive." Likewise: "It is called the mystery of faith, because you ought to believe that upon it our salvation rests."

If moreover anyone asks whether we should daily communicate, hear what St. Augustine says of it: "Daily," he says, "to receive the Eucharist, is a practice I neither praise, nor condemn; however I urge that persons should communicate every Lord's day. But if the mind is in the disposition to sin, I say that it is rather burdened than purified by the receiving of the Eucharist. And although anyone be grieved with sin; if he does not have the will to sin in the future, and make satisfaction with tears and prayers, let him approach secure, but I say this of him who is not burdened by mortal sins."—"If not more frequently, at least three times a year let men communicate, unless by chance someone is hindered by crimes: at Easter, that is, and Pentecost, and at Christmas." "Let all therefore communicate, who do not wish to be outside the doors of the Church."

DISTINCTION XIV

PART I

I. *Of penance, and why it is called penance.*

Next we must discuss penance. Penance is needful to those who are far from God, that they may come near. For it is, as Jerome says, "the second plank after shipwreck"; because if anyone be sinning sullies the robe of innocence received in baptism, he can restore it by the remedy of penance. The first plank is baptism, where the old man is laid aside and the new put on; the second, penance, by which after a fall we rise again, while the old state which had returned is disdained, and the new one which had been lost is resumed. Those who have lapsed after baptism can be restored by penance, but not by baptism. A man is allowed to do penance often, but not to be baptized often. Baptism is called only a sacrament, but penance is called both a sacrament and virtue of the mind. For there is an inner penance, and an outer: the outer is the sacrament, the inner is the virtue of the mind; and both are for the sake of salvation and justification.—But whether all outer penance is a sacrament, or if not all, what is to be classed under this name, we shall investigate later.—With penance began the preaching of John who said: "Do penance, for the kingdom of heaven is at hand." "And what the herald taught, the Truth afterwards preached, beginning his discourse with penance."

II. *What penance is, and what it is to do penance.*

"It is called penance from punishment, for by it a man punishes the sins which he has committed. The virtue of penance is conceived in fear." Wherefore Isaiah: "By the fear of thee, oh Lord, have we conceived, and have brought forth the spirit of salvation." "Moreover penance is, as Ambrose says, to lament past evils, and not commit again what must be lamented." Likewise Gregory: "To repent is to bewail the sins committed previously, and not to commit what must be bewailed. For he who deplores some, so that he may commit others, is either as yet ignorant of how to do penance, or he dissembles. For what value is there if he bewails his sins of luxury, and yet pants with the fever of avarice?"

PART II

Some persons clinging vehemently to these words, contend that the truly penitent cannot again sin to condemnation; and if he does sin grievously, he did not earlier do true penance. This view they even defend by other testimonies. For Isidore says: "He is a scoffer and not a penitent, who still does that of which he repents. Nor does he seem to desire to call on God humbly, but to mock him proudly: 'a dog is returned to his vomit, and the penitent to his sin.' Many shed their tears without ceasing, and do not cease to sin. I observe that some have tears for penance and have not the effect of penance, because in the inconstancy of their minds they now shed tears in remembrance of sin; now when the habit reasserts itself, they commit again the things which they bewailed. Isaiah says concerning sinners: "Wash yourselves, be clean." He is both washed and is clean who both laments the past, and does not again commit the deeds he has bewailed. He is washed, and is not clean, who laments the things he does, and does not forsake them, and after his tears repeats the things which he has wept over." Also Augustine: "Penance is vain, which subsequent guilt contaminates entirely. Lamentations are of no avail, if sins are repeated. It is of no value to ask pardon for sins, and repeat the sins afresh." Also Gregory: "He who laments what he has committed, yet does not abandon it, subjects himself to more severe punishment." Also Ambrose: "There are men who think that penance should be done repeatedly, who luxuriate in Christ. For if they did penance truly in Christ, they would not think that they needed to repeat it afterwards; because, just as there is one baptism, so there is one penance."—These and many other authorities they use for the support of their opinion. But

Ambrose says: "This is true penance, to cease from sin." And again: "It is of great profit to renounce error." "For to free and purify souls steeped in vice is the work of perfect virtue and heavenly grace."

And therefore it may be certainly defined: penance is the virtue or grace by which we lament and hate the evils committed, with the purpose of amendment and do not wish to commit further what must be lamented; because true penance is to grieve in spirit and to hate the offences.—Wherefore the preceding words: "to do penance is to bewail what has been done and not to commit what must be bewailed," may be thus rightly understood, that they refer not to different times, but to the same time, so that at the time a man bewails the sins committed, he does not commit in will or in deed what he must bewail; this is implied in the following words: "For whoever thus deplores some things," etc. Hence Augustine says: "We must beware, lest anyone suppose that he may daily perpetrate these heinous offences, and redeem them by almsgiving, who do such things 'shall not possess the kingdom of God.' For life must be changed to better, and by almsgiving God may be propitiated for past sins, but not bought in any way, so as to allow wrongs to be committed with impunity. For to no one did he give freedom to sin, even if by lamenting he wiped out sins committed, when the proper satisfaction was not neglected." Also Pope Pius: "It is of no profit to a man to fast and pray, and to do the other acts of religion, unless he recalls his mind from iniquity."—Whoever therefore so recalls his mind from evil, that he laments what was committed, and does not wish to commit what must be lamented, and does not neglect to make satisfaction, does penance truly. Nor can it be said that it was not true penance, if afterwards, not purposely, but accidentally, or through infirmity, he may perhaps sin. But he is a scoffer and not a penitent who laments what he has committed, in such a way that he does not cease to commit in word and deed what he has lamented. He who repeats after tears what he has bewailed, is washed for the time being, but is not clean, that is, the cleansing is not sufficient for him unto salvation, because it is momentary, not permanent. And also this statement: "Penance is in vain, which succeeding sin stains," is thus to be interpreted: It is in vain, that is, wanting in the fruit of that penance, which succeeding sin stains. For the fruit of penance is the avoiding of gehenna and the attainment of glory. And that penance and other preceding good deeds are annihilated by the succeeding sin, so that they do not obtain the reward which they deserved when they were done, and which they would have had if sin had not followed. But if penance be done also for that following sin, both the penance which preceded and the other previous good deeds revive; but only those which sprang from charity. For those deeds alone live, which are done in charity; and on that account if they are annihilated by following sins, they may revive by subsequent penance. But those deeds which are done without charity are brought forth dead and void; and therefore they are not able to revive by penance. Similarly this saying is to be understood: "Lamentations avail nothing," etc.; and this: "Nothing is able," etc. For if sins are repeated, preceding lamentation avails nothing for salvation or for pardon in the end, because nothing is left of the cleanness of life; because either the sins which have been remitted return, as some think when they are repeated, or if they do not return, and even though they are forgiven, the man becomes as guilty and unclean on account of ingratitude, since he is still involved in sins to be expiated, as if the sins already forgiven returned. This question however, that is, whether sins return, we shall treat more fully afterwards. Likewise it avails nothing for obtaining salvation, or for having cleanness of life, to ask pardon for evils done, and then to repeat afresh the evils.—In this way must be understood that which Augustine says elsewhere: "Penance is a sort of vengeance of the one who grieves, always punishing in himself what he grieves to have committed." And below: "We should grieve daily for sin, as the very nature of the word declares. For to do penance is to do punishment, so that one may always punish in himself by vengeance what he committed by sinning. Now he does punishment, who always avenges what he laments that he has committed." "What remains to us, except to lament in life? for where grief is ended, penance also is lacking. But if penance is ended, what is left of pardon? Let a man praise and hope for grace only as long as he is sustained by penance. For the Lord says: 'Go, and do not desire to sin any more.' He did not say, do not sin, but let not the will to sin rise in you. How will this commandment be observed, unless grief be continually preserved in penance? But let a man always grieve, and rejoice in grief; and let it not be enough that he should grieve, but let him grieve from faith, and let him grieve that he has not always grieved."

Of the penance of the perfect, sufficing even unto salvation, we must understand what I said above, that is: "Penance is a vengeance always punishing what one has committed"; and other things of the same sort. But this statement: "If penance is finished, nothing is left of pardon," may be received in two ways. For if according to the belief of some persons, sins which have been forgiven return, it is easy to understand that nothing of pardon is left; because the sins forgiven are again repeated. For just as one who is manumitted from slavery into freedom, for a time is truly free, and yet on account of an offense is afterward returned to slavery; so also sins are truly remitted in penance, and yet on account of the repetition of the offense they return again.—But if the sins are said not to return, it may reasonably be said also that nothing of pardon is left, not because forgiven sins are imputed again, but because on account of ingratitude the man becomes as guilty and unclean, as if they did return.

* * * * *

IV. *That sins are forgiven frequently by penance.*

But that penance is done not once only, but is frequently repeated, and by it frequently pardon is again afforded; is proved by many testimonies of the saints. For Augustine says, writing against certain heretics who asserted that penance was useful only once for those who sin after baptism: "The faithless still assail us, who know more than they should, not sober, but out of bounds; they say: 'And if penance has value for those who sin once after baptism, yet repeated it is not of value to those who sin often; otherwise remission would be an encouragement to sin.' For they say: 'Who would not always sin, if he could always be restored through penance?' For they call the Lord an encourager of evil, if he always aids sinners; and says that sins are pleasing to him, for which grace is always at hand. But they err. For it is evident that sins much displease him, who is always ready to destroy them; if he loved them, he would not always destroy them." The same to Macedonius: "To such lengths does the iniquity of men sometimes go, even after penance has been performed, and reconciliation to the altar, they commit either similar or more grievous sins. And yet God causes his sun to rise even upon them, nor does he grant less freely than before the most abundant gifts of life and salvation. And although an opportunity for penance is not granted them in the Church, yet God does not forget his patience towards them. If anyone of their number should say to you: Tell me whether it avails anything for a future life, if in this life I have contempt for the most enticing allurements of pleasure, if I distress myself more vehemently than before by doing penance, if I weep more copiously, if I live better, if I help the poor more abundantly, if I am aflame more ardently with charity; who of you would be so foolish as to say to this man: These things will profit you nothing in the future? Go, at least enjoy the pleasantness of this life. May God avert such monstrous and sacrilegious madness." Also John Chrysostom, on the restoration of the fallen: "Such, believe me, such is the pity of God towards men: never does he spurn penance, if it be offered him sincerely and in simplicity; even if a man reach the extreme of wickedness, and wishes then to return to the life of virtue; he receives him freely and embraces him, and does everything until he brings him back to his former state. And what is still more excellent and more extraordinary, even if one is not able to perform the whole order of rendering satisfaction, he does not reject a penance, however small and done in however short a time; he accepts even that, nor does he suffer the reward of conversion, however humble, to be lost." This same view may also be supported by examples. For David, by penance, obtained pardon at the same time for adultery and murder; and yet afterwards he sinned grievously in the numbering of the people, as was shown by the multitude of the people destroyed. "But this is admirable, that he offered himself to the angel who smote the people saying, 'Let they hand be turned upon me, and upon my father's house.' When he had done this, he was immediately judged worthy of sacrifice, though he had been judged unworthy of absolution. Nor is it strange if by so great an oblation of himself, for the people, he obtained pardon of sin for himself; since Moses by offering himself for the error of the people, removed their sins."

From these and from many other testimonies it is clearly shown, that by penance not only once, but often, we rise from our sins, and that true penance may be done repeatedly. "For if we sin wilfully," as says the Apostle, "There is now left no sacrifice for sins," that is, because once only must Christ have to suffer; nor is a second baptism left; but there is left a second penance, and a third, and after that another, as John Chrysostom says on this passage: "It must be known," he says, "that some arise at this point doing away with penance on the pretext of these words; just as if by penance a sinner after a fall could not rise a second time, and a third, and after that. But indeed in this passage the apostle does not exclude penance nor propitiation, which is often accomplished by penance; but a second baptism, and a (second) sacrifice."

* * * * *

DISTINCTION XXIII

I. *Of the sacrament of extreme unction.*

"Beside the preceding, there is also another sacrament, that is, the unction of the sick, which is administered at the end of life, with oil consecrated by the bishop." "And there are three kinds of unction."

II. *Of the three kinds of unction.*

"For there is the unction, which is performed with the chrism, which is called the principal unction, because through it especially the Paraclete is given. Wherefore also on account of the abundance of grace it contains two liquids mixed, namely, oil and balsam, the oil of conscience, the balsam of good report. And it is called 'Chrism' in Greek, 'unction' in Latin. But not all oil sanctified for unction is called chrism, but only that which is mixed with balsam, with which the heads of kings and bishops are anointed, and with which the priest anoints the baptized on the head, and the bishop anoints those who are to be confirmed on the brow with the laying on of hands. And there is another unction with which catechumens and neophytes are anointed on the breast and between the shoulders, when they receive baptism. But the third unction is that which is called the oil of the sick; and of this we will now treat."

III. *By whom this sacrament was instituted.*

"This sacrament of the unction of the sick is said to have been instituted by the apostles. For James says: 'Is any sick among you? Let him call in the priests of the Church, and let them pray over him, anointing him with oil in the name of the Lord, and the Lord shall raise him up; and if he be in sins, they shall be forgiven him.' In this passage we are shown that the sacrament was instituted for a double purpose, namely for the remission of sins, and for the relief of bodily infirmity. Wherefore it is plain that he who receives this unction faithfully and devoutly, is relieved both in body and in soul, provided it is expedient that he be relieved in both. But if perhaps it is not expedient for him to have bodily health, he acquires in this sacrament that health which is of the soul." "And as in the other sacraments, so also in this, the 'sacrament' is one thing, and the 'thing of the sacrament' another. The 'sacrament' is the outer unction itself, the 'thing of the sacrament' the inner unction, which is accomplished by the remission of sins and the increase of virtues. And if this sacrament is omitted from contempt or neglect, it is dangerous and damnable."

IV. *Of the repetition of this sacrament.*

Some persons ask whether this sacrament can be repeated, since baptism and some other sacraments when once received are not to be repeated. Augustine says, "The sacrament must not be repeated, and injury must not be done to the sacrament"; but he says this where he treats of the sacraments of baptism, of confirmation and of ordination. Wherefore it does not seem that this rule is to be accepted generally, but only for the sacraments of baptism, of confirmation and of ordination, which must never be repeated, because baptism, confirmation and ordination are given once for all and not more frequently. But the sacraments of the altar, and of penance and of marriage are evidently often repeated; for the sacrament of the body is often received, penance is frequently done, marriage is repeatedly contracted. Why therefore cannot unction be similarly repeated? If the disease does not return, the medicine is not to be repeated; but if the disease cannot be checked, why ought the medicine be prohibited? Even as prayer can be repeated, so it seems unction can also be repeated; for James in that passage mentions both, and both work together to bring relief of body and soul. Why therefore do some persons deny that unction can be repeated on one who is sick, in order to obtain again the health of mind and body, when the same prayer may be often repeated for the same infirmity?—But some wish it understood that the whole sacrament should not be repeated, namely everything which belongs to the sacrament, saying that some sacraments can be often received, but some not; and that those which are often received, are not completely repeated, as the sacrament of the altar and of unction; for although they are often received, yet because the same host is not blessed again, nor the same oil, the sacrament is not repeated with injury.—But someone will say: "in this sense baptism also is not repeated, even if one is frequently baptized, since the same water is not blessed again."—"But it is one thing," they say, the blessing of the water, by which baptism is conferred, another the blessing of the bread and oil. For baptism can be celebrated even in unblessed water, because the blessing is only for reverence and decorum, not for the virtue of the sacrament. But the body of Christ cannot be made, except of consecrated bread; nor can unction be performed, except with oil consecrated by the bishop; and therefore this sanctification seems to be a part of the virtue of the sacrament. In marriage also, a man is blessed only once, not oftener.—"For he is blessed," as Ambrose says, "with his first and not with his second wife. If therefore when you say that a sacrament must not be repeated, nor injury done it, you apply the meaning of the term to the sanctification of the 'thing' by which the sacrament is completed, the rule is generally true of every sacrament. But if you apply it to the receiving of the 'sacrament,' it is true of some that they are not repeated or frequently received, but it is not true of others, because they are frequently received like this sacrament of unction, which is often repeated in almost every Church.

DISTINCTION XXIV

PART I

I. *Of ecclesiastical orders, how many they are.*

Now we come to the consideration of holy ordination. There are seven grades or orders of spiritual office, as is clearly taught us in the words of the holy Fathers, and is shown by the example of our head, that is Jesus Christ, who performed in his own person the duties of them all, and left the same orders to be observed in his body which is the Church.

II. *Why there are seven.*

And there are seven on account of the sevenfold grace of the holy Spirit, and those who do not participate in this grace, enter the ecclesiastical grades unworthily. But when men in whose minds the seven-fold grace of the holy Spirit is diffused, enter the ecclesiastical orders, they are believed to receive a fuller grace in the very promotion to the spiritual rank.

III. *What kind of men are to be taken into the clergy.*

"And such clergy are to be elected to the spiritual ministry, as can worthily perform the Lord's sacraments. For it is better for the Lord to have few ministers who can worthily do the work of God, than many useless ones, who bring a heavy burden on him who ordained them." For it is fitting that such be ministers of Christ as are adorned with the sevenfold grace of the holy Spirit; from whose doctrine and form of conversation the same grace may be transmitted to others, lest they trample the celestial pearls of spiritual words and divine ministrations under the feet of a vile life. Now in the sacrament of the sevenfold Spirit there are seven ecclesiastical ranks, that is: doorkeepers, readers, exorcists, acolytes, subdeacons, deacons, priests; but all are called clergy, that is, chosen.

* * * * *

XI. *Of presbyters.*

The seventh order is that of presbyters. "Presbyter in Greek is senior in Latin. They are called presbyters not only because of their years or advanced age, but on account of the honor and dignity which they receive"; "for they ought to excel among the people by the prudence of their ways and the maturity of their conversation, as it is written: 'Old age is venerable, not for its length nor for the number of years computed. For it is the thoughts of a man that are hoary, and an immaculate life is old age.' " "Presbyters are also called priests, because they give what is sacred; yet, although they are priests, they have not the crown of the pontificate as bishops have, because they do not sign the forehead with the chrism nor give the Paraclete, which functions are shown by a reading of the Acts of the Apostles to belong to bishops only." Wherefore also among men of old times bishops and presbyters were the same, because it is the name of a dignity, not of an age. "The name priest (*sacerdos*) is composed from the Greek and the Latin, that is *sacrum dans,* or *sacer dux.* For as a king (*rex*) is called from ruling (*regendo*), so a priest from sanctifying (*sanctificando*); for he consecrates and sanctifies. A priest is also called antistes from the fact that he stands before (*ante stat*), for he is first in the order of the Church." "Moreover the duty of a presybter is to perform the sacrament of the body and blood of the Lord on the altar of God, to say prayers and to bless the gifts of God"; when he is ordained he has his hands anointed, that he may know he has received the grace of consecrating and that he ought to extend the deeds of charity to all. He also receives the stole which falls on both sides, because he ought to be protected by the arms of justice against both adversity and prosperity. He also receives the chalice with the wine and the paten with the host, that he may thereby know he receives the power of offering "sacrifices acceptable to God."–This order had its origin with the sons of Aaron. For God instituted high-priests and lesser priests through Moses, who at God's command anointed Aaron to be high-priest and his sons lesser priests. Christ also first "chose twelve disciples, whom he likewise called Apostles"; whose place is now occupied by the greater bishops in the Church. Next he appointed also seventy-two other disciples, whose place in the Church is filled by the presbyters. But one among the apostles became chief, Peter, whose vicar and successor is the Supreme Pontiff, wherefore he is called "apostolic" and is also known as Pope (Papa), that is, father of fathers. And the Apostle, when he wrote to Timothy, showed what manner of man ought to be elected presbyter; for there he means presbyter when he uses the name of "bishop."—And Christ performed this office when he "offered himself on the altar of the cross." When he was both priest and victim, and when after supper he changed the bread and wine into his own body and blood.—Behold, we have spoken briefly of the seven grades of the Church, and have mentioned what the duty of each is.

XII. *Which are called holy orders.*

And although all orders are spiritual and holy, yet the canons rightly ordain that two should be called holy orders, namely the diaconate and the presbyterate; because "the primitive church is said to have had only these," and we have the command of the Apostle for these only. "For the Apostle ordained bishops and presbyters in each city"; we read also that Levites were ordained by the Apostles, of whom the greatest was the blessed Stephen; but the Church established subdeacons and acolytes for herself as time went on.

XIII. *Why it is called order.*

Now if we are asked what that is which we here call order; we can say rightly that it is a sign, that is, something sacred, by which spiritual power and office are delivered to one ordained. Therefore the spiritual marking when the bestowal of power occurs, is called the order or grade. And these orders are called sacraments, because in the reception of them, a sacred thing, that is, grace is received, which is symbolized by the procedure at that time.

XIV. *Of the names of the dignities or offices.*

And there are other names, not of orders, but of dignities or of offices. Bishop is the name both of a dignity and of an office.

XV. *Of the bishop.*

"Now the word episcopate comes from the fact that he who is made bishop superintends, that is, has the care of those under him. For *scopein* in Greek is to superintend (*intendere*) in Latin; *episcopi* in Greek are in Latin overseers (*speculatores*). For the overseer (*speculator*) is placed over the Church, and is so called from the fact that he oversees and watches the customs and life of the people under him."

XVI. *Of the bishop.*

"The bishop is the head of the priests, as it were a way for those who follow; and he is also called the 'high-priest.' For he makes the Levites and priests, he assigns all the ecclesiastical orders."

XVII. *Of the four-fold order of bishops.*

"And the order of bishops is four-fold, that is, patriarchs, archbishops, metropolitans and bishops. *Patriarcha* in Greek means the chief of the fathers, because the patriarch holds the first, that is the apostolic place, like the Roman, the Antiochian, the Alexandrian"; but the chief of all is the Roman. "The *archbishop* is the head of the bishops; for *archos* in Greek is head (*princeps*) in Latin. But metropolitans are so called from the importance of their cities; for they preside over single provinces; and the other priests are subject to their authority and doctrine. For the care of the whole province is committed to the bishops themselves. And all the orders designated above are called bishops."—Note, that evidently primates were meant above by the name archbishops, and by metropolitans, those whom we now call archbishops. "Also the distinction between these seems to have been introduced by Gentiles who called some of their flamens simply flamens, other archflamens, others chief-flamens." "For the priests of the Gentiles were called flamens, because they wore on their heads a felt cap, on which there was a short rod, with wool upon it, and when they could not wear it for the heat, they bound a thread only about their heads. For it was wrong for them to take their places with bare heads. Wherefore they are called flamens or filamines from the thread (*fils*) which they wore. But on feast-days they laid aside the thread and assumed the cap for the dignity of the priesthood.

* * * * *

DISTINCTION XXVI

I. *Of the sacrament of marriage.*

"Although the other sacraments took their rise after sin and on account of sin, we read that the sacrament of marriage was instituted by the Lord even before sin, yet not as a remedy, but as a duty." For the Scripture relates in Genesis that a sleep was sent upon Adam and one of his ribs was taken, and from it a woman formed, and that the man understanding in spirit for what purpose the woman was made, said prophetically after his trance: "This is now bone of my bones and flesh of my flesh; for this reason shall a man leave his father and his mother, and shall cleave unto his wife, and they shall be two in one flesh."

II. *Of its institution and purpose.*

Now the institution of marriage is two-fold: one was instituted before sin in paradise as a duty, that there might be a blameless couch and honorable nuptials; as a result of which they might conceive without passion and bring forth without pain; the other was instituted after sin outside paradise for a remedy, to prevent unlawful desires; the first, that nature might be multiplied; the second, that nature might be protected, and sin repressed. For even before sin God said: "Increase and multiply"; and again after sin, when most men had been destroyed by the Deluge. But Augustine testifies that before sin marriage was instituted for a duty, and after sin allowed for a remedy, when he says: "What is a duty for the sound is a remedy for the sick." For the infirmity of incontinence which exists in the flesh that is dead through sin, is protected by honorable marriage lest it fall into the ruin of vice. If the first men had not sinned, they and their descendants would have united without the incentive of the flesh and the heat of passion; and as any good deed deserves reward, so their union would have been good and worthy of reward. But because on account of sin the law of deadly concupiscence has beset our members, without which there is no carnal union, an evil union is reprehensible unless it be excused by the blessings of marriage.

III. *When marriage was contracted by command and when by permission.*

The first institution was commanded, the second permitted. For we learn from the Apostle, that marriage was permitted to the human race for the purpose of preventing fornication. But this permission, because it does not select better things, is a remedy, not a reward; if anyone rejects it, he will deserve judgment of death. An act which is allowed by permission is voluntary, not necessary; otherwise the one who did not do it would be a transgressor. And we can rightly understand that it was said to the first men as a command before sin: "Increase and multiply"; and they were bound by the command even after sin, until the multiplication was achieved, after which marriage was contracted by permission. So after the deluge when nearly the whole human race was wiped out, the sons of Noah were commanded: "Increase and multiply"; but when man had multiplied, marriage was contracted by permission, not by command.

IV. *In what ways the permission should be received.*

Now permission is received in various ways, as concession, as remission, as toleration. And there is toleration in the New Testament, for lesser good deeds and lesser evils; among the lesser good deeds is marriage, which does not deserve a palm, but is a remedy; among the lesser evils, that is, the venial ones, is a union which is due to incontinency. For such a marriage is permitted, that is, is allowed; and such a marriage, that is such a union, is tolerated, that is suffered, in so far as it is not forbidden.

V. *That marriage is good.*

Now there have been some heretics who denounced marriage, who were called Tatians. "These condemn marriage altogether and make it equal to fornication and other corruptions, and they do not receive into their number any male or female living in marriage." "But that marriage is good is proved not only by the fact that we read that the Lord instituted marriage between our first parents, but also that Christ was present at a marriage in Cana of Galilee and commended it by a miracle, changing the water into wine; and that afterwards he forbade a man to put away his wife, save for the cause of fornication. The Apostle also says: 'A virgin does not sin if she marries.' It is therefore clear that marriage is a good thing," otherwise it would not be a sacrament; for a sacrament is a sacred sign.

VI. *Of what thing marriage is a sacrament.*

Since therefore marriage is a sacrament, it is also a sacred sign and of a sacred thing, namely, of the union of Christ and the Church, as the Apostle says: It is written, he says: "A man shall leave father and mother and shall cleave to his wife, and they shall be two in one flesh. This is a great sacrament, but I speak of Christ and of the Church." For as between husband and wife there is union in the harmony of their spirits and in the joining of their bodies, so the Church is joined to Christ by will and nature in that she wills the same as he, and that he himself assumed the form of the nature of man. Therefore the bride is united to the bridegroom spiritually and physically, that is by love and by a conformity to nature. And the symbol of both these unions is in marriage; for the harmony of the husband and wife signifies the spiritual union of Christ and the Church which takes place through love; and the union of the sexes signifies the union which takes place through a conformity to nature.

Hence it is that some doctors have said that a woman does not belong in marriage who does not know union in the flesh. For Augustine says: "There is no doubt that a woman does not belong in marriage, in whose case it is shown that there has been no sexual union." Also Pope Leo: "Since the bond of marriage was so instituted from the beginning that without sexual union it does not contain the sacrament of Christ and the Church; there is not doubt that a woman does not belong in marriage in whose case it is shown that there has been no mystery of marriage." Also Augustine: "Marriage is not complete without sexual union."–If one accepts this according to the superficial meaning of the words, he is led into such error as to say that without carnal union, matrimony cannot be contracted, and that there was no marriage between Mary and Joseph, or that it was not perfect; to think which is a sin. For it was the more holy and perfect, as it was the more free from carnal acts. But the passages above are to be understood in this way, not that a woman does not belong in marriage, in whose case there is no sexual union; but that she does not belong in a marriage which contains the express and full symbol of the union of Christ and the Church. For her marriage represents the union of Christ and the Church, which is in love, but not that which is in a conformity to nature. There is therefore in her marriage a type of the union of Christ and the Church, but only of that union in which the Church is united to Christ by love, not of that in which through Christ's assumption of the flesh the members are joined to the head; but her marriage is not for that reason less holy, because as Augustine says, "in marriage the sanctity of the sacrament is more important than the fruitfulness of the womb." Marriage is also a sign of the spiritual union and affection of souls, by which husbands and wives ought to be united. Wherefore the Apostle says: "Husbands, love your wives as your own bodies."

St. Bonaventure
1217-1274

Bonaventure was born near Viterbo, Italy, the son of a well-to-do physician. He went to Paris around 1234 and was deeply impressed with the Franciscan teacher, Alexander of Hales. He joined the Franciscans himself, probably in 1243. In 1248 he became a bachelor of Scripture, lecturing especially on Luke's Gospel. After commenting on the Sentences *of Peter Lombard from 1250 to 1252, he received the licentiate and doctorate, probably in 1253, a time when the strife between the masters and the mendicants was coming to a head.*

In 1257 at a chapter held in Rome he was elected general of the Franciscans. He devoted himself vigorously to correcting abuses and resolving conflicts for the next decade and a half. In 1273 Pope Gregory X made him cardinal bishop of Albano, and for the final months of his life he worked as a papal legate, preparing for and taking part in the Second Council of Lyons. He died unexpectedly on July 15, 1274, as the fourth session of that Council was about to begin. A brief notice in the record of the time states simply: "At the funeral there was much sorrow and tears; for the Lord had given him this grace, that all who saw him were filled with an immense love for him." He was declared a saint in 1482.

Bonaventure's Commentaries on the Four Books of Sentences of Peter Lombard *constitute over half of his written works. They cover the entire range of technical theology as practiced at that time. It is his next longest work, however,* The Breviloquium, *that is drawn upon here. It consists of a prologue and seven parts, embracing the full spectrum of theological concerns, but in a more abbreviated form. It has been described as more "a canticle of praise than a manual of theology," an exposition that has few, if any, counterparts on the medieval scene.*

The particular achievement and fascination of Bonaventure is his success in having removed any conflict between the vision of the mystic and the logic of the theologian. In realizing that reason and faith are not the same, he does not find it necessary to pair them off as enemies, but looks for the necessary harmony that must exist between two instruments leading to one truth.

It can certainly be maintained that this is not Bonaventure at his best. The shortcomings of the scholastic approach to the sacraments have been recognized and remedied to a degree by the liturgical renewal of our day. But the effort must be made to appreciate why a more positive and dynamic understanding did not develop in an age that otherwise saw such progress in Christian theology. Each age, it seems, has its own insights and its own blind spots; honesty requires that one try to acknowledge both of these phenomena in evaluating the past. If the Church today goes beyond the limited perspective on the sacraments found here in Bonaventure, it also proclaims insistently that he attained in spectacular fashion the Reality which all of the liturgy is meant to signify and, by signifying, accomplish.

THE BREVILOQUIUM

PART VI–ON THE SACRAMENTAL REMEDY

CHAPTER I

ON THE ORIGIN OF THE SACRAMENTS

Now that we have considered the Trinity of God, the creation of the world, the corruption of sin, the incarnation of the Word, and the grace of the Holy Spirit, there remains in the sixth place to study the sacramental remedy. Seven points are to be developed in this regard: the origin, diversity, division, institution, administration, and renewal of the sacraments, and finally the integrity of each one in particular.

2. Concerning the origin of the sacraments, the following must be held. They are sensible signs divinely instituted as remedies through which "beneath the cloak of material species God's power operates in a hidden manner"; so that, "being likenesses, they represent; from their mode of institution, they signify; being made holy, they are means of conferring a certain spiritual grace" by which the soul is healed of its weaknesses due to vice. And it is to this as to their final end that they are principally ordained; but as subordinate ends, they also procure humility, knowledge, and the practice of virtue.

3. This should be understood as follows. Because the restoring Principle, Christ crucified, the incarnate Word, governs all things most wisely, being God, and heals them most mercifully, being incarnate as God: therefore He must so restore and heal the diseased human race as to conform with the needs of the patient, of the disease, of its occasion, and of its cure. He Himself, the Physician, is the incarnate Word, that is, God invisible existing in a visible nature. Man, the patient, is not pure spirit, nor is he flesh alone, but a spirit in mortal flesh. The disease is original sin, which infects the mind through ignorance, and the flesh through concupiscence. Although the

origin of this sin was principally the consent of reason, its occasion was brought about by the bodily senses.

Now, that a medicine should fit all these requirements, not only did it have to be spiritual, but it also had to possess something of the nature of sensible signs, in order that, as sensible objects had been the occasion of the fall of the soul, so also they would become the occasion of its rising. But because in themselves the sensible signs [of the sacraments] cannot produce any effect in the order of grace, although they are by nature distant representations of grace, it was necessary that the Author of grace *institute* [appoint] them for the sake of signifying and *bless* them for the sake of sanctifying; so that through natural similitude they would represent, through conjoined institution they would signify, and through superadded benediction they would sanctify and prepare for grace, by which our soul is healed and cured.

4. Again, because curative grace is not granted to the proud, the unbelieving, or the slothful, it was fitting that God gave signs which not only would confer sanctification and grace, and thus healing, but would also teach through their signification, humble when received, and prompt to action through their diversity. So that, sloth being removed from the concupiscible power by prompting, ignorance from the rational power by teaching, and pride from the irascible power by humbling, the whole soul would become open to healing by the grace of the Holy Spirit, which forms us once more, as regards these three powers, in the likeness of the Trinity and of Christ.

5. Finally, because it is through these sensible signs divinely instituted that the grace of the Holy Spirit is received, and within them that those who approach discover it: therefore these sacraments are called "vessels of grace" and likewise its cause; not that grace is substantially present in them or causally effected by them—for grace dwells only in the soul and is infused by none but God—but that, by divine command, we are to draw the grace of our healing from Christ the supreme Physician through and by these sensible signs, "although God has not made His power depend upon the sacraments."

6. What has been said so far indicates not only the origin of the sacraments but also their function and their fruit. Their

origin is Christ the Lord; their function is to produce a prompting, teaching, and humbling effect; and their fruit is the healing and salvation of men.

Also apparent are: their efficient cause–institution by God; their material cause–representation through sensible signs; their formal cause–sanctification through grace; and their final cause–the healing of men through a proper medicine. And because "a thing is named after its form and end," these are called "sacraments," as being "sacred medicaments." Through them, in very truth, the soul is led away from the filth of vice, and toward perfect holiness. Wherefore these signs, although material and sensible, must be respected as sacred, since they are signs of sacred mysteries, prepare for sacred gifts, were provided by the most sacred God, divinely consecrated through a sacred institution and blessing, and established in the sacred Church for the most sacred worship of God. Hence, they are rightly called "sacraments."

CHAPTER 2

ON THE DIVERSITY OF THE SACRAMENTS

1. Concerning the diversity of the sacraments, the following must be held. For the sake of the healing of man, sacraments were instituted from the very beginning, and always ran parallel to his disease, and will last until the end of ages; but they were different at the time of the law of nature, at the time of the law of Scripture, and at the time of grace. Of all these sacraments, the last-named have the most evident signification and the greatest worth because of the grace they impart.

Oblations, sacrifices, and tithes existed under the law of nature. Then, under the law of Scripture, circumcision was introduced, expiation added, and an elaborate distinction superadded between the various oblations, tithes, and sacrifices. But under the new law [of grace], "sacraments were imposed, lesser in number but greater in effect and more powerful in virtue," and also higher in dignity: and in these, all the sacraments of earlier days were both fulfilled and voided.

2. This should be understood as follows. The incarnate Word–principle of our restoration, fountainhead and origin of

the sacraments—is most merciful and wise. Being most merciful, He saw to it that the rampant disease of sin should not go without sacramental remedy; being most wise, in accord with the immutable wisdom that governs the universe with supreme order, He made use of diverse and various medicines well suited to the changing conditions of the successive ages. Because "from the very beginning, as time went by and the advent of the Saviour came ever closer, the fruits of salvation and the knowledge of truth grew more and more, therefore it was fitting that the very signs of salvation should vary with the flow of time, so that as divine grace became increasingly effective toward this salvation, the signification of the visible signs might become more and more evident." Hence, "the sacrament of expiation and justification was established first as an offering, later as circumcision, and finally as baptismal cleansing, because the form and symbol of purification are somewhat hidden in an offering, more clearly expressed in circumcision, and manifestly revealed in baptism." And that is why, as Hugh writes, "the sacraments of the early days were like the shadow of truth, those of intermediate times, like its figure or image, and those of the later age, the age of grace, like its very body," for when they are taken together they contain the truth and healing grace they represent, and they actually impart what they promise.

3. Again, because the presence of truth and grace, demonstrated in the law of grace, could not—by reason of the loftiness and variety of their effects and powers—be properly expressed by any single sign, therefore in every age and law several sacraments were given to manifest this truth and grace: more at the time of the law of figures [i. e., law of Scripture], whose purpose is symbolical, for then the many and varied signs were intended to express in many ways the grace of Christ, and to commend it more forcefully; and, through this manifold commendation, to feed the little ones, train the imperfect, and impose upon the stubborn a heavy burden, taming them for the yoke of grace and in a measure softening them.

4. Finally, at the appearance of truth, darkness disappears and the foreshadowing figure attains its destined end, at which point both its use and its existence necessarily cease. Wherefore,

at the advent of grace, the ancient sacraments and signs were both fulfilled and abolished, for they were signs *announcing* things to come, so to speak, *foretelling* from afar. New sacraments were then instituted *demonstrating* the presence of grace, and each in its way *commemorating* the passion of the Lord, which is the origin and fountainhead of healing grace, for those who lived before Christ as well as for us: for the former, a price promised; for the latter, a price paid. Now, because grace is not due to a promise of payment except in view of its acquittal; and because it is due more abundantly to the price paid than to the promise of payment: therefore the passion of Chirst more immediately sanctifies the sacraments of the time of the new law, and a more abundant measure of grace flows from them. Whence the former sacraments were preparations and guides toward the latter, as the road leads to destination, the sign to the thing signified, the figure to truth, and as the imperfect both prepares for and leads to the perfect.

CHAPTER 3

ON THE NUMBER AND DIVISION OF THE SACRAMENTS

1. Concerning the number and division of the sacraments of the new law, the following must be held. There are seven sacraments corresponding to the sevenfold grace which, through the seven ages of time, leads us to the Principle, to repose, to the circle of eternity, as to an eighth age, that of universal resurrection.

Now, the door to these sacraments is Baptism; then follow Confirmation, Holy Eucharist, Penance, Extreme Unction, Orders, and finally Matrimony, which although it occupies the last place because of the disease of concupiscence attached to it, was yet established in paradise before all the others, and even before sin.

2. This should be understood as follows. Our restoring Principle, Christ the Lord, the incarnate Word, being *the power of God and the wisdom of God,* and unto us mercy, would establish His sacraments in the law of grace so powerfully, so wisely, so mercifully, and so fittingly that no means were lacking for our healing in this present life. Now, for the perfect

cure of a disease, three things must concur: expulsion of the actual disease, restoration of health, and preservation of the health restored.

First, because perfect cure requires the perfect and complete *expulsion* of disease, and the disease [here] is sevenfold, comprising three forms of sin, original, mortal, and venial, and four forms of penalty, ignorance, malice, weakness, and concupiscence; and because, as Jerome says, "what heals the foot does not heal the eye"—therefore, seven different remedies are needed to expel completely this sevenfold disease. These are: Baptism, against original sin; Penance, against mortal sin; Extreme Unction, against venial sin; Orders, against ignorance; Holy Eucharist, against malice; Confirmation, against weakness; and Matrimony, against concupiscence, which it tempers and excuses.

3. Again, there is no perfect cure without *restoration* of perfect health, and perfect health of the soul consists in the practice of the seven virtues, the three theological and the four cardinal. Hence, for the restoring of their healthful practice, seven sacraments are needed. Baptism leads to faith, Confirmation to hope, Holy Eucharist to charity, penance to justice, Extreme Unction to perseverance which is the complement and summit of fortitude, Orders to prudence, and Matrimony to the preservation of temperance, which is threatened mostly by the weakness of the flesh but is saved through honest marriage.

4. Finally, there can be no perfect healing without *preservation* of the health restored. In the battle of life, this health may be preserved only by means of the sevenfold armament of grace, and nowhere else but in the army of the Church as *awe-inspiring as bannered troops*; wherefore there must necessarily be seven sacraments. Since this army consists of elements subject to weakening, in order to be perfectly and permanently strengthened, it needs sacraments to fortify, restore, and revive its members: to fortify the combatants, restore the wounded, and revive the dying. Now, a fortifying sacrament fortifies either those who are entering the battle, and this is Baptism; or those who are fighting, and this is Confirmation; or those who are leaving, and this is Extreme Unction. A restoring sacrament

restores either from venial sin, and this is Holy Eucharist, or from mortal sin, and this is Penance. And a reviving sacrament revives either in the spiritual life, and this is Orders, which has the function of administering the sacraments, or in the natural life, and this is Matrimony, which, because it revives the multitude in its natural existence, the foundation of all existence, was the first to be instituted. Because Matrimony is connected with the disease of concupisence and is the sacrament with the least sanctifying power—even though, in its signification, it is *a great sacrament*—it is listed as the last and lowest of the spiritual remedies.

Hence, because Baptism is for those entering the battle, Confirmation for those fighting, Holy Eucharist for those recuperating, Penance for those rising anew, Extreme Unction for those about to leave, Orders for those bringing in new recruits, and Matrimony for those providing these recruits—it is clear that the sacramental remedies and means of defense are sufficient and orderly.

CHAPTER 4

IN THE INSTITUTION OF THE SACRAMENTS

1. Concerning the institution of the sacraments, the following must be held. Christ, as the Mediator and supreme Lawgiver of the New Testament, instituted seven sacraments by the law of grace, that law whereby He called to eternal promises, gave directing precepts, and instituted these sacraments in words and material elements for the sake of conveying clear meaning and effective sanctification; but in such a way that while they would always signify truly, they would not always heal effectively, by reason of a defect, nor of their own, but of the recipient.

These sacraments Christ instituted in different ways. Some, He confirmed, approved, and brought to full perfection, to wit, Matrimony and Penance; others He established implicitly in their original form, to wit, Confirmation and Extreme Unction; others again, He originated, brought to full perfection, and received in Person, to wit, Baptism, Holy Eucharist, and Orders. He fully instituted these three, and was also their first Recipient.

2. This should be understood as follows. Our restoring Principle is Christ crucified, the incarnate Word. Being the Word, He is coequal and consubstantial with the Father; He is the Word of supreme power, truth, and goodness, and so also of supreme authority. Wherefore it was His proper part to bring forth the New Testament, and to provide a complete and sufficient law as required by His supreme power, truth, and goodness. In His supreme goodness, He made beatifying promises; in His supreme truth, He gave directing commands; and in His supreme power, He established helpful sacraments. Through these sacraments, man may regain strength to obey the directing commands, may attain to the eternal promises. All this is effected in the evangelical law by the eternal Word, Christ the Lord, in as much as He is *the way, and the truth, and the life.*

3. Again, the restoring Principle is the Word, not only as such, but also as incarnate. In His incarnation, He offers Himself to all, in order to reveal truth, and gives Himself to those who worthily come to Him, in order to impart the grace of healing. Wherefore, being *full of grace and truth,* He instituted the sacraments in both material elements and words, in order to signify more clearly and to sanctify more effectively. For when, through sight and hearing—the most informative of the senses—these elements are seen and these words heard, they clearly reveal the meaning of the sign itself. Also, the words sanctify the material elements and make them more effective for the healing of man. And because this healing is not granted to him who, in the depth of his heart, refuses and opposes the fountain of grace, the sacraments, though so instituted as to have signification always and universally, would bring sanctification only to those who would receive them worthily and sincerely.

4. Finally, while the incarnate Word is the fountain of every sacramental grace, some sacramental graces existed before the incarnation, others only after the sending of the Holy Spirit, and still others in between. That is why the sacraments had to be instituted by different methods.

Penitential sorrow and matrimonial procreation existed before the incarnation. Christ, therefore, did not institute as novelties the two corresponding sacraments; but, having already established them and imprinted them in a certain manner upon natural reason, He completed and confirmed them in the evangelical law by preaching penance, attending a wedding feast, and reasserting the law of marriage, as may be gathered from various passages of the Gospel. But the Spirit was not given in full for man's strengthening and his public confession of the name of Christ until the Holy Spirit was sent, nor was there, before that time, full spiritual unction to help the soul rise aloft. Christ, therefore, merely originated and shadowed forth the two corresponding sacraments, Confirmation and Extreme Unction: Confirmation, by imposing His hands upon the little ones, and by foretelling that His disciples would be baptized with the Holy Spirit; and Extreme Unction, by sending the disciples to care for the sick whom they *anointed with oil,* as is said in Mark.

In the meantime there was a time of regeneration, of organization of the Church, and of spiritual refection. Christ, therefore, both fully and clearly instituted the three corresponding sacraments: Baptism, Holy Eucharist, and Orders. He instituted Baptism first by being baptized Himself, then by determining the form of Baptism, and by making it universal. He instituted the sacrament of Orders by giving first the power to bind and absolve the sins of mankind, and then the power to offer the sacrifice of the altar. He instituted the Holy Eucharist, by comparing Himself to a grain of wheat, and, immediately before the passion, by consecrating and giving to His disciples the sacrament of His Body and Blood. Wherefore these three sacraments had to be distinctly and entirely established by Christ Himself, and they were frequently prefigured in the Old Testament, being as they were the substantial sacraments of the new law and the proper works of the Lawgiver, the incarnate Word.

CHAPTER 5

ON THE ADMINISTRATION OF THE SACRAMENTS

1. Concerning the administration of the sacraments, the following must be held. The power of administering the sacraments belongs, as a general rule, to none but men. The administration of any sacrament necessarily implies the proper intention in the mind of the minister. Some sacraments require,

besides this proper intention, the presence of either priestly or pontifical Orders: Confirmation and Ordination require pontifical Orders, while the Holy Eucharist, Penance, and Extreme Unction require priestly Orders. As regards Baptism and Matrimony, although they are the concern of the priest, they may in fact be administered without priestly Orders, particularly in cases of necessity.

Once these conditions [intention and Orders] are present, the sacraments may be conferred by either the good or the wicked, the faithful or the heretical, within the Church or outside it: but within the Church, they are conferred both in fact and in effect, while outside it, although conferred in fact, they are not effective.

2. This should be understood as follows. Since it was as God-Man that our restoring Principle, the incarnate Word, instituted the sacraments for the salvation of men, He ordained, and properly so, that they were to be dispensed to men through the ministry of men, so that the minister would conform both to Christ the Saviour and to man in need of salvation. Christ the Saviour brought about the salvation of mankind in a manner befitting the equity of justice, the dignity of order and the assurance of salvation itself—for He *wrought salvation* in a just, orderly, and sure way; therefore He entrusted the administration of these sacraments to men in a way that conformed to these three perfections.

First, *equity of justice* demands that the actions of man, as man, be not performed unthinkingly; that the actions of man, as minister of Christ, be referred in some way to Christ; and that the actions of man, as minister of salvation, be referred in some general or particular way to salvation. Because the administration of the sacraments is a work of man as rational, as minister of Christ, and as minister of salvation, therefore it must necessarily proceed from intention: an intention by which a man proposes to perform that which Christ has instituted for man's salvation, or at least to do that which the Church does; which would generally include the same purpose, since the Church, as it receives the sacraments from Christ, also dispenses them for the salvation of the faithful.

3. The *order of Dignity* demands that the greater men be entrusted with the greater sacraments, the lesser men with the lesser, and those of intermediate rank with the intermediate. Now some sacraments are principally concerned with the excellence of virtue or dignity, to wit, the sacraments of Confirmation and Orders; others, with the poverty of need, to wit, Baptism and Matrimony—the former generating, and the latter regenerating, to a life of virtue; others again are mainly concerned with intermediate matters, to wit, Holy Eucharist, Penance, and Extreme Unction. Hence, under general law, the first may be conferred only by bishops and pontiffs; the last, being the least may be administered by those who have received merely the lower Orders, or even by laymen, particularly in case of need—i.e., as regards Baptism; the intermediate may be conferred only by priests, who stand, so to speak, in the middle, between bishops and laymen.

4. Finally, the *assurance of salvation* requires that the sacraments be so administered as to exclude any doubt. Now, no one could ever be certain of the morality or faith of the minister, nor could the minister himself be certain whether he is *worthy of love, or hatred.* And so, if the administration of the sacraments were reserved to the virtuous, no one would be certain of having received them validly: they would have to be repeated again and again, and one man's sin might hamper the salvation of another. Neither would there be any stability in the hierarchical degrees of the Church Militant, which are founded mainly upon the administration of the different sacraments. It was fitting, therefore, that such administration be entrusted in consideration, not of a man's personal holiness, which depends upon the will, but of his authority, which is essentially constant. Properly, then, this power was given to good and bad alike, to those within the Church and to those without.

But because none may be saved outside the communion of faith and love which makes us children and members of the Church, whenever the sacraments are received outside it, they are received with no effect toward salvation, although they are true sacraments. They may become effective, however, when the recipient returns to Holy Mother Church, the only Bride of Christ, whose sons are the only ones Christ the Spouse deems worthy of the eternal inheritance. Wherefore Augustine writes against the Donatists: "A comparison of the Church with paradise reveals that while strangers to the Church may receive its Baptism, no one outside the Church may receive or possess beatific salvation. For, as the Scriptures testify, the rivers from the fountain of paradise flowed abundantly even on the outside. Indeed, they are remembered by name, and we all know through which countries they ran, and that they did in fact exist outside of paradise. Yet neither in Mesopotamia nor in Egypt, both washed by these rivers, is there anything left of that blissful life remembered of paradise. The waters of paradise, then, are found outside it, but beatitude only within. Likewise, the Baptism of the Church may be obtained outside it, but the reward of beatific life is found only within this Church built upon a rock; and endowed with the keys to bind and absolve. And this Church is one, and it holds and possesses all the power of its Spouse and Lord, and by virtue of this conjugal power, it may give birth even through slave-girls to children who shall be called to the state of heirs if they are not proud; whereas, if they are proud, they shall remain outside. Even more: because we are fighting for the honor and unity of the Church, let us not give credit to heretics for any of its truth we find in them, but teach them instead by demonstration that they have it through union, and that it shall be of no salutary use to them unless they return to this same union."

CHAPTER 6

ON THE REPETITION OF THE SACRAMENTS

1. Concerning the repetition of the sacraments, the following must be held. Although, generally speaking, none of the sacraments should be conferred several times upon the same person, as regards the same matter, and for the same reason, lest there be lack of respect for the sacrament, there are in particular three sacraments, Baptism, Confirmation, and Orders, which are never to be repeated; for by each of these three a unique inner character is imprinted which is never deleted. Among these characters, that of Baptism is fundamental, for the other two cannot be imprinted unless this has first been given. Thus, if a

man goes through the ordination ceremony without having been baptized, nothing is effected, but [after Baptism is conferred] everything has to be done over again: "for when a thing [ordination] in fact was not done in the first place, it cannot be said to be repeated."

2. This should be understood as follows. Although our restoring Principle, the incarnate Word, in His supreme power, wisdom, and goodness never does anything inefficacious, improper, or fruitless in any circumstances, this is true all the more in His most noble works such as those through which the human race is restored. Since the sacraments belong to this category of divine works, it follows that a certain disrespect is shown to them when they are repeated on the same matter and person and for the same reason. For this would indicate that their first administration was inefficacious, improper, and fruitless, which contradicts the requirements of the supreme power, wisdom, and goodness of the restoring Principle, always present and active in and through the sacraments.

3. Again, among the sacraments, whose general purpose is to restore mankind through the efficacy of divine power, there are some which were introduced merely as remedies against disease, and others not only for this purpose but also for the sake of establishing, dividing, and ordaining the hierarchical dignities within the Church. Now, diseases may vary, yield to remedies, and yet recur, but the dignities of the Church must remain firm, solid, and unshaken. That is why the sacraments concerned with recurring diseases have transitory effects, and consequently they may be repeated if a new reason appears; while those concerned with the hierarchical dignities and the different states of faith must necessarily have some effects that remain beyond their remedial action in order to establish a fixed and stable distinction between the dignities and states within the Church. Since this can be attained neither by natural means nor even by the gift of sanctifying grace, it must necessarily come about through certain signs impressed upon the incorruptible substance, that is, the incorruptible soul, by the incorruptible Principle, according to incorruptible nature, that is, indelibly and gratuitously: and such signs are called characters. These characters, because they are indelible, may never

be assumed a second time, nor may the sacraments imprinting them ever be repeated.

4. Finally, there is a threefold functioning of faith whereby a distinction is made among the Christian people, which is to say, among the orderly ranks of the Church: the states of faith born, faith strengthened, and faith multiplied; the first dividing the faithful from unbelievers, the second dividing the strong from the weak or infirm, the third dividing clerics from laymen. That is why the sacraments related to this threefold state of faith always impress a character distinguishing those indelibly marked by it, wherefore these sacraments may never be repeated. And because Baptism concerns the state of faith born whereby the people of God is distinguished from unbelievers, as were the Israelites from the Egyptians; because Confirmation concerns the state of faith strengthened whereby the strong are distinguished from the weak, as are fighters from those who cannot fight; and because Orders concerns the state of faith multiplied whereby clerics are distinguished from laymen, as were the Levites from the other tribes: therefore it is only in these three sacraments that a character is imprinted.

5. Moreover, since the distinction between God's people and the others is first and fundamental, it follows that the character of Baptism is the foundation of all the others. Therefore, in the absence of this foundation, nothing may be built, and thus everything [that may have been attempted] must be done anew; while if this character has been laid down, the others may be impressed, each once and for all. The three said sacraments that imprint these characters may not be repeated for any reason whatsoever; and a severe penalty must be imposed upon those who do repeat them for they insult a sacrament of God.

The other four sacraments, however, may be repeated without offense when new occasions arise.

CHAPTER 7

ON THE NATURE AND INTEGRITY OF BAPTISM

1. Now, in the seventh place, we come to the consideration of the integrity of each sacrament. Of the seven, we must speak first of Baptism which is the door to the others.

2. Concerning the sacrament of Baptism, the following must be held. For anyone to be validly and fully baptized, the form established by the Lord must be said aloud: "I baptize thee in the name of the Father, and of the Son, and of the Holy Spirit. Amen." No word should be omitted, none added, nor should the order given here be changed, nor should the word "name" in the beginning be altered. There must also be immersion or ablution of the whole body, or at least of its most noble part, by means of the element water, in such a way that the immersion [or ablution] and the vocal expression are performed simultaneously by one and the same minister.

If these conditions are fulfilled, and if there is no feigning in the one to be baptized, there is given to him a grace that regenerates and rectifies him, and cleanses him of every sin. For the sake of greater effectiveness, a preparatory instruction and exorcism precede the baptism of both children and adults. In the case of adults, personal faith is required, whereas in the case of children, the faith of another suffices.

3. This should be understood as follows. Because our restoring Principle, the incarnate Word, as an utterly perfect and sufficient Principle, must in restoring mankind through remedial sacraments employ nothing superfluous, out of order, or incomplete: therefore He necessarily made the sacraments of Baptism and the others as complete as required by His power, by our salvation, and also by our disease.

Now this power which restores us is the power of the whole Trinity, whom Holy Mother Church accepts in her soul, confesses in words, and professes with signs, under the distinctness and properness, order and natural origin, of three Persons. This power is also the power of the passion of Christ, who died and was buried and *rose again the third day*. Hence, in order to express both [the Trinity and Christ] in the sacrament which is the first of all the sacraments, and the one in which this power is first and radically active, there must be in Baptism an expression of the Trinity through a distinct, proper, and orderly mentioning of names; this at least in the common form, for in the early days of the Church, Baptism could be conferred in the name of Christ, which comprised the Trinity by implication. The formula of Baptism also must be pronounced in a proper and orderly sequence, concurrently with the threefold immersion [or ablution] fittingly representing Christ's death, burial, and resurrection the third day. And because these powers [of the Trinity and of the passion] act simultaneously and within a single Christ and Saviour, both must be applied by one and the same minister at one and the same time in order to preserve the oneness of the sacrament and to signify the oneness of the Mediator.

Again, because our salvation required first a regeneration or renovation into the state of grace, that is, the state of spiritual life—a regeneration or renovation through the cleansing of impurity, the expelling of darkness, and the cooling of concupiscence, the downfall of every man born of Adam's seed—therefore the first sacrament, which brings about regeneration, most fittingly was performed with that element which applies by its natural signification to the aforesaid threefold effect of the grace initiating our salvation. For water cleanses by its purity, transmits light by its limpidity, and cools by its freshness. It is also the commonest of all liquids. That is why the sacrament of our regeneration is fittingly performed with water—any water whatsoever, for "any water is of the same species as any other water"; and thus also is obviated the danger that someone's salvation might be imperiled through lack of the proper material element.

5. Finally, the disease in us which Baptism radically opposes is original sin. This disease denies to the soul the life of grace; [it denies it] the enabling rectitude of all the virtues; it inclines the soul in a certain measure toward every kind of sin. Being inherited, "it makes a child potentially concupiscent and a man actually so," and also reduces the soul to diabolical servitude, submitting it to the power of the prince of darkness. And so, for the efficient cure of the disease, this sacrament must provide a grace that regenerates, to offset the loss of the spiritual life; a grace that rectifies by means of a sevenfold power, to offset the loss of the enabling virtues; and a grace that cleanses of all sin, to offset every tendency to vicious disorder.

6. Now, because original sin, received from another, makes a child potentially concupiscent and an adult actually so: there-

fore the adult must necessarily have personal faith and personal contrition, while the child needs no more than the faith and contrition of another, that is, of the universal Church. And because the purpose of Baptism is to deliver both children and adults from the power of the prince of darkness, both should be exorcised, that the hostile spirits may be expelled, and both instructed, that the adults may be delivered from the darkness of error and formed to the faith, and that the godparents representing the children may learn what to teach them; lest the sacrament of Baptism be prevented by human default from achieving its intended end.

CHAPTER 8

ON THE INTEGRITY OF CONFIRMATION

1. Concerning the sacrament of Confirmation, the following must be held. For this sacrament to be complete, a formula must be pronounced, usually in these terms: "I sign thee with the sign of the cross, and I confirm thee with the chrism of salvation, in the name of the Father, and of the Son, and of the Holy Spirit. Amen."

The chrism required is made of olive oil and balm.

When the bishop anoints the forehead with chrism in the form of a cross while pronouncing the formula of confirmation, the sacrament is received. By this sacrament, a man is strengthened as a soldier of Christ, prepared to confess His name publicly and courageously.

2. This should be understood as follows. As our restoring Principle, the incarnate Word, was eternally conceived in the bosom of the Father and temporally appeared to man in sensible flesh, He likewise restores none but the one who also conceives Him is his heart by believing, and who brings forth by fitting confession of faith Him in whom he believes. Now, a fitting confession of faith is one that is sincere and characterized by absolute truthfulness: that is, one that is not only speculative but also practical. It implies not only "conformity between thought, expression, and object," but also conformation of the whole man to truth, in which the reason understands, the will agrees, and the faculties co-operate, so that the confession of

faith comes forth from the whole heart, the whole soul, and the whole mind: *from a pure heart and a good conscience and faith unfeigned.* And such a confession of faith is whole, acceptable, and courageous: whole in regard to the One of whom it is made, acceptable in regard to the one[s] before whom it is made, and courageous in the one who makes it. But since man is too fainthearted for this without the strengthening hand of heavenly grace, therefore the sacrament of Confirmation was divinely instituted as an immediate complement to Baptism.

3. Now, because "the end determines the means," for this sacrament to be complete, it must meet the three aforesaid conditions of a proper confession of faith.

First, it must be *whole*, and there is no whole confession of faith unless a man confesses that Christ is true Man crucified for the sake of men, and that He is also true incarnate Son of God, coequal within the Trinity in all respects with the Father and the Holy Spirit. Hence, the formula expresses, not only the act of confirming, but also the sign of the cross itself, and the name of the blessed Trinity.

4. Next, a fitting confession of faith must be *acceptable* to the one[s] before whom it is made—that is God and men. It cannot be acceptable to God unless the mind is enlightened and the conscience purified, nor can it be acceptable to men without the fragrance of a good name and a virtuous life. Hence, the external element [of the sacrament] combines clear olive oil and scented balm in order to signify that the confessing toward which this sacrament disposes and leads must combine clarity of conscience and understanding with the fragrance of a good life and name, lest there be contradiction between words and conscience, or between words and reputation, which would prevent a confession of faith from being accepted by man or approved by Christ.

5. Finally, a fitting confession of faith must be *courageous.* No one should avoid confessing the truth out of reluctance or timidity; nor, in time of persecution, should anyone be afraid or ashamed of publicily confessing Christ ignominiously put to death on the cross, out of fear of suffering pain or disgrace similar to those of the passion. Such shame and fear show mostly in the face, and more particularly on the fore-

head: that is why a strength-conferring hand is imposed upon us for our strengthening and a cross imprinted upon our brow, so that we may not blush to acknowledge this cross openly, nor fear to confess when we must the name of Christ, come pain or shame—like a true wrestler rubbed with oil before the bout, or a hardy soldier bearing before him the sign of his King, the triumphal standard of the cross, wherewith to penetrate in safety the ranks of the enemy. Indeed, the glory of the cross cannot be preached if there is present any fear of its suffering or shame. This accords with the words of St. Andrew: "As for me, if I were afraid of the disgrace of the cross, I would not be preaching its glory."

CHAPTER 9

ON THE INTEGRITY OF THE HOLY EUCHARIST

1. Concerning the sacrament of the Holy Eucharist, the following must be held. Therein are not only represented but actually contained, under the two species of bread and wine, yet forming not two sacraments but one, Christ's true body and true blood. This is brought about through consecration of the priest, using the vocal form instituted by the Lord: over the bread, "[For] this is My body"; over the wine, "[For] this is the chalice of My blood . . ." When these words are said by the priest with the intention of consecrating, the substance of the elements is transubstantiated into the body and the blood of Christ. While the species remain unchanged in their sensible form, both contain the whole Christ, not as confining Him in space, but sacramentally. Under these same species, He is offered to us as sustainment. Whoever receives it worthily, eating not merely in fact but also spiritually through faith and love, is more fully incorporated into the mystical body of Christ, being also refreshed and cleansed in himself. But he who approaches it *unworthily, without distinguishing the body* of Christ, *eats and drinks judgment to himself.*

2. This should be understood as follows. Because our restoring Principle, the incarnate Word, is utterly sufficient in His power and utterly wise in His expression, therefore He so

conferred the sacraments upon us as to conform with the demands of both His wisdom and His sufficiency.

Because of His supreme sufficiency, in providing disease-healing remedies and charismatic graces, He instituted sacraments not only to bring us forth to the life of grace, as Baptism; or to increase and strengthen us in this life once we were born to it, as Confirmation; but also to nourish us in it once we were born and strengthened, and this is the sacrament of the Holy Eucharist. Wherefore these three sacraments are conferred upon all who have attained faith. Now, because nourishment in the life of grace consists for any one of the faithful in preserving devotion toward God, love for neighbor, and inner delight; and devotion toward God is practiced through the offering of a sacrifice, love for neighbor through union within a single sacrament, and inner delight through partaking of the pilgrim's food: therefore our restoring Principle gave us this sacrament of the Holy Eucharist as a sacrificial offering, as a sacramental union, and as sustainment on the way.

3. But because our restoring Principle is not only utterly sufficient but also utterly wise, and as such, does all things in orderly fashion: therefore He so gave us and disposed for us this sacrifice, this sacrament, and this food, as to conform with the time in which grace was revealed, with our state of wayfaring, and with our capacity to receive.

First, then, because the *time* in which grace was revealed demanded the offering, not of a victim of any kind, but of one that would be pure, acceptable, and all-sufficient; and none such exists but the One offered on the cross, that is, the body and blood of Christ: the body and blood of Christ had to be present in this sacrament, not only figuratively but in reality, as a gift to suit the time.

Likewise, because the time of grace demands that the sacrament of union and love not only signify this union and love, but also be a means inflaming the heart toward them so as to bring about what it represents; and because what chiefly inflames toward mutual love, and chiefly unites the members, is the oneness of the Head from whom the stream of mutual affection flows into us through the all-pervading, uniting, and transforming power of love: therefore this sacrament contains the true body and immaculate flesh of Christ, in such a way that it penetrates our being, unites us to one another, and transforms us into Him through that burning love by which He gave Himself to us [in the incarnation], offered Himself up for us [in the passion], and now gives Himself back to us, to remain with us until the end of the world.

For the same reason, a sustainment fitting for the state [time] of grace must be spiritual, universal, and salutary. Now, the spirit is sustained by the Word of life: wherefore the spiritual soul in the flesh is properly sustained by the incarnate Word, or the flesh of the Word, which is a universal and salutary food; for although one, it is the means of salvation unto all. Because no spiritual, universal, and salutary food can be given, except the body of Christ, it follows that this body must in all reality be contained within the Holy Eucharist for the sacrifice to be perfectly propitiative, the sacrament perfectly unitive, and the food perfectly refective: all of which must occur in the time of the new law, of grace revealed, and of the truth of Christ.

4. Again, because it does not accord with the *state of wayfaring* that Christ be seen, since the mystery should be veiled and the merit of faith thereby secured; and because it is unseemly that the flesh of Christ be torn with the teeth, by reason of the loathsomeness of such crudity and the immortality of the same body: therefore it was necessary that the body and blood of Christ be imparted under the veil of the most sacred symbols and by means of congruous and expressive similitudes. Now, nothing is better suited for refection than bread as food and wine as drink, and nothing is a more appropriate symbol of the unity of the body of Christ, physical and mystical, than the one bread made of a number of the cleanest grains and the one wine pressed from a number of the purest grapes; therefore it was fittingly under these species, in preference to any others, that this sacrament was proffered. And because Christ was to be present under these species by means of a change occurring not in Himself but in them, therefore when the two aforementioned formulas are pronounced, indicating the presence of Christ under the species, there occurs a change of substance of both into His body and blood, while the accidents alone remain as signs containing and expressing them.

5. Since in truth the blessed and glorious body of Christ cannot be divided into its physical parts nor separated from the soul or from the supreme Godhead, therefore under each of the species there is present one Christ, whole and undivided, body, soul, and God. Hence under the two species there is but one utterly simple sacrament containing the whole Christ. And because any portion of the species represents the body of Christ, it follows that He is as fully present in any part as in the whole, whether the species be divided or not: and thus He is not present there in the sense of being spatially confined, as occupying a place, as having a position, or as being perceptible to any of the bodily and human senses: He is hidden to every sense so that faith may have its field and acquire merit. For this reason also—to maintain the mystery—the accidents retain their full operation (although they are not related to that which underlies them) as long as they contain within themselves the body of Christ: and that is as long as they keep their natural properties and are fit to provide nourishment.

6. Finally, because *our capacity* to receive Christ fruitfully resides, not in the flesh but in the spirit, not in the stomach but in the mind; and because the mind does not attain Christ except through understanding and love, through faith and charity, so that faith gives us light to recognize Him and charity gives us ardor to love Him: therefore, if anyone is to approach this sacrament worthily, he must partake in the spirit so as to eat in the acknowledgment of faith and to receive in the devotion of love, whereby he will not be transforming Christ into himself, but instead will be passing over into the mystical body of Christ.

Clearly, then, the one who receives with a lukewarm, irreverent, and careless heart *eats and drinks judgment to himself,* because he offends such a great sacrament. Wherefore those who know themselves to be insufficiently clean of bodily or spiritual sin, or lacking in devotion, are advised to wait until they are ready to receive the true and pure Lamb in a manner both devout and attentive.

7. Wherefore also it is commanded that this sacrament be surrounded with great solemnity, of place as well as time, of words and prayers as well as of vestments, in the celebration of

Masses; so that both the celebrating priests and the communicants may realize the gift of grace through which they are cleansed, enlightened, perfected, restored, vivified, and most ardently transformed into Christ by rapturous love.

CHAPTER 10

ON THE INTEGRITY OF PENANCE

1. Concerning the sacrament of Penance, the following must be held. It is "a life-saving plank after shipwreck," a plank to which any man drowning in mortal sin may cling as long as he lives, whenever and as often as he chooses to implore the divine mercy.

Integral parts of this sacrament are: contrition in spirit, confession in words, and satisfaction in deed. Wherefore penance is entire when the sinner has abandoned in fact, confessed in word, detested in spirit, every mortal sin he ever committed, and has firmly purposed never to sin again. When these conditions properly concur with absolution by one who possesses Orders, the power of the keys, and jurisdiction, the penitent is absolved of his sin, reunited with the Church, and reconciled with Christ by means of the aforesaid priestly keys; furthermore, to the judgment of this same one [endowed with the keys] pertain matters not only of absolving but also of excommunicating and of granting indulgences, the latter two properly belonging to a bishop as the spouse of the Church.

2. This should be understood as follows. Because our restoring Principle, the incarnate Word, being the Word, is the fountainhead of truth and wisdom, and being incarnate, is the fountainhead of kindness and leniency: therefore it belongs to Him to restore humanity through the medicine of the sacraments, and most of all to heal it of its principal disease, mortal sin, as befits the kind High Priest, the able Physician, and the just Judge; so that our healing may demonstrate the supreme mercy, prudence, and justice of the incarnate Word.

3. Our healing from mortal sin through penance demonstrates, in the first place, the supreme *mercy* of Christ, most kind High Priest. This mercy more than suffices to offset any human sin, whatever its nature, gravity, or frequency. That

is why Christ, in His supreme mercy, receives and pardons sinners, not only once or twice, but as often as they prayerfully beg for God's mercy. Now, because divine mercy is implored sincerely and humbly only when the spirit is sorrowful and repentant; and because the way of repentance is open to man during his whole lifetime, for he is then free to turn toward either good or evil: therefore, whatever the gravity, circumstances, or frequency of his sins, the sinner may always seek refuge in the sacrament of Penance, through which his transgressions will be remitted unto him.

4. Again, our healing must demonstrate the supreme *prudence* of Christ, most able Physician. Now, because a physician's prudence consists in applying remedies specific to the disease, removing not only the disease itself but also its cause; and because sins are committed against God through pleasure, assent, and execution, that is, in the heart, in the mouth, and in action: therefore the Physician most prudent ordained that this disease in the affective, expressive, and operative powers of the sinner, originating as it does from hidden acceptance of the pleasure, be cured in terms of the same three powers by means of penitential sorrow conceived in the heart through compunction, expressed orally through confession, and consummated in deed through satisfaction.

And because every mortal sin leads away from the one God, opposes the one grace, and distorts the one and essential righteousness of man, therefore, in order to assure the complete sufficiency of the penitential remedy, the sinner must repent of all his misdeeds, regretting those of the past, breaking away from those of the present, and proposing firmly never to commit in the future sins of the same or of any other kind. Hence, by completely withdrawing from sin through Penance, the sinner receives that divine grace which brings about the remission of all sins.

5. Finally, because our healing must demonstrate the true *justice* of Christ the Judge, and since He is not to judge in person before the last and final judgment, therefore it was necessary to appoint judges who would pass particular judgments before the end of time. And because these judges, placed between the offended God and offending man, are like mediators,

being close to Christ and appointed over the people; and because priests are particularly close to the Lord and familiar with Him by reason of their office, having been especially consecrated to His ministry: therefore all priests, and none but priests, receive the power of the two keys—the key of knowledge for discerning and the key of binding and loosing for judgment and for imparting the grace of absolution.

6. Now, lest there be confusion, prelates are not appointed indiscriminately over others, for the hierarchy of the Church must be organized according to judiciary power. Hence this [judiciary] use of binding and loosing is granted primarily to a single and sovereign Pontiff, upon whom universal jurisdiction is conferred as upon the supreme head. Thence it is apportioned to the different Churches [dioceses], first to the bishops and thence to the priests. Thus, although every priest possesses ordination and the keys, their use extends only to those subjects who are under his ordinary jurisdiction, except when he receives delegated power over others from one who has jurisdiction over them. Since such jurisdiction exists primarily in the supreme head, then [within his diocese] in the bishop, and finally [within his parish] in the pastor, it may be delegated by any one of them, sufficiently by the lowest in rank, to a wider extent by the intermediate, and most extensively by the highest.

7. Now, this jurisdiction, as it is found in the supreme Pontiff, and also in the bishops, extends not only to matters of the inner conscience in man's relationship with God, but also to matters of public relationship between man and man—for instance, in the case of those who are responsible for the administration and care of the Church, as the spouse is responsible for the bride. Therefore prelates have the power of the sword by which they may strike, through excommunication, in the defense of right, and the power of largess by which they may distribute, through indulgences, the Church's treasures of merit entrusted to their care by both the Head and the members. Thus, as true judges appointed by God, they possess the full power of binding and loosing, of striking the impenitent and cowing the rebellious, of absolving the truly repentant and reconciling them with God and Holy Mother Church.

CHAPTER 11

ON THE INTEGRITY OF EXTREME UNCTION

1. Concerning the sacrament of Extreme Unction, this, in sum, must be held. It is the sacrament of those who are leaving this life, preparing and disposing them for *perfect* [spiritual] health. It also has the power of obliterating venial sins, and of restoring *temporal* health if that is for the good of the patient.

For this sacrament to be complete, pure consecrated oil must be used, certain prayers must be said, and the patient must be anointed on seven parts of the body: on the eyes, ears, nostrils, lips, hands, feet, and loins. And the sacrament must be conferred upon none but adults in danger of death who ask for it, and only by the hand and ministration of a priest. Wherefore, between this sacrament and the sacrament of Confirmation there are seven differences: in effect, matter, form, recipient, minister, place, and time.

2. This should be understood as follows. Because our restoring Principle, the incarnate Word, restores us as the *Mediator between God and men, Himself man, Christ Jesus,* and as it pertains to Jesus [Saviour] to save and to Christ the Anointed to pour upon men the grace of anointment: therefore it is for Him to impart to His members a saving unction. Now, for the sake of perfect healing, the soul needs to be made well in regard to three things—the strife of action, the sweetness of contemplation, and the delight of possession; and the first pertains to the recruits of the Church Militant, the second to its leaders who are to teach others, and the third to those who are leaving this same Church through death. Wherefore the Lord was not content to institute a [first] sacramental unction, as He did in Confirmation, but He also instituted an intermediate one in priestly Orders, and an Extreme Unction at the approach of death.

3. Now, because "the end determines the means," this sacrament must act, and be constituted, received, and conferred, in a manner to conform to its end.

First, therefore, the *action* of this sacrament must be determined by its end, which is to make the attaining of salvation, that is, eternal happiness, swifter and easier. Now, these effects come about through devotion that lifts up the soul, and through remission of venial sins and their consequences, that drag it down; therefore this sacrament must effectively prompt devotion, remit venial sin, and more easily remove the dross of sin. Moreover, because many are sick who need to live longer in order to increase their merit, this sacrament, while strengthening the soul toward good and disburdening it of evil, often also gives relief from the physical disease. And that is what blessed James means when he says that: *the prayer of faith will save the sick man . . . and if he be in sins, they shall be forgiven him.*

4. In the second place, the *constitution* of this sacrament must be determined by its end, which is to restore spiritual health through deliverance from sin. Now, such health depends on soundness and purity of the inner conscience upon which the heavenly Judge will pass judgment. Hence, the matter of this sacrament must be oil, pure and consecrated, symbol of a conscience both clean and holy; and since mortal man has not the power to restore spiritual health, the prayer and words must be an appeal for grace.

Again, the soul contracts spiritual infirmities in the body through the agency of the four leading powers of that body—the perceptive, the rationally expressive, the generative, and the locomotive: wherefore the organs to be anointed are those serving these same four powers. Now, there are five organs serving the senses—the eyes providing vision, the ears hearing, the nose olfaction, the hands feeling, the mouth both taste and another power, that of rational expression; while the feet provide locomotion and the loins generation (for it would not be proper or modest here to touch or even mention the genitals). Therefore the *conferring of the unction* must be on the seven parts here named, so that by this sacrament a man may be disposed toward the fullness of spiritual health through the removal of all venial sin.

5. Finally, the *reception* of this sacrament must also be determined by the end, which is to make swifter man's passage to heaven by taking away his burden of venial sin and turning his mind to God. Therefore Extreme Unction should be administered to none but adults, that is, those capable of venial sin; to

none but those requesting it with a devout heart; and to none but those in danger of death and almost at the point of passing into another state. And because this is a sacrament of those in danger of death, and, on the other hand, a sacrament whose matter is holy—that is, consecrated oil—in order to avoid any risk, its dispensation is entrusted to priests in general. And, because of the consecration of the oil, it should be touched by none but consecrated hands.

6. Confirmation and Extreme Unction, differing as they do in their end, differ also in their effect, matter, form, place, occasion, recipient, and minister. In effect: one prepares for a more courageous fight, the other for a swifter ascent; in matter: one uses oil mixed with balm, the other pure oil; in form: one is indicative, the other deprecative; in place: one is applied to the forehead only, the other to several parts; in occasion: one is given in health, the other in sickness; in the recipient: one may be given not only to adults but also to infants, the other to adults only; in the minister: one is conferred by a bishop, the other by any priest. All these differences are determined by the difference in the ends, for it is clear that a difference in proximate ends causes a difference in the means to them.

CHAPTER 12

ON THE INTEGRITY OF ORDERS

1. Concerning the sacrament of Orders, this is, in sum, what must be held. "Orders is a certain sign through which a spiritual power is conferred upon the ordained."

Although Orders is but one of seven sacraments, there are within it seven states: the first, of *porters*, the second of *lectors*, the third, of *exorcists*, the fourth, of *acolytes*, the fifth, of *subdeacons*, the sixth, of *deacons*, the seventh, of *priests*. Below these stages as preparation, are clerical *tonsure* and *psalmody*; and above them as fulfilled states are *episcopacy*, *patriarchate*, and *papacy*. It is from these [the latter three states] that all Orders derive; and to them it pertains to confer all, under the proper signs both seen and heard, and in accordance with the proper ritual as regards time, place, office, and recipient.

2. This should be understood as follows. Our restoring Principle, the incarnate Word, being both man and God, instituted the sacramental remedy for the salvation of man in a way that was ordinating, distinguishing, and power-imparting, thus conforming to the requirements of His goodness, wisdom, and might. Therefore, in entrusting to men the dispensation of this same sacramental remedy, He willed it to be, not haphazard, but in accordance with the demands of order, separation, and power. It was fitting, then, that definite persons be distinguished and set apart for the performing of this office, and that the necessary power be given them as a matter of ordinary jurisdiction. And because a distinction of this nature could not be brought about properly except by means of some sacred sign such as a sacrament, therefore a sacrament was properly instituted to be such a sign imparting order, distinction, and power, for the purpose of dispensing the other sacraments in a distinctive, effective, and orderly manner. Hence, Orders is defined as "a certain sign through which a spiritual power is conferred upon the ordained"; which definition contains the three aforesaid characters making up its essential constituents.

3. First, Orders being a sign that *distinguishes* a man and sets him apart from others as one totally consecrated to the worship of God, the Orders are preceded by a certain distinctive mark; this consists in the tonsure or corona, which signifies withdrawal from temporal desires and elevation of the mind toward the eternal, thus indicating that the cleric is entirely devoted to the service of God. Wherefore, on receiving the corona, he says: "O Lord, the portion of my inheritance. . . ." And because he should be well versed in the praise of God, which consists primarily in the recitation of the Psalms, the office of Psalmodist also is conferred, as a preamble to the Orders. Isidore, however, in a broad interpretation, considers this function as one of the Orders.

4. Secondly, because Orders is an *ordinating* sign and is in itself orderly, and Orders consists in a complete distinction and differentiation of ranks, conforming to the sevenfold grace for the dispensation of which the sacrament of Orders is chiefly intended: therefore there are seven Orders gradually rising to culminate in the priesthood, in which is the fulfillment of all

Orders: for it is the priest who consecrates the sacrament of the body of Christ, in which is the fullness of all graces. Thus the other six degrees are attendants upon this one, and resemble the steps leading to the throne of Solomon. There are six degrees here, because of the perfection of that number, six being the first perfect number, and because that number is needed for the perfection and effectiveness of the ministry. For it is fitting that some serve as from a distance, others more closely, and others again very closely so that nothing be lacking in the sacred rites. And because each of these functions may be paired with another according as they concern either cleansing or enlightenment, it follows that there are six ministering Orders, and the most perfect of all, the seventh, in which the Sacrament of the Altar is performed, and which is consummated as a single Order, as a full and final end.

5. Finally, because Orders is a *power-imparting* sign as regards the dispensation, not only of the other sacraments, but also of itself; and because such power over power is an excelling power: therefore it implies not only simple power, as found in simple [priestly] Orders, but also the eminence of power, as found in those to whom the conferring of Orders pertains by ordinary jurisdiction. And because the lower the degree of authority, the more widely it is distributed, and the higher the degree, the more narrowly it is concentrated: therefore there are many bishops, a lesser number of archbishops, very few patriarchs, and but one father of fathers, rightly called Pope [Father], as the unique, first, and supreme spiritual father, not only of all fathers, but likewise of all the faithful; as first hierarch, only spouse, undivided head, supreme pontiff, vicar of Christ, fountainhead, origin and law in relation to all the authorities of the Church; the one from whom all orderly power descends as from the summit to the very lowest members of the Church, according to what the loftiest dignity in the hierarchy of the Church demands.

6. And because such dignity resides chiefly in Orders, therefore this sacrament may be conferred only with great prudence and solemnity, and hence, not indiscriminately through the ministry of any one at random, nor upon any one no matter whom, nor in any place or time indifferently. It is to be conferred

upon men who are educated, virtuous, free from impediments, and in a state of fasting; in a consecrated building, during the celebration of Mass, within the time designated by ecclesiastical law; and only by bishops, to whom the dispensation of Orders is reserved because of the eminence of their rank—as also are confirmation by imposition of the hands, the consecration of nuns and abbots, and the dedication of churches; all being functions which, because of their solemnity, may not be performed by any but those endowed with eminent power.

CHAPTER 13

ON THE INTEGRITY OF MATRIMONY

1. Concerning the sacrament of Matrimony, this in sum must be held; that "Matrimony is a legitimate union of a man and a woman, establishing an indissoluble community of life." This state of union existed not only after the fall, but also before it; though originally the sacrament of union was established solely in view of its function, now it serves not merely in its function, but also as a remedy against the disease of lust. In addition, it was originally a symbol of the union of God with the soul; now it further signifies the union of Christ with the Church, and the union of the two natures in the one Person.

Matrimony is effected by free consent of the mind on the part of two persons of opposite sex, expressed externally through a certain sensible sign and consummated by physical union. For marriage, which is said to be initiated by words concerning the future and ratified by words concerning the present, is consummated by physical union.

There are three benefits attached to this sacrament, "faithfulness, offspring, and the sacrament itself." There are twelve impediments which prevent an intended marriage and void a marriage that has been contracted. They are expressed in these verses: "Error, condition, vow, consanguinity, crime, disparity of cult, force, Orders, prior marriage, public honesty, affinity, impotency: these prevent intended marriage and void marriage already contracted."

2. This should be understood as follows. Our restoring Principle, the incarnate Word, being *the Word of God, . . . is*

the fountain of wisdom on high; being incarnate, is the source of mercy on earth. As the uncreated Word, He is, by His supreme wisdom, the formative cause of mankind; and as the incarnate Word, He is, by His supreme mercy, its reformative cause. Therefore He restores mankind through His mercy precisely because, in His wisdom, He had originally made it restorable; for such wisdom required as a condition of supreme order that, in making the human race, God make it able to stand, to fall, and to be restored, as we have shown above. Because, then, the Word of God, in His wisdom, did give man the capacity to stand, to fall, and to be restored, as it behooved Him to do: therefore He ordained the continuance of the human race in such a way that in the very [sacramental] means employed man would possess what would lead him to stand firm, and also what he would need as a remedy, since in the very function of propagation there is something of sin, that is, lust, which hands down the disease.

Now, man's original perfection consisted in the union of his soul with God through an utterly chaste, *singular, and individual* union of love; moreover, the remedy came from the union of the divine and the human natures within the oneness of a hypostasis or Person, a oneness, that is to say, effected by divine grace as *singular and individual.* Therefore God decreed from the very beginning that propagation would be brought about by means of a *singular and individual* union of male and female. This union was to signify, before the fall, the union of God with the soul, that is, of God with the sub-celestial hierarchy [of spirits]; but after the fall, the union of God with human nature, or of Christ with the Church. Hence, Matrimony was a sacrament both before and after the fall, but it differed as to its meaning and purpose. Since Matrimony was a sacrament before the occurrence of the disease, therefore lust, which appeared later through sin, is something excused by Matrimony rather than something able to vitiate it: for the disease does not vitiate the medicine, but the medicine cures the disease.

From this may be clearly seen what Matrimony is, and how it was divinely brought about.

3. Again, because any one of the said spiritual unions signified by Matrimony consists in the conjunction of [two parties], one active and influencing and the other passive and receiving,

this being brought about through the action of a bond of love which proceeds from free will alone: therefore Matrimony must be the conjunction of two persons who differ as agent and patient, that is, as male and female, their union proceeding from consent of the will alone. And because the will is not visible externally except through a sign that manifests it, therefore the mutual consent must be expressed in an external manner. Now, a consent regarding the future is not a true consent, but merely the promise of a consent to come; and actual consent without intercourse does not produce complete union, since the parties are not yet *one flesh.* Therefore, the *words concerning the future* [i.e., the betrothal] are the inception of marriage, and the *words concerning the present* [i.e., the marriage vows] are its ratification, but the union of sexes alone is its consummation; for then only do the parties become one flesh and one body, and in this only is the union between Christ and ourselves fully signified. Then indeed is the body of the one fully surrendered to that of the other, in virtue of each one's respective power toward the procreation of offspring.

4. Thus there are three goods in Matrimony: the sacrament, consisting in the indissoluble bond; faithfulness, in the fulfillment of the conjugal duty; and offspring, in the effect proceeding from both.

5. Finally, because this matrimonial union must result from a free consent of the will, leading to the conjunction, under a single matrimonial obligation, of two persons [properly] distant, and because there are twelve ways in which this may be impeded, therefore there are twelve impediments to marriage, which is evident from what follows.

Matrimonial consent implies freedom of the consent itself, freedom in the consenting subject, and fitness for the union. But freedom of consent may be broken in two ways, corresponding to the two causes of involuntary acts, that is, ignorance and violence. Thus, there are here two impediments: *error* and *force.*

Freedom in the consenting subject may be destroyed by this, that someone is bound to another, either God or man. If he is bound to God, this may be through a religious vow, or through a state of which a vow is an integral condition; the first is the impediment of vow, the second, the impediment of Holy Orders. If he is bound to man, this may be in two ways, either present or antecedent; the first consists in a contract by which one is bound to a spouse; the second consists in the crime by which an adulterer or adulteress has contrived the death of the legitimate spouse, or promised to marry after his or her death from some other cause. Hence, there are here four impediments: *vow, Holy Orders, bond,* and *crime.*

Fitness for the union consists in the adequacy of the distance between the parties, and is destroyed by excessive closeness or excessive disparity.

Now, the parties may be too closely related either by reason of a blood tie, or through something similar to it, such as legal or spiritual parenthood; or again, they may be too closely related through the union of the sexes, or betrothal. Hence, there are three impediments: *parenthood, affinity,* and *breach of public honesty.*

There may be excessive disparity between the parties [in three ways]. These are: matters related to physical nature, such as the inability to consummate the carnal union; or matters related to a situation beyond control by the parties, such as one of them being a slave and the other free; or again, matters related to the Christian religion, such as one party being baptized and the other not. Hence, there are here three impediments: *impotency, disparity of condition,* and *disparity of cult.*

And so there are altogether twelve impediments introduced, under the guidance of the Holy Spirit, in the teaching of the Church; for to the Church is entrusted the care of all the sacraments, but in a special way of Matrimony, because of the variations which may occur in relation to it, and because of the concomitant disease, which is the most infectious and the hardest to moderate. That is why it pertains to the Church to determine the acceptable degree of blood relationship as it sees fit at any given time; to determine which persons may or may not validly marry; and to verify separation. But the Church may not, and in fact could not, annul a marriage legitimately effected; for what God has united, no man, whatever his power, may set asunder, since all men are to be judged by the judgment of God alone.

St. Thomas Aquinas
1225-1274

The impact of Thomas Aquinas is all-pervasive in the theology of the Western Church. This is all the more remarkable in view of the comparative brevity of his teaching career. He received the Dominican habit in 1244 and died in 1274. The intervening three decades were filled with unceasing activity: study, travel from Italy to France to Germany and back again, teaching, preaching, writing, and demonstrating an originality of unparalleled proportions. The majestic calm conveyed by the simple, flowing Latin of his theological works belies the turmoil that surrounded him for most of his career.

From a contemporary standpoint the liturgy as it had come to be practiced and understood in the Middle Ages left much to be desired. Social conditions had contributed to the decline in understanding and appropriate participation in the Mass. The Roman liturgy as modified by Gallican influences since Charlemagne had become too privatized, too clericalized, too monastic, and its significance had been distorted by excessive allegorizing. To be fair in evaluating Aquinas in this regard, one must acknowledge all of these problems, see him as a child of his times, and then measure the magnitude of his achievement in spite of these limitations.

The very term "scholastic" reminds us of some of the parameters within which the work of Aquinas had to be done.

Theology was more of a corporate enterprise than perhaps at any other time of Christian history. Even though new questions were encouraged, there was a body of material, a catalogue of questions already formulated, which every theologian was expected to, required to, address. The chief compendium of these set questions was the work of Peter Lombard, the "textbook" of the Schoolmen.

A full appreciation of the creativity of Aquinas would require a detailed examination of how he handled, synthesized, went beyond, and clarified the Scholastic tradition presented to him. His novel use of Aristotle was a major factor in his achievement and the cause for suspicion about his work during his lifetime. But time was to vindicate the validity of his synthesis.

The following selection contains four questions from the third part of his Summa Theologica *(qq. 73-76). This part of the* Summa *was written shortly before his death. He had completed his second teaching assignment in Paris and returned to Naples in 1272, and it was in that and the following year that he composed his treatment of the Eucharist, shortly before he ceased his theological work altogether. It is at the same time a summary of all his earlier writings on the subject and a work of numerous innovations. He reorganizes the order of treatment, putting the question of the "matter" of the sacrament first because, unlike the other sacraments, in this one "what is both reality and sacrament is in the matter itself."*

The rigorous format of the Scholastic method does not recommend itself to us today. The style is so devoid of personal intrusion that it seems boring to modern taste. That it has its shortcomings must readily be granted, but this should not detract from our appreciation for its achievements. The best proof of this is to see that in the current renewal in Catholic eucharistic theology it is invariably those who have built upon Aquinas, not those who have ignored or abandoned him, who have had the most to contribute.

SUMMA THEOLOGICA ON THE SACRAMENT OF THE EUCHARIST

QUESTION LXXIII

(In Six Articles)

We have now to consider the sacrament of the Eucharist; and first of all we treat of the sacrament itself; secondly, of its matter; thirdly, of its form; fourthly, of its effects; fifthly, of the recipients of this sacrament; sixthly, of the minister; seventhly, of the rite.

Under the first heading there are six points of inquiry: (1) Whether the Eucharist is a sacrament? (2) Whether it is one or several sacraments? (3) Whether it is necessary for salvation? (4) Its names. (5) Its institution. (6) Its figures.

FIRST ARTICLE

WHETHER THE EUCHARIST IS A SACRAMENT?

We proceed thus to the First Article:—

Objection 1. It seems that the Eucharist is not a sacrament. For two sacraments ought not to be ordained for the same end, because every sacrament is efficacious in producing its effect. Therefore, since both Confirmation and the Eucharist are ordained for perfection, as Dionysius says (*Eccl. Hier.* iv.), it seems that the Eucharist is not a sacrament, since Confirmation is one, as stated above (Q. LXV., A. 1; Q. LXXII., A. 1).

Obj. 2. Further, in every sacrament of the New Law, that which comes visibly under our senses causes the invisible effect of the sacrament, just as cleansing with water causes the baptismal character and spiritual cleansing, as stated above (Q. LXIII., A. 6; Q. LXVI., AA. 1, 3, 7). But the species of bread and wine, which are the objects of our senses in this sacrament, neither produce Christ's true body, which is both reality and sacrament, nor His mystical body, which is the reality only in the Eucharist. Therefore, it seems that the Eucharist is not a sacrament of the New Law.

Obj. 3. Further, Sacraments of the New Law, as having matter, are perfected by the use of the matter, as Baptism is by ablution, and Confirmation by signing with chrism. If, then, the Eucharist be a sacrament, it would be perfected by the use of the matter, and not by its consecration. But this is manifestly false, because the words spoken in the consecration of the matter are the form of this sacrament, as will be shown later on (Q. LXXVIII., A. 1). Therefore the Eucharist is not a sacrament.

On the contrary, It is said in the Collect: *May this Thy Sacrament not make us deserving of punishment.*

I answer that, The Church's sacraments are ordained for helping man in the spiritual life. But the spiritual life is analogous to the corporeal, since corporeal things bear a resemblance to spiritual. Now it is clear that just as generation is required for corporeal life, since thereby man receives life; and growth, whereby man is brought to maturity: so likewise food is required for the preservation of life. Consequently, just as for the spiritual life there had to be Baptism, which is spiritual generation; and Confirmation, which is spiritual growth: so there needed to be the sacrament of the Eucharist, which is spiritual food.

Reply Obj. 1. Perfection is twofold. The first lies within man himself; and he attains it by growth: such perfection belongs to Confirmation. The other is the perfection which comes to man from the addition of food, or clothing, or something of the kind; and such is the perfection befitting the Eucharist, which is the spiritual refreshment.

Reply Obj. 2. The water of Baptism does not cause any spiritual effect by reason of the water, but by reason of the power of the Holy Ghost, which power is in the water. Hence on John v. 4, *An angel of the Lord at certain times,* etc., Chrysostom observes: *The water does not act simply as such upon the baptized, but when it receives the grace of the Holy Ghost, then it looses all sins.* But the true body of Christ bears the same relation to the species of the bread and wine, as the power of the Holy Ghost does to the water of Baptism: hence the species of the bread and wine produce no effect except from the virtue of Christ's true body.

Reply Obj. 3. A sacrament is so termed because it contains something sacred. Now a thing can be styled sacred from two causes; either absolutely, or in relation to something else. The difference between the Eucharist and other sacraments having sensible matter, is that whereas the Eucharist contains something which is sacred absolutely, namely, Christ's own body; the baptismal water contains something which is sacred in relation to something else, namely, the sanctifying power: and the same holds good of chrism and suchlike. Consequently, the sacrament of the Eucharist is completed in the very consecration of the matter, whereas the other sacraments are completed in the application of the matter for the sanctifying of the individual. And from this follows another difference. For, in the sacrament is in the matter itself; but what is reality only, namely, the grace bestowed, is in the recipient; whereas in Baptism both are in the recipient, namely, the character, which is both reality and sacrament, and the grace of pardon of sins, which is reality only. And the same holds good of the other sacraments.

SECOND ARTICLE

WHETHER THE EUCHARIST IS ONE SACRAMENT OR SEVERAL?

We proceed thus to the Second Article:—

Objection 1. It seems that the Eucharist is not one sacrament but several, because it is said in the Collect: *May the sacraments which we have received purify us, O Lord:* and this is said on account of our receiving the Eucharist. Consequently the Eucharist is not one sacrament but several.

Obj. 2. Further, it is impossible for genera to be multiplied without the species being multiplied: thus it is impossible for one man to be many animals. But, as stated above (Q. LX., A. 1), sign is the genus of sacrament. Since, then, there are more signs than one, to wit, bread and wine, it seems to follow that here must be more sacraments than one.

Obj. 3. Further, this sacrament is perfected in the consecration of the matter, as stated above (A. 1 *ad* 3). But in this sacrament there is a double consecration of the matter. Therefore, it is a twofold sacrament.

On the contrary, The Apostle says (1 Cor. x. 17): *For we, being many, are one bread, one body, all that partake of one bread:* from which it is clear that the Eucharist is the sacrament of the Church's unity. But a sacrament bears the likeness of the reality whereof it is the sacrament. Therefore the Eucharist is one sacrament.

I answer that, As stated in *Metaph.* v., a thing is said to be one, not only from being indivisible, or continuous, but also when it is complete; thus we speak of one house, and one man. A thing is one in perfection, when it is complete through the presence of all that is needed for its end; as a man is complete by having all the members required for the operation of his soul, and a house by having all the parts needful for dwelling therein. And so this sacrament is said to be one. Because it is ordained for spiritual refreshment, which is conformed to corporeal refreshment. Now there are two things required for corporeal refreshment, namely, food, which is dry sustenance, and drink, which is wet sustenance. Consequently, two things concur for the integrity of this sacrament, to wit, spiritual food and spiritual drink, according to John: *My flesh is meat indeed, and My blood is drink indeed.* Therefore, this sacrament is materially many, but formally and perfectively one.

Reply Obj. 1. The same Collect at first employs the plural: *May the sacraments which we have received purify us;* and afterwards the singular number: *May this sacrament of Thine not make us worthy of punishment:* so as to show that this sacrament is in a measure several, yet simply one.

Reply Obj. 2. The bread and wine are materially several signs, yet formally and perfectively one, inasmuch as one refreshment is prepared therefrom.

Reply Obj. 3. From the double consecration of the matter no more can be gathered than that the sacrament is several materially, as stated above.

THIRD ARTICLE

WHETHER THE EUCHARIST IS NECESSARY FOR SALVATION?

We proceed thus to the Third Article:—

Objection 1. It seems that this sacrament is necessary for salvation. For Our Lord said (John vi. 54): *Except you eat the flesh of the Son of Man, and drink His blood, you shall not have life in you.* But Christ's flesh is eaten and His blood drunk in this sacrament. Therefore, without this sacrament man cannot have the health of spiritual life.

Obj. 2. Further, this sacrament is a kind of spiritual food. But bodily food is requisite for bodily health. Therefore, also is this sacrament, for spiritual health.

Obj. 3. Further, as Baptism is the sacrament of Our Lord's Passion, without which there is no salvation, so also is the Eucharist. For the Apostle says (1 Cor. xi. 26): *For as often as you shall eat this bread, and drink the chalice, you shall show the death of the Lord, until He come.* Consequently, as Baptism is necessary for salvation, so also is this sacrament.

On the contrary, Augustine writes (*Ad Bonifac., contra Pelag. I.*): *Nor are you to suppose that children cannot possess life, who are deprived of the body and blood of Christ.*

I answer that, Two things have to be considered in this sacrament, namely, the sacrament itself, and what is contained in it. Now it was stated above (A. 1, *Obj.* 2) that the reality of the sacrament is the unity of the mystical body, without which there can be no salvation; for there is no entering into salvation outside the Church, just as in the time of the deluge there was none outside the Ark, which denotes the Church, according to 1 Pet. iii. 20, 21. And it has been said above (Q. LXVIII., A. 2), that before receiving a sacrament, the reality of the sacrament can be had through the very desire of receiving the sacrament. Accordingly, before actual reception of this sacrament, a man can obtain salvation through the desire of receiving it, just as he can before Baptism through the desire of Baptism, as stated above (Q. LXVIII., A. 2). Yet there is a difference in two respects. First of all, because Baptism is the beginning of the spiritual life, and the door of the sacraments; whereas the Eucharist is, as it were, the consummation of the spiritual life, and the end of all the sacraments, as was observed above (Q. LXIII., A. 6): for by the hallowings of all the sacraments preparation is made for receiving or consecrating the Eucharist. Consequently, the reception of Baptism is necessary for starting the spiritual life, while the receiving of the Eucharist is requisite for its consummation; by partaking not indeed actually, but in desire, as an end is possessed in desire and intention. Another difference is because by Baptism a man is ordained to the Eucharist, and therefore from the fact of children being baptized, they are destined by the Church to the Eucharist; and just as they believe through the Church's faith, so they desire the Eucharist through the Church's intention, and, as a result, receive its reality. But they are not disposed for Baptism by any previous sacrament, and consequently, before receiving Baptism, in no way have they Baptism in desire; but adults alone have: consequently, they cannot have the reality of the sacrament without receiving the sacrament itself. Therefore this sacrament is not necessary for salvation in the same way as Baptism is.

Reply Obj. 1. As Augustine says, explaining John vi. 54, *This food and this drink,* namely, of His flesh and blood: *He would have us understand the fellowship of His body and members, which is the Church in His predestinated, and called, and justified, and glorified, His holy and believing ones.* Hence, as he says in his Epistle to Boniface (Pseudo-Beda, *in* 1 *Cor.* x 17): *No one should entertain the slightest doubt, that then every one of the faithful becomes a partaker of the body and blood of Christ, when in Baptism he is made a member of Christ's body; nor is he deprived of his share in that body and chalice even though he depart from this world in the unity of Christ's body, before he eats that bread and drinks of that chalice.*

Reply Obj. 2. The difference between corporeal and spiritual food lies in this, that the former is changed into the substance of the person nourished, and consequently it cannot avail for supporting life except it be partaken of; but spiritual food changes man into itself, according to that saying of Augustine (*Conf.* vii.), that he heard the voice of Christ as it were saying to him: *Nor shalt thou change Me into thyself, as food of thy flesh, but thou shalt be changed into Me.* But one can be changed into Christ, and be incorporated in Him by mental desire, even without receiving this sacrament. And consequently the comparison does not hold.

Reply Obj. 3. Baptism is the sacrament of Christ's death and Passion, according as a man is born anew in Christ in virtue of His Passion; but the Eucharist is the sacrament of Christ's Passion according as a man is made perfect in union with Christ Who suffered. Hence, as Baptism is called the sacrament of Faith, which is the foundation of the spiritual life, so the Eucharist is termed the sacrament of Charity, which is *the bond of perfection* (Col. iii. 14).

FOURTH ARTICLE

WHETHER THIS SACRAMENT IS SUITABLY CALLED BY VARIOUS NAMES?

We proceed thus to the Fourth Article:—

Objection 1. It seems that this sacrament is not suitably called by various names. For names should correspond with things. But this sacrament is one, as stated above (A. 2). Therefore, it ought not to be called by various names.

Obj. 2. Further, a species is not properly denominated by what is common to the whole genus. But the Eucharist is a sacrament of the New Law; and it is common to all the sacraments for grace to be conferred by them, which the name *Eucharist* denotes, for it is the same thing as *good grace.* Furthermore, all the sacraments bring us help on our journey through this present life, which is the notion conveyed by *Viaticum.* Again something sacred is done in all the sacraments, which belongs to the notion of *Sacrifice;* and the faithful intercommunicate through all the sacraments, which this Greek word Σύναξις and the Latin *Communio* express. Therefore, these names are not suitably adapted to this sacrament.

Obj. 3. Further, a host seems to be the same as a sacrifice. Therefore, as it is not properly called a sacrifice, so neither is it properly termed *a Host.*

On the contrary, Is the use of these expressions by the faithful.

I answer that, This sacrament has a threefold significance: one with regard to the past, inasmuch as it is commemorative of Our Lord's Passion, which was a true sacrifice, as stated above (Q. XLVIII., A. 3), and in this respect it is called a *Sacrifice.*

With regard to the present it has another meaning, namely, that of Ecclesiastical unity, in which men are aggregated through this Sacrament; and in this respect it is called *Communion* or Σύναξις. For Damascene says (*De Fide Orthod.* iv.) that *it is called Communion because we communicate with Christ through it, both because we partake of His flesh and Godhead, and because we communicate with and are united to one another through it.*

With regard to the future it has a third meaning, inasmuch as this sacrament foreshadows the Divine fruition, which shall come to pass in heaven; and according to this it is called *Viaticum,* because it supplies the way of winning thither. And in this respect it is also called the *Eucharist,* that is, *good grace,* because *the grace of God is life everlasting* (Rom. vi. 23); or because it really contains Christ, Who is *full of grace.*

In Greek, moreover, it is called Μετάληψις, *i.e., Assumption,* because, as Damascene says (*loc. cit.*), *we thereby assume the Godhead of the Son.*

Reply Obj. 1. There is nothing to hinder the same thing from being called by several names, according to its various properties or effects.

Reply Obj. 2. What is common to all the sacraments is attributed antonomastically to this one on account of its excellence.

Reply Obj. 3. This sacrament is called a *Sacrifice* inasmuch as it represents the Passion of Christ; but it is termed a *Host* inasmuch as it contains Christ, Who is *a host* (Douay,—*sacrifice*) . . . *of sweetness* (Eph. v. 2).

FIFTH ARTICLE

WHETHER THE INSTITUTION OF THIS SACRAMENT WAS APPROPRIATE?

We proceed thus to the Fifth Article:—

Objection 1. It seems that the institution of this sacrament was not appropriate, because as the Philosopher says (*De Gener.* ii.): *We are nourished by the things from whence we spring.* But by Baptism, which is spiritual regeneration, we receive our spiritual being, as Dionysius says (*Eccl. Hier.* ii.). Therefore we are also nourished by Baptism. Consequently there was no need to institute this sacrament as spiritual nourishment.

Obj. 2. Further, men are united with Christ through this sacrament as the members with the head. But Christ is the Head of all men, even of those who have existed from the beginning of the world, as stated above (Q. VIII., AA. 3, 6). Therefore the institution of this sacrament should not have been postponed till the Lord's supper.

Obj. 3. Further, this sacrament is called the memorial of Our Lord's Passion, according to Matth. xxvi. (Luke xxii. 19): *Do this for a commemoration of Me.* But a commemoration is of things past. Therefore, this sacrament should not have been instituted before Christ's Passion.

Obj. 4. Further, a man is prepared by Baptism for the Eucharist, which ought to be given only to the baptized. But Baptism was instituted by Christ after His Passion and Resurrection, as is evident from Matth. xxviii. 19. Therefore, this sacrament was not suitably instituted before Christ's Passion.

On the contrary, This sacrament was instituted by Christ, of Whom it is said (Mark vii. 37) that *he did all things well.*

I answer that, This sacrament was appropriately instituted at the supper, when Christ conversed with His disciples for the last time. First of all, because of what is contained in the sacrament: for Christ is Himself contained in the Eucharist sacramentally. Consequently, when Christ was going to leave His disciples in His proper species, He left Himself with them under the sacramental species; as the Emperor's image is set up to be reverenced in his absence. Hence Eusebius says: *Since He was going to withdraw His assumed body from their eyes, and bear it away to the stars, it was needful that on the day of the supper He should consecrate the sacrament of His body and blood for our sakes, in order that what was once offered up for our ransom should be fittingly worshipped in a mystery.*

Secondly, because without faith in the Passion there could never be any salvation, according to Rom. iii. 25: *Whom God hath proposed to be a propitiation, through faith in His blood.* It was necessary accordingly that there should be at all times among men something to show forth Our Lord's Passion; the chief sacrament of which in the Old Law was the Paschal Lamb. Hence the Apostle says (1 Cor. v. 7): *Christ our Pasch is sacrificed.* But its successor under the New Testament is the sacrament of the Eucharist, which is a remembrance of the Passion now past, just as the other was figurative of the Passion to come. And so it was fitting that when the hour of the Passion was come, Christ should institute a new Sacrament after celebrating the old, as Pope Leo (I.) says (*Serm. lviii.*).

Thirdly, because last words, chiefly such as are spoken by departing friends, are committed most deeply to memory; since then especially affection for friends is more enkindled, and the things which affect us most are impressed the deepest in the soul. Consequently, since, as Pope Alexander (I.) says, *among sacrifices there can be none greater than the body and blood of Christ, nor any more powerful oblation;* Our Lord instituted this sacrament at His last parting with His disciples, in order that it might be held in the greater veneration. And this is what Augustine says (*Respons. ad Januar.* i.): *In order to commend more earnestly the depth of this mystery. Our Saviour willed this last act to be fixed in the hearts and memories of the disciples whom He was about to quit for the Passion.*

Reply Obj. 1. *We are nourished from the same things of which we are made,* but they do not come to us in the same way; for those out of which we are made come to us through generation, while the same, as nourishing us, come to us through being eaten. Hence, as we are new-born in Christ through Baptism, so through the Eucharist we eat Christ.

Reply Obj. 2. The Eucharist is the perfect sacrament of Our Lord's Passion, as containing Christ crucified; consequently it could not be instituted before the Incarnation; but then there was room for only such sacraments as were prefigurative of the Lord's Passion.

Reply Obj. 3. This sacrament was instituted during the supper, so as in the future to be a memorial of Our Lord's Passion as accomplished. Hence He said expressively: *As often as ye shall do these things,* speaking of the future.

Reply Obj. 4. The institution responds to the order of intention. But the sacrament of the Eucharist, although after Baptism in the receiving, is yet previous to it in intention; and therefore it behoved to be instituted first. Or else it can be said that Baptism was already instituted in Christ's Baptism; hence some were already baptized with Christ's Baptism, as we read in John iii. 22.

SIXTH ARTICLE

WHETHER THE PASCHAL LAMB WAS THE CHIEF FIGURE OF THIS SACRAMENT?

We proceed thus to the Sixth Article:—

Objection 1. It seems that the Paschal Lamb was not the chief figure of this sacrament, because (Ps. cix. 4) Christ is called *a priest according to the order of Melchisedech,* since Melchisedech bore the figure of Christ's sacrifice, in offering bread and wine. But the expression of likeness causes one thing to be named from another. Therefore, it seems that Melchisedech's offering was the *principal* figure of this sacrament.

Obj. 2. Further, the passage of the Red Sea was a figure of Baptism, according to 1 Cor. x. 2: *All . . . were baptized in the cloud and in the sea.* But the immolation of the Paschal Lamb was previous to the passage of the Red Sea, and the Manna came after it, just as the Eucharist follows Baptism. Therefore the Manna is a more expressive figure of this sacrament than the Paschal Lamb.

Obj. 3. Further, the principal power of this sacrament is that it brings us into the kingdom of heaven, being a kind of *viaticum.* But this was chiefly prefigured in the sacrament of expiation when the *high-priest entered once a year into the Holy of Holies with blood,* as the Apostle proves in Heb. ix. Consequently, it seems that that sacrifice was a more significant figure of this sacrament than was the Paschal Lamb.

On the contrary, The Apostle says (1 Cor. v. 7, 8): *Christ our Pasch is sacrificed; therefore let us feast . . . with the unleavened bread of sincerity and truth.*

I answer that, We can consider three things in this sacrament: namely, that which is sacrament only, and this is the bread and wine; that which is both reality and sacrament, to wit, Christ's true body; and lastly that which is reality only, namely, the effect of this sacrament. Consequently, in relation to what is sacrament only, the chief, figure of this sacrament was the oblation of Melchisedech, who offered up bread and wine.—In relation to Christ crucified, Who is contained in this sacrament, its figures were all the sacrifices of the Old Testament, especially the sacrifice of expiation, which was the most solemn of all. While with regard to its effect, the chief figure was the Manna, *having in it the sweetness of every taste* (Wisd. xvi. 20), just as the grace of this sacrament refreshes the soul in all respects.

The Paschal Lamb foreshadowed this sacrament in these three ways. First of all, because it was eaten with unleavened loaves, according to Exod. xii. 8: *They shall eat flesh . . . and unleavened bread.* As to the second, because it was immolated by the entire multitude of the children of Israel on the fourteenth day of the moon; and this was a figure of the Passion of Christ, Who is called the Lamb on account of His innocence. As to the effect, because by the blood of the Paschal Lamb the children of Israel were preserved from the destroying Angel, and brought from the Egyptian captivity; and in this respect the Paschal Lamb is the chief figure of this sacrament, because it represents it in every respect.

From this the answer to the objections is manifest.

* * * * *

QUESTION LXXV

OF THE CHANGE OF BREAD AND WINE INTO THE BODY AND BLOOD OF CHRIST

(In Eight Articles)

We have now to consider the change of the bread and wine into the body and blood of Christ; under which head there are eight points of inquiry: (1) Whether the substance of bread and wine remain in this sacrament after the consecration? (2) Whether it is annihilated? (3) Whether it is changed into the body and blood of Christ? (4) Whether the accidents remain after the change? (5) Whether the substantial form remains there? (6) Whether this change is instantaneous? (7) Whether it is more miraculous than any other change? (8) By what words it may be suitably expressed?

FIRST ARTICLE

WHETHER THE BODY OF CHRIST BE IN THIS SACRAMENT IN VERY TRUTH, OR MERELY AS IN A FIGURE OR SIGN?

We proceed thus to the First Article:—

Objection 1. It seems that the body of Christ is not in this sacrament in very truth, but only as in a figure, or sign. For it is written (John vi. 54) that when Our Lord had uttered these words: *Except you eat the flesh of the Son of Man, and drink His blood,* etc., *Many of His disciples on hearing it said: 'this is a hard saying':* to whom He rejoined: *'It is the spirit that quickeneth; the flesh profiteth nothing':* as if He were to say, according to Augustine's exposition on Ps. iv.: *Give a spiritual meaning to what I have said. You are not to eat this body which you see, nor to drink the blood which they who crucify Me are to spill. It is a mystery that I put before you: in its spiritual sense it will quicken you; but the flesh profiteth nothing.*

Obj. 2. Further, Our Lord said (Matth. xxviii. 20): *Behold I am with you all days even to the consummation of the world.* Now in explaining this, Augustine makes this observation (*Tract.* xxx. *in Joan.*): *The Lord is on high until the world be ended; nevertheless the truth of the Lord is here with us; for the body, in which He rose again, must be in one place; but His truth is spread abroad everywhere.* Therefore, the body of Christ is not in this sacrament in very truth, but only as in a sign.

Obj. 3. Further, no body can be in several places at the one time. For this does not even belong to an angel; since for the same reason it could be everywhere. But Christ's is a true body, and it is heaven. Consequently, it seems that it is not in very truth in the sacrament of the altar, but only as in a sign.

Obj. 4. Further, the Church's sacraments are ordained for the profit of the faithful. But according to Gregory in a certain Homily (xxviii. *in Evang.*), the ruler is rebuked *for demanding Christ's bodily presence.* Moreover the apostles were prevented from receiving the Holy Ghost because they were attached to His bodily presence, as Augustine says on John xvi. 7: *Except I go, the Paraclete will not come to you* (*Tract.* xciv. *in Joan.*). Therefore Christ is not in the sacrament of the altar according to His bodily presence.

On the contrary, Hilary says (*De Trin.* viii.): *There is no room for doubt regarding the truth of Christ's body and blood; for now by Our Lord's own declaring and by our faith His flesh is truly food, and His blood is truly drink.* And Ambrose says (*De Sacram.* vi): *As the Lord Jesus Christ is God's true Son, so is it Christ's true flesh which we take, and His true blood which we drink.*

I answer that, The presence of Christ's true body and blood in this sacrament cannot be detected by sense, nor understanding, but by faith alone, which rests upon Divine authority. Hence, on Luke xxii. 19: *This is My body, which shall be delivered up for you,* Cyril says: *Doubt not whether this be true; but take rather the Saviour's words with faith; for since He is the Truth, He lieth not.*

Now this is suitable, first for the perfection of the New Law. For, the sacrifices of the Old Law contained only in figure that true sacrifice of Christ's Passion, according to Heb. x. 1: *For the law having a shadow of the good things to come, not the very image of the things.* And therefore it was necessary that the sacrifice of the New Law instituted by Christ should have something more, namely, that it should contain Christ Himself crucified, not merely in signification or figure, but also in very truth. And therefore this sacrament which contains Christ Himself, as Dionysius says (*Eccl. Hier.* iii.), is perfective of all the other sacraments, in which Christ's virtue is participated.

Secondly, this belongs to Christ's love, out of which for our salvation He assumed a true body of our nature. And because it is the special feature of friendship to live together with friends, as the Philosopher says (*Ethic.* ix.), He promises us His bodily presence as a reward, saying (Matth. xxiv. 38): *Where the body is, there shall the eagles be gathered together.* Yet meanwhile in our pilgrimage He does not deprive us of His bodily presence; but unites us with Himself in this sacrament through the truth of His body and blood. Hence (John vi. 57) he says: *He that eateth My flesh, and drinketh My blood, abideth in Me, and I in him.* Hence this sacrament is the sign of supreme charity, and the uplifter of our hope, from such familiar union of Christ with us.

Thirdly, it belongs to the perfection of faith, which concerns His humanity just as it does His Godhead, according to John xiv. 1: *You believe in God, believe also in Me.* And since faith is of things unseen, as Christ shows us His Godhead invisibly, so also in this sacrament He shows us His flesh in an invisible manner.

Some men accordingly, not paying heed to these things, have contended that Christ's body and blood are not in this sacrament except as in a sign, a thing to be rejected as heretical, since it is contrary to Christ's words. Hence Berengarius, who had been the first deviser of this heresy, was afterwards forced to withdraw his error, and to acknowledge the truth of the faith.

Reply Obj. 1. From this authority the aforesaid heretics have taken occasion to err from evilly understanding Augustine's words. For when Augustine says: *You are not to eat this body which you see,* he means not to exclude the truth of Christ's body, but that it was not to be eaten in this species in which it was seen by them. And by the words: *It is a mystery that I put before you; in its spiritual sense it will quicken you,* he intends not that the body of Christ is in this sacrament merely according to mystical signification, but *spiritually,* that is, invisibly, and by the power of the spirit. Hence (*Tract.* xxvii.), expounding John vi. 64—*the flesh profiteth nothing,* he says: *Yea, but as they understood it, for they understood that the flesh was to be eaten as it is divided piecemeal in a dead body, or as sold in the shambles, not as it is quickened by the spirit . . . Let the spirit draw nigh to the flesh . . . then the flesh profiteth very much: for if the flesh profiteth nothing, the Word had not been made flesh, that It might dwell among us.*

Reply Obj. 2. That saying of Augustine and all others like it are to be understood of Christ's body as it is beheld in its proper species; according as Our Lord Himself says (Matth. xxvi. 11): *But Me you have not always.* Nevertheless He is invisibly under the species of this sacrament, wherever this sacrament is performed.

Reply Obj. 3. Christ's body is not in this sacrament in the same way as a body is in a place, which by its dimensions is commensurate with the place; but in a special manner which is proper to this sacrament. Hence we say that Christ's body is upon many altars, not as in different places, but *sacramentally:* and thereby we do not understand that Christ is there only as in a sign, although a sacrament is a kind of sign; but that Christ's body is here after a fashion proper to this sacrament, as stated above.

Reply Obj. 4. This argument holds good of Christ's bodily presence, as He is present after the manner of a body, that is, as it is in its visible appearance, but not as it is spiritually, that is, invisibly, after the manner and by the virtue of the spirit. Hence Augustine (*Tract.* xxvii. *in Joan.*) says: *If thou hast understood* Christ's words spiritually concerning His flesh, *they are spirit and life to thee; if thou hast understood them carnally, they are also spirit and life, but not to thee.*

SECOND ARTICLE

WHETHER IN THIS SACRAMENT THE SUBSTANCE OF THE BREAD AND WINE REMAINS AFTER THE CONSECRATION?

We proceed thus to the Second Article:—

Objection 1. It seems that the substance of the bread and wine does remain in this sacrament after the consecration: because Damascene says (*De Fide Orthod.* iv.): *Since it is customary for men to eat bread and drink wine, God has wedded his Godhead to them, and made them His body and blood:* and further on: *The bread of communication is not simple bread, but is united to the Godhead.* But wedding together belongs to things actually existing. Therefore the bread and wine are at the same time, in this sacrament, with the body and the blood of Christ.

Obj. 2. Further, there ought to be conformity between the sacraments. But in the other sacraments the substance of the matter remains, like the substance of water in Baptism, and the substance of chrism in Confirmation. Therefore the substance of the bread and wine remains also in this sacrament.

Obj. 3. Further, bread and wine are made use of in this sacrament, inasmuch as they denote ecclesiastical unity, as *one bread is made from many grains and wine from many grapes,* as Augustine says in his book on the Creed (*Tract.* xxvi. *in Joan.*). But this belongs to the substance of bread and wine. Therefore, the substance of the bread and wine remains in this sacrament.

On the contrary, Ambrose says (*De Sacram.* iv.): *Although the figure of the bread and wine be seen, still, after the Consecration, they are to be believed to be nothing else than the body and blood of Christ.*

I answer that, Some have held that the substance of the bread and wine remain in this sacrament after the consecration. But this opinion cannot stand: first of all, because by such an opinion the truth of this sacrament is destroyed, to which it belongs that Christ's true body exists in this sacrament; which indeed was not there before the consecration. Now a thing cannot be in any place, where it was not previously, except by change of place, or by the conversion of another thing into itself; just as fire begins anew to be in some house, either because it is carried thither, or because it is generated there. Now it is evident that Christ's body does not begin to be present in this sacrament by local motion. First of all, because it would follow that it would cease to be in heaven: for what is moved locally does not come anew to some place unless it quit the former one. Secondly, because every body moved locally passes through all intermediary spaces, which cannot be said here. Thirdly, because it is not possible for one movement of the same body moved locally to be terminated in different places at the one time, whereas the body of Christ under this sacrament begins at the one time to be in several places. And consequently it remains that Christ's body cannot begin to be anew in this sacrament except by change of the substance of bread into itself. But what is changed into another thing, no longer remains after such change. Hence the conclusion is that, saving the truth of this sacrament, the substance of the bread cannot remain after the consecration.

Secondly, because this position is contrary to the form of this sacrament, in which it is said: *This is My body,* which would not be true if the substance of the bread were to remain there; for the substance of bread never is the body of Christ. Rather should one say in that case: *Here is My body.*

Thirdly, because it would be opposed to the veneration of this sacrament, if any substance were there, which could not be adored with adoration of latria.

Fourthly, because it is contrary to the rite of the Church, according to which it is not lawful to take the body of Christ after bodily food, while it is nevertheless lawful to take one consecrated host after another. Hence this opinion is to be avoided as heretical.

Reply Obj. 1. God *wedded His Godhead, i.e.,* His Divine power, to the bread and wine, not that these may remain in this sacrament, but in order that He may make from them His body and blood.

Reply Obj. 2. Christ is not really present in the other sacraments, as in this; and therefore the substance of the matter remains in the other sacraments, but not in this.

Reply Obj. 3. The species which remain in this sacrament, as shall be said later (A.5), suffice for its signification; because the nature of the substance is known by its accidents.

THIRD ARTICLE

WHETHER THE SUBSTANCE OF THE BREAD OR WINE IS ANNIHILATED AFTER THE CONSECRATION OF THIS SACRAMENT, OR DISSOLVED INTO THEIR ORIGINAL MATTER?

We proceed thus to the Third Article:—

Objection 1. It seems that the substance of the bread is annihilated after the consecration of this sacrament, or dissolved into its original matter. For whatever is corporeal must be somewhere. But the substance of bread, which is something corporeal, does not remain, in this sacrament, as stated above (A. 2); nor can we assign any place where it may be. Consequently it is nothing after the consecration. Therefore, it is either annihilated, or dissolved into its original matter.

Obj. 2. Further, what is the term *wherefrom* in every change exists no longer, except in the potentiality of matter; *e.g.*, when air is changed into fire, the form of the air remains only in the potentiality of matter; and in like fashion when what is white becomes black. But in this sacrament the substance of the bread or of the wine is the *term wherefrom*, while the body or the blood of Christ is the *term whereunto:* for Ambrose says in *De Officiis* (*De Myster.* ix.): *Before the blessing it is called another species, after the blessing the body of Christ is signified.* Therefore, when the consecration takes place, the substance of the bread or wine no longer remains, unless perchance dissolved into its (original) matter.

Obj. 3. Further, one of two contradictories must be true. But this proposition is false: *After the consecration the substance of the bread or wine is something.* Consequently, this is true: *The substance of the bread or wine is nothing.*

On the contrary, Augustine says (Qq. 83): *God is not the cause of tending to nothing.* But this sacrament is wrought by Divine power. Therefore, in this sacrament the substance of the bread or wine is not annihilated.

I answer that, Because the substance of the bread and wine does not remain in this sacrament, some, deeming that it is impossible for the substance of the bread and wine to be changed into Christ's flesh and blood, have maintained that by the consecration, the substance of the bread and wine is either dissolved into the original matter, or that it is annihilated.

Now the original matter into which mixed bodies can be dissolved is the four elements. For dissolution cannot be made into primary matter, so that a subject can exist without a form, since matter cannot exist without a form. But since after the consecration nothing remains under the sacramental species except the body and the blood of Christ, it will be necessary to say that the elements into which the substance of the bread and wine is dissolved, depart from thence by local motion, which would be perceived by the senses.—In like manner also the substance of the bread or wine remains until the last instant of the consecration; but in the last instant of the consecration there is already present there the substance of the body or blood of Christ, just as the form is already present in the last instant of generation. Hence no instant can be assigned in which the original matter can be there. For it cannot be said that the substance of the bread or wine is dissolved gradually into the original matter, or that it successively quits the species, for if this began to be done in the last instant of its consecration, then at the one time under part of the host there would be the body of Christ together with the substance of bread, which is contrary to what has been said above (A. 2). But if this begin to come to pass before the consecration, there will then be a time in which under one part of the host there will be neither the substance of bread nor the body of Christ, which is not fitting. They seem indeed to have taken this into careful consideration; wherefore they formulated their proposition with an alternative, viz., that (the substance) may be annihilated. But even this cannot stand, because no way can be assigned whereby Christ's true body can begin to be in this sacrament, except by the change of the substance of bread into it, which change is excluded the moment we admit either annihilation of the substance of the bread, or dissolution into the original matter.—Likewise no cause can be assigned for such dissolution or annihilation, since the effect of the sacrament is signified by the form: but neither of these is signified by these words of the form: *This is My body.* Hence it is clear that the aforesaid opinion is false.

Reply Obj. 1. The substance of the bread or wine, after the consecration, remains neither under the sacramental species, nor elsewhere; yet it does not follow that it is annihilated; for it is changed into the body of Christ; just as, if the air, from which fire is generated, be not there or elsewhere, it does not follow that it is annihilated.

Reply Obj. 2. The form, which is the term *wherefrom,* is not changed into another form; but one form succeeds another in the subject; and therefore the first form remains only in the potentiality of matter. But here the substance of the bread is changed into the body of Christ, as stated above. Hence the conclusion does not follow.

Reply Obj. 3. Although after the consecration this proposition is false: *The substance of the bread is something,* still that into which the substance of the bread is changed, is something, and consequently the substance of the bread is not annihilated.

FOURTH ARTICLE

WHETHER BREAD CAN BE CONVERTED INTO THE BODY OF CHRIST?

We proceed thus to the Fourth Article:—

Objection 1. It seems that bread cannot be converted into the body of Christ. For conversion is a kind of change. But in every change there must be some subject, which from being previously in potentiality is now in act; because as is said in *Phys.* iii.: *motion is the act of a thing existing in potentiality.* But no subject can be assigned for the substance of the bread and of the body of Christ, because it is of the very nature of substance for it *not to be in a subject,* as it is said in *Prædic.* iii. Therefore it is not possible for the whole substance of the bread to be converted into the body of Christ.

Obj. 2. Further, the form of the thing into which another is converted, begins anew to inhere in the matter of the thing converted into it: as when air is changed into fire not already existing, the form of fire begins anew to be in the matter of the air; and in like manner when food is converted into non-pre-existing man, the form of the man begins to be anew in the matter of the food. Therefore, if bread be changed into the body of Christ, the form of Christ's body must necessarily begin to be in the matter of the bread, which is false. Consequently, the bread is not changed into the substance of Christ's body.

Obj. 3. Further, when two things are diverse, one never becomes the other, as whiteness never becomes blackness, as is stated in *Phys.* i. But since two contrary forms are of themselves diverse, as being the principles of formal difference, so two signate matters are of themselves diverse, as being the principles of material distinction. Consequently, it is not possible for this matter of bread to become this matter whereby Christ's body is individuated, and so it is not possible for this substance of bread to be changed into the substance of Christ's body.

On the contrary, Eusebius Emesenus says: *To thee it ought neither to be a novelty nor an impossiblity that earthly and mortal things be changed into the substance of Christ.*

I answer that, As stated above (A. 2), since Christ's true body is in this sacrament, and since it does not begin to be there by local motion, nor is it contained therein as in a place, as is evident from what was stated above (A. 1 *ad* 2), it must be said then that it begins to be there by conversion of the substance of bread into itself.

Yet this change is not like natural changes, but is entirely supernatural, and effected by God's power alone. Hence Ambrose says [(*De Sacram.* iv.): *See how Christ's word changes nature's laws, as He wills: a man is not wont to be born save of man and woman: see therefore that against the established law and order a man is born of a Virgin:* and] (*De Myster.* iv.): *It is clear that a Virgin begot beyond the order of nature: and what we make is the body from the Virgin. Why, then, do you look for nature's order in Christ's body, since the Lord Jesus was Himself brought forth of a Virgin beyond nature?* Chrysostom likewise (*Hom.* xlvii.), commenting on John vi. 64,—*The words which I have spoken to you,* namely, of this sacrament, *are spirit and life,* says: *i.e., spiritual, having nothing carnal, nor natural consequence; but they are rent from all such necessity which exists upon earth, and from the laws here established.*

For it is evident that every agent acts according as it is in act. But every created agent is limited in its act, as being of a determinate genus and species: and consequently the action of every created agent bears upon some determinate act. Now the determination of every thing in actual existence comes from its form. Consequently, no natural or created agent can act except by changing the form in something; and on this account every change made according to nature's laws is a formal change. But God is infinite act, as stated in the First Part (Q. VII., A. 1; Q. XXV., A. 2); hence His action extends to the the whole nature of being. Therefore He can work not only formal conversion, so that diverse forms succeed each other in the same subject; but also the change of all being, so that, to wit, the whole substance of one thing be changed into the whole substance of another. And this is done by Divine power in this sacrament; for the whole substance of the bread is changed into the whole substance of Christ's body, and the whole substance of the wine into the whole substance of Christ's blood. Hence this is not a formal, but a substantial conversion; nor is it a kind of natural movement: but, with a name of its own, it can be called *transubstantiation.*

Reply Obj. 1. This objection holds good in respect of formal change, because it belongs to a form to be in matter or in a subject; but it does not hold good in respect of the change of the entire substance. Hence, since this substantial change implies a certain order of substances, one of which is changed into the other, it is in both substances as in a subject, just as order and number.

Reply Obj. 2. This argument also is true of formal conversion or change, because, as stated above (A. *ad* 1), a form must be in some matter or subject. But this is not so in a change of the entire substance; for in this case no subject is possible.

Reply Obj. 3. Form cannot be changed into form, nor matter into matter by the power of any finite agent. Such a change, however, can be made by the power of an infinite agent, which has control over all being, because the nature of being is common to both forms and to both matters; and whatever there is of being in the one, the author of being can change into whatever there is of being in the other, withdrawing that whereby it was distinguished from the other.

FIFTH ARTICLE

WHETHER THE ACCIDENTS OF THE BREAD AND WINE REMAIN IN THIS SACRAMENT AFTER THE CHANGE?

We proceed thus to the Fifth Article:—

Objection 1. It seems that the accidents of the bread and wine do not remain in this sacrament. For when that which comes first is removed, that which follows is also taken away. But substance is naturally before accident, as is proved in *Metaph.* vii. Since, then, after consecration, the substance of the bread does not remain in this sacrament, it seems that its accidents cannot remain.

Obj. 2. Further, there ought not to be any deception in a sacrament of truth. But we judge of substance by accidents. It seems, then, that human judgment is deceived, if, while the accidents remain, the substance of the bread does not. Consequently this is unbecoming to this sacrament.

Obj. 3. Further, although our faith is not subject to reason, still it is not contrary to reason, but above it, as was said in the beginning of this work (P. I., Q. I., A. 6 *ad* 2; A. 8). But our reason has its origin in the senses. Therefore our faith ought not to be contrary to the senses, as it is when sense judges that to be bread which faith believes to be the substance of Christ's body. Therefore it is not befitting this sacrament for the accidents of bread to remain subject to the senses, and for the substance of bread not to remain.

Obj. 4. Further, what remains after the change has taken place seems to be the subject of change. If therefore the accidents of the bread remain after the change has been effected, it seems that the accidents are the subject of the change. But this is impossible; for *an accident cannot have an accident* (*Metaph.* iii.). Therefore the accidents of the bread and wine ought not to remain in this sacrament.

On the contrary, Augustine says in his book on the Sentences of Prosper (Lanfranc, *De Corp. et Sang. Dom.* xiii.): *Under the species which we behold, of bread and wine, we honour invisible things, i.e., flesh and blood.*

I answer that, It is evident to sense that all the accidents of the bread and wine remain after the consecration. And this is reasonably done by Divine providence. First of all, because it is not customary, but horrible, for men to eat human flesh, and to drink blood. And therefore Christ's flesh and blood are set before us to be partaken of under the species of those things which are the more commonly used by men, namely, bread and wine. Secondly, lest this sacrament might be derided by unbelievers, if we were to eat Our Lord under His own species. Thirdly, that while we receive Our Lord's body and blood invisibly, this may redound to the merit of faith.

Reply Obj. 1. As is said in the book *De Causis,* an effect depends more on the first cause than on the second. And therefore by God's power, which is the first cause of all things, it is possible for that which follows to remain, while that which is first is taken away.

Reply Obj. 2. There is no deception in this sacrament; for the accidents which are discerned by the senses are truly present. But the intellect, whose proper object is substance, as is said in *De Anima* iii., is preserved by faith from deception.

And this serves as answer to the third argument; because faith is not contrary to the senses, but concerns things to which sense does not reach.

Reply Obj. 4. This change has not properly a subject, as was stated above (A. 4 *ad* 1); nevertheless the accidents which remain have some resemblance of a subject.

SIXTH ARTICLE

WHETHER THE SUBSTANTIAL FORM OF THE BREAD REMAINS IN THIS SACRAMENT AFTER THE CONSECRATION?

We proceed thus to the Sixth Article:—

Objection 1. It seems that the substantial form of the bread remains in this sacrament after the consecration. For it has been said (A. 5) that the accidents remain after the consecration. But since bread is an artificial thing, its form is an accident. Therefore it remains after the consecration.

Obj. 2. Further, the form of Christ's body is His soul: for it is said in *De Anima* ii., that the soul *is the act of a physical body which has life in potentiality.* But it cannot be said that the substantial form of the bread is changed into the soul. Therefore it appears that it remains after the consecration.

Obj. 3. Further, the proper operation of a thing follows its substantial form. But what remains in this sacrament, nourishes, and performs every operation which bread would do were it present. Therefore the substantial form of the bread remains in this sacrament after the consecration.

On the contrary, The substantial form of bread is of the substance of bread. But the substance of the bread is changed into the body of Christ, as stated above (AA. 2, 3, 4). Therefore the substantial form of the bread does not remain.

I answer that, Some have contended that after the consecration not only do the accidents of the bread remain, but also its substantial form. But this cannot be. First of all, because if the substantial form of the bread were to remain, nothing of the bread would be changed into the body of Christ, excepting the matter; and so it would follow that it would be changed, not into the whole body of Christ, but into its matter, which is repugnant to the form of the sacrament, wherein it is said: *This is My body.*

Secondly, because if the substantial form of the bread were to remain, it would remain either in matter, or separated from matter. The first cannot be, for if it were to remain in the matter of the bread, then the whole substance of the bread would remain, which is against what was said above (A. 2). Nor could it remain in any other matter, because the proper form exists only in its proper matter.—But if it were to remain separate from matter, it would then be an actually intelligible form, and also an intelligence; for all forms separated from matter are such.

Thirdly, it would be unbefitting this sacrament: because the accidents of the bread remain in this sacrament, in order that the body of Christ may be seen under them, and not under its proper species, as stated above (A. 5).

And therefore it must be said that the substantial form of the bread does not remain.

Reply Obj. 1. There is nothing to prevent art from making a thing whose form is not an accident, but a substantial form; as frogs and serpents can be produced by art: for art produces such forms not by its own power, but by the power of natural energies. And in this way it produces the substantial forms of bread, by the power of fire baking the matter made up of flour and water.

Reply Obj. 2. The soul is the form of the body, giving it the whole order of perfect being, *i.e.,* being, corporeal being, and animated being, and so on. Therefore the form of the bread is changed into the form of Christ's body, according as the latter gives corporeal being, but not according as it bestows animated being.

Reply Obj. 3. Some of the operations of bread follow it by reason of the accidents, such as to affect the senses, and such operations are found in the species of the bread after the consecration on account of the accidents which remain. But some other operations follow the bread either by reason of the matter, such as that it is changed into something else, or else by reason of the substantial form, such as an operation consequent upon its species, for instance, that it *strengthens man's heart* (Ps. ciii. 15); and such operations are found in this sacrament, not on account of the form or matter remaining, but because they are bestowed miraculously upon the accidents themselves, as will be said later (Q. LXXVII., A. 3 *ad* 2, 3; AA. 5, 6).

SEVENTH ARTICLE

WHETHER THIS CHANGE IS WROUGHT INSTANTANEOUSLY?

We proceed thus to the Seventh Article:—

Objection 1. It seems that this change is not wrought instantaneously, but successively. For in this change there is first the substance of bread, and afterwards the substance of Christ's body. Neither, then, is in the same instant, but in two instants. But there is a mid-time between every two instants. Therefore this change must take place according to the succession of time, which is between the last instant in which the bread is there, and the first instant in which the body of Christ is present.

Obj. 2. Further, in every change something is *in becoming* and something is *in being.* But these two things do not exist at the one time, for, what is *in becoming,* is not yet, whereas what is *in being,* already is. Consequently, there is a before and an after in such change: and so necessarily the change cannot be instantaneous, but successive.

Obj. 3. Further, Ambrose says (*De Sacram.* iv.) that this sacrament *is made by the words of Christ.* But Christ's words are pronounced successively. Therefore the change takes place successively.

On the contrary, This change is effected by a power which is infinite, to which it belongs to operate in an instant.

I answer that, A change may be instantaneous from a threefold reason. First on the part of the form, which is the terminus of the change. For, if it be a form that receives more and less, it is acquired by its subject successively, such as health; and therefore because a substantial form does not receive more and less, it follows that its introduction into matter is instantaneous.

Secondly on the part of the subject, which sometimes is prepared successively for receiving the form; thus water is heated successively. When, however, the subject itself is in the ultimate disposition for receiving the form, it receives it suddenly, as a transparent body is illuminated suddenly. Thirdly on the part of the agent, which possesses infinite power: wherefore it can instantly dispose the matter for the form. Thus it is written (Mark vii. 34) that when Christ had said, *'Ephpheta,' which is 'Be thou opened,' immediately his ears were opened, and the string of his tongue was loosed.*

For these three reasons this conversion is instantaneous. First, because the substance of Christ's body which is the term of this conversion, does not receive more or less.—Secondly, because in this conversion there is no subject to be disposed successively.—Thirdly, because it is effected by God's infinite power.

Reply Obj. 1. Some do not grant simply that there is a mid-time between every two instants. For they say that this is true of two instants referring to the same movement, but not if they refer to different things. Hence between the instant that marks the close of rest, and another which marks the beginning of movement, there is no mid-time. But in this they are mistaken, because the unity of time and of instant, or even their plurality, is not taken according to movements of any sort, but according to the first movement of the heavens, which is the measure of all movement and rest.

Accordingly others grant this of the time which measures movement depending on the movement of the heavens. But there are some movements which are not dependent on the movement of the heavens, nor measured by it, as was said in the First Part (Q. LIII., A. 3) concerning the movements of the angels. Hence between two instants responding to those movements there is no mid-time.—But this is not to the point, because although the change in question has no relation of itself to the movement of the heavens, still it follows the pronouncing of the words, which (pronouncing) must necessarily be measured by the movement of the heavens. And therefore there must of necessity be a mid-time between every two signate instants in connection with that change.

Some say therefore that the instant in which the bread was last, and the instant in which the body of Christ is first, are indeed two in comparison with the things measured, but are one comparatively to the time measuring; as when two lines touch, there are two points on the part of the two lines, but one point on the part of the place containing them. But here there is no likeness, because instant and time is not the intrinsic measure of particular movements, as a line and point are of a body, but only the extrinsic measure, as place is to bodies.

Hence others say that it is the same instant in fact, but another according to reason. But according to this it would follow that things really opposite would exist together; for diversity of reason does not change a thing objectively.

And therefore it must be said that this change, as stated above, is wrought by Christ's words which are spoken by the priest, so that the last instant of pronouncing the words is the first instant in which Christ's body is in the sacrament; and that the substance of the bread is there during the whole preceding time. Of this time no instant is to be taken as proximately preceding the last one, because time is not made up of successive instants, as is proved in *Phys.* vi. And therefore a first instant can be assigned in which Christ's body is present; but a last instant cannot be assigned in which the substance of bread is there, but a last time can be assigned. And the same holds good in natural changes, as is evident from the Philosopher (*Phys.* viii.).

Reply Obj. 2. In instantaneous changes a thing is *in becoming,* and is *in being* simultaneously; just as becoming illuminated and to be actually illuminated are simultaneous: for in such, a thing is said to be *in being* according as it now is; but to be *in becoming,* according as it was not before.

Reply Obj. 3. As stated above (*ad.* 1), this change comes about in the last instant of the pronouncing of the words; for then the meaning of the words is finished, which meaning is efficacious in the forms of the sacraments. And therefore it does not follow that this change is successive.

EIGHTH ARTICLE

WHETHER THIS PROPOSITION IS FALSE: THE BODY OF CHRIST IS MADE OUT OF BREAD?

We proceed thus to the Eighth Article:—

Objection 1. It seems that this proposition is false: *The Body of Christ is made out of bread.* For everything out of which another is made, is that which is made the other; but not conversely: for we say that a black thing is made out of a white thing, and that a white thing is made black: and although we may say that a man becomes black, still we do not say that a black thing is made out of a man, as is shown in *Phys.* i. If it be true, then, that Christ's body is made out of bread, it will be true to say that bread is made the body of Christ. But this seems to be false, because the bread is not the subject of the making, but rather its term. Therefore, it is not said truly that Christ's body is made out of bread.

Obj. 2. Further, the term of *becoming* is something that *is,* or something that *is made.* But this proposition is never true: *The bread is the body of Christ;* or *The bread is made the body of Christ;* or again, *The bread will be the body of Christ.* Therefore it seems that not even this is true: *The body of Christ is made out of bread.*

Obj. 3. Further, everything out of which another is made is converted into that which is made from it. But this proposition seems to be false: *The bread is converted into the body of Christ,* because such conversion seems to be more miraculous than the creation of the world, in which it is not said that non-being is converted into being. Therefore it seems that this proposition likewise is false: *The body of Christ is made out of bread.*

Obj. 4. Further, that out of which something is made, can be that thing. But this proposition is false: *Bread can be the body of Christ.* Therefore this is likewise false: *The body of Christ is made out of bread.*

On the contrary, Ambrose says (*De Sacram.* iv.): *When the consecration takes place, the body of Christ is made out of the bread.*

I answer that, This conversion of bread into the body of Christ has something in common with creation, and with natural transmutation, and in some respect differs from both. For the order of the terms is common to these three; that is, that after one thing there is another (for, in creation there is being after non-being; in this sacrament, Christ's body after the substance of bread; in natural transmutation white after black, or fire after air); and that the aforesaid terms are not coexistent.

Now the conversion, of which we are speaking, has this in common with creation, that in neither of them is there any common subject belonging to either of the extremes; the contrary of which appears in every natural transmutation.

Again, this conversion has something in common with natural transmutation in two respects, although not in the same fashion. First of all because in both, one of the extremes passes into the other, as bread into Christ's body, and air into fire; whereas non-being is not converted into being. But this comes to pass differently on the one side and on the other; for in this sacrament the whole substance of the bread passes into the whole body of Christ; whereas in natural transmutation the matter of the one receives the form of the other, the previous form being laid aside. Secondly, they have this in common, that on both sides something remains the same; whereas this does not happen in creation: yet differently; for the same matter or subject remains in natural transmutation; whereas in this sacrament the same accidents remain.

From these observations we can gather the various ways of speaking in such matters. For, because in no one of the aforesaid three things are the extremes coexistent, therefore in none of them can one extreme be predicated of the other by the substantive verb of the present tense: for we do not say, *Non-being is being,* or, *Bread is the body of Christ,* or, *Air is fire,* or, *White is black.* Yet because of the relationship of the extremes in all of them we can use the preposition *ex* (*out of*), which denotes order; for we can truly and properly say that *being is made out of non-being,* and *out of bread, the body of Christ,* and *out of air, fire,* and *out of white, black.*

But because in creation one of the extremes does not pass into the other, we cannot use the word *conversion* in creation, so as to say that *non-being is converted into being:* we can, however, use the word in this sacrament, just as in natural transmutation. But since in this sacrament the whole substance is converted into the whole substance, on that account this conversion is properly termed transubstantiation.

Again, since there is no subject of this conversion, the things which are true in natural conversion by reason of the subject, are not to be granted in this conversion. And in the first place indeed it is evident that potentiality to the opposite follows a subject, by reason whereof we say that *a white thing can be black,* or that *air can be fire;* although the latter is not so proper as the former: for the subject of whiteness, in which there is potentiality to blackness, is the whole substance of the white thing; since whiteness is not a part thereof; whereas the subject of the form of air is part thereof: hence when it is said, *Air can be fire,* it is verified by synecdoche by reason of the part. But in this conversion, and similarly in creation, because there is no subject, it is not said that one extreme can be the other, as that *non-being can be being,* or that *bread can be the body of Christ:* and for the same reason it cannot be properly said that *being is made of (de) non-being,* or that *the body of Christ is made of bread,* because this preposition *of* (*de*) denotes a consubstantial cause, which consubstantiality of the extremes in natural transmutations is considered according to something common in the subject. And for the same reason it is not granted that *bread will be the body of Christ,* or that it *may become the body of Christ,* just as it is not granted in creation that *non-being will be being,* or that *non-being may become being,* because this manner of speaking is verified in natural transmutations by reason of the subject: for instance, when we say that *a white thing becomes black,* or *a white thing will be black.*

Nevertheless, since in this sacrament, after the change, something remains the same, namely, the accidents of the bread, as stated above (A. 5), some of these expressions may be admitted by way of similitude, namely, that *bread is the body of Christ,* or, *bread will be the body of Christ,* or *the body of*

Christ is made of bread; provided that by the word *bread* is not understood the substance of bread, but in general *that which is contained under the species of bread,* under which species there is first contained the substance of bread, and afterwards the body of Christ.

Reply Obj. 1. That out of which something else is made, sometimes implies together with the subject, one of the extremes of the transmutation, as when it is said *a black thing is made out of a white one;* but sometimes it implies only the opposite or the extreme, as when it is said—*out of morning comes the day.* And so it is not granted that the latter becomes the former, that is, *that morning becomes the day.* So likewise in the matter in hand, although it may be said properly that *the body of Christ is made out of bread,* yet it is not said properly that *bread becomes the body of Christ,* except by similitude, as was said above.

Reply Obj. 2. That out of which another is made, will sometimes be that other because of the subject which is implied. And therefore, since there is no subject of this change, the comparison does not hold.

Reply Obj. 3. In this change there are many more difficulties than in creation, in which there is but this one difficulty, that something is made out of nothing; yet this belongs to the proper mode of production of the first cause, which presupposes nothing else. But in this conversion not only is it difficult for this whole to be changed into that whole, so that nothing of the former may remain (which does not belong to the common mode of production of a cause), but furthermore it has this difficulty that the accidents remain while the substance is destroyed, and many other difficulties of which we shall treat hereafter (Q. LXXVII.). Nevertheless the word *conversion* is admitted in this sacrament, but not in creation, as stated above.

Reply Obj. 4. As was observed above, potentiality belongs to the subject, whereas there is no subject in this conversion. And therefore it is not granted that bread can be the body of Christ: for this conversion does not come about by the passive potentiality of the creature, but solely by the active power of the Creator.

QUESTION LXXVI

OF THE WAY IN WHICH CHRIST IS IN THIS SACRAMENT

(In Eight Articles)

We have now to consider the manner in which Christ exists in this sacrament; and under this head there are eight points of inquiry: (1) Whether the whole Christ is under this sacrament? (2) Whether the entire Christ is under each species of the sacrament? (3) Whether the entire Christ is under every part of the species? (4) Whether all the dimensions of Christ's body are in this sacrament? (5) Whether the body of Christ is in this sacrament locally? (6) Whether after the consecration, the body of Christ is moved when the host or chalice is moved? (7) Whether Christ's body, as it is in this sacrament, can be seen by the eye? (8) Whether the true body of Christ remains in this sacrament when He is seen under the appearance of a child or of flesh?

FIRST ARTICLE

WHETHER THE WHOLE CHRIST IS CONTAINED UNDER THIS SACRAMENT?

We proceed thus to the First Article:—

Objection 1. It seems that the whole Christ is not contained under this sacrament, because Christ begins to be in this sacrament by conversion of the bread and wine. But it is evident that the bread and wine cannot be changed either into the Godhead or into the soul of Christ. Since therefore Christ exists in three substances, namely, the Godhead, soul and body, as shown above (Q. II., A. 5; Q. V., AA. 1, 3), it seems that the entire Christ is not under this sacrament.

Obj. 2. Further, Christ is in this sacrament, forasmuch as it is ordained to the refection of the faithful, which consists in food and drink, as stated above (Q. LXXIV., A. 1). But Our Lord said (John vi. 56): *My flesh is meat indeed, and My blood is drink indeed.* Therefore, only the flesh and blood of Christ are contained in this sacrament. But there are many other parts of Christ's body, for instance, the nerves, bones, and suchlike. Therefore the entire Christ is not contained under this sacrament.

Obj. 3. Further, a body of greater quantity cannot be contained under the measure of a lesser. But the measure of the bread and wine is much smaller than the measure of Christ's body. Therefore it is impossible that the entire Christ be contained under this sacrament.

On the contrary, Ambrose says (*De Offic.*): *Christ is in this sacrament.*

I answer that, It is absolutely necessary to confess according to Catholic faith that the entire Christ is in this sacrament. Yet we must know that there is something of Christ in this sacrament in a twofold manner: first, as it were, by the power of the sacrament; secondly, from natural concomitance. By the power of the sacrament, there is under the species of this sacrament that into which the pre-existing substance of the bread and wine is changed, as expressed by the words of the form, which are effective in this as in the other sacraments; for instance, by the words—*This is My body,* or, *This is My blood.* But from natural concomitance there is also in this sacrament that which is really united with that thing wherein the aforesaid conversion is terminated. For if any two things be really united, then wherever the one is really, there must the other also be: since things really united together are only distinguished by an operation of the mind.

Reply Obj. 1. Because the change of the bread and wine is not terminated at the Godhead or the soul of Christ, it follows as a consequence that the Godhead or the soul of Christ is in this sacrament not by the power of the sacrament, but from real concomitance. For since the Godhead never set aside the assumed body, wherever the body of Christ is, there, of necessity, must the Godhead be; and therefore it is necessary for the Godhead to be in this sacrament concomitantly with His body. Hence we read in the profession of faith at Ephesus (P. I., chap. xxvi.): *We are made partakers of the body and blood of Christ, not as taking common flesh, nor as of a holy man united to the Word in dignity, but the truly life-giving flesh of the Word Himself.*

On the other hand, His soul was truly separated from His body, as stated above (Q. L., A. 5). And therefore had this sacrament been celebrated during those three days when He was dead, the soul of Christ would not have been there, neither by the power of the sacrament, nor from real concomitance. But since *Christ rising from the dead dieth now no more* (Rom. vi. 9), His soul is always really united with His body. And therefore in this sacrament the body indeed of Christ is present by the power of the sacrament, but His soul from real concomitance.

Reply Obj. 2. By the power of the sacrament there is contained under it, as to the species of the bread, not only the flesh, but the entire body of Christ, that is, the bones, the nerves, and the like. And this is apparent from the form of this sacrament, wherein it is not said: *This is My flesh,* but—*This is My body*. Accordingly, when Our Lord said (John vi. 56): *My flesh is meat indeed,* there the word flesh is put for the entire body, because according to human custom it seems to be more adapted for eating, as men commonly are fed on the flesh of animals, but not on the bones or the like.

Reply Obj. 3. As has been already stated (Q. LXXV., A. 5), after the consecration of the bread into the body of Christ, or of the wine into His blood, the accidents of both remain. From which it is evident that the dimensions of the bread or wine are not changed into the dimensions of the body of Christ, but substance into substance. And so the substance of Christ's body or blood is under this sacrament by the power of the sacrament, but not the dimensions of Christ's body or blood. Hence it is clear that the body of Christ is in this sacrament *by way of substance,* and not by way of quantity. But the proper totality of substance is contained indifferently in a small or large quantity; as the whole nature of air in a great or small amount of air, and the whole nature of a man in a big or small individual. Wherefore, after the consecration, the whole substance of Christ's body and blood is contained in this sacrament, just as the whole substance of the bread and wine was contained there before the consecration.

SECOND ARTICLE

WHETHER THE WHOLE CHRIST IS CONTAINED UNDER EACH SPECIES OF THIS SACRAMENT?

We proceed thus to the Second Article:—

Objection 1. It seems that the whole Christ is not contained under both species of this sacrament. For this sacrament is ordained for the salvation of the faithful, not by virtue of the species, but by virtue of what is contained under the species, because the species were there even before the consecration, from which comes the power of this sacrament. If nothing, then, be contained under one species, but what is contained under the other, and if the whole Christ be contained under both, it seems that one of them is superfluous in this sacrament.

Obj. 2. Further, it was stated above (A. 1 *ad* 1) that all the other parts of the body, such as the bones, nerves, and the like, are comprised under the name of flesh. But the blood is one of the parts of the human body, as Aristotle proves (*De Anima. Histor.* i.). If, then, Christ's blood be contained under the species of bread, just as the other parts of the body are contained there, the blood ought not to be consecrated apart, just as no other part of the body is consecrated separately.

Obj. 3. Further, what is once *in being* cannot be again *in becoming.* But Christ's body has already begun to be in this sacrament by the consecration of the bread. Therefore, it cannot begin again to be there by the consecration of the wine; and so Christ's body will not be contained under the species of the wine, and accordingly neither the entire Christ. Therefore the whole Christ is not contained under each species.

On the contrary, The gloss on 1 Cor. xi. 25, commenting on the word *Chalice,* says that *under each species,* namely, of the bread and wine, *the same is received;* and thus it seems that Christ is entire under each species.

I answer that, After what we have said above (A. 1), it must be held most certainly that the whole Christ is under each sacramental species yet not alike in each. For the body of Christ is indeed present under the species of bread by the power of the sacrament, while the blood is there from real concomitance, as stated above (A. 1 *ad* 1) in regard to the soul and Godhead of Christ; and under the species of wine the blood is present by the power of the sacrament, and His body by real concomitance, as is also His soul and Godhead: because now Christ's blood is not separated from His body, as it was at the time of His Passion and death. Hence if this sacrament had been celebrated then, the body of Christ would have been under the species of the bread, but without the blood; and, under the species of the wine, the blood would have been present without the body, as it was then, in fact.

Reply Obj. 1. Although the whole Christ is under each species, yet it is so not without purpose. For in the first place this serves to represent Christ's Passion, in which the blood was separated from the body; hence in the form for the consecration of the blood mention is made of its shedding. Secondly, it is in keeping with the use of this sacrament, that Christ's body be shown apart to the faithful as food, and the blood as drink. Thirdly, it is in keeping with its effect, in which sense it was stated above (Q. LXXIV., A. 1) that *the body is offered for the salvation of the body, and the blood for the salvation of the soul.*

Reply Obj. 2. In Christ's Passion, of which this is the memorial, the other parts of the body were not separated from one another, as the blood was, but the body remained entire, according to Exod. xii. 46: *You shall not break a bone thereof.* And therefore in this sacrament the blood is consecrated apart from the body, but no other part is consecrated separately from the rest.

Reply Obj. 3. As stated above, the body of Christ is not under the species of wine by the power of the sacrament, but by real concomitance: and therefore by the consecration of the wine the body of Christ is not there of itself, but concomitantly.

THIRD ARTICLE

WHETHER CHRIST IS ENTIRE UNDER EVERY PART OF THE SPECIES OF THE BREAD AND WINE?

We proceed thus to the Third Article:—

Objection 1. It seems that Christ is not entire under every part of the species of bread and wine. Because those species can be divided infinitely. If therefore Christ be entirely under every part of the said species, it would follow that He is in this sacrament an infinite number of times: which is unreasonable; because the infinite is repugnant not only to nature, but likewise to grace.

Obj. 2. Further, since Christ's is an organic body, it has parts determinately distant; for a determinate distance of the individual parts from each other is of the very nature of an organic body, as that of eye from eye, and eye from ear. But this could not be so, if Christ were entire under every part of the species; for every part would have to be under every other part, and so where one part would be, there another part would be. It cannot be then that the entire Christ is under every part of the host or of the wine contained in the chalice.

Obj. 3. Further, Christ's body always retains the true nature of a body, nor is it ever changed into a spirit. Now it is the nature of a body for it to be *quantity having position* (*Predic.* iv.). But it belongs to the nature of this quantity that the various parts exist in various parts of place. Therefore, apparently it is impossible for the entire Christ to be under every part of the species.

On the contrary, Augustine says in a sermon (Gregory, *Sacramentarium*): *Each receives Christ the Lord, Who is entire under every morsel, nor is He less in each portion, but bestows Himself entire under each.*

I answer that, As was observed above (A. 1 *ad* 3), because the substance of Christ's body is in this sacrament by the power of the sacrament, while dimensive quantity is there by reason of real concomitance, consequently Christ's body is in this sacrament substantively, that is, in the way in which substance is under dimensions, but not after the manner of dimensions, which means, not in the way in which the dimensive quantity of a body is under the dimensive quantity of place.

Now it is evident that the whole nature of a substance is under every part of the dimensions under which it is contained; just as the entire nature of air is under every part of air, and the entire nature of bread under every part of bread; and this indifferently, whether the dimensions be actually divided (as when the air is divided or the bread cut), or whether they be actually undivided, but potentially divisible. And therefore it is manifest that the entire Christ is under every part of the species of the bread, even while the host remains entire, and not merely when it is broken, as some say, giving the example of an image which appears in a mirror, which appears as one in the unbroken mirror, whereas when the mirror is broken, there is an image in each part of the broken mirror: for the comparison is not perfect, because the multiplying of such images results in the broken mirror on account of the various reflections in the various parts of the mirror; but here there is only one consecration, whereby Christ's body is in this sacrament.

Reply Obj. 1. Number follows division, and therefore so long as quantity remains actually undivided, neither is the substance of any thing several times under its proper dimensions, nor is Christ's body several times under the dimensions of the bread; and consequently not an infinite number of times, but just as many times as it is divided into parts.

Reply Obj. 2. The determinate distance of parts in an organic body is based upon its dimensive quantity; but the nature of substance preceded even dimensive quantity. And since the conversion of the substance of the bread is terminated at the substance of the body of Christ, and since according to the manner of substance the body of Christ is properly and directly in this sacrament; such distance of parts is indeed in Christ's true body, which, however, is not compared to this sacrament according to such distance, but according to the manner of its substance, as stated above (A. 1 *ad* 3).

Reply Obj. 3. This argument is based on the nature of a body, arising from dimensive quantity. But it was said above (*ad* 2) that Christ's body is compared with this sacrament not by reason of dimensive quantity, but by reason of its substance, as already stated.

FOURTH ARTICLE

WHETHER THE WHOLE DIMENSIVE QUANTITY OF CHRIST'S BODY IS IN THIS SACRAMENT?

We proceed thus to the Fourth Article:—

Objection 1. It seems that the whole dimensive quantity of Christ's body is not in this sacrament. For it was said (A. 3) that Christ's entire body is contained under every part of the consecrated host. But no dimensive quantity is contained entirely in any whole, and in its every part. Therefore it is impossible for the entire dimensive quantity of Christ's body to be there.

Obj. 2. Further, it is impossible for two dimensive quantities to be together, even though one be separate from its subject, and the other in a natural body, as is clear from the Philosopher (*Metaph.* iii.). But the dimensive quantity of the bread remains in this sacrament, as is evident to our senses. Consequently, the dimensive quantity of Christ's body is not there.

Obj. 3. Further, if two unequal dimensive quantities be set side by side, the greater will overlap the lesser. But the dimensive quantity of Christ's body is considerably larger than the dimensive quantity of the consecrated host, according to every dimension. Therefore, if the dimensive quantity of Christ's body be in this sacrament together with the dimensive quantity of the host, the dimensive quantity of Christ's body is extended beyond the quantity of the host, which nevertheless is not without the substance of Christ's body. Therefore, the substance of Christ's body will be in this sacrament even outside the species of the bread, which is unreasonable, since the substance of Christ's body is in this sacrament, only by the consecration of the bread, as stated above (A. 2). Consequently, it is impossible for the whole dimensive quantity of Christ's body to be in this sacrament.

On the contrary, The existence of the dimensive quantity of any body cannot be separated from the existence of its substance. But in this sacrament the entire substance of Christ's body is present, as stated above (AA. 1, 3). Therefore the entire dimensive quantity of Christ's body is in this sacrament.

I answer that, As stated above (A. 1), any part of Christ is in this sacrament in two ways: in one way, by the power of the sacrament; in another, from real concomitance. By the power of the sacrament the dimensive quantity of Christ's body is not in this sacrament; for, by the power of the sacrament that is present in this sacrament, whereat the conversion is terminated. But the conversion which takes place in this sacrament is terminated directly at the substance of Christ's body, and not at its dimensions; which is evident from the fact that the dimensive quantity of the bread remains after the consecration, while only the substance of the bread passes away.

Nevertheless, since the substance of Christ's body is not really deprived of its dimensive quantity and its other accidents, hence it comes that by reason of real concomitance the whole dimensive quantity of Christ's body and all its other accidents are in this sacrament.

Reply Obj. 1. The manner of being of every thing is determined by what belongs to it of itself, and not according to what is coupled accidentally with it: thus an object is present to the sight, according as it is white, and not according as it is sweet, although the same object may be both white and sweet; hence sweetness is in the sight after the manner of whiteness, and not after that of sweetness. Since, then, the substance of Christ's body is present on the altar by the power of this sacrament, while its dimensive quantity is there concomitantly and as it were accidentally, therefore the dimensive quantity of Christ's body is in this sacrament, not according to its proper manner (namely, that the whole is in the whole, and the individual parts in individual parts), but after the manner of substance, whose nature is for the whole to be in the whole, and the whole in every part.

Reply Obj. 2. Two dimensive quantities cannot naturally be in the same subject at the same time, so that each be there according to the proper manner of dimensive quantity. But in this sacrament the dimensive quantity of the bread is there after its proper manner, that is, according to commensuration: not so the dimensive quantity of Christ's body, for that is there after the manner of substance, as stated above (*ad* 1).

Reply Obj. 3. The dimensive quantity of Christ's body is in this sacrament not by way of commensuration, which is proper to quantity, and to which it belongs for the greater to be extended beyond the lesser; but in the way mentioned above (*ad* 1, 2).

FIFTH ARTICLE

WHETHER CHRIST'S BODY IS IN THIS SACRAMENT AS IN A PLACE?

We proceed thus to the Fifth Article:—

Objection 1. It seems that Christ's body is in this sacrament as in a place. Because, to be in a place definitively or circumscriptively belongs to being in a place. But Christ's body seems to be definitively in this sacrament, because it is so present where the species of the bread and wine are, that it is nowhere else upon the altar: likewise it seems to be there circumscriptively, because it is so contained under the species of the consecrated host, that it neither exceeds it nor is exceeded by it. Therefore Christ's body is in this sacrament as in a place.

Obj. 2. Further, the place of the bread and wine is not empty, because nature abhors a vacuum; nor is the substance of the bread there, as stated above (Q. LXXV., A. 2); but only the body of Christ is there. Consequently the body of Christ fills that place. But whatever fills a place is there locally. Therefore the body of Christ is in this sacrament locally.

Obj. 3. Further, as stated above (A. 4), the body of Christ is in this sacrament with its dimensive quantity, and with all its accidents. But to be in a place is an accident of a body; hence *where* is numbered among the nine kinds of accidents. Therefore Christ's body is in this sacrament locally.

On the contrary, The place and the object placed must be equal, as is clear from the Philosopher (*Phys.* iv.). But the place, where this sacrament is, is much less than the body of Christ. Therefore Christ's body is not in this sacrament as in a place.

I answer that, As stated above (A. 1 *ad* 3; A. 3), Christ's body is in this sacrament not after the proper manner of dimensive quantity, but rather after the manner of substance. But every body occupying a place is in the place according to the manner of dimensive quantity, namely, inasmuch as it is commensurate with the place according to its dimensive quantity. Hence it remains that Christ's body is not in this sacrament as in a place, but after the manner of substance, that is to say, in that way in which substance is contained by dimensions; because the substance of Christ's body succeeds the substance of bread in this sacrament: hence as the substance of bread was not locally under its dimensions, but after the manner of substance, so neither is the substance of Christ's body. Nevertheless the substance of Christ's body is not the subject of those dimensions, as was the substance of the bread: and therefore the substance of the bread was there locally by reason of its dimensions, because it was compared with that place through the medium of its own dimensions; but the substance of Christ's body is compared with that place through the medium of foreign dimensions, so that, on the contrary, the proper dimensions of Christ's body are compared with that place through the medium of substance; which is contrary to the notion of a located body.

Hence in no way is Christ's body locally in this sacrament.

Reply Obj. 1. Christ's body is not in this sacrament definitively, because then it would be only on the particular altar where this sacrament is performed; whereas it is in heaven under its own species, and on many other altars under the sacramental species. Likewise it is evident that it is not in this sacrament circumscriptively, because it is not there according to the commensuration of its own quantity, as stated above. But that it is not outside the superficies of the sacrament, nor on any other part of the altar, is due not to its being there definitively or circumscriptively, but to its being there by consecration and conversion of the bread and wine, as stated above (A. 1; Q. LXXV., A. 2 *sqq*.).

Reply Obj. 2. The place in which Christ's body is, is not empty; nor yet is it properly filled with the substance of Christ's body, which is not there locally, as stated above; but it is filled with the sacramental species, which have to fill the place either because of the nature of dimensions, or at least miraculously, as they also subsist miraculously after the fashion of substance.

Reply Obj. 3. As stated above (A. 4), the accidents of Christ's body are in this sacrament by real concomitance. And therefore those accidents of Christ's body which are intrinsic to it are in this sacrament. But to be in a place is an accident when compared with the extrinsic container. And therefore it is not necessary for Christ to be in this sacrament as in a place.

SIXTH ARTICLE

WHETHER CHRIST'S BODY IS IN THIS SACRAMENT MOVABLY?

We proceed thus to the Sixth Article:—

Objection 1. It seems that Christ's body is movably in

this sacrament, because the Philosopher says (*Topic.* ii.) that *when we are moved, the things within us are moved:* and this is true even of the soul's spiritual substance. *But Christ is in this sacrament,* as shown above (Q. LXXIV., A. 1). Therefore He is moved when it is moved.

Obj. 2. Further, the truth ought to correspond with the figure. But, according to the commandment (Exod. xii. 10), concerning the Paschal Lamb, a figure of this sacrament, *there remained nothing until the morning.* Neither, therefore, if this sacrament be reserved until morning, will Christ's body be there; and so it is not immovably in this sacrament.

Obj. 3. Further, if Christ's body were to remain under this sacrament even until the morrow, for the same reason it will remain there during all coming time; for it cannot be said that it ceases to be there when the species pass, because the existence of Christ's body is not dependent on those species. Yet Christ does not remain in this sacrament for all coming time. It seems, then, that straightway on the morrow, or after a short time, He ceases to be under this sacrament. And so it seems that Christ is in this sacrament movably.

On the contrary, It is impossible for the same thing to be in motion and at rest, else contradictories would be verified of the same subject. But Christ's body is at rest in heaven. Therefore it is not movably in this sacrament.

I answer that, When any thing is one, as to subject, and manifold in being, there is nothing to hinder it from being moved in one respect, and yet to remain at rest in another just as it is one thing for a body to be white, and another thing, to be large; hence it can be moved as to its whiteness, and yet continue unmoved as to its magnitude. But in Christ, being in Himself and being under the sacrament are not the same thing, because when we say that He is under this sacrament, we express a kind of relationship to this sacrament. According to this being, then, Christ is not moved locally of Himself, but only accidentally, because Christ is not in this sacrament as in a place, as stated above (A. 5). But what is not in a place, is not moved of itself locally, but only according to the motion of the subject in which it is.

In the same way neither is it moved of itself according to the being which it has in this sacrament, by any other change whatever, as for instance, that it ceases to be under this sacrament: because whatever possesses unfailing existence of itself, cannot be the principle of failing; but when something else fails, then it ceases to be in it; just as God, Whose existence is unfailing and immortal, ceases to be in some corruptible creature because such corruptible creature ceases to exist. And in this way, since Christ has unfailing and incorruptible being, He ceases to be under this sacrament, not because He ceases to be, nor yet by local movement of His own, as is clear from what has been said, but only by the fact that the sacramental species cease to exist.

Hence it is clear that Christ, strictly speaking, is immovably in this sacrament.

Reply Obj. 1. This argument deals with accidental movement, whereby things within us are moved together with us. But with things which can of themselves be in a place, like bodies, it is otherwise than with things which cannot of themselves be in a place, such as forms and spiritual substances. And to this mode can be reduced what we say of Christ, being moved accidentally, according to the existence which He has in this sacrament, in which He is not present as in a place.

Reply Obj. 2. It was this argument which seems to have convinced those who held that Christ's body does not remain under this sacrament if it be reserved until the morrow. It is against these that Cyril says (*Ep.* lxxxiii.): *Some are so foolish as to say that the mystical blessing departs from the sacrament, if any of its fragments remain until the next day: for Christ's consecrated body is not changed, and the power of the blessing, and the life-giving grace is perpetually in it.* Thus are all other consecrations irremovable so long as the consecrated things endure; on which account they are not repeated.—And although the truth corresponds with the figure, still the figure cannot equal it.

Reply Obj. 3. The body of Christ remains in this sacrament not only until the morrow, but also in the future, so long as the sacramental species remain: and when they cease, Christ's body ceases to be under them, not because it depends on them, but because the relationship of Christ's body to those species is taken away, in the same way as God ceases to be the Lord of a creature which ceases to exist.

SEVENTH ARTICLE

WHETHER THE BODY OF CHRIST, AS IT IS IN THIS SACRAMENT, CAN BE SEEN BY ANY EYE, AT LEAST BY A GLORIFIED ONE?

We proceed thus to the Seventh Article:—

Objection 1. It seems that the body of Christ, as it is in this sacrament, can be seen by the eye, at least by a glorified one. For our eyes are hindered from beholding Christ's body in this sacrament, on account of the sacramental species veiling it. But the glorified eye cannot be hindered by anything from seeing bodies as they are. Therefore, the glorified eye can see Christ's body as it is in this sacrament.

Obj. 2. Further, the glorified bodies of the saints will be *made like to the body* of Christ's *glory,* according to Phil. iii. 21. But Christ's eye beholds Himself as He is in this sacrament. Therefore, for the same reason, every other glorified eye can see Him.

Obj. 3. Further, in the resurrection the saints will be equal to the angels, according to Luke xx. 36. But the angels see the body of Christ as it is in this sacrament, for even the devils are found to pay reverence thereto, and to fear it. Therefore, for like reason, the glorified eye can see Christ as He is in this sacrament.

On the contrary, As long as a thing remains the same, it cannot at the same time be seen by the same eye under diverse species. But the glorified eye sees Christ always, as He is in His own species, according to Isa. xxxiii. 17: (*His eyes*) *shall see the king in his beauty.* It seems, then, that it does not see Christ, as He is under the species of this sacrament.

I answer that, The eye is of two kinds, namely, the bodily eye properly so-called, and the intellectual eye, so-called by similitude. But Christ's body as it is in this sacrament cannot be seen by any bodily eye. First of all, because a body which is visible brings about an alteration in the medium, through its accidents. Now the accidents of Christ's body are in this sacrament by means of the substance; so that the accidents of

Christ's body have no immediate relationship either to this sacrament or to adjacent bodies; consequently they do not act on the medium so as to be seen by any corporeal eye. Secondly, because, as stated above (A. 1 *ad* 3; A. 3), Christ's body is substantially present in this sacrament. But substance, as such, is not visible to the bodily eye, nor does it come under any one of the senses, nor under the imagination, but solely under the intellect, whose object is *what a thing is* (*De Anima* iii.).

And therefore, properly speaking, Christ's body, according to the mode of being which it has in this sacrament, is perceptible neither by the sense nor by the imagination, but only by the intellect, which is called the spiritual eye.

Moreover it is perceived differently by different intellects. For since the way in which Christ is in this sacrament is entirely supernatural, it is visible in itself to a supernatural, *i.e.*, the Divine, intellect, and consequently to a beatified intellect, of angel or of man, which, through the participated glory of the Divine intellect, sees all supernatural things in the vision of the Divine Essence. But it can be seen by a wayfarer through faith alone, like other supernatural things. And not even the angelic intellect of its own natural power is capable of beholding it; consequently the devils cannot by their intellect perceive Christ in this sacrament, except through faith, to which they do not pay willing assent; yet they are convinced of it from the evidence of signs, according to James ii. 19: *The devils believe, and tremble.*

Reply Obj. 1. Our bodily eye, on account of the sacramental species, is hindered from beholding the body of Christ underlying them, not merely as by way of veil (just as we are hindered from seeing what is covered with any corporeal veil), but also because Christ's body bears a relation to the medium surrounding this sacrament, not through its own accidents, but through the sacramental species.

Reply Obj. 2. Christ's own bodily eye sees Himself existing under the sacrament, yet it cannot see the way in which it exists under the sacrament, because that belongs to the intellect. But it is not the same with any other glorified eye, because Christ's eye is under this sacrament, in which no other glorified eye is conformed to it.

Reply Obj. 3. No angel, good or bad, can see anything with a bodily eye, but only with the mental eye. Hence there is no parallel reason, as is evident from what was said above.

EIGHTH ARTICLE

WHETHER CHRIST'S BODY IS TRULY THERE WHEN FLESH OR A CHILD APPEARS MIRACULOUSLY IN THIS SACRAMENT?

We proceed thus to the Eighth Article:—

Objection 1. It seems that Christ's body is not truly there when flesh or a child appears miraculously in this sacrament. Because His body ceases to be under this sacrament when the sacramental species cease to be present, as stated above (A. 6). But when flesh or a child appears, the sacramental species cease to be present. Therefore Christ's body is not truly there.

Obj. 2. Further, wherever Christ's body is, it is there either under its own species, or under those of the sacrament. But when such apparitions occur, it is evident that Christ is not present under His own species, because the entire Christ is contained in this sacrament, and He remains entire under the form in which He ascended to heaven: yet what appears miraculously in this sacrament is sometimes seen as a small particle of flesh, or at times as a small child. Now it is evident that He is not there under the sacramental species, which is that of bread or wine. Consequently, it seems that Christ's body is not there in any way.

Obj. 3. Further, Christ's body begins to be in this sacrament by consecration and conversion, as was said above (Q. LXXV., AA. 2, 3, 4). But the flesh and blood which appear by miracle are not consecrated, nor are they converted into Christ's true body and blood. Therefore the body or the blood of Christ is not under those species.

On the contrary, When such apparition takes place, the same reverence is shown to it as was shown at first, which would not be done if Christ were not truly there, to Whom we show reverence of *latria.* Therefore, when such apparition occurs. Christ is under the sacrament.

I answer that, Such apparition comes about in two ways, when occasionally in this sacrament flesh, or blood, or a child, is seen. Sometimes it happens on the part of the beholders, whose eyes are so affected as if they outwardly saw flesh, or blood, or a child, while no change takes place in the sacrament. And this seems to happen when to one person it is seen under the species of flesh or of a child, while to others it is seen as before under the species of bread; or when to the same individual it appears for an hour under the appearance of flesh or a child, and afterwards under the appearance of bread. Nor is there any deception there, as occurs in the feats of magicians, because such species is divinely formed in the eye in order to represent some truth, namely, for the purpose of showing that Christ's body is truly under this sacrament; just as Christ without deception appeared to the disciples who were going to Emmaus. For Augustine says (*De Qq. Evang.* ii.) that *when our pretence is referred to some significance, it is not a lie, but a figure of the truth.* And since in this way no change is made in the sacrament, it is manifest that, when such apparition occurs, Christ does not cease to be under this sacrament.

But it sometimes happens that such apparition comes about not merely by a change wrought in the beholders, but by an appearance which really exists outwardly. And this indeed is seen to happen when it is beheld by everyone under such an appearance, and it remains so not for an hour, but for a considerable time; and, in this case some think that it is the proper species of Christ's body. Nor does it matter that sometimes Christ's entire body is not seen there, but part of His flesh, or else that it is not seen in youthful guise, but in the semblance of a child, because it lies within the power of a glorified body for it to be seen by a non-glorified eye either entirely or in part, and under its own semblance or in strange guise, as will be said later (Suppl. Q. LXXXV., AA. 2, 3).

But this seems unlikely. First of all, because Christ's body under its proper species can be seen only in one place, wherein it is definitively contained. Hence since it is seen in its proper species, and is adored in heaven, it is not seen under its proper species in this sacrament. Secondly, because a glorified body, which appears at will, disappears when it wills after the apparition; thus it is related (Luke xxiv. 31) that Our Lord *vanished out of sight* of the disciples. But that which appears under the likeness of flesh in this sacrament, continues for a long time; indeed, one reads of its being sometimes enclosed, and, by order of many bishops, preserved in a pyx, which it would be wicked to think of Christ under His proper semblance.

Consequently, it remains to be said, that, while the dimensions remain the same as before, there is a miraculous change wrought in the other accidents, such as shape, colour, and the rest, so that flesh, or blood, or a child, is seen. And, as was said already, this is not deception, because it is done *to represent the truth,* namely, to show by this miraculous apparition that Christ's body and blood are truly in this sacrament. And thus it is clear that as the dimensions remain, which are the foundation of the other accidents, as we shall see later on (Q. LXXVII., A. 2), the body of Christ truly remains in this sacrament.

Reply Obj. 1. When such apparition takes place, the sacramental species sometimes continue entire in themselves; and sometimes only as to that which is principal, as was said above.

Reply Obj. 2. As stated above, during such apparitions Christ's proper semblance is not seen, but a species miraculously formed either in the eyes of the beholders, or in the sacramental dimensions themselves, as was said above.

Reply Obj. 3. The dimensions of the consecrated bread and wine continue, while a miraculous change is wrought in the other accidents, as stated above.

Prosper Guéranger
1805-1875

Guéranger was born in Sable-sur-Sarthe, France, in 1805. He entered the seminary and was ordained for the diocese of Le Mans in 1827. He had already developed a keen interest in the liturgy because of his growing conviction that spirituality and worship were intimately connected. In 1833 with the help of friends he purchased the long-deserted priory of Solesmes, only a short distance from his birthplace. There, with five other priests, he had the opportunity to test his thesis that a proper union of liturgy and monasticism would result in the renewal of each. A strict observance of the Rule of St. Benedict was adopted with everything revolving around the daily chanting of the Divine Office in choir.

His bishop supported him as he initiated negotiations with Rome to have his community approved and incorporated into the Order of St. Benedict. Pope Gregory XVI granted this request in 1837, making Solesmes an abbey. Guéranger had already made his profession as a Benedictine in Rome a few months before, and he was then elected the first abbot of Solesmes.

The abbey gradually became known as the center for liturgical revival that was looked to by kindred spirits in France, and Guéranger took up his pen to give his ideas wider circulation. He prepared two broad works that had greater impact than any other writings on the liturgy in the nineteenth century. The first was negative, the second positive. The negative was a three-volume polemic against the liturgical usages of his day. It was called Institutions Liturgiques *(1840-1852), and eventually accomplished the goal of eliminating much of what it was protesting, despite the fact that some of the history used in its arguments was less than accurate.*

The positive work which has come to be identified with the very name of Guéranger was his L'Année Liturgique, *the first three chapters of which are given in the following selection. The first volume appeared in 1841 and the last volume (15, completed by L. Fromage) came out in 1866. Guéranger died at Solesmes in 1875.*

In the liturgical renewal of recent years it has become common-place to point out the shortcomings of Guéranger: his view of liturgy was too monastic, insufficiently pastoral, too prone to archaism with his emphasis on restoring Gregorian Chant, insufficiently grounded in either the more advanced historical findings or the more enlightened biblical insights of our day. All of that is true, but unfair. The man ought to be judged in terms of what he found in his day and what access he had to fuller appreciation. There is simply no way to deny that Guéranger's Liturgical Year *started the modern liturgical renewal in the Catholic Church. Its German translation had a great impact on that country, from which so much of the subsequent renewal was to stem. In fact, all of those whose works follow must be viewed as standing on the shoulders of Dom Guéranger.*

The three chapters that follow provide the setting for the liturgical celebration of Christmas. This was the pattern adopted for all of the volumes: first the background, then the actual texts of the liturgy, so that the whole being, mind and heart, might be involved in the worship experience. Thus the battle was launched against irrelevant and unintelligible forms in the liturgy, and the way was opened back to the recovery of biblical and patristic riches. Much progress has been made since, but Guéranger's pioneering efforts are an indispensable part of that story.

THE LITURGICAL YEAR

CHAPTER ONE

THE HISTORY OF CHRISTMAS

We apply the name of *Christmas* to the forty days which begin with the *Nativity of our Lord,* December 25, and end with the *Purification of the Blessed Virgin*, February 2. It is a period which forms a distinct portion of the Liturgical Year, as distinct, by its own special spirit, from every other, as are Advent, Lent, Easter, or Pentecost. One same Mystery is celebrated and kept in view during the forty days. Neither the Feasts of the Saints, which so abound during this Season; nor the time of Septuagesima, with its mournful Purple, which often begins before Christmastide is over, seem able to distract our Holy Mother the Church from the immense *joy* of which she received the *good tidings* from the Angels on that glorious Night for which the world had been longing four thousand years. The Faithful will remember that the Liturgy commemorates this long expectation by the four penitential weeks of Advent.

The custom of celebrating the Solemnity of our Saviour's Nativity by a feast or commemoration of forty days' duration is founded on the holy Gospel itself; for it tells us that the Blessed Virgin Mary, after spending forty days in the contemplation of the Divine Fruit of her glorious Maternity, went to the Temple, there to fulfil, in most perfect humility, the ceremonies which the Law demanded of the daughters of Israel, when they became mothers.

The Feast of Mary's Purification is, therefore, part of that of Jesus' Birth; and the custom of keeping this holy and glorious period of forty days as one continued Festival has every appearance of being a very ancient one, at least in the Roman Church. And firstly, with regard to our Saviour's Birth on December 25, we have St. John Chrysostom telling us, in his Homily for this Feast, that the Western Churches had, from the very commencement of Christianity, kept it on this day. He is not satisfied with merely mentioning the tradition; he undertakes to show that it is well founded, inasmuch as the Church of Rome had every means of knowing the true day of our Saviour's Birth, since the acts of the Enrolment, taken in Judea by command of Augustus, were kept in the public archives of Rome. The holy Doctor adduces a second argument, which he founds upon the Gospel of St. Luke, and he reasons thus: we know from the sacred Scriptures that it must have been *in the fast of the seventh month* that the Priest Zachary had the vision in the Temple; after which Elizabeth, his wife, conceived St. John the Baptist: hence it follows that the Blessed Virgin Mary having, as the Evangelist St. Luke relates, received the Angel Gabriel's visit, and conceived the Saviour of the world *in the sixth month* of Elizabeth's pregnancy, that is to say, in March, the Birth of Jesus must have taken place in the month of December.

But it was not till the fourth century that the Churches of the East began to keep the Feast of our Saviour's Birth in the month of December. Up to that period they had kept it at one time on the sixth of January, thus uniting it, under the generic term of *Epiphany,* with the *Manifestation* of our Saviour made to the Magi, and in them to the Gentiles; at another time, as Clement of Alexandria tells us, they kept it on the 25th of the month *Pachon* (May 15), or on the 25th of the month *Pharmuth* (April 20). St. John Chrysostom, in the Homily we have just cited, which he gave in 386, tells us that the Roman custom of celebrating the Birth of our Saviour on December 25 had then only been observed ten years in the Church of Antioch. It is probable that this change had been introduced in obedience to the wishes of the Apostolic See, wishes which received additional weight by the edict of the Emperors Theodosius and Valentinian, which appeared towards the close of the fourth century, and decreed that the Nativity and Epiphany of our Lord should be made two distinct Festivals. The only Church that has maintained the custom of celebrating the two mysteries on January 6 is that of Armenia; owing, no doubt, to the circumstance of that country not being under the authority of the Emperors; as also because it was withdrawn at an early period from the influence of Rome by schism and heresy.

The Feast of our Lady's Purification, with which the forty days of Christmas close, is, in the Latin Church, of very great antiquity; so ancient, indeed, as to preclude the possibility of our fixing the date of its institution. According to the unanimous opinion of Liturgists, it is the most ancient of all the Feasts of the Holy Mother of God; and as her Purification is related in the Gospel itself, they rightly infer that its anniversary was solemnized at the very commencement of Christianity. Of course, this is only to be understood of the Roman Church; for as regards the Oriental Church, we find that this Feast was not definitely fixed to February 2 until the reign of the Emperor Justinian, in the sixth century. It is true that the Eastern Christians had previously to that time a sort of commemoration of this Mystery, but it was far from being a universal custom, and it was kept a few days after the Feast of our Lord's Nativity, and not on the day itself of Mary's going up to the Temple.

But what is the characteristic of Christmas in the Latin Liturgy? It is twofold: it is *joy,* which the whole Church feels at the coming of the divine Word in the Flesh; and it is *admiration* of that glorious Virgin, who was made the Mother of God. There is scarcely a prayer, or a rite, in the Liturgy of this glad Season, which does not imply these two grand Mysteries: an Infant-God, and a Virgin-Mother.

For example, on all Sundays and Feasts which are not *Doubles,* the Church, throughout these forty days, makes a commemoration of the *fruitful virginity* of the Mother of God, by three special Prayers in the Holy Sacrifice of the Mass. She begs the *suffrage* of Mary by proclaiming her quality of *Mother of God* and her *inviolate* purity, which remained in her even after she had given birth to her Son. And again the magnificent Anthem, *Alma Redemptoris,* composed by the Monk Herman Contractus, continues, up to the very day of the Purification, to be the termination of each Canonical Hour. It is by such manifestations of her love and veneration that the Church, honouring the Son in the Mother, testifies her holy joy during this season of the Liturgical Year, which we call *Christmas.*

Our readers are aware that, when Easter Sunday falls at its latest—that is, in April—the Ecclesiastical Calendar counts as many as six Sundays after the Epiphany. Christmastide (that is, the forty days between Christmas Day and the Purification) includes sometimes four out of these six Sundays; frequently only two; and sometimes only one, as in the case when Easter comes so early as to necessitate keeping Septuagesima, and even Sexagesima Sunday, in January. Still, nothing is changed, as we have already said, in the ritual observances of this joyous season, excepting only that on those two Sundays, the fore-runners of Lent, the Vestments are purple, and the *Gloria in excelsis* is omitted.

Although our holy Mother the Church honours with especial devotion the Mystery of the Divine Infancy during the whole season of Christmas; yet, she is obliged to introduce into the Liturgy of this same season passages from the holy Gospels which seem premature, inasmuch as they relate to the *active life* of Jesus. This is owing to there being less than six months allotted by the Calendar for the celebration of the entire work of our Redemption: in other words, Christmas and Easter are so near each other, even when Easter is as late as it can be, that Mysteries must of necessity be crowded into the interval; and this entails anticipation. And yet the Liturgy never loses sight of the Divine Babe and his incomparable Mother, and never tires in their praises, during the whole period from the Nativity to the day when Mary comes to the Temple to present her Jesus.

The Greeks, too, make frequent *commemorations* of the Maternity of Mary in their Offices of this Season: but they have a special veneration for the twelve days between Christmas Day and the Epiphany, which, in their Liturgy, are called the *Dodecameron.* During this time they observe no days of Abstinence from flesh-meat; and the Emperors of the East had, out of respect for the great Mystery, decreed that no servile work should be done, and that the Courts of Law should be closed, until after January 6.

From this outline of the history of the holy season, we can understand what is the characteristic of this second portion of the Liturgical Year, which we call *Christmas,* and which has ever been a season most dear to the Christian world. What are the *Mysteries* embodied in its Liturgy will be shown in the following chapter.

CHAPTER TWO

THE MYSTERY OF CHRISTMAS

Everything is Mystery in this holy season. The Word of God, whose generation is *before the day-star*, is born in time—a Child is God—a Virgin becomes a Mother, and remains a Virgin—things divine are commingled with those that are human—and the sublime, the ineffable antithesis, expressed by the Beloved Disciple in those words of his Gospel, *the Word was made flesh*, is repeated in a thousand different ways in all the prayers of the Church;—and rightly, for it admirably embodies the whole of the great portent which unites in one Person the nature of Man and the nature of God.

The splendour of this Mystery dazzles the understanding, but it inundates the heart with joy. It is the consummation of the designs of God in time. It is the endless subject of admiration and wonder to the Angels and Saints; nay, is the source and cause of their beatitude. Let us see how the Church offers this Mystery to her children, veiled under the symbolism of her Liturgy.

The four weeks of our preparation are over—they were the image of the four thousand years which preceded the great coming—and we have reached the twenty-fifth day of the month of December, as a long-desired place of sweetest rest. But why is it that the celebration of our Saviour's Birth should be the perpetual privilege of this one fixed day; whilst the whole liturgical Cycle has, every year, to be changed and remodelled, in order to yield that ever-varying day which is to be the feast of his Resurrection—Easter Sunday?

The question is a very natural one, and we find it proposed and answered, even so far back as the fourth century; and that, too, by St. Augustine, in his clebrated Epistle *to Januarius.* The holy Doctor offers this explanation: We solemnize the day of our Saviour's Birth, in order that we may honour that Birth, which was for our salvation; but the precise day of the week, on which he was born, is void of any mystical signification. *Sunday,* on the contrary, the day of our Lord's Resurrection, is the day marked, in the Creator's designs, to express a mystery which was to be commemorated for all ages. St. Isidore of Seville, and the ancient Interpreter of Sacred Rites who, for a long time, was supposed to be the learned Alcuin, have also adopted this explanation of the Bishop of Hippo; and our readers may see their words interpreted by Durandus, in his *Rationale.*

These writers, then, observe that as, according to a sacred tradition, the creation of man took place on a Friday, and our Saviour suffered death also on a Friday for the redemption of man; that as, moreover, the Resurrection of our Lord was on the third day after his death, that is, on a Sunday, which is the day on which the Light was created, as we learn from the Book of Genesis—'the two Solemnities of Jesus' Passion and Resurrection,' says St. Augustine, 'do not only remind us of those divine facts; but they moreover represent and signify some other mysterious and holy thing.'

And yet we are not to suppose that because the Feast of Jesus' Birth is not fixed to any particular day of the week, there is no mystery expressed by its being always on the twenth-fifth of December. For firstly we may observe, with the old Liturgists, that the Feast of Christmas is kept by turns on each of the days of the week, thus its holiness may cleanse and rid them of the curse which Adam's sin had put upon them. But secondly, the great mystery of the twenty-fifth of December, being the Feast of our Saviour's Birth, has reference, not to the division of time marked out by God himself, which is called the Week; but to the course of that great Luminary which gives life to the world, because it gives it light and warmth. Jesus, our Saviour, *the Light of the World,* was born when the night of idolatry and crime was at its darkest; and the day of his Birth, the twenty-fifth of December, is that on which the material Sun begins to gain his ascendency over the reign of gloomy night, and show to the world his triumph of brightness.

In our *'Advent'* we showed, after the Holy Fathers, that the diminution of the physical light may be considered as emblematic of those dismal times which preceded the Incarnation. We joined our prayers with those of the people of the Old Testament; and, with our holy Mother the Church, we cried out to the Divine *Orient, the Sun of Justice,* that he would deign to come and deliver us from the twofold death of body and soul.

God has heard our prayers; and it is on the day of the Winter Solstice—which the Pagans of old made so much of by their fears and rejoicings—that he gives us both the increase of the natural light, and him who is the Light of our souls.

St. Gregory of Nyssa, St. Ambrose, St. Maximus of Turin, St. Leo, St. Bernard, and the principal Liturgists, dwell with complacency on this profound mystery, which the Creator of the universe has willed should mark both the natural and the supernatural world. We shall find the Church also making continual allusion to it during this season of *Christmas,* as she did in that of Advent.

'On this the Day which the Lord hath made,' says St. Gregory of Nyssa, 'darkness decreases, light increases, and Night is driven back again. No, brethren, it is not by chance, nor by any created will, that his natural change begins on the day when he shows himself in the brightness of his coming, which is the *spiritual* Life of the world. It is Nature revealing, under this symbol, a secret to them whose eye is quick enough to see it; to them, I mean, who are able to appreciate this circumstance of our Saviour's coming. Nature seems to me to say: Know, O Man! that under the things which I show thee Mysteries lie concealed. Hast thou not seen the night, that had grown so long, suddenly checked? Learn hence, that the black night of Sin, which had reached its height by the accumulation of every guilty device, is this day stopped in its course. Yes, from this day forward its duration shall be shortened, until at length there shall be naught but Light. Look, I pray thee, on the Sun; and see how his rays are stronger, and his position higher in the heavens: learn from that how the other Light, the Light of the Gospel is now shedding itself over the whole earth.'

'Let us, my Brethren, rejoice,' cries out St. Augustine: 'this day is sacred, not because of the visible sun, but because of the Birth of him who is the invisible Creator of the sun. . . . He chose this day whereon to be born, as he chose the Mother of whom to be born, and he made both the day and the Mother. The day he chose was that on which the light begins to increase, and it typifies the work of Christ, who renews our interior man day by day. For the eternal Creator having willed to be born in time, his Birthday would necessarily be in harmony with the rest of his creation.'

The same holy Father, in another sermon for the same Feast, gives us the interpretation of a mysterious expression of St. John Baptist, which admirably confirms the tradition of the Church. The great Precursor said on one occasion, when speaking of Christ: *He must increase, but I must decrease.* These prophetic words signify, in their literal sense, that the *Baptist's* mission was at its close, because Jesus was entering upon *his.* But they convey, as St. Augustine assures us, a second meaning: 'John came into this world at the season of the year when the length of the day decreases; Jesus was born in the season when the length of the day increases.' Thus, there is mystery both in the rising of that glorious Star, the Baptist, at the summer solstice; and in the rising of our Divine Sun in the dark season of winter.

There have been men who dared to scoff at Christianity as a *superstition,* because they discovered that the ancient Pagans used to keep a feast of the sun on the winter solstice! In their shallow erudition they concluded that a Religion could not be divinely instituted, which had certain rites or customs originating in an analogy to certain phenomena of this world: in other words, these writers denied what Revelation asserts, namely, that God only created this world for the sake of his Christ and his Church. The very facts which these enemies of our holy Religion brought forward as objections to the true Faith are, to us Catholics, additional proof of its being worthy of our most devoted love.

Thus, then, have we explained the fundamental Mystery of these Forty Days of Christmas, by having shown the grand secret hidden in the choice made by God's eternal decree, that the twenty-fifth day of December should be the Birthday of God upon this earth. Let us now respectfully study another mystery: that which is involved in the *place* where this Birth happened.

This place is Bethlehem. *Out of Bethlehem,* says the Prophet, *shall he come forth that is to be the Ruler in Israel.* The Jewish Priests are well aware of the prophecy, and a few days hence will tell it to Herod. But why was this insignificant town chosen in preference to every other to be the birth-place of Jesus? Be attentive, Christians, to the mystery! The name of this

City of David signifies *the House of Bread*: therefore did he, who is *the living Bread come down from heaven,* choose it for his first visible home. *Our Fathers did eat manna in the desert and are dead;* but lo! here is the Saviour of the world, come to give life to his creature Man by means of his own divine Flesh, which *is meat indeed.* Up to this time the Creator and the creature had been separated from each other; henceforth they shall abide together in closest union. The Ark of the Covenant, containing the manna which fed but the body, is now replaced by the Ark of a New Covenant, purer and more incorruptible than the other: the incomparable Virgin Mary, who gives us Jesus, *the Bread of Angels,* the nourishment which will give us a divine transformation; for this Jesus himself has said: *He that eateth my flesh abideth in me, and I in him.*

It is for this *divine transformation* that the world was in expectation for four thousand years, and for which the Church prepared herself by the four weeks of *Advent.* It has come at last, and Jesus is about to enter within us, if we will but *receive him.* He asks to be united to each one of us in particular, just as he is united by his Incarnation to the whole human race; and for this end he wishes to become our *Bread,* our spiritual nourishment. His coming into the souls of men at this mystic season has no other aim than this union. He comes *not to judge the world, but that the world may be saved by him,* and that all *may have life, and may have it more abundantly.* This divine Lover of our souls will not be satisfied, therefore, until he have substituted himself in our place, so that we may live not we ourselves, but he in us; and in order that this mystery may be effected in a sweeter way, it is under the form of an Infant that this Beautiful Fruit of Bethlehem wishes first to enter into us, there to *grow* afterwards *in wisdom and age before God and men.*

And when, having thus visited us by his grace and nourished us in his love, he shall have changed us into himself, there shall be accomplished in us a still further mystery. Having become one in spirit and heart with Jesus, the Son of the heavenly Father, *we* shall also become sons of this same God our Father. The Beloved Disciple, speaking of this our dignity, cries out: *Behold! what manner of charity the Father hath bestowed upon us, that we should be called, and should be the Sons of God!* We will not now stay to consider this immense happiness of the Christian soul, as we shall have a more fitting occasion, further on, to speak of it, and show by what means it is to be maintained and increased.

There is another subject, too, which we regret being obliged to notice only in a passing way. It is, that, from the day itself of our Saviour's Birth even to the day of our Lady's Purification, there is, in the Calendar, an extraordinary richness of Saints' Feasts, doing homage to the master feast of Bethlehem, and clustering in adoring love round the Crib of the Infant-God. To say nothing of the four great Stars which shine so brightly near our Divine Sun, from whom they borrow all their own grand beauty—St. Stephen, St. John the Evangelist, the Holy Innocents, and our own St. Thomas of Canterbury: what other portion of the Liturgical Year is there that can show within the same number of days so brilliant a constellation? The Apostolic College contributes its two grand luminaries, St. Peter and St. Paul: the first in his Chair of Rome; the second in the miracle of his Conversion. The Martyr-host sends us the splended champions of Christ, Timothy, Ignatius of Antioch, Polycarp, Vincent, and Sebastian. The radiant line of Roman Pontiffs lends us four of its glorious links, named Sylvester, Telesphorus, Hyginus and Marcellus. The sublime school of holy Doctors offers us Hilary, John Chrysostom, and Ildephonsus; and in their company stands a fourth Bishop—the amiable Francis de Sales. The Confessor-kingdom is represented by Paul the Hermit, Anthony the conqueror of Satan, Maurus the Apostle of the Cloister, Peter Nolasco the deliverer of captives, and Raymond of Pennafort, the oracle of Canon Law and guide of the consciences of men. The army of defenders of the Church deputes the pious King Canute, who died in defence of our Holy Mother, and Charlemagne, who loved to sign himself 'the humble champion of the Church.' The choir of holy Virgins gives us the sweet Agnes, the generous Emerentiana, the invincible Martina. And lastly, from the saintly ranks which stand below the Virgins—the holy Widows—we have Paula, the enthusiastic lover of Jesus' Crib. Truly, our Christmastide is a glorious festive season! What magnificence in its Calendar! What a banquet for us in its Liturgy!

A word upon the symbolism of the colours used by the Church during this season. *White* is her Christmas Vestment; and she employs this colour at every service from Christmas Day to the Octave of the Epiphany. To honour her two Martyrs, Stephen and Thomas of Canterbury, she vests in *red*; and to condole with Rachel wailing her murdered Innocents, she puts on *purple:* but these are the only exceptions. On every other day of the twenty she expresses, by her white Robes, the gladness to which the Angels invited the world, the beauty of our Divine Sun that has risen in Bethlehem, the spotless purity of the Virgin-Mother, and the clean-heartedness which they should have who come to worship at the mystic Crib.

During the remaining twenty days, the Church vests in accordance with the Feast she keeps; she varies the colour so as to harmonize either with the red Roses which wreathe a Martyr, or with the white Amaranths which grace her Bishops and her Confessors, or again, with the spotless Lilies which crown her Virgins. On the Sundays which come during this time—unless there occur a Feast requiring red or white or, unless Septuagesima has begun its three mournful weeks of preparation for Lent—the colour of the Vestments is *green.* This, say the interpreters of the Liturgy, is to teach us that in the Birth of Jesus, who is the *flower of the fields,* we first received the hope of salvation, and that after the bleak winter of heathendom and the Synagogue, there opened the verdant spring-time of grace.

With this we must close our mystical interpretation of those rites which belong to *Christmas* in general. Our readers will have observed that there are many other sacred and symbolical usages, to which we have not even alluded; but as the mysteries to which they belong are peculiar to certain days, and are not, so to speak, *common* to this portion of the Liturgical Year, we intend to treat fully of them all, as we meet with them on their proper Feasts.

CHAPTER THREE

PRACTICE DURING CHRISTMAS

The time has now come for the faithful soul to reap the fruit of the efforts she made during the penitential weeks of

Advent to prepare a dwelling-place for the Son of God, who desires to be born within her. The *Nuptials of the Lamb are come, and his Spouse hath prepared herself.* Now the Spouse is the Church; the Spouse is also every faithful soul. Our Lord gives his whole self to the whole flock, and to each sheep of the flock with as much love as though he loved but that one. What garments shall we put on, to go and meet the Bridegroom? Where shall we find the pearls and jewels wherewith to deck our soul for this happy meeting? Our holy Mother the Church will tell us all this in her Liturgy. Our best plan for spending Christmas is, undoubtedly, to keep close to her, and do what she does; for she is most dear to God, and being our Mother, we ought to obey all her injunctions.

But, before we speak of the mystic Coming of the Incarnate Word into our souls; before we tell the secrets of that sublime familiarity between the Creator and the Creature; let us, first, learn from the Church the duties which human nature and each of our souls owes to the Divine Infant, whom the Heavens have at length given to us as the refreshing *Dew* we asked them to *rain down* upon our earth. During Advent, we united with the Saints of the Old Law, in praying for the coming of the Messias, our Redeemer; now that he is come, let us consider what is the homage we must pay him.

The Church offers to the Infant-God, during this holy season, the tribute of her profound adoration, the enthusiasm of her exceeding joy, the return of her unbounded gratitude, and the fondness of her intense love. These four offerings, *adoration, joy, gratitude,* and *love,* must be also those of every Christian to his Jesus, his Emmanuel, the Babe of Bethlehem. The prayers of the Liturgy will express all four sentiments in a way that no other Devotions could do. But, the better to appropriate to ourselves these admirable formulas of the Church, let us understand thoroughly the nature of each of these four sentiments.

The first of our duties at our Saviour's Crib is *Adoration.* Adoration is Religion's first act; but there is something in the Mystery of our Lord's Birth which seems to make this duty doubly necessary. In heaven the Angels veil their faces, and prostrate themselves before the throne of Jehovah; the Four-and-Twenty Elders are for ever *casting their crowns before the throne* of the Lamb; what, then, shall we do—we who are sinners, and unworthy members of the Tribe of the Redeemer—now that this same great God shows himself to us, humbled for our sakes, and stript of all his glory? now that the duties of the creature to his Creator are fulfilled by the Creator himself? now that the eternal God bows down not only before the Sovereign Majesty of the Godhead, but even before sinful man, his creature?

Let us endeavour to make, by our profound adorations, some return to the God who thus humbles himself for us; let us thus give him back some little of that whereof he has deprived himself out of love for us, and in obedience to the will of his Father. It is incumbent on us to emulate, as far as possible, the sentiments of the Angels in heaven, and never to approach the Divine Infant without bringing with us the incense of our soul's adoration, the protestation of our own extreme unworthiness, and lastly, the homage of our whole being. All this is due to the infinite Majesty of the Babe of Bethlehem, who is the more worthy of every tribute we can pay him, because he has made himself thus little for our sakes. Unhappy we, if the apparent weakness of the Divine Child, or the familiarity wherewith he is ready to caress us, should make us negligent in this our first duty, or forget what he is, and what we are!

The example of his Blessed Mother will teach us to be thus humble. Mary was humble in the presence of her God, even before she became his Mother; but, once his Mother, she comported herself before him who was her God and her Child with greater humility than ever. We too, poor sinners, sinners so long and so often, we must adore with all the power of our soul him who has come down so low: we must study to find out how by our self-humiliation to make him amends for this Crib, these swathing-bands, this eclipse of his glory. And yet all our humiliations will never bring us so low as that we shall be on a level with his lowliness. No; only God could reach the humiliations of God.

But our Mother, the Church, does not only offer to the Infant God the tribute of her profound *adoration.* The mystery of Emmanuel, that is, of *God with us*, is to her a source of singular *joy.* Look at her sublime Canticles for this holy Season, and you will find the two sentiments admirably blended—her deep reverence for her God, and her glad joy at his Birth. Joy! did not the very Angels come down and urge her to it? She therefore studies to imitate the blithe Shepherds, who ran for joy to Bethlehem, and the glad Magi, who were well-nigh out of themselves with delight when, on quitting Jerusalem, the star again appeared and led them to the Cave *where the Child was.* Joy at Christmas is a Christian instinct, which originated those many *Carols,* which, like so many other beautiful traditions of the ages of Faith, are unfortunately dying out amongst us; but which Rome still encourages, gladly welcoming each year those rude musicians, the *Pifferari,* who come down from the Apennines, and make the streets of the Eternal City re-echo with their shrill melodies.

Come, then, faithful Children of the Church, let us take our share in her joy! This is not the season for sighing or for weeping. *For unto us a Child is born!* He for whom we have been so long waiting is come; and he is come to *dwell among us.* Great, indeed, and long was our suspense; so much the more let us love our possessing him. The day will too soon come when this Child, *now born to us,* will be the *Man of Sorrows,* and then we will compassionate him; but at present we must rejoice and be glad at his coming and sing round his Crib with the Angels. Heaven sends us a present of its own joy: we need joy, and forty days are not too many for us to get it well into our hearts. The Scripture tells us that *a secure mind is like a continual feast,* and a secure mind can only be where there is *peace*; now it is *Peace* which these blessed days bring to the *earth; Peace,* say the Angels, *to men of good will!*

Intimately and inseparably united with this exquisite mystic joy is the sentiment of *gratitude. Gratitude* is indeed due to him who, neither deterred by our unworthiness nor restrained by the infinite respect which becomes his sovereign Majesty, deigned to be born of his own creature, and have a stable for his birthplace. Oh! how vehemently must he not have desired to advance the work of our salvation, to remove everything which could make us afraid of approaching him, and to encourage us, by his own example, to return, by the path of humility, to the heaven we had strayed from by pride!

Gratefully, therefore, let us receive the precious gift—this Divine Babe, our Deliverer. He is the Only-Begotten Son of the

Father, that Father *who hath so loved the world as to give his only Son.* He, the Son, unreservedly ratifies his Father's will, and comes to *offer* himself *because it is his own will. How,* as the Apostle expresses it, *hath not the Father with him given us all things?* O gift inestimable! How shall we be able to repay it by suitable gratitude, we who are so poor as not to know how to appreciate it? God alone, and the Divine Infant in his Crib, know the value of the mystery of Bethlehem, which is given to us.

Shall our debt, then, never be paid? Not so: we can pay it by *love,* which, though finite, gives itself without measure, and may grow for ever in intensity. For this reason, the Church, after she has offered her adorations and hymns and gratitude, to her Infant Saviour, gives him also her tenderest *Love.* She says to him: '*How beautiful art thou, my Beloved One, and how comely!* How sweet to me is thy rising, O Divine Sun of Justice! How my heart glows in the warmth of thy beams! Nay, dearest Jesus, the means thou usest for gaining me over to thyself are irresistible—the feebleness and humility of a Child! Thus do all her words end in *love*; and her *adoration, praise,* and *thanksgiving,* when she expresses them in her Canticles, are transformed into *love.*

Christians! let us imitate our Mother, and give our hearts to our Emmanuel. The Shepherds offer him their simple gifts, the Magi bring him their rich presents, and no one must appear before the Divine Infant without something worthy his acceptance. Know, then, that nothing will please him, but that which he came to seek—our *love.* It was for this that he came down from heaven. Hard indeed is that heart which can say, *He shall not have my love!*

These, then, are the duties we owe to our Divine Master in this his first *Coming,* which, as St. Bernard says, is *in the flesh and in weakness,* and is for the salvation, not for the judgement, of the world.

As regards that other *Coming,* which is to be in majesty and power on the Last Day, we have meditated upon it during Advent. The fear of the *Wrath to come* should have roused our souls from their lethargy, and have prepared them, by humility of heart, to receive the visit of Jesus in that secret *Coming* which he makes to the soul of man. It is the ineffable mystery of this *intermediate* Coming that we are now going to explain.

We have shown elsewhere how the time of *Advent* belongs to that period of the spiritual life which is called, in Mystic Theology, *the Purgative Life,* during which the soul cleanses herself from sin and the occasions of sin, by the fear of God's judgements, and by combating against evil concupiscence. We are taking it for granted that every faithful soul has journeyed through these rugged paths, which must be gone through before she could be admitted to the Feast to which the Church invites all mankind, saying to them, on the Saturday of the Second Week of Advent, these words of the Prophet Isaias: *Lo! this is our God: we have waited for him, and he will save us. We have patiently waited for him, and we shall rejoice and be joyful in his Salvation! As in the house of our heavenly Father there are many mansions,* so likewise, on the grand Solemnity of Christmas, when those words of Isaias are realized, the Church sees, amongst the countless throng who receive the Bread of Life, a great variety of sentiments and dispositions. Some were dead, and the graces given during the holy Season of Advent have restored them to life: others, whose spiritual life had long been healthy, have so spent their Advent that its holy exercises have redoubled their love of their Lord, and their entrance into Bethlehem has been to them a renewal of their Soul's life.

Now every soul that has been admitted to Bethlehem, that is to say, into the *House of Bread,* and has been united with him who is the *light of the World*—that soul no longer walks in darkness. The mystery of Christmas is one of Illumination; and the grace it produces in the soul that corresponds with it, places her in the second *stage* of the Mystic Life, which is called the *Illuminative Life.* Henceforward, then, we need no longer weary ourselves watching for our Saviour's arrival; he has come, he has shone upon us, and we are resolved to keep up the light, nay, to cherish its growth within us, in proportion as the Liturgical Year unfolds its successive seasons of mysteries and graces. God grant that we may reflect in our souls the Church's progressive development of this divine Light; and be led by its brightness to that *Union* which crowns both the year of the Church, and the faithful soul which has spent the year under the Church's guidance!

But, in the mystery of Christmastide, this Light is given to us, so to speak, softened down; our weakness required that it should be so. It is indeed the Divine Word, the Wisdom of the Father, that we are invited to know and imitate; but this Word, this Wisdom, are shown us under the appearance of *a Child.* Let nothing keep us from approaching him. We might fear were he seated on a throne in his palace; but he is lying on a crib in a stable! Were it the time of his Fatigues, his Bloody Seat, his Cross, his Burial, or even of his Glory and his Victory, we might say we had not courage enough: but what courage is needed to go near him in Bethlehem, where all is sweetness and silence, and a simple Little Babe! *Come to him,* says the Psalmist, *and be enlightened!*

Where shall we find an interpreter of the twofold mystery which is wrought at this holy season—the mystery of the Infancy of Jesus in the soul of man, and the mystery of the infancy of man's soul in his Jesus? None of the Holy Fathers has so admirably spoken upon it as St. Leo: let us listen to his grand words.

'Although that Childhood, which the majesty of the Son of God did not disdain to assume, has developed, by growth of age, into the fulness of the perfect man, and, the triumph of his Passion and Resurrection having been achieved, all the humiliations he submitted to for our sakes are passed; nevertheless, the Feast we are now keeping brings back to us the sacred Birth of the Virgin Mary's Child, Jesus our Lord. So that whilst adoring *his* Birth, we are, in truth, celebrating *our own* commencement of life; for the Generation of Christ is the origin of the Christian people, and the Birth Day of him that is our Head is the Birth Day of us that are his Body. It is true, that each Christian has his own rank, and the children of the Church are born each in their respective times; yet the whole mass of the Faithful, once having been regenerated in the font of Baptism, are born, on this Day of Christmas, together with Christ; just as they are crucified together with *him* in his Passion, and have risen together with *his* Resurrection, and in *his* Ascension are placed at the right hand of the Father. For every believer, no matter in what part of the world he may be living, is born again in Christ; his birth according to nature is not taken into account; he becomes a man by his second birth; neither is he any longer called of the family of his father in the flesh, but of the family of our Redeemer, who unto this was made a Son of Man, that we might become the Sons of God.'

Yes, this is the Mystery achieved in us by the holy Season of Christmas! It is expressed in those words of the passage from St. John's Gospel which the Church has chosen for the third Mass of the great Feast: *As many as received him, he gave them power to be made the Sons of God, to them that believe in his name; who are born, not of blood, nor of the will of the flesh, nor of the will of man, but of God.* So that all they who, having purified their souls, freed themselves from the slavery of *flesh* and *blood,* and renounced everything which is of *man,* inasmuch as *man* means *sinner,* wish now to open their hearts to the Divine Word, that is, to the *Light which shineth in darkness,* which *darkness did not comprehend,* these, I say, are born with Jesus; they are born *of God;* they begin a new life, as did the Son of God himself in this mystery of his Birth in Bethlehem.

How beautiful are these first beginnings of the Christian Life! How great is the glory of Bethlehem, that is, of our holy Mother the Church, the true *House of Bread!* for in her midst there is produced, during these days of Christmas, and everywhere throughout the world, a countless number of *sons of God.* Oh! the unceasing vitality of our mysteries! As *the Lamb, who was slain from the beginning of the world,* sacrifices himself without ceasing, ever since his real sacrifice; so also, once born of the Holy Virgin his Mother, he makes it a part of his glory to be ceaselessly born in the souls of men. We are not, therefore, to think for a moment that the dignity of Mary's divine Maternity is lessened, or that *our* souls enjoy the same grand honour which was granted to her: far from that, 'let us,' as Venerable Bede says, 'raise our voice from amid the crowd, as did the woman in the Gospel, and say to our Saviour, with the Catholic Church, of which that woman was the type: *Blessed is the Womb that bore thee, and the Breasts that gave thee suck!"* Mary's prerogative is indeed incommunicable, and it makes her the Mother of God, and the Mother of men. But we must also remember the answer made by our Saviour to the woman, who spoke those words: *Yea rather,* said Jesus, *blessed are they who hear the word of God, and keep it;* 'hereby declaring,' continues

Venerable Bede, 'that not only is she blessed, who merited to conceive in the flesh the Word of God, but they also who endeavour to conceive this same Word spiritually, by the hearing of faith, and to give him birth and nourish him by *keeping* and doing what is good, either in their own or their neighbour's heart. For the Mother of God herself was *Blessed* in that she was made, for a time, the minister to the wants of the Incarnate Word; but much *more Blessed* was she, in that she was and ever will be the *keeper* and doer of the love due to that same her Son.'

Is it not this same truth which our Lord teaches us on that other occasion, where he says: *Whosoever shall do the will of my Father that is in heaven, he is my brother and sister and mother?* And why was the Angel sent to Mary in preference to all the rest of the daughters of Israel, but because she had already conceived the Divine Word in her heart by the vehemence of her undivided love, the greatness of her profound humility, and the incomparable merit of her virginity? Why, again, is this *Blessed among women* holy above all creatures, but because, having once conceived and brought forth a Son of God, she continues for ever his *Mother*, by her fidelity in doing the will of the heavenly Father, by her love for the uncreated light of the Divine Word, and by her union as Spouse with the Spirit of sanctification?

But no member of the human race is excluded from the honour of imitating Mary, though at a humble distance, in this her spiritual Maternity: for, by that real birth which she gave him in Bethlehem, which we are now celebrating, and which initiated the world into the myseries of God, this ever Blessed Mother of Jesus has shown us how we may bear the resemblance of her own grand prerogative. We ought to have *prepared the way of the Lord* during the weeks of Advent; and if so, our hearts have conceived him: therefore now our good works must bring him forth, that thus our heavenly Father, seeing not us ourselves, but his own Son Jesus now living within us, may say of each of us, in his mercy, what he heretofore said in very truth of the Incarnate Word: *This is my beloved Son, in whom I am well pleased.*

Let us give ear to the words of the Seraphic St. Bonaventure, who in one of his sermons for Christmas Day thus explains the mystery of the birth of Jesus in the soul of man: 'This happy birth happens when the soul, prepared by long thought and reflection, passes at length to action; when the flesh being made subject to the spirit, good works are produced in due time: then do interior peace and joy return to the soul. In this birth there is neither travail nor pain nor fear; everything is admiration and delight and glory. If then, O devout soul! thou art desirous for this birth, imagine thyself to be like Mary. *Mary* signifies *bitterness;* bitterly bewail thy sins: it signifies *illuminatrix,* be thou illumined by thy virtues: and lastly, it signifies *Mistress;* learn how to be mistress and controller of thy evil passions. Then will Christ be born of thee, and oh! with what happiness to thyself! For it is then that the soul tastes and sees how sweet is her Lord Jesus. She experiences this sweetness when, in holy meditation, she nourishes this Divine Infant; when she covers him with her tears; when she clothes him with her holy longings; when she presses him to her heart in the embrace of holy tenderness; when, in a word, she cherishes him in the warmth of her glowing love. O happy Crib of Bethlehem! in thee I find the King of glory: but happier still than thou, the pious soul which holds within itself him whom thou couldst hold but corporally!'

Now that we may pass on from this spiritual conception to the birth of our Lord Jesus; in other words, that we may pass from *Advent* to *Christmas,* we must unceasingly keep the eyes of our soul on him who wishes to be born within us, and in whom the world is born to a new life. Our study and ambition should be, how best to become like Jesus, by imitating him; for, though the imitation must needs be imperfect, yet we know from the Apostle that our heavenly Father himself gives this as the sign of the elect—that they are made like to the *image of his Son.*

Let us, therefore, hearken to the invitation of the Angels, and *go over to Bethlehem.* We know what *sign* will be given to us of our Jesus—*a Child wrapped in swaddling-clothes, and laid in a crib.* So that you, O Christians! must become *children*; you must not disdain to be tied in the *bonds* of a spiritual childhood; you must come down from your proud spirit, and meet your Saviour who has come down from heaven, and with him hide yourselves in the humility of the *crib.* Thus will you begin, with him, a new life. Thus will the *Light that goeth forwards and increaseth even to perfect day,* illumine your *path* the whole remaining length of your journey. Thus the sight of God which leaves room for faith, which you receive at Bethlehem, will merit for you the face-to-face vision on Thabor, and prepare you for the blissful *Union*, which is not merely *Light*, but the *plenitude* and *repose* of Love.

So far we have been speaking only of the living members of the Church, whether they began the life of grace during the holy Season of Advent, or were already living in the grace of the Holy Ghost when the ecclesiastical year commenced, and spent their Advent in preparing to be born with Jesus to a new year of higher perfection. But how shall we overlook those of our Brethren who are dead in sin; and so dead, that neither the coming of their Emmanuel, nor the example of the Christians throughout the universal Church earnestly preparing for that coming, could rouse them? No, we cannot forget them: we love them, and come to tell them (for even now they may yield to grace, and live), that *there hath appeared the goodness and kindness of God our Saviour.* If this volume of ours should perchance fall into the hands of any of those who have not yielded to the solicitations of grace, which press them to be converted to the sweet Babe of Bethlehem, their Lord and their God; who, instead of spending the weeks of Advent in preparing to receive him at Christmas, lived them out, as they began them, in indifference and in sin: we shall, perhaps, be helping them to a knowledge of the grievousness of their state, by reminding them of the ancient discipline of the Church, which obliged all the Faithful, *under pain of being considered as no longer Catholics*, to receive Holy Communion on Christmas Day, as well as on Easter and Whit Sundays. We find a formal decree of this obligation given in the fifteenth Canon of the Council of Agatha (Agde) held in 506. We would also ask these poor sinners to reflect on the joy the Church feels at seeing, throughout the whole world, the immense number of her children, who still, in spite of the general decay of piety, keep the Feast of the birth of the Divine Lamb, by the sacramental participation of his Body and Blood.

Sinners! take courage; this Feast of Christmas is one of grace and mercy, on which all, both just and sinners, meet in the fellowship of the same glad Mystery. The heavenly Father has resolved to honour the Birthday of his Son, by granting pardon to all save those who obstinately refuse it. Oh! how worthy is the Coming of our dear Emmanuel to be honoured by this divine amnesty!

Nor is it we that give this invitation; it is the Church herself. Yes, it is she that with divine authority invites you to begin the work of your new life on this day whereon the Son of God begins the career of his human life. That we may the more worthily convey to you this her invitation, we will borrow the words of a great and saintly Bishop of the Middle Ages, the pious Rabanus Maurus, who, in a homily on the Nativity of our Lord, encourages sinners to come and take their place, side by side with the just, in the stable of Bethlehem, where even the ox and the ass recognize their Master in the Babe who lies there.

'I beseech you, dearly beloved Brethren, that you receive with fervent hearts the words our Lord speaks to you through me on this most sweet Feast, on which even infidels and sinners are touched with compunction; on which the wicked man is moved to mercy, the contrite heart hopes for pardon, the exile despairs not of returning to his country, and the sick man longs for his cure; on which is born the Lamb who taketh away the sins of the world, that is, Christ our Saviour. On such a Birthday, he that has a good conscience rejoices more than usual; and he whose conscience is guilty fears with a more useful fear. . . . Yes, it is a sweet Feast, bringing true sweetness and forgiveness to all true penitents. My little children, I promise you without hesitation that every one who, on this day, shall repent from his heart, and return not to the vomit of his sins, shall obtain all whatsoever he shall ask; let him only ask with a firm faith, and not return to sinful pleasures.

'On this day are taken away the sins of the entire world: why needs the sinner despair? . . . On this day of our Lord's Birth let us, dearest Brethren, offer our promises to this Jesus, and keep them, as it is written: *Vow ye, and pay to the Lord your God.* Let *us* make our promises with confidence and love; *he* will enable us to keep them. . . . And when I speak of promises, I would not have anyone think that I mean the promise of fleeting and earthly goods. No—I mean, that each of us should offer what our Saviour redeemed, namely, our soul. "But how," someone will say, "how shall we offer our souls to him, to whom they already belong?" I answer: by leading holy lives, by chaste thoughts, by fruitful works, by turning away from evil, by following that which is good, by loving God, by loving our neighbour, by showing mercy (for we ourselves were in need of it, before we were redeemed), by forgiving them that sin against us (for we ourselves were once in sin), by trampling on pride, since it was by pride that our first parent was deceived and fell.'

It is thus our affectionate Mother the Church invites sinners to the Feast of the Divine Lamb; nor is she satisfied until her *House be filled.* The grace of a *New Birth,* given her by the Sun of Justice, fills this Spouse of Jesus with joy. A new year has begun for her, and, like all that have preceded it, it is to be rich in flower and fruit. She renews her youth as that of an eagle. She is about to unfold another Cycle, or Year, of her mysteries, and to pour forth upon her faithful children the graces of which God has made the Cycle to be the instrument. In this season of Christmas, we have the first-fruits of these graces offered to us; they are the knowledge and the love of our Infant God: let us accept them with attentive hearts, that so we may merit to *advance,* with our Jesus, *in wisdom and age and grace before God and men.* The Christmas Mystery is the gate of all the others of the rest of the year; but it is a gate which we may all enter, for, though most heavenly, yet it touches earth; since, as St. Augustine beautifully remarks in one of his sermons for Christmas: 'We cannot as yet contemplate the splendour of him who was *begotten* of the Father *before the Day Star*; let us, then, visit him who was born of the Virgin in the nighthour. We cannot understand how *his Name continueth before the sun*; let us, then, confess that he hath set *his tabernacle* in her that is purer than *the sun.* We cannot as yet see the Only-Begotten Son dwelling in the Father's Bosom; let us, then, think on the *Bridegroom that cometh out of his bridechamber.* We are not yet ready for the banquet of our heavenly Father; let us, then, keep to *the Crib of Jesus, our Master.*'

Louis Duchesne
1843-1922

Louis Duchesne was born in Saint-Servan, France, in 1843. He went to Rome for his theological studies and was ordained a priest in 1867. After a few years of teaching and then some higher studies in Paris, he was appointed a member of the French archeological school in Rome, and sent to do scholarly research in Epirus, Thessaly, Mount Athos, and Asia Minor (1874-1876). He then accepted the chair of Church history at the Institut Catholique in Paris, where he taught from 1877 to 1885. Controversy over some of his views of the development of doctrine before the Council of Nicaea and of the founding of the Church in France led to his resignation. From 1885 to 1895 he held a chair at the Ecole supérieur des lettres, and from 1895 to his death he was director of the French archeological school in Rome. In 1900 Pope Leo XIII made him a prothonotary apostolic and in 1910 he was made a member of the French Academy.

Duchesne possessed boundless energy for research, had a highly developed critical sense, and deplored the use of whitewash in history. Such a spirit was bound to draw ultra-conservative fire in the troubled days of the first decade of our century. His three-volume Early History of the Church *(1906-1910) appeared during the Modernist crisis and was put on the Index of Forbidden Books even though it had received the imprimatur before publication. Many of his opinions have been modified in the light of subsequent research, but his basic insights and judgments have been vindicated. His work received wide recognition as a most valuable introduction to the first five centuries of the Church's history.*

Duchesne's chief contribution to the liturgy, however came in his earlier (1889) work, Les Origines du Culte Chrétien, *which was first translated into English in 1902. It is from that work that the following selection is taken. As Duchesne himself says in the Preface: "This volume contains the description and explanation of the chief ceremonies of Catholic worship as they were performed in the Latin Churches of the West from the fourth to the ninth century." If the* Liturgical Year *of Dom Guéranger did much to awaken interest and begin the liturgical movement on the popular level, it was the scholarship of Msgr. Duchesne that provided the other necessary pillar.*

As a perceptive historian Duchesne was well aware of his transitional position. On the one hand, he paid full homage to pioneers like Mabillon and Martène. On the other hand, he knew his limitations as an individual scholar: "With regard to these primitive liturgical forms, I have not said all that we might wish to know about them, or indeed all that might be made known." But he also knew that his purpose should be the honest pursuit of truth rather than edification. "This book is by no means one to take to church to help the faithful to follow ceremonial worship more intelligently." Its importance was more subtle than that.

CHRISTIAN WORSHIP, ITS ORIGIN AND EVOLUTION

CHAPTER III

THE TWO LITURGICAL USES OF THE LATIN WEST

1.—The Roman and Gallican Uses

The liturgical uses of the East, varying at first with the patriarchates, or, rather, with the great ecclesiastical groups of the fourth century, gave way at length, one after the other, to the distinctive ritual of the Church of Constantinople. Provincial peculiarities were maintained only among the dissentient Churches outside the sphere of orthodoxy, and beyond the bounds of the Greek language and even of the Byzantine Empire. In the West also diversity of use preceded unity. It is easy to show that towards the end of the fourth century the Latin Churches did not all follow the same use. Judged in the whole, and apart from certain local peculiarities, these different liturgical uses can be reduced to two—the Roman and the Gallican.

There is something strange in this duality. The history of the evangelisation of the West gives support to the assertion of Pope Innocent that it proceeded entirely from Rome, and that on this ground the Roman Liturgy alone has the primordial right to be the liturgy of Latin Christendom:—

> Quis enim nesciat aut non advertat id quod a principe apostolorum Petro Romanae ecclesiae traditum est ac nunc usque custoditur ab omnibus debere servari, nec superduci aut introduci aliquid quod auctoritatem non habeat, aut aliunde accipere videatur exemplum? Praesertim cum sit manifestum in omnem Italiam, Galliam, Hispanias, Africam, atque Siciliam insulasque interjacentes nullum instituisse ecclesias, nisi eos quos venerabilis apostolus Petrus aut ejus successores constituerunt sacerdotes? Aut

> legant si in his provinciis alius apostolorum invenitur aut legitur docuisse. Quod si non legunt, quia nusquam inveniunt, oportet eos hoc sequi quod ecclesia Romana custodit, a qua eos principium accepisse non dubium est.

However strange the fact may seem to us, it is none the less certain that, from the time of Pope Innocent, the Roman liturgical use was not the only one followed in the West, or even in Italy itself. The bishop to whom the letter, from which I have just quoted, was addressed was Bishop of Eugubium (Gubbio), in the district of Umbria, which belonged to the metropolitan diocese of the Pope. As an immediate suffragan of the Pope he had special reasons for conforming to Roman customs, and notwithstanding this he was tempted to introduce others. The practice of Rome was thus attacked in its own domain.

The letter belongs to the year 416. The liturgical and disciplinal peculiarities which were therein found to be opposed to the Roman customs are all characteristic of the use which is conventionally called the Gallican. The latter was, therefore, already in existence at the beginning of the fifth century; it had even sufficient vigour to enter into competition with the Roman Liturgy, and that, too, up to the surburbicarian diocese itself. This use, as is evident from very numerous documents, was followed by the Churches of Northern Italy (metropolitan diocese of Milan) and by those in Gaul, Spain, Britain, and Ireland. From what we can learn, however, from allusions by the Christian orators and synodical decrees of Africa, the use there seems to have been in absolute conformity with the use of Rome and of Southern Italy. We thus find Rome and Carthage on one side, and on the other Milan and the countries beyond the Alps.

In grouping the transalpine countries with Milan, I imply that the Ambrosian Liturgy is identical with the Gallican. This is a view which is not generally accepted. There is no difficulty, on the other hand, in the identification of the liturgy of the Churches of Spain, or Mozarabic Liturgy, up to the eleventh century, with that which was followed by the Churches of Gaul before Charlemagne, and with that which obtained in the British Isles before the Roman missions of the seventh century. With regard to the Ambrosian Liturgy it is, in its present state, very different from other types of the Gallican Liturgy, but we must not lose sight of the fact that it has been for centuries subject to continuous modification in the direction of bringing it more and more into conformity with the Roman use. This movement suffered no check from the discovery of printing. Editions after editions of the Ambrosian Missal became more and more Romanised. But the beginning of this process goes back to some time before Charlemagne. It was natural that such should be the case, for Milan was too near Rome to escape from its influence in this as in other respects. It adopted at an early date the Gregorian Canon. In spite, however, of the many modifications it has experienced, the Ambrosian Liturgy preserves sufficient Gallican features to establish clearly its primitive identity, in my opinion, at least, with the transalpine liturgies. The facts I intend to adduce later on will put this in a clear light. I do not bring them forward here because they would lose something of their significance if I isolated them from the comparative analysis of the Gallican rites; but I think no one will regret giving me credit in the mean time.

2.—*Origin of the Gallican Use*

Assuming that the domain of the Gallican Liturgy extended up to the metropolitan diocese of the Pope, embracing North Italy, or, at the least, the metropolitan diocese of Milan, the way becomes open for the solution of an obscure and contentious question: that of the origin of the Gallican Liturgy.

The English liturgiologists, who have been much occupied with this question, have in general resolved it as follows: The Gallican Liturgy, according to them, is the Liturgy of Ephesus, of the ancient Church of the Roman province of Asia, and was imported into Gaul by the founders of the Church of Lyons. From this Church it spread throughout the whole transalpine West.

I believe that this position cannot be maintained, and for the following reasons: The Gallican Liturgy, as far as it is distinct from the Roman, is a very complicated affair, and there is something very formal in its complication. While it implies numerous and varied rites arranged in a certain order, it consists of formularies which are identical in theme and style, and sometimes in tenor. It departs widely from those simple and still unfixed forms which can be definitely assigned to, or may be assumed to have existed in, the liturgy of the second century. Its development corresponds at the earliest with the condition of things in the fourth century. It shows an advance upon that of the Apostolic Constitutions. Its importation into, and propagation throughout, the West cannot be assigned to the second century. We have here before us a text which must be ascribed, at the very earliest, to the middle of the fourth century.

Now, in the fourth century, the ecclesiastical influence of Lyons was almost non-existent. This city, after the new provincial organisation under Diocletian, had lost its position as metropolis of the three Gauls. The glory and influence of Treves, Vienne, and Arles had passed away. The Bishop of Lyons, whatever may have been his importance in the second century, occupied no special prominence after Constantine. He was scarcely more than metropolitan of *Lugdunensis Prima* until the time of Gregory VII., who was the founder of the primacy of Lyons, ineffective as it was. It was not in conditions such as these that this Church could become the model of all Western Churches, the focus of an ecclesiastical radiation sufficiently intense to make itself felt beyond the Pyrenees and the English Channel, and, crossing the Alps, strong enough to withdraw from the area of Roman influence half the Churches of Italy.

It is manifest that another solution of the question must be sought for. The solution I have to offer is based on the assumption that Milan was the principal centre of this development.

I have shown above that the Church of Milan had been, towards the end of the fourth century and in the early years of the fifth, a kind of superior metropolis to which the whole of the West was inclined to look. We have seen that the Bishops of Gaul and Spain were accustomed to proceed thither frequently to procure solutions of difficulties and rules of conduct. The imperial city was admirably situated to afford a model in the matter of worship and of liturgy. What cannot be allowed to Lyons is readily granted in the case of Milan. From the moment when Rome became no longer the centre of attraction, from the moment when inspiration was sought elsewhere, Milan could not fail to have the preference over all other Churches. And it is worthy of note that the time to which we have assigned these relations between Milan and the transalpine Churches of the West corresponds with a period in which a considerable number of these Churches were undergoing an internal organisation and development, or even in process of being founded. This was the time in which the masses in the towns were converted, in which Churches were reconstructed on a larger scale, in which it was necessary to increase the number of the clergy and to lay down with precision the rules regulating discipline and public worship. The influence of Milan was asserting itself just at the moment when the Gallican Liturgy had reached that stage of development which it possessed when it spread throughout the West, and at the very moment when the West experienced the need of a definitely fixed liturgy.

This is not all. It is well known that the Gallican Liturgy, in the features distinguishing it from the Roman use, betrays all the characteristics of the Eastern liturgies. We shall see, further on, that some of its formularies are to be found word for word in the Greek texts in use in the Churches of the Syro-Byzantine rite either in the fourth century or somewhat later. This close resemblance implies an importation. The Gallican Liturgy is an Oriental liturgy, introduced into the West towards the middle of the fourth century. Now, apart from the presence of the Court at Milan, and the numerous assemblies of Oriental bishops held there, we have to take into account the important fact that the Church of Milan had at its head for nearly twenty years (355-374) a Cappadocian, Auxentius, who had been designated by the Emperor Constantius to occupy the see of St. Dionysius, when the latter was exiled for the Catholic faith. Auxentius belonged to the clergy of the Court, who were out of sympathy with St. Athanasius and the defenders of "consubstantial" orthodoxy. He played a distinguished part at the Council of Ariminum (359). After the defeat of the Arianising party which, in the West, followed closely upon the breaking up of this council, Auxentius maintained his position, and remained fifteen years in his see, notwithstanding the efforts made to dislodge him. This would seem to indicate that he had a strength of mind beyond the common. We can readily believe, therefore, that during his long episcopate he made some impression upon his clergy and upon the internal organisation of his Church. St. Ambrose, his successor, found many customs established which did not all seem to require correction. His broad-mindedness on this score is shown by his retention of the whole of the clerical staff left or organised by his predecessor. Possibly, doctrine being safeguarded by the very fact of his elevation to the see of Milan, Ambrose thought it inopportune to introduce useless changes in the domain of ritual. Certainly many of the most important Milanese peculiarities in discipline and worship go back to his episcopate, and, seeing that these peculiarities have a distinctly Oriental character, they could not have been introduced by him. It is more natural to believe that they existed before him, and that he had only sanctioned customs previously imported.

I do not wish to be dogmatic on this point. Milan was in easy communication with Constantinople and Asia Minor through Aquileia and the Illyrian provinces. Auxentius was not the only Greek who in the fourth century may have exercised episcopal functions in a Latin country. His action in the liturgical domain may have been but an episode in a larger movement. Others might have acted as he did in adopting the same models. Nevertheless, it is very difficult to regard the development in Gaul and Spain as having proceeded from a Latin source further removed than Milan.

However this may be, the political position of Milan was not maintained later than cir. 400. The glory of its see was dimmed at the same time, and Rome was thus relieved from a competition which might have ended in the establishment of a rival. It was scarcely possible, indeed, to undo an accomplished fact. The Popes no doubt considered that no inconvenience would arise if liturgical usages differing from their own were allowed to continue; in any case, there were more urgent questions seeking solution. They confined their efforts to defending their metropolitan diocese from the invasion of the Gallican ritual, and left the Churches of other provinces to arrange on this point as they felt inclined. Circumstances, moreover, did not favour the development of ecclesiastical centralisation. National barriers soon rose up between Rome and the Churches of the barbaric kingdoms founded in Gaul and Spain.

3.—*Fusion of the Two Uses*

If the countries of the Gallican rite found themselves increasingly isolated from Rome, their liturgical use, deprived of a common religious centre, escaped all regulation and all superior ecclesiastical authority capable of controlling its development. Numerous varieties were the consequence, and many details not settled at the beginning were determined later on without any common understanding. The provincial synods attempted here and there to establish some uniformity: *e.g.* the decrees of the Council of Vannes (cir. 465) may be cited for the province of Tours, those of the Council of Agde (506) for the Visigothic kingdom of Gaul, and those of the Council of Gerona (517) for the province of Tarragona.

The most remarkable results were obtained in Spain, in the seventh century, when that country had attained its religious and political unity. There, at least, there had been, in the Councils of Toledo and in the primacy of that see, a firm basis for legislation and for the reformation of public worship. It was in this country that the Gallican use maintained its hold the longest.

Outside the Visigothic kingdom this use fell into irremediable decadence. Rome, on the contrary, continued always to appear as a model Church, as well regulated in its worship as in its discipline and its faith. Relations between it and the Churches of the West were not impossible, though they had become less close and less easy. The bishops of the regions of the Gallican rite resorted from time to time to the apostolic see, after, as well as before, the invasions of the fifth century, to obtain from it a ruling in their difficulties. When liturgical matters were in question, the Popes could not reply otherwise than by sending their own books and recommending their own use. In this manner, little by little, the influence of the Roman ritual made itself felt. The result was at first the combination of the two uses; then the Roman use gained the ascendency over the other until at length it ended by almost completely eliminating the Gallican. The following are the main facts of the history of this change.

In 538, Profuturus, Bishop of Braga, the metropolitan of the Suevic kingdom of Galicia, wrote to Pope Vigilius to consult him on certain liturgical points. We still possess the Pope's reply.

Added to this reply were certain appendices containing decisions on matters of discipline, and, in the way of liturgical texts, the order of the baptismal ceremonies and of the Roman Mass. The latter contained merely what we call the Ordinary of the Mass, that is, the part which does not vary, but the Pope notified to the Bishop of Braga that it was customary to add to it in various places formularies peculiar to the solemnity of the day. Of these formularies, which represent the greater part of what is called the *Liber Sacramentorum*, or Sacramentary, Vigilius confines himself to giving only one specimen, that of the festival of Easter. He assumes that the Bishop of Braga could draw up his own Sacramentary for himself, in case he thought proper to conform to the Roman ritual. The Pope gives expression to no order or advice on this point. The liturgical documents sent by him were nevertheless received in Galicia with the greatest respect. This was manifested a little later on, when, after the conversion of the king of the Suevi to Catholicism, the bishops of this country considered it opportune to put their ecclesiastical regulations on a definite basis. In the National Council held in 561 the liturgical texts sent from Rome to Profuturus were made obligatory.

From this there must have arisen a mixed liturgy, in which there were naturally blended with the Roman *ordines* of the Mass and of baptism certain other elements either of an indigenous origin, or borrowed from the Gallican Liturgy. As no Suevic Liturgy has come down to us, it is not possible to form an idea of what these combinations were, but they did not at any rate enjoy a lengthy existence. In 588, the Suevic kingdom having been annexed to the Visigothic, the Churches of this country passed under the jurisdiction of the National Councils of Toledo, which were very eager for liturgical uniformity. The Roman usages introduced into Galicia were treated as departures from the normal, and were carefully deleted in favour of the Gallican Liturgy.

The Roman mission which was sent to England at the end of the sixth century naturally introduced the use of the Roman Liturgy into the Christian communities which it had newly founded there. But this first mission was not attended with permanent success. The work of evangelising the Anglo-Saxons was again taken in hand, shortly afterwards, by Irish missionaries from the North, where at Lindisfarne, a small island on the east coast of Northumberland, they had their headquarters. With the advent of these new apostles the liturgy used in Ireland, that is to say, the Gallican rite, was imported into the Anglo-Saxon Churches. Hence arose a conflict as to use between the Irish missions from Lindisfarne and the somewhat inactive mission in Kent, which was always Roman in principle, even if its members were not all Roman. The episcopal succession of Canterbury having come to an end, Pope Vitalian sent to England (668), as its new archbishop, Theodore, a Greek monk of Tarsus in Cilicia. It was to this man, as able and energetic as he was conscientious, that the English Church owed its definitive foundation. He managed to reconcile the various and somewhat conflicting elements which he found in the missions entrusted to his care. By his wise and strong rule he was able to secure unity, and the work of evangelisation prospered in consequence. He doubtless made concessions in liturgical matters, and condoned the customs introduced by the Irish missionaries, for the oldest Anglo-Saxon books by no means contain the Roman Liturgy in an absolutely pure form; they abound, indeed, in Gallican details.

The attitude of Theodore, however, as far as the liturgy was concerned, was in harmony with the instructions which had been given by St. Gregory to his disciple Augustine, the first Archbishop of Canterbury:—

> Cum una sit fides, cur sunt ecclesiarum consuetudines tam diversae, et altera consuetudo missarum est in Romana ecclesia atque altera in Galliarum ecclesiis tenetur?
>
> —Novit fraternitas tua Romanae ecclesiae consuetudinem in qua se meminit enutritam. Sed mihi placet ut sive in Romana, sive in Galliarum, sive in qualibet ecclesia aliquid invenisti quod plus omnipotenti Deo possit placere, sollicite eligas et in Anglorum ecclesia, quae adhuc in fide nova est, institutione praecipua quae de multis ecclesiis colligere potuisti infundas. Non enim pro locis res, sed pro rebus loca nobis amanda sunt. Ex singulis ergo quibusque ecclesiis quae pia, qua religiosa, quae recta sunt

> collige, et haec quasi in fasciculum collect apud Anglorum mentes in consuetudinem depone.

There were, in England, moreover, even in the lifetime of Theodore, some who were more zealous than he was for the purity of the Roman use. We may gather this much from his disputes with St. Wilfrid. This ultramontane tendency, as we should say at the present time, was introduced on the Continent by St. Boniface, the Apostle of Germany and the reformer of the Frankish Church. It was he who inaugurated that movement towards Rome, which, favoured by later political relations, brought about, among other consequences, the suppression of the Gallican Liturgy in the Churches of the Frankish kingdom.

Even before St. Boniface the influence of the Roman Liturgy had been felt in Gaul. During the seventh century this country was constantly traversed by the Roman missionaries on their way to England. The English converts, on their side, were accustomed to undertake the journey to Rome, from whence they brought back relics, pictures, books, and above all, liturgical documents. Some of the latter may have been dropped on the way, or copies taken of them in the dwellings of the bishops, or in the monasteries where these pious travellers were accustomed to put up. Finally, the monks of St. Columbanus, who did so much to propagate the Benedictine rule, must also have contributed to the spread of the liturgical customs of the Roman Church.

The few Gallican books which have come down to us date back to the last period of the Merovingian rule. Nearly all of them contain formularies of Roman origin and Masses in commemoration of Roman saints. As early as the time of Gregory of Tours, the *Hieronymian Martyrology,* a book of Roman origin, though not of an official nature, was introduced into Gaul and adapted to the Use of the country. The Sacramentary of St. Denis, known as the *Gelasian Sacramentary*—a work which is, in fact, fundamentally Roman—was drawn up at the latest in the time of Charles Martel. Some other books, or fragments of books, of both Roman and mixed origin, belong to this period, that is to say, to a time when the influence of St. Boniface had not yet made itself felt in the Frankish Church, at all events, within the limits of ancient Gaul.

That St. Boniface gave a strong impulse to liturgical reform and to the adoption of Roman customs is indubitable. We know little, however, of the details of his activity in this direction. He must have been vigorously supported by the Popes, whose counsellor he was, as well as their legate. There was introduced into the matter, moreover, a zeal and an acrimonious heat far removed from the spirit manifested in the Gregorian document I have just cited. One of the most impressive rites in the Gallican Mass was the benediction of the people by the bishop at the moment of communion. So much importance was attached to this rite that it was retained even after the adoption of the Roman Liturgy. Almost all the Sacramentaries of the Middle Ages contain formularies of benediction; they are even still in use in the Church of Lyons. I quote here a letter to Boniface from Pope Zacharias, which shows how the latter speaks of them:

> Pro benedictionibus autem quas faciunt Galli, ut nosti, frater, multis vitiis variant. Nam non ex apostolica traditione hoc faciunt, sed per vanam gloriam hoc operantur, sibi ipsis damnationem adhibentes, dum scriptum est: *Si quis vobis evangelizaverit praeter id quod evangelizatum est, anathema sit.* Regulam catholicae traditionis susepisti, frater amantissime: sic omnibus praedica omnesque doce, sicut a sancta Romana, cuit Deo auctore deservimus, accepisti ecclesia.

It was during the episcopate of St. Chrodegang (732-766), and very probably after his return from Rome in 754, that the Church of Metz adopted the Roman Liturgy. Among all the liturgical innovations, the most obvious and most striking was the chant, the *Romana Cantilena.* This has left more traces than any other innovation in the books and correspondence of the time. Pope Paul sent from Rome to King Pepin, about the year 760, an *Antiphonary* and a *Responsorial.* In the same year, Remedius, son of Charles Martel, and Bishop of Rouen, having been sent on an embassy to Rome, obtained permission from the Pope to take back with him the sub-director (*secundus*) of the *Schola Cantorum*, in order to initiate his monks "in the modulations of psalmody" according to the Roman method. This teacher having been shortly afterwards recalled by the Pope, the bishop sent his Neustrian monks to finish their musical education at Rome itself, where they were admitted to the School of Cantors.

These are mere isolated facts. It was owing to a general measure, a decree of King Pepin, that the Gallican Use was suppressed. This decree is not forthcoming, but mention of it is found in the *admonitio generalis* put forth by Charlemagne in 789. The passage (cap. 80) reads as follows:—

> *Omni clero.*—Ut cantum Romanum pleniter discant et ordinabiliter per nocturnale vel gradale officium peragatur, secundum quod beatae memoriae genitor noster Pippinus rex decertavit ut fieret, quando Gallicanum tulit, ob unanimitatem apostolicae sedis et sanctae Dei Ecclesiae pacificam concordiam.

It was not, therefore, Charlemagne, as has often been stated, but Pepin the Short, who abolished the Gallican Liturgy. This reform had become necessary. The Frankish Church, during the reigns of the latest Merovingians, had fallen into a sad state of corruption, disorganisation, and ignorance. There was no religious centre anywhere, no metropolis whose customs being better regulated and better preserved might serve as a model and become the point of departure for a reformation. The Visigothic Church had a centre at Toledo, a recognised head in the metropolitan of this town, and an unique disciplinary code—the *Hispana* collection. The Liturgy of Toledo was then the liturgy of the whole of Spain. The Frankish Church possessed frontiers only, and lacked a capital. The Frankish Episcopate, except when the king or the Pope took the direction of it, was an acephalous episcopate. Each Church possessed its book of canons and its liturgical use. There was no order anywhere, nothing but the most complete anarchy—a lawless state of affairs which would have been irremediable if the Carlovingian monarchs had made no appeal to tradition and to the authority of the Roman Church.

The intervention of Rome in the reformation of the liturgy was neither spontaneous nor very active. The Popes contented themselves with sending copies of their liturgical books without troubling themselves as to the use which might be made of them. The individuals who were charged by the Frankish kings—Pepin, Charlemagne, and Louis the Pious—with the execution of the liturgical reform did not regard themselves as prohibited from supplementing the Roman books or from combining with them whatever seemed worth preserving in the Gallican rite. Hence arose a somewhat composite liturgy, which from its source in the Imperial chapel spread throughout all the Churches of the Frankish Empire, and at length, finding its way to Rome, gradually supplanted there the ancient use. The Roman Liturgy, from the eleventh century at the least, is nothing else than the Frankish Liturgy, such as men like Alcuin, Helisachar, and Amalarius had made it. It is even extraordinary that the ancient Roman books—representing the genuine use of Rome up to the ninth century—have been so completely displaced by others, that not a single example of them is now to be found.

It would appear that the liturgical reform taken in hand by the Carlovingian kings never reached Milan. The particularities of the Milanese ritual were not unknown in France, but this important Church, being better governed, doubtless, than those of Merovingian Gaul, seems to have been able to dispense with reform. The use of the Church, moreover, had already approximated considerably to the Roman rite. It was protected by the name of St. Ambrose. The fables related by Landulf as to the hostility displayed by Charlemagne to the Ambrosian ritual are not worthy of credit.

CHAPTER VI

THE ROMAN MASS

The *Ordines Romani* describe to us the stational Mass as celebrated by the Pope in person in the great liturgical assemblies to which all the clergy and people were convoked, and at which it was taken for granted that they were present. The priests, in their titulary churches, in the churches and chapels of cemeteries, in the oratories of monasteries, of deaconries, and of private houses, were accustomed to celebrate according to a form fundamentally the same, but without the solemn ceremonial. The cardinal priest had at his disposition only clerics of an inferior order—the acolytes—and he was obliged to take upon himself many functions which in a solemn Mass would be assigned to the deacons. The disparity in the ceremonial was not occasioned by the difference in rank between the priest and a bishop, for it often happened that when the Pope could not celebrate, the stational Mass was taken by a simple priest, and the ceremonial in this case was not less imposing and complicated than if the Pope himself were present. It was not, moreover, the place of the station which made the difference. Private Masses might be said at St. Peter's, or at Constantine's basilica at the Lateran, or at Santa Maria Maggiore; and, on the other hand, it often happened that the stational Mass, in all its ceremony, was celebrated in a simple presbyteral church. We may even safely say that all such churches, or almost all, had at least once in each year, the honour of being designated for the stational Mass. The difference in place depended on the character of the congregation. At the Masses celebrated in chapels, cemeteries, presbyteral churches, and even in the great basilicas, there were present, the stational days excepted, only a private congregation, consisting of a family, or a corporation, or the inhabitants of a quarter, or any kind of association of the faithful, whether resident or pilgrims. The Mass said on such occasions was a private Mass. The public Mass, that is to say, the stational Mass, was that in which the whole Roman church was considered to take part.

This public Mass is that which agrees best with the primitive type of the institution, and on that account its study is the more important. As we find it described in the *Ordines* of the eighth or ninth century, it implied a ceremonial which corresponded more with the exigencies of a later date than with those of primitive times. The pontifical court, which had then reached a considerable development, played in it an important part. The different classes of the clergy, arranged according to their orders and to their regions, the corporation of cantors, the crucifers of the quarter, the military and civil rulers, and, in fact, everybody, had his part in these high ceremonials of worship. I will put on one side everything in the *Ordo* which has to do with this high ceremonial, and will confine myself to those rites which are essential, and which are common to the Roman and other liturgies.

1.–The Entry of the Officiating Priest

The congregation of the faithful having assembled, the priests, accompanied by the bishops then in Rome, took their places in the apse of the church which was reserved for the superior clergy. The pontiff and his deacons set out from the *secretarium*, or sacristy (which was situated close to the entrance of the church), and proceeded to the altar. The *Ordines* of the eighth century represent them as wearing their liturgical vestments, and as preceded by the sub-deacons, one of whom swings a censer, and by seven acolytes carring tapers. During the procession the choir (*schola cantorum*) sings the antiphon *ad introitum.* Originally this antiphon consisted of the singing of a complete psalm, or, at least, of several verses of it. It continued to be sung until the pontiff had reached the altar. Before he did so, he was met by a cleric, who brought to him a fragment of consecrated bread, which was reserved from a previous Mass. The eucharistic portion was intended to be placed in the chalice before the ceremony of the "fraction of the bread." On entering the sanctuary the Pope gave the kiss of peace to the senior bishop and senior priest, and then to all his deacons. He thereupon proceeded to prostrate himself before the holy table. A few minutes before his arrival there, the book of the Gospels had been solemnly brought and placed upon the altar. After the Pope's prostration, the deacons proceeded two by two and kissed the altar on its sides. The pontiff also, drawing near, kissed the altar, as well as the book of the Gospels.

It is difficult to assign a precise date to this ceremony. In all rituals the entry of the officiating minister was from an early time associated with some pomp. We shall not go far wrong, however, if we refer to the fifth century, at the earliest, the majority of the details which have just been described.

2.–Introductory Chants

The *Kyrie eleison* may be considered as a remnant of the Litany form of prayer, or dialogue between one of the sacred ministers and the whole congregation. This form of prayer occupies, as we have seen, a prominent place in the Greek liturgies. The Liturgy of Constantinople, for instance, contains a litany to be said at the beginning of the Mass, before the entry of the celebrants. It would appear also that at Rome, in early times, it formed the initial portion of the Liturgy. It was customary in the eighth century on the Litany days, that is, the days on which the people went in general procession to the church of the station, to sing neither *Kyrie* nor *Gloria.* The service at the church began directly with the *Pax vobis* and the first prayer. The *Kyrie*, in like manner, was omitted on the days appointed for ordinations, because on such occasions the Litany was sung after the gradual. Even at the present time the *Kyrie eleison* in the Mass for Easter Eve is nothing more than the conclusion of the Litany with which that Mass commenced. St. Gregory is the authority for the statement that in his time the words *Kyrie eleison* and *Christe eleison* were accompanied, except in the daily Masses, by other formularies. These formularies were, doubtless, a litany more or less elaborated.

The Litany of the Saints at present in use has preserved this ancient form of dialogue-prayer as it was accustomed to be said in the Roman Church. It has, doubtless, been subject to considerable development, especially in the first part of it, which contains the invocation of Saints. But the conclusion, in which the response occurs, *Te rogamus, audi nos,* has quite an ancient ring about it, and possesses a great resemblance to the petitions in the litanies used in the Greek Church. Although the earliest text in which it occurs goes back only to the eighth century, it is probable that it is much more ancient.

It is evident, moreover, that the place assigned to the *Kyrie eleison* in the Roman Litany is not that given to it in the Eastern Churches. In the Roman Litany it occurs at the beginning and the end, and is said alternately by the precentor and the congregation. In the East it formed the people's response to the petitions in the Diaconal Litany. St. Gregory was already aware of this difference. It rose from the fact that the *Kyrie* was adventitious in the Roman Church, as it was throughout the entire West. The formulary *Te rogamus, audi nos,* however could not be omitted, since it occupies in the Roman Litany the same place as the *Kyrie eleison* in the Greek. Another place had to be found for the latter. It is a somewhat singular thing that the *Kyrie*, which is of later date at Rome than the Litany, should not be preserved in the Mass, whereas from the Litany, a more ancient service, it has been almost eliminated.

The *Gloria in excelsis.*—This hymn, like the *Kyrie,* is of Greek origin. We find it, in a slightly different form, however, in the *Apostolic Constitutions* (vii. 47), and in the appendices to the Bible at the end of the *Codex Alexandrinus,* which belongs to the fifth century. It was a morning hymn, and formed part of the office for Matins, and did not belong to the Liturgy properly so called. It was originally introduced at Rome into the first Mass of the Nativity, which was celebrated before daybreak. Pope Symmachus extended its use to Sundays and the feasts of martyrs, but only in the case of episcopal Masses. Priests were allowed to say it only on Easter Day, when they were regarded as taking the place of the absent Pope, or on the day of their first performance of sacerdotal functions.

3.—The First Prayer

After saluting the congregation, the celebrant calls upon them to pray with him in the introductory prayer, which was called the *collecta,* because it was said as soon as the people had fully assembled. This is the first of the three "collective prayers," or collects, allowed in the Roman Mass. The other two are the prayer *super oblata (secreta),* and that called the *post communio.*

4.—The Lections and the Chanting of Psalms

From the beginning of the sixth century there were in use in Rome only two lections, viz. the Epistle and Gospel. The first was taken, sometimes from the Old Testament and sometimes from the New (the four evangelists excepted), but most frequently from the Epistles of St. Paul, or from the General Epistles, from whence its name.

Originally the lections were more numerous. In the existing use, indeed, more than one trace is found of the *prophetic* lection, which has now disappeared. This form of lesson, indeed, is still employed on certain days—for instance, on the Ember days and in Lent. The most remarkable thing in this connection is the arrangement of the chants between the Epistle and Gospel. These chants are always two in number, a *psalmus responsorius,* or response, which is entitled the *Gradual,* and the *Alleluia,* to which there is still attached a verse of a psalm. During Lent and other penitential seasons, and at Masses for the dead, the *Alleluia* is replaced by a psalm, with a melody of a special character, called the *Psalmus tractus,* or tract. There is in every case a second chant after the gradual. Whence this duality? The reason will occur to us if we consider that in the few Masses which have preserved the "prophetic" lection, the gradual is sung between that lection and the Epistle, whilst the *Alleluia,* or the tract, is used between the Epistle and Gospel. The two chants were at first thus inserted respectively between the lections, but when the first of the latter was removed, both chants were united and sung between the Epistle and Gospel.

The suppression of the prophetic lection must have taken place at Rome in the course of the fifth century. About the same time it suffered similar treatment at Constantinople. The Armenian Liturgy, which is an ancient form of the Byzantine, still retains the three lections, but in the most ancient books of the Byzantine use which have come down to us there are but two.

I have already pointed out that the practice of chanting psalms between the lections in the Mass is as old as these lections themselves, and that both go back in direct line to the religious services of the Jewish Synagogue. In the Christian Liturgy these psalms constitute the most ancient and most solemn representation of the Davidic Psalter. We must take care not to put them on the same footing as the other chants, the Introit, Offertory, and Communion, which were introduced later, and then merely to occupy attention during long ceremonies. The gradual and similar chants had an intrinsic value, and during the time in which they were sung there was nothing else going on. This was the ancient chanting of the psalms, which in the primitive Church alternated with the lections from Holy Scripture.

The *gradual,* as has been said, was so called because it was sung at the *gradus*, or ambo, where the lections also were read. It was sung always by a single cantor, and the office of the choir was confined to taking up the final musical phrase. The other chants were executed *in plano* by the choir, or *schola cantorum.* It was also customary, up to the time of St. Gregory, that the gradual and its additions should be sung like the Gospel, by deacons only; and this function had quite a special importance in the ministry of that order. Mention of it frequently occurs in epitaphs:

"Psallere et in populis volui modulante propheta
sic merui plebem Christi retinere sacerdos,"

says a bishop, explaining in this manner how the faithful, being ravished by his singing, had raised him to the episcopate. We read also in the epitaph of the deacon Redemptus, a contemporary of Pope Damasus—

Dulcia nectareo promebat mella canore
prophetam celebrans placido modulamine senem;

and in that of the archdeacon Deusdedit (fifth century)—

Hic levitarum primus in ordine vivens
Davitici cantor carminis iste fruit;

and in that of the archdeacon Sabinus (fifth century)—

[Ast eg] *o qui voce psalmos modulatus et arts*
[dive] *rsis cecini verba sacrata sonis.*

Thus the possession of a good voice and of a thorough knowledge of music was a necessary qualification for a deacon.

In the pursuit of this knowledge, many other more essential things were neglected. St. Gregory thought to obviate this evil by suppressing the monopoly of deacons in regard to chanting the psalms. But if the gradual came to be no longer sung by the deacons, it still continued to be executed as a solo.

The reading of the lections was formerly prefaced by an injunction to silence, of which the formulary is preserved in the order of the ceremony called "opening of the Ears," or "Traditio Symboli," one of the ceremonies preparatory to baptism. The deacon said in a loud voice, *State cum silentio, audientes intente!*

After the lections we ought to find the homily. But the homily appears to have fallen into guise at Rome at a somewhat early period. St. Gregory, and St. Leo before him, were the only early Popes who left homilies behind them, or indeed, seem, as far as we know, to have preached them. The homilies of St. Leo are, moreover, short, and restricted to certain solemn festivals. Roman priests had no authority to preach, and the Popes looked askance at the permission to do so granted to their clergy by other bishops. Sozomen, who wrote about the time of Pope Xystus III., tells us that no one preached at Rome.

There is no trace to be found in the liturgical books of the eighth century of the dismissal of catechumens and penitents. This is owing to the fact that they were drawn up at a time when discipline in regard to catechumens and penitents had been largely modified. There were no longer any adult catechumens, and public penitents were usually shut up in monasteries. The ancient formularies of the *missa catechumenorum* and of the *missa paenitentium* were preserved, notwithstanding, and occur respectively in the order of baptism already referred to, and in one of St. Gregory's dialogues. On the day of the "opening of the Ears" the deacon dismissed the candidates for baptism with the words, *Catechumeni recedant! Si quis catechumenus est recedat! Omnes catechumeni exeant foras!* St. Gregory relates that two nuns, who had been excommunicated by St. Benedict, were buried in a certain church, and that whenever the deacon cried out, at each Mass celebrated there, the words, *Si quis non communicat, det locum!* their foster mother used to see them arise from their graves and go out of the holy place. The manner in which St. Gregory explains *Cumque . . . ex more diaconus clamaret,* seems to indicate that this form of dismissal, or one equivalent to it, was still in use in his time, that is, at the end of the sixth century.

5.—The Prayer of the Faithful

After the Mass of the catechumens had been said, that of the faithful began. The bishop, having once more saluted the congregation with the words *Dominus vobiscum!* calls upon them to pray: *Oremus!* It is a strange thing that this exhortation was as barren of result in the eighth century as it is in the present day. No one prayed. The Pope and his assistants proceeded to collect the offerings of the people and clergy, the choir executed some chant or other, but no prayer was provided by the liturgical books, and there was no rubric implying that any prayer was to be said privately or secretly. There is, therefore, a hiatus here; something has disappeared, and that something is nothing else than the "Prayer of the Faithful," which, in all other liturgies, occurs at this place.

I am inclined to believe that the disappearance is not altogether complete, and that the form used in ancient times in the Roman Church is still preserved in the series of solemn prayers employed on Good Friday.

In the eighth century these prayers were said, not only on the Friday, but also on the Wednesday in Holy Week. There is nothing in their tenor which connects them especially with the solemnities of the Passion and of Easter. They are prayers for the ordinary needs of the Church, for peace, for the bishop, for the whole hierarchy down to the confessors (*ascetae*), virgins, and widows; for the Roman emperor; for the sick, the poor, captives, travellers, sailors; for heretics, schismatics, Jews, and heathen. These are the same petitions which we encounter, frequently repeated, in the daily liturgies of the Eastern Church. I am of opinion, therefore, that these prayers once formed part of the ordinary Roman Mass, and that they were said after the lections, that is, at the place in which they long continued to be recited on Wednesday and Friday in Holy Week.

6.—The Offering

If the Roman Liturgy was deprived at an early date of the Prayer of the Faithful, it still preserved in the ninth century, as a compensation, that of the oblation, which had disappeared at an early date from all other liturgies. The faithful, including not only the laity, but also the priests and other clerics, together with the Pope himself, brought each their gifts of bread and wine, for each was obliged to make his own offering. The Pope himself, assisted by the bishops and priests, received the loaves;

the archdeacon and his colleagues the *amulae,* or phials of wine. This distinction of functions was observed throughout the entire ceremony, the species of wine being considered as within the special province of the deacons.

During the offering the choir chanted a responsory psalm, called the *Offertorium.* This chant is of ancient use. It was introduced into Carthage while St. Augustine was yet alive. As is the case with all novelties, this introduction was adversely criticised. A certain Hilary, an individual of the rank of a tribune (*vir tribunitius*), made such a stir over the matter that the Bishop of Hippo was asked to write a treatise to confute him. This was the occasion of the book, now lost, called *Contra Hilar[*i*]um,* in which the celebrated doctor defended *morem qui tunc esse apud Carthaginem coeperat, ut hymni ad altara dicerentur de Psalmorum libro, sive ante oblationem, sive cum distribueretur populo quod fuisset oblatum.*

The *Offertory* at present consists of a single verse without response, but in the ancient antiphonaries it presents a longer and more complicated form.

The offerings having been made, the archdeacon chooses from the loaves those which are to be employed in the communion, and places them upon the altar. He places there also the vessel (*scyphus*) containing the wine for the communion of the faithful, the two loaves offered by the Pope himself, and lastly the chalice, which, together with these two loaves, is to serve for communicating the pontiff and the higher clergy. He takes care to pour into this chalice, together with the wine offered by the Pope, a little of that offered by the priests and deacons, and of that which is contained in the *scyphus* which represents the offering of the faithful. He adds, last of all, a small quantity of water.

No prayer accompanies these ceremonies. The Pope takes no part in them, but sits all the time in his seat at the end of the apse. The offertory prayers now in use are not indicated in the ancient books. They are, however, complete counterparts, as far as the meaning is concerned, of those employed by the Greek priests, and, doubtless, also by the Gallican priests before the beginning of the Mass at the table of Prothesis.

7.–The Consecration Prayers

As the preparation of the oblation takes place, according to the Roman custom, at the altar itself, and during the time of Mass, there is no room in it for the solemn entry with the oblation previously prepared, of the Oriental and Gallican ritual. The kiss of peace and the reading of the diptychs are relegated to a later place. As soon as the archdeacon has finished placing on the altar the loaves and chalices to be consecrated, the Pope, after washing his hands, proceeds to the altar and begins the consecration prayers. He calls the faithful, in the first place, to join in a prayer, which is the second of the two *collective* prayers of the Roman Mass, and is known by the appellation *super oblata*, or *Secreta.* It is preceded by an invitatory of a special form: *Orate, fratres, ut meum ac vestrum sacrificium acceptabile fiat apud Deum Patrem omnipotentem.* The form of prayer which follows, and which at the beginning was merely the conclusion of the prayer offered up in silence by the faithful, was said in a low voice, and hence its name of *Secreta.* It was terminated by an *ecphony,* that is, by an ending on a high note, to which *Amen* was responded.

At this point came the eucharistic prayer which corresponded to the *Anaphora* of the Greek liturgies. It was divided by the chanting of the *Sanctus* into two parts of unequal length, of which the first, sung on a high note, was called the *Preface*, and the second, recited in a low tone, named the *Canon.* The Roman *Anaphora* possesses testimony to its great antiquity. The form at present in use existed already, word for word, at the beginning of the seventh century. St. Gregory gave to it its final touch, adding to the prayer *Hanc igitur* the following words: *diesque nostros in tua pace disponas, atque ab eterna damnatione nos eripi et in electorum tuorum jubeas grege numerari.* The author of the *Liber Pontificalis,* which dates from the beginning of the sixth century, speaks of the Canon as fixed in form, and of known content. He implies also that it had been a long time in existence, for he relates that St. Leo (440-461) had added some words to it. But we can go still further back, and show conclusively that the prayer to which St. Leo added four words was already in being in the time of Pope Damasus. The proof is to be found in a criticism levelled at it by the author of the *Quaestiones Veteris et Novi Testamenti*, who was a contemporary of Damasus. In the misleading theology of this writer, Melchisedec is identified with the Holy Spirit, and, while he is still recognised as the priest of God, Melchisedec's priesthood is considered as inferior to that of Christ: *Similiter et Spiritus sanctus quasi antistes sacerdos appellatus est excelsi Dei, non summus, sicut nostri in oblatione praesumunt. Quia quamvis unius substantiae Christus et Spiritus sanctus, uniuscujusque tamen ordo observandus est.* The words *non summus sicut nostri in oblatione praesumunt* have evidently in view the form of the Roman Epiclesis, *summus sacerdos tuus Melchisedech.*

We find, furthermore, in a work not much later than the time of Damasus—the *De sacramentis* of the pseudo-Ambrose—large portions of the Roman Canon. Although we cannot assign a precise date to this work, or give the name of its author, it would seem, in my opinion, to have been drawn up in some North Italian Church, where the Roman use was combined with that of Milan, probably at Ravenna. As it assumes that the population of the towns is still made up of pagans and Christians, and as it is, moreover, partly borrowed from a similar work of St. Ambrose, we cannot go far wrong in fixing its date as somewhere about 400. The portions of the Roman Canon which appear in it run as follows:—

> Vis scire quia verbis caelestibus consecratur? Accipe quae sunt verba. Dicit sacerdos: *Fac nobis,* inquit, *hanc oblationem ascriptam, ratam, rationabilem, acceptabilem, quod figura est corporis et sanguinis Iesus Christi. Qui pridie quam pateretur, in sanctis manibus suis accepit panem, respexit in caelum ad te, sancte Pater omnipotens, aeterne Deus, gratias agens, benedixit, fregit, fractumque apostolis suis et discipulis suis tradidit, dicens: "Accipite et edite ex hoc omnes: hoc est enim corpus memum, quod pro multis confringertur." Similiter etiam caliecm, postquam caenatum est, pridie quam pateretur, accepit, respexit in caleum ad te, sancte Pater omnipotens, aeterne Deus, gratias agens, benedixit, apostolis suis et discipulis suis tradidit, dicens: "Accipite et bibite*

ex hoc omnes: hic est enim sanguis meus. . . . Quoties cumque hoc feceritis, toties commemorationem mei facietis, donec iterum adveniam."

Et sacerdos dicit: Ergo memores gloriosissimae ejus passionis et zb inferis resurrectionis et in caelum ascensionis, offerimus tibi hanc immaculatam hostiam, hunc panem sanctum et calicem vitae aeternae; et petimus et precamur, ut hanc oblationem suscipias in sublimi altari tuo per manus angelorum turoum, sicut suscipere dignatus es munera pueri tui justi Abel et sacrificium patriarchae nostri Abrahae et quod tibi obtulit summus sacerdos Melchisedech.

This text, while it does not correspond word for word, agrees very closely with that of the present Roman Canon from the conclusion of the formulary of the diptychs up to and including the *Epiclesis.*

But let us return to our consideration of the Roman *Anaphora.*

After the injunction to lift up the heart to God, and to render thanks to Him, the officiating priest goes on: *Vere dignum et justum est,* etc. In the Sacramentary of Adrian, this form, that is to say, the *Preface,* admits only a small number of variations for the chief festivals. Previously these variations were much more numerous. We would gather from the Leonian Sacramentary that improvisation, or at the least the intercalation of certain sentences previously composed by the officiating priest, was still the practice in the sixth century. The Preface ends with an ascription to the glory of God, and the *Sanctus.*

After the *Sanctus* the Roman Canon, instead of proceeding at once to the account of the Last Supper, intercalates a long passage appropriated to the enumeration of the persons in whose name the oblation is made—the whole Catholic Church, the Pope (or, if occasion requires it, the bishop of the locality), and all the orthodox bishops; then the Sovereign and the congregation; and finally, as representing the Communion of Saints, all the righteous who have already attained the heavenly beatitude—the Virgin Mary, the Apostles, and their successors the Popes, martyrs, and other saints. The oblation is thus made by the whole Christian family, and God is asked to accept it, and to transform it into the Body and Blood of Christ.

The existing texts for this part of the Canon give forms which are definitely fixed, but not so much so, however, that provision has not been made for additions with the object of commemorating the festival of the day or for the enumeration of certain persons or classes of persons. Thus, there is no doubt that the names of the four patriarchs of the East, and possibly of certain Western primates, were formerly mentioned in the *Te igitur* after that of the Roman pontiff. The *Memento,* which follows it, admits of a break where many names and petitions might have been intercalated. As for the prayer beginning with *Communicantes,* the Sacramentary of Adrian furnishes variations suited to the solemnity of the day. Later in the same prayer the list of Popes, now reduced to the first three names, Linus, Cletus, and Clement, must have been recited at length. It is not impossible that the ancient pontifical catalogue, of which we have a relic in the Hieronymian Martyrology, was extracted from some copy of the Canon. The names of martyrs which follow are also merely a selection. The Churches which adopted the Roman Liturgy were within their rights in completing that list by adding to it the names of the saints which they held in special honour. Finally, the *Hanc igitur* admits the insertion at the festivals of Easter and Pentecost of a commemoration of the newly baptised. Formerly the names of the candidates for baptism were therein recited on the days of the scrutiny, while those of their godfathers and godmothers found a place in the *Memento.* Similar additions were made in Masses for ordinations.

All this part of the Canon corresponds, on the whole, with the recitation of the diptychs prescribed in the Gallican and Eastern liturgies, but which are placed in these liturgies before the beginning of the Preface. This latter disposition may seem the more natural one, and we may perhaps admit that the former is not altogether primitive. It is at the same time certain, that from the beginning of the fifth century the order of the Roman Canon was already that which it is to-day. The final formulary, in fact, in all this series of enumerations, namely, that which appears before the *Qui pridie,* is already met with in the *De sacramentis,* in terms almost identical with those of the present

Quam oblationem. The letter of Pope Innocent to Decentius assumes, moreover, that the recitation of the diptychs occupied at Rome in 416, and for a long time previously, the place which it holds at present.

The account of the institution (*Qui pridie*) and the *Anamnesis (Unde et memores),* which follows it, present nothing peculiar. The same may be said of the *Epiclesis.*

This portion of the Canon runs as follows:—

> Supra quae (the oblations) propitio ac sereno vultu respicere digneris et accepta habere, sicuti accepta habere dignatus es munera pueri tui justi Abel et sacrificium patriarchae nostri Abrahae, et quod tibi obtulit summus sacerdos tuus Melchisedech [sanctum sacrificium, immaculatam hostiam]. Supplices te rogamus, omnipotens Deus, jube haec perferri per manus sancti angeli tui in sublime altare tuum, in conspectu divinae majestatis tuae, ut quotquot ex hac altaris participatione sacrosanctum Filii tui corpus et sanguinem sumpserimus, omni benedictione caelesti et gratia repleamur.

This prayer is far from exhibiting the precision of the Greek formularies, in which there is a specific mention of the grace prayed for, that is, the intervention of the Holy Spirit to effect the transformation of the bread and wine into the Body and Blood of Jesus Christ. It is true, nevertheless, (1) that it occupies, in regard to the subject-matter and the logical connection of the formulary, the exact place of the Greek *Epiclesis*; and (2) that it also is a prayer to God for His intervention in the mystery. But whilst the Greek Liturgies use here clear and simple terms, the Roman Liturgy embodies its meaning in symbolical forms. It prays that the angel of the Lord may take the oblation from the visible altar and bear it to the highest heaven, to the invisible altar, before the shrine of the Divine Majesty. This symbolical transference is in a contrary sense to that implied in the Greek formulary; it involves not the descent of the Holy Spirit upon the oblation, but the elevation by God's angel of the oblation to heaven. But in both cases alike it is after it has been brought near to, and has participated in, the Divine Virtue that it is called the Body and Blood of Christ.

The prayers which follow correspond with the Great Intercession of the Greek Liturgies, and occupy the same place as that assigned to it in the Syro-Byzantine rite.

It is certain that this formulary has been much curtailed. It begins with the commemoration of the faithful departed (*Memento*) for whom it requests eternal beatitude. This is also asked for those still living (*Nobis quoque*) by the mention of the saints into whose society it desires they should be admitted. After this prayer . . . *largitor admitte, per Christum Dominum nostrum,* there is apparently a *hiatus.* The text continues: *per quen haec omnia, Domine, semper bona creas, sanctificas, benedicis et praestas nobis.* It is clear that the words *haec omnia bona* have no reference to what immediately precede them; if we take the word *omnia,* moreover, into account it is difficult to make them apply to the consecrated oblation. The easiest explanation of the difficulty is that there was formerly here a mention of the fruits of the earth, with an enumeration of the various kinds—wheat, wine, oil, etc. This view is confirmed, moreover, by the fact that the blessing of aliments took place, on certain days, at this point in the Mass, as, for instance, the drink made of water, milk and honey, which was given to the neophytes at Easter and Pentecost. I append the formulary of this benediction, according to the Leonian Sacramentary, for the first Mass at Pentecost—

> Benedic, Domine, et has tuas creaturas fontis, mellis et lactis et pota famulos tuos ex hoc fonte aquae vitae perennis qui est Spiritus veritatis, et enutri eos de hoc lacte et melle, quemadmodum patribus nostris Abraham, Issac et Jacob [promisisti] introducere te eos in terram promissionis, terram fluentem melle et lacte. Conjunge ergo famulos tuos, Domine, Spiritui sancto, sicut conjunctum est hoc mel et lac, quo caelestis terrenaeque substantiae significatur unitio in Christo Jesu Domino nostro, per quem haec omnia, etc.

It was also at this place that the new beans were blessed on Ascension Day, and the new grapes on the day of St. Sixtus (August 6).

Benedic, Domine, et has fruges novas fabae, etc.
Benedic, Domine, et hos fructus novos uvae, etc.

Finally, it was at this point that the oil for the unction of the sick was blessed, and still is blessed, on Maundy Thursday.

There is no doubt, therefore, that the formulary *per quem haec omnia* was originally preceded, and that, too, apart from these extraordinary occasions, by a prayer for the fruits of the earth. This furnishes a further instance of the resemblance of the Roman Canon to the corresponding portion of the Greek and Eastern Liturgies.

8.–The Fraction of the Bread

The Canon having come to an end, the *Pater noster* follows. According to universal custom, it has a short introductory preface, and at the end an elaboration of the last petition (*Libera nos*).

Before the time of St. Gregory, the fraction of the bread followed immediately upon the Canon. It was he who transferred the *Pater noster* to this place, on the ground that it was hardly proper that the formulary of the Canon, the work of some unknown scholar, should alone be recited over the oblation, to the exclusion of the prayer composed by our Lord Himself. This transposition, although St. Gregory defends himself from the accusation of having followed any authority in introducing it, had the effect of bringing the Roman use into conformity with that of Constantinople.

The ceremony which follows is seemingly complicated. It begins with the kiss of peace, which is placed immediately after the salutation, *Pax Domini sit semper vobiscum.* The Pope places in the chalice the fragment of consecrated bread which had been brought to him at the beginning of the Mass; he then breaks one of his own two *oblatae*, and places one half of it upon the altar. We have not yet come to the fraction of the bread, properly speaking, but as all the loaves upon the altar intended for the Communion are about to be removed, and as it was customary to observe the prescription, *dum missarum solemnia peraguntur, altare sine sacrificio non sit*, the half-loaf placed on the altar by the Pope is meant to maintain this idea of permanence.

It was a matter of importance in the Roman Church that the ritual of the Communion should contain a clear and striking expression of ecclesiastical unity. Hence the custom of the *fermentum,* that is, of sending consecrated bread from the bishop's Mass to the priests whose duty it was to celebrate in the *Tituli*; hence also the significance of the rite of the *Sancta,* that is, of putting into the chalice at the *Pax Domini* a fragment consecrated at the preceding Mass and brought forth at the beginning of the present one. Thus, in all the Churches at Rome, and at every assembly there for liturgical worship past or present, there was always the same Sacrifice, the same Eucharist, the same Communion. Thus, in order to show clearly that the bread broken and distributed away from the altar was the same as that which had been consecrated on the altar, a fragment of it was allowed to remain on the holy table.

The other half of the first *oblata* and the second in its entirety were placed on the paten and brought before the Pope, who, after the *Pax Domini,* had returned to his seat. As for the other consecrated loaves, the archdeacon had caused them to be brought before the bishops and priests by acolytes, who carried them in linen bags suspended from their necks. Thereupon followed the fraction of the bread by the whole *presbyterium.* The Pope also took part in it, but only through his intermediaries the deacons, whose office it was to break the *oblata* and demi-*oblata* placed upon the paten. From the time of Pope Sergius (687-701) this ceremony was accompanied by the chanting of the *Agnus Dei.* It is probable that before the time of St. Gregory the *Pater noster* was said at this time, that is, after the fraction.

9.—The Communion

The fraction having been performed, the deacons present to the Pope the paten, from which, taking a fragment, he detaches a particle and consumes the rest. He then puts the detached portion into the chalice, which the archdeacon, who has brought it from the altar, holds before him. This is the rite of the *Commixtio.* The Pope thereupon drinks from the chalice, which is presented to him and held by the archdeacon.

Then comes the communion of the superior clergy. The bishops and priests approach the Pope, who puts into the hands of each a fragment taken from the paten. They then proceed to the altar, and each one, putting on the holy table his hand containing the consecrated bread, then communicates. The deacons do the same after them. The archdeacon brings back the chalice to the altar and puts it into the hands of the senior bishop present, who, after having drunk from it, presents it to the other bishops, and then to the priests and deacons. The communion of the congregation then follows. The Pope and the bishops and priests distribute the Eucharist under the species of bread. The archdeacon, following the Pope, and the other deacons following the bishops and priests, administer the chalice. As the Pope's chalice is used only for communicating the higher clergy, the archdeacon takes care to pour, beforehand, into the vessels containing the consecrated wine for the communion of the people, some drops from that used by the Pope, and, afterwards, what remains in it after the communion of the bishops, priests, and deacons. By this it is intended to show, that, although all do not touch with their lips the same vessel, yet they all drink the same spiritual drink. The rite of the *Commixtio,* having been performed by the Pope in the principal chalice, is repeated by the bishops and priests in all the other chalices, from which the faithful are communicated under the species of wine.

Before the communion of the people, the archdeacon announces the day and place of the next Station. There was an object in choosing this moment for the announcement. Those who did not communicate were, doubtless, accustomed to go out before the communion began. While the faithful were communicating, the choir chanted the antiphon *ad communionem.* At present it is chanted after communion, and is restricted to the anthem, which is sung only once. But the liturgical books of the ninth century still presuppose here a *real* antiphon, the psalm being chanted either in its entirety, or in part, according as the time occupied in the communion is long or short. It was terminated by the doxology *Gloria Patri,* etc., and the antiphon [*antienne*] was repeated. This chant, like that of the offertory, must go back to somewhere about the end of the fourth century.

The communion having ended, the pope returns to the altar, and salutes the congregation, inviting them to join in an act of thanksgiving, the *post communio.* This is the third of the *collective* prayers of the Roman Mass. It is followed by a final salutation, whereupon the deacon accounces the dismissal in a special formulary: *Ite missa est.* The procession is then reformed in the same order as it had at entrance, and as it proceeds to the sacrarium the Pope gives his blessing successively to the different groups of clergy and the faithful which he encounters on his way.

Romano Guardini
1885-1968

Guardini's 58 years as a priest saw unparalleled changes take place in the Catholic Church in Europe. From his professorial chair in Berlin before World War II and in Munich after World War II, he was one of the most respected pioneers in that turbulent era. The most fascinating thing about him was the way in which he personified the most fruitful polarities. Italian-German, scholar-pastor, historian-reformer, he invariably brought new insight to bear on every question.

Even for one of such originality, however, his 1918 book on the liturgy is difficult to account for. A dozen years passed before it was translated into English, and even then it was still so far ahead of most other work in the field that it had no real rivals. When Sheed & Ward put it into the series of "Catholic Masterpieces" in 1940, it was assured the attention it deserved.

Guardini's participation in the liturgical movement in Germany guaranteed it a prominent doctrinal component that it did not always enjoy elsewhere. This was certainly a factor in the support and growth which that movement enjoyed in Germany years before it found comparable acceptance in some other countries. The practical need for reform would soon be obvious once basic perspectives were accepted; e.g., he says in chapter one: "It is of paramount importance that the whole gathering should take an active share in the proceedings. If those composing the gathering merely listen, while one of the number acts as spokesman, the interior movement soon stagnates. All present, therefore, are obliged to take part." With such a principle it was only a matter of time till the necessity for the vernacular would become insistent.

The Spirit of the Liturgy *had an impact all out of proportion to its size. It is only some 90 pages long. Ranging over the entire field of human knowledge for examples and insights, he finds a significance and importance in the liturgy that would be taken up by thousands in the following decades. When the author died, 50 years after the publication of this book, the most extensive, systematic liturgical reform in the history of the Church had been mandated by Vatican II and was being implemented under Pope Paul VI. Few men live to see such a harvest from seeds they helped to sow in younger days.*

THE SPIRIT OF THE LITURGY

CHAPTER V

THE PLAYFULNESS OF THE LITURGY

Grave and earnest people, who make the knowledge of truth their whole aim, see moral problems in everything, and seek for a definite purpose everywhere, tend to experience a peculiar difficulty where the liturgy is concerned. They incline to regard it as being to a certain extent aimless, as superfluous pageantry of a needlessly complicated and artificial character. They are affronted by the scrupulously exact instructions which the liturgy gives on correct procedure, on the right direction in which to turn, on the pitch of the voice, and so on. What is the use of it all? The essential part of Holy Mass—the action of Sacrifice and the divine Banquet—could be so easily consummated. Why, then, the need for the solemn institution of the priestly office? The necessary consecration could be so simply accomplished in so few words, and the sacraments so straightforwardly administered—what is the reason of all the prayers and ceremonies? The liturgy tends to strike people of this turn of mind as—to use the words which are really most appropriate—trifling and theatrical.

The question is a serious one. It does not occur to everyone, but in the people whom it does affect it is a sign of the mental attitude which concentrates on and pursues that which is essential. It appears to be principally connected with the question of purpose.

That which we call purpose is, in the true sense of the word, the distributive, organising principle which subordinates actions or objects to other actions or objects, so that the one is directed towards the other, and one exists for the sake of the other. That which is subordinate, the means, is only significant in so far as it is capable of serving that which is superior, the end. The purpose does not infuse a spiritual value into its medium; it uses it as a passage to something else, a thoroughfare merely; aim and fulcrum alike reside in the former. From this point of view, every instrument has to prove in the first place whether, and in the second to what extent, it is fitted to accomplish the purpose for which it is employed. This proof will primarily be headed by the endeavour to eliminate from the instrument all the non-essential, unimportant, and superfluous elements. It is a scientific principle that an end should be attained with the minimum expenditure of energy, time, and material. A certain restless energy, an indifference to the cost involved, and accuracy in going to the point, characterise the corresponding turn of mind.

A disposition like this is, on the whole, both appropriate and necessary to life, giving it earnestness and fixity of purpose. It also takes reality into consideration, to the extent of viewing everything from the standpoint of purpose. Many pursuits and professions can be shown to have their origin almost entirely in the idea of purpose. Yet no phenomenon can be entirely, and many can be, to a minor degree only, comprehended in this category. Or, to put it more plainly, that which gives objects and events their right to existence, and justifies their individuality, is in many cases not the sole, and in others not even the primary reason for their usefulness. Are flowers and leaves useful? Of course; they are the vital organs of plants. Yet because of this, they are not tied down to any particular form, colour, or smell. Then what, upon the whole, is the use of the extravagance of shapes, colours and scents, in Nature? To what purpose the multiplicity of species? Things could be so much more simple. Nature could be entirely filled with animate beings, and they could thrive and progress in a far quicker and more suitable manner. The indiscriminate application to Nature of the idea of purpose is, however, open to objection. To go to the root of the matter, what is the object of this or that plant, and that of this or that animal, existing at all? Is it in order to afford nourishment to some other plant or animal? Of course not. Measured merely by the standard of apparent and external utility, there is a great deal in Nature which is only partially, and nothing which is wholly and entirely, intended for a purpose, or, better still, purpose*ful*. Indeed, considered in this light, a great deal is purposeless. In a mechanical structure—a machine, say, or a bridge—everything has a purpose; and the same thing applies to business enterprises or to the government of a State; yet even where these phenomena are concerned, the idea of purpose is not far-reaching enough to give an adequate reply to the query, whence springs their right to existence?

If we want to do justice to the whole question, we must shift our angle of vision. The conception of purpose regards an object's centre of gravity as existing outside that object, seeing it lie instead in the transition to further movement, *i.e.*, that towards the goal which the object provides. But every object is to a certain extent, and many are entirely, self-sufficient and an end in itself—if, that is, the conception can be applied at all in this extensive sense. The conception of meaning is more adaptable. Objects which have no purpose in the strict sense of the term have a meaning. This meaning is not realised by their extraneous effect or by the contribution which they make to the stability or the modification of another object, but their significance consists in being what they are. Measured by the strict sense of the word, they are purposeless, but still full of meaning.

Purpose and meaning are the two aspects of the fact that an existent principle possesses the motive for, and the right to, its own essence and existence. An object regarded from the point of view of purpose is seen to dovetail into an order of things which comprehends both it and more beyond it; from the standpoint of meaning, it is seen to be based upon itself.

Now what is the meaning of that which exists? That it should exist and should be the image of God the Everlasting. And what is the meaning of that which is alive? That it should live, bring forth its essence, and bloom as a natural manifestation of the living God.

This is true of Nature. It is also true of the life of the soul. Has science an aim or an object in the real sense of the word? No. Pragmatism is trying to foist one upon it. It insists that the aim of science is to better humanity and to improve it from the moral point of view. Yet this constitutes a failure to appreciate the independent value of knowledge. Knowledge has no aim, but it has a meaning, and one that is rooted in itself—truth. The legislative activity of Parliament, for instance, has an end in view; it is intended to bring about a certain agreed result in the life of the State. Jurisprudence, on the contrary, has no object; it merely indicates where truth lies in questions of law. The same thing applies to all real science. According to its nature, it is either the knowledge of truth or the service of truth, but nothing else. Has art any aim or purpose? No, it has not. If it had, we should be obliged to conclude that art exists in order to provide a living for artists, or else, as the eighteenth century German thinkers of the *Aufklärung*—the 'age of enlightenment'—considered, it is intended to offer concrete examples of intelligent views and to inculcate virtue. This is absolutely untrue. The work of art has no purpose, but it has a meaning—'*ut sit*'—that it should exist, and that it would clothe in clear and genuine form the essence of things and the inner life of the human artist. It is merely to be '*splendor veritatis*,' the glory of truth.

When life lacks the austere guidance of the sense of purpose it degenerates into pseudo-æstheticism. But when it is forced into the rigid framework that is the purely purposeful conception of the world, it droops and perishes. The two conceptions are interdependent. Purpose is the goal of all effort, labour and organisation, meaning is the essence of existence, of flourishing, ripening life. Purpose and meaning, effort and growth, activity and production, organisation and creation—these are the two poles of existence.

The Life of the Universal Church is also organised on these lines. In the first place, there is the whole tremendous system of purposes incorporated in the Canon Law, and in the constitution and government of the Church. Here we find every means directed to the one end, that of keeping in motion the great machinery of ecclesiastical government. The first-mentioned point of view will decide whether adjustment or modification best serves the collective purpose, and whether the latter is attained with the least possible expenditure of time and energy. The scheme of labour must be arranged and controlled by a strictly practical spirit.

The Church, however, has another side. It embraces a sphere which is in a special sense free from purpose. And that is the liturgy. The latter certainly comprehends a whole system of aims and purposes, as well as the instruments to accomplish them. It is the business of the Sacraments to act as the channels of certain graces. This mediation, however, is easily and quickly accomplished when the necessary conditions are present. The administration of the Sacraments is an example of a liturgical action which is strictly confined to the one object. Of course, it can be said of the liturgy, as of every action and every prayer which it contains, that it is directed towards the providing of spiritual instruction. This is perfectly true. But the liturgy has no thought-out, deliberate, detailed plan of instruction. In order to sense the difference it is sufficient to compare a week of the ecclesiastical year with the Spiritual Exercises of St. Ignatius. In the latter every element is determined by deliberate choice, everything is directed towards the production of a certain spiritual and didactic result; each exercise, each prayer, even the way in which the hours of repose are passed, all aim at the one thing, the conversion of the will. It is not so with the liturgy. The fact that the latter has no place in the Spiritual Exercises is a proof of this. The liturgy wishes to teach, but not by means of an artificial system of aim-conscious educational influences; it simply creates an entire spiritual world in which the soul can live according to the requirements of its nature. The difference resembles that which exists between a gymnasium, in which every detail of the apparatus and every exercise aims at a calculated effect, and the open woods and fields. In the first everything is consciously directed towards discipline and development, in the second life is lived with Nature, and internal growth takes place in her. The liturgy creates a universe brimming with fruitful spiritual life, and allows the soul to wander about in it at will and to develop itself there. The abundance of prayers, ideas, and actions, and the whole arrangment of the calendar are incomprehensible when they are measured by the objective standard of strict suitability for a purpose. The liturgy has no purpose, or, at least, it cannot be considered from the standpoint of purpose. It is not a means which is adapted to attain a certain end—it is an end in itself. This fact is important, because if we overlook it, we labour to find all kinds of didactic purposes in the liturgy which may certainly be stowed away somewhere, but are not actually evident.

When the liturgy is rightly regarded, it cannot be said to have a purpose, because it does not exist for the sake of humanity, but for the sake of God. In the liturgy man is no longer concerned with himself; his gaze is directed towards God. In it man is not so much intended to edify himself as to contemplate God's majesty. The liturgy means that the soul exists in God's presence, originates in Him, lives in a world of divine realities, truths, mysteries and symbols, and really lives its true, characteristic and fruitful life.

There are two very profound passages in Holy Scripture, which are quite decisive on the point. One is found in the description of Ezekiel's vision. Let us consider the flaming Cherubim, who 'every one of them went straight forward, whither the impulse of the Spirit was to go . . ., and they turned not when they went . . ., ran and returned like flashes of lightning . . ., went . . . and stood . . . and were lifted up from the earth . . ., the noise of their wings was like the noise of many waters . . ., and when they stood, their wings were let down.' How 'aimless' they are! How discouraging for the zealous partisans of reasonable suitability for a purpose! They are only pure motion, powerful and splendid, acting according to the direction of the Spirit, desiring nothing save to express Its inner drift and Its interior glow and force. They are the living image of the liturgy.

In the second passage it is Eternal Wisdom which speaks: 'I was with Him, forming all things, and was delighted every day, playing before Him at all times, playing in the world. . . .'

This is conclusive. It is the delight of the Eternal Father that Wisdom (the Son, the perfect Fullness of Truth) should pour out Its eternal essence before Him in all Its ineffable splendour, without any 'purpose'—for what purpose should It have?—but full of decisive meaning, in pure and vocal happiness; the Son 'plays' before the Father.

Such is the life of the highest beings, the angels, who, without a purpose and as the Spirit stirs them, move before God, and are a mystic diversion and a living song before Him.

In the earthly sphere there are two phenomena which tend in the same direction: the play of the child and the creation of the artist.

The child, when it plays, does not aim at anything. It has no purpose. It does not want to do anything but to exercise its youthful powers, pour forth its life in an aimless series of movements, words and actions, and by this to develop and to realise itself more fully; all of which is purposeless, but full of meaning nevertheless, the significance lying in the unchecked revelation of this youthful life in thoughts and words and movements and actions, in the capture and expression of its nature, and in the fact of its existence. And because it does not aim at anything in particular, because it streams unbroken and spontaneously forth, its utterance will be harmonious, its form clear and fine; its expression will of itself become picture and dance, rhyme, melody and song. That is what play means; it is life, pouring itself forth without an aim, seizing upon riches from its own abundant store, significant through the fact of its existence. It will be beautiful, too, if it is left to itself, and if no futile advice and pedagogic attempts at enlightenment foist upon it a host of aims and purposes, thus denaturising it.

Yet, as life progresses, conflicts ensue, and it appears to grow ugly and discordant. Man sets before himself what he wants to do and what he should do, and tries to realise this in his life. But in the course of these endeavours he learns that many obstacles stand in his way, and he perceives that it is very seldom that he can attain his ideal.

It is in a different order, in the imaginary sphere of representation, that man tries to reconcile the contradiction between that which he wishes to be and that which he is. In art he tries to harmonise the ideal and actuality, that which he ought to be and that which he is, the soul within and nature without, the body and the soul. Such are the visions of art. It has no didactic aims, then; it is not intended to inculcate certain truths and virtues. A true artist has never had such an end in view. In art, he desires to do nothing but to overcome the discord to which we have referred, and to express in the sphere of representation the higher life of which he stands in need, and to which in actuality he has only approximately attained. The artist merely wants to give life to his being and its longings, to give external form to the inner truth. And people who contemplate a work of art should not expect anything of it but that they should be able to linger before it, moving freely, becoming conscious of their own better nature, and sensing the fulfilment of their most intimate longings. But they should not reason and chop logic, or look for instruction and good advice from it.

The liturgy offers something higher. In it man, with the aid of grace, is given the opportunity of realising his fundamental essence, of really becoming that which according to his divine destiny he should be and longs to be, a child of God. In the liturgy he is to go 'unto God, Who giveth joy to his youth.' All this is, of course, on the supernatural plane, but at the same time it corresponds to the same degree to the inner needs of man's nature. Because the life of the liturgy is higher than that to which customary reality gives both the opportunity and form of expression, it adopts suitable forms and methods from that sphere in which alone they are to be found, that is to say, from art. It speaks measuredly and melodiously; it employs formal, rhythmic gestures; it is clothed in colours and garments foreign to everyday life; it is carried out in places and at hours which have co-ordinated and systematised according to sublimer laws than ours. It is in the highest sense the life of a child, in which everything is picture, melody and song.

Such is the wonderful fact which the liturgy demonstrates; it unites art and reality in a supernatural childhood before God. That which formerly existed in the world of unreality only, and was rendered in art as the expression of mature human life, has here become reality. These forms are the vital expression of real and frankly supernatural life. But this has one thing in common with the play of the child and the life of art—it has no purpose, but it is full of profound meaning. It is not work, but play. To be at play, or to fashion a work of art in God's sight—not to create, but to exist—such is the essence of the liturgy. From this is derived its sublime mingling of profound earnestness and divine joyfulness. The fact that the liturgy gives a thousand strict and careful directions on the quality of the language, gestures, colours, garments and instruments which it employs, can only be understood by those who are able to take art and play seriously. Have you ever noticed how gravely children draw up the rules of their games, on the form of the melody, the position of the hands, the meaning of this stick and that tree? It is for the sake of the silly people who may not grasp their meaning and who will persist in seeing the justification of an action or object only in its obvious purpose. Have you ever read of or even experienced the deadly earnestness with which the artist-vassal labours for art, his lord? Of his sufferings on the score of language? Or of what an overweening mistress form is? And all this for something that has no aim or purpose! No, art does not bother about aims. Does anyone honestly believe that the artist would take upon himself the thousand anxieties and feverish perplexities incident to creation if he intended to do nothing with his work but to teach the spectator a lesson, which he could just as well express in a couple of facile phrases, or one or two historical examples, or a few well-taken photographs? The only answer to this can be an emphatic negative. Being an artist means wrestling with the expression of the hidden life of man, avowedly in order that it may be given existence; nothing more. It is the image of the Divine creation, of which it is said that it has made things '*ut sint.*'

The liturgy does the same thing. It too, with endless care, with all the seriousness of the child and the strict conscientiousness of the great artist, has toiled to express in a thousand forms the sacred, God-given life of the soul to no other purpose than that the soul may therein have its existence and live its life. The liturgy has laid down the serious rules of the sacred game which the soul plays before God. And, if we are desirous of touching bottom in this mystery, it is the Spirit of fire and of holy discipline 'Who has knowledge of the world'—the Holy Ghost—Who has ordained the game which the Eternal Wisdom plays before the Heavenly Father in the Church, Its kingdom on earth. And 'Its delight' is in this way 'to be with the children of men.'

Only those who are not scandalised by this understand what the liturgy means. From the very first every type of rationalism has turned against it. The practice of the liturgy means that by the help of grace, under the guidance of the Church, we grow into living works of art before God, with no other aim or purpose than that of living and existing in His sight; it means fulfilling God's word and 'becoming as little children'; it means foregoing maturity with all its purposefulness, and confining oneself to play, as David did when he danced before the Ark. It may, of course, happen that those extremely clever people, who merely from being grown-up have lost all spiritual youth and spontaneity, will misunderstand this and jibe at it. David probably had to face the derision of Michal.

It is in this very aspect of the liturgy that its didactic aim is to be found, that of teaching the soul not to see purposes everywhere, not to be too conscious of the end it wishes to attain, not to be desirous of being over-clever and grown-up, but to understand simplicity in life. The soul must learn to abandon, at least in prayer, the restlessness of purposeful activity; it must learn to waste time for the sake of God, and to be prepared for the sacred game with sayings and thoughts and gestures, without always immediately asking 'why?' and 'wherefore?' It must learn not to be continually yearning to *do* something, to attack something, to accomplish something useful, but to play the divinely ordained game of the liturgy in liberty and beauty and holy joy before God.

In the end, eternal life will be its fulfilment. Will the people who do not understand the liturgy be pleased to find that the heavenly consummation is an eternal song of praise? Will they not rather associate themselves with those other industrious people who consider that such an eternity will be both boring and unprofitable?

CHAPTER VI

THE SERIOUSNESS OF THE LITURGY

The liturgy is art, translated into terms of life. Sensitive people clearly recognise its wealth of expression, its symmetry of form, and its delicate sense of proportion. As a result, such people are in danger of appreciating the Church's worship merely for the sake of its æsthetic value. It is on the whole understandable that poetic literature should apprehend the liturgy from its artistic side. It is a more serious matter when this is so emphatically stressed in writings which are particularly dedicated to liturgical worship. It is sufficient for our purpose to recall valuable works such as Staudenmaier's *Geist des Christentums,* or many of J. K. Huysman's books, *L'Oblat,* for instance. The present writer is anxious that this little work should not gravitate, however unconsciously, in the same direction. For this reason, in the chapter which has been begun, the question will be more closely examined.

It is an incontrovertible proposition that people who consider a work of art merely from the artistic point of view do it an injustice. Its significance as a composition can only be fully estimated when it is viewed in connection with the whole of life. A work of art is in less danger from the logician or the moral philosopher pure and simple, because they stand in no particular relation to it. Deadly destructive to the work of art, however, is the purely artistic perception of the æsthete—both word and matter being taken in the worst and most extreme sense which they have possessed since, for instance, Oscar Wilde.

Still more does this hold good when it is a question, not of the representation of a work of art, but of actual people, and even of that tremendous unity—the *Opus Dei,* that is the liturgy in which the Creator-Artist, the Holy Ghost, has garnered and expressed the whole fulness of reality and of creative art. Æsthetes are everywhere looked upon as unwelcome guests, as drones and as parasites sponging on life, but nowhere are they more deserving of anger and contempt than in the sphere of sacred things. The careworn man who seeks nothing at Mass but the fulfilment of the service which he owes to his God; the busy woman, who comes to be a little lightened of her burden; the many people who, barren of feeling and perceiving nothing of the beauty and splendour of word and sound which surrounds them, but merely seek strength for their daily toil—all these penetrate far more deeply into the essence of the liturgy than does the connoisseur who is busy savouring the contrast between the austere beauty of a Preface and the melodiousness of a Gradual.

All of which impels us to the fundamental question, what is the importance of beauty in relation to the entire liturgical scheme?

First, however, a light but necessary digression. We have already seen that the Church's life functions in two directions. On the one side there exists an active communal life, a tremendous driving force of systematically directed activities, which, however, coalesce in the many-membered but strongly centralised organisation. Such a unity alike presupposes and manifests power. But what is the purpose of power in the spiritual sphere?

This query deeply concerns every one of us, each according to his disposition. For the one, it is a question of satisfying himself as to the truth of the axiom that every type of society, including the spiritual, needs power if it is to subsist. The truth of this does not degrade the ideal, even if it ranks power next in order to doctrine, exhortation, and organisation. This external power must not of course be allowed to usurp the place of truth and of justice, nor permitted to influence convictions. Where, however, a religion is concerned which does not confine itself to presenting ideals and opinions, but undertakes the moulding and adapting of human entities on behalf of the Kingdom of God, there power is necessary. It is this which adapts a truth, or a spiritual or ethical system, to the needs of actual existence.

But if there are people who find it hard to bear that things like justice and power should be named in the same breath with such intimate matters as religious convictions and spiritual life, there are others who are entirely differently constituted. Upon such people a tremendous force like the Catholic Church produces so direct an effect that they easily forget the real significance of such power. It is merely a means to an end. It is a tool, used to carve the Kingdom of God from the raw material of the world; it is the servant of Divine truth and grace. If an attempt were to be made to constitute a form of spiritual society without a powerful discipline, it would inevitably dissolve into fleeting shadows. But if power, the servant, were to be promoted to the position of master, the means to that of the end, the tool to that of the guiding hand, religion would then be stifled by despotism and its consequence, slavery.

Somewhat analogous to the position of power in the Church's active life is that of beauty in relation to her contemplative side. The Church not only exists for a purpose, but she is of herself significant, viewed from her other aspect of art transformed into life—or, better still, in the process of transformation. For that is what the Church is in the liturgy.

The preceding chapter endeavoured to demonstrate that artistic self-sufficiency is actually compatible with the liturgy. Only a sophist could argue that the justification of a form of life resides exclusively in its manifest purposes. On the other hand, one must not forget as well that artistic worth—beauty—is as dangerous to the susceptible person as is power in the corresponding sphere of active communal life. The danger inherent in the idea of power is only to be overcome by those who are clear about its nature and the method of employing it. Similarly, only those who force their way into perception of its import can break free from the illusive spell of beauty.

Apart from this stands the question, whence a spiritual value derives its currency, whether from itself or from an extraneous superior value? Associated with it, but entirely distinct, is the second question, as to the quality of the relation which exists between one value which is admittedly based upon itself and other independent values. The first question endeavours to trace one value back to another, *e.g.*, the validity of the administration of justice to justice in the abstract. The second investigates the existence, between two values of equal validity, of a determinate order which may not be inverted.

Truth is of itself a value, because it is truth, justice because it is justice, and beauty because and in so far as it is beauty. No one of these qualities can derive its validity from another, but only from itself. The most profound and true thought does not make a work beautiful, and the best intentions of the artist avail as little, if his creation, in addition to a concrete, vivid and robust form, has not—in a word—beauty. Beauty as such is valid of itself, entirely independent of truth and other values. An object or a work of art is beautiful, when its inner essence and significance find perfect expression in its existence. This perfection of expression embraces the fact of beauty, and is its accepted form of currency. Beauty means that the essence of an object or action has, from the first moment of its existence and from the innermost depths of its being, formulated its relation to the universe and to the spiritual world; that this interior formation, from which has developed a phenomenon susceptible of expression, has resolved upon symbolic unity; that everything is said which should be said, and no more; that the essential form is attained, and no other; that in it there is nothing that is lifeless and empty, but everything that is vivid and animated; that every sound, every word, every surface, shade and movement, emanates from within, contributes to the expression of the whole, and is associated with the rest in a seamless, organic unity. Beauty is the full, clear and inevitable expression of the inner truth in the external manifestation. *'Pulchritudo est splendor veritatis'—'est species boni,'* says ancient philosophy, 'beauty is the splendid perfection which dwells in the revelation of essential truth and goodness.

Beauty, therefore, is an independent value; it is not truth and not goodness, nor can it be derived from them. And yet it stands in the closest relation to these other values. As we have already remarked, in order that beauty may be made manifest, something must exist which will reveal itself externally; there must be an essential truth which compels utterance, or an event which will out. Pride of place, therefore, though not of rank or worth, belongs, not to beauty, but to truth. Although this applies incontestably to life as a whole, and to the fundamentals of art as well, it will perhaps be difficult for the artist to accept without demur.

'Beauty is the splendour of truth,' says scholastic philosophy. To us moderns this sounds somewhat frigid and superficially dogmatic. But if we remember that this axiom was held and taught by men who were incomparable constructive thinkers, who conceived ideas, framed syllogisms, and established systems, which still tower over others like vast cathedrals, we shall feel it incumbent upon us to penetrate more deeply into the meaning of these few words. Truth does not mean mere lifeless accuracy of comprehension, but the right and appropriate regulation of life, a vital spiritual essence; it means the intrinsic value of existence in all its force and fulness. And beauty is the triumphant splendour which breaks forth when the hidden truth is revealed, when the external phenomenon is at all points the perfect expression of the inner essence. Perfection of expression, then, not merely superficial and external, but interior and contemporaneous with every step in the creation—can the essence of beauty be more profoundly and at the same time more briefly defined?

Beauty cannot be appreciated unless this fact is borne in mind, and it is apprehended as the splendour of perfectly expressed intrinsic truth.

But there is a grave risk, which many people do not escape, of this order being reversed, and of beauty being placed before truth, or treated as entirely separate from the latter, the perfection of form from the content, and the expression from its substance and meaning. Such is the danger incurred by the æsthetic conception of the world, which ultimately degenerates into nerveless æstheticism.

No investigation of the æsthetic mind and ideas can be undertaken here. But we may premise that its primary characteristic is a more or less swift withdrawal from discussion of the reason for a thing's existence to the manner of it, from the content to the method of presentation, from the intrinsic value of the object to its value as a form, from the austerity of truth and the inflexible demands of morality to the relaxing harmony of beauty. This will happen more or less consistently, and more or less consciously, until everything terminates finally in a frame of mind which no longer recognises intrinsic truth, with its severe 'thus and not otherwise,' nor the moral idea with its unconditional 'either–or,' but seeks for significance in form and expression alone. That which is objective, whether it is a natural object, a historical event, a man, a sorrow, a preference, a work, a legal transaction, knowledge, an idea, is merely viewed as a fact without significance. It serves as a pretext for expression, that is all. Thus originates the shadowy image of absolute form, a manner without a matter, a radiance without heat, a fact without force.

People who think like this have lost the ability to grasp the profundity of a work of art, and the standard by which to measure its greatness. They no longer comprehend it as being what it is, as a victory and as an avowal. They do not even do justice to the form which is the exclusive object of their preoccupation; for form means the expression of a substance, or the mode of life of an existent being.

Truth is the soul of beauty. People who do not understand what the one and the other are really worth turn their joyful play into mere empty trifling. There is something heroic in every great and genuine creation, in which the interior essence has won through opposition to its true expression. A good fight has been fought, in which some essential substance, conscious of the best elements within itself, has set aside that which is extraneous to itself, submitted all disorder and confusion to a strict discipline, and obeyed the laws of its own nature. A tremendous ebullition takes place, and an inner substance gives external testimony to its essence and to the essential message which it holds. But the æsthete looks upon all this as pointless trifling.

Nay, more. Æstheticism is profoundly shameless. All true beauty is modest. This word is not used in a superficial sense. It has no relation as to the suitability of this or that for utterance, portrayal, or existence. What it means is that all expression has been impelled by an interior urge, justified by immutable standards, and permitted, even offered existence by the latter. This permission and obligation, however, only reside in the intrinsic truth of an entity or a genuine spiritual experience. Expression on the other hand for the sake of expression, self-elected as both matter and form, has no longer any value.

We are led yet further afield by these considerations. In spite of the most genuine impulse, and even when truth not only emphatically justifies the proceeding, but also imperatively demands it, all true inwardness still shrinks from self-revelation, just because it is full of all goodness. The desire for revelation, however, and the realisation that it is only in articulation that it can obtain release from the tyranny of silence, compel the expression of an inwardness; yet it still shrinks from disclosure, because it fears that by this it will lose its noblest elements. The fulfilment of all inwardness lies in the instant when it discloses itself in a form appropriate to its nature. But it is immediately conscious of a painful reaction, of a sensation as of having irrevocably lost something inexpressibly precious.

This applies—or is it too sweeping a statement?—to all genuine creative art. It is like a blush after the word, readily enough spoken, but followed by a secret reproach, and often incomprehensible pain, arising from depths till now unexplored; it is like the quick compression of the lips which would give much to recall the hasty avowal. People who understand this are aware that further depths and modestly concealed riches still lie beyond that which, surrendering itself, has taken shape. This generosity, while at the same time the store remains undiminished, this advance, followed by withdrawal into resplendent fastnesses, this grappling with expression, triumphant expansion, and timid, dolorous contraction, together constitute the tenderest charm of beauty.

But all this—the restrained yet youthful fulness of candour—vanishes before the glance, at once disrespectful and obtuse, of those who seek after articulation for the sake of articulation, and after beauty for the sake of beauty.

Those who aspire to a life of beauty must, in the first place, strive to be truthful and good. If a life is true it will automatically become beautiful, just as light shines forth when flame is kindled. But if they seek after beauty in the first place, it will fare with them as it fared with Hedda Gabler, and in the end everything will become nauseating and loathsome.

In the same way—however strange it may sound—the creative artist must not seek after beauty in the abstract, not, that is, if he understands that beauty is something more than a certain grace of external form and a pleasing and elegant effect. He must, on the contrary, with all his strength endeavour to become true and just in himself, to apprehend truth and to live in and by it, and in this way fully realise both the internal and external world. And then the artist, as the enemy of all vanity and showiness, must express truth as it should be expressed, without the alteration of a single stroke or trait. It follows that his work, if he is an artist at all, will, and not only will, but *must* be beautiful. If, however, he tries to avoid the toilsome path of truth, and to distil form from form, that which he represents is merely empty illusion.

People who have not enjoyed—repulsive word, which puts beauty on a par with a titbit, and originates from the worthless conception which we have just now censured—human perfection or the beauty of a work of art, but desire closer familiarity with it, must take the inner essence for their starting-point. They will be well advised to ignore expression and harmony of form at first, but to endeavour to penetrate instead to the inner truth of the vital essence. Viewed from this standpoint, the whole process by which the matter transposes itself into its form becomes apparent, and the spectators witness a miraculous flowering. This means that they are familiar with beauty, although perhaps they may not consciously recognise it for what it is, but are merely aware of a sentiment of perfect satisfaction at the visible and adequate fulfilment of an object or of an existence.

Beauty eludes those who pursue it for its own sake, and their life and work are ruined because they have sinned against the fundamental order of values. If a man, however, desires to live for truth alone, to be truthful in himself and to speak the truth, and if he keeps his soul open, beauty—in the shape of richness, purity, and vitality of form—will come to meet him, unsought and unexpected.

What profound penetration and insight was shown by Plato, the master of æsthetics, in his warnings against the dangers of excessive worship of beauty! We need a new artist-seer to convince the young people of our day, who bend the knee in idolatrous homage before art and beauty, what must be the fruit of such perversion of the highest spiritual laws.

We must now refer what has already been propounded to the liturgy. There is a danger that in the liturgical sphere as well æstheticism may spread; that the liturgy will first be the subject of general eulogy, then gradually its various treasures will be estimated at their æsthetic value, until finally the sacred beauty of the House of God comes to provide a delicate morsel for the connoisseur. Until, that is, the 'house of prayer' becomes once more, in a different way, a 'den of thieves.' But for the sake of Him who dwells there and for that of our own souls, this must not be tolerated.

The Church has not built up the *Opus Dei* for the pleasure of forming beautiful symbols, choice language, and graceful, stately gestures, but she has done it—in so far as it is not completely devoted to the worship of God—for the sake of our desperate spiritual need. It is to give expression to the events of the Christian's inner life: the assimilation, through the Holy Ghost, of the life of the creature to the life of God in Christ; the actual and genuine rebirth of the creature into a new existence; the development and nourishment of this life, its stretching forth from God in the Blessed Sacrament and the means of grace, towards God in prayer and sacrifice; and all this in the continual mystic renewal of Christ's life in the course of the ecclesiastical year. The fulfilment of all these processes by the set forms of language, gesture, and instruments, their revelation, teaching, accomplishment and acceptance by the faithful, together constitute the liturgy. We see, then, that it is primarily concerned with reality, with the approach of a real creature to a real God, and with the profoundly real and serious matter of redemption. There is here no question of creating beauty, but of finding salvation for sin-stricken humanity. Here truth is at stake, and the fate of the soul, and real—yes, ultimately the only real—life. All this it is which must be revealed, expressed, sought after, found and imparted by every possible means and method; and when this is accomplished, lo! it is turned into beauty.

This is not a matter for amazement, since the principle here at work is the principle of truth and of mastery over form. The interior element has been expressed clearly and truthfully, the whole superabundance of life has found its utterance, and the fathomless profundities have been plainly mapped out. It is only to be expected that a gleam of the utmost splendour should shine forth at such a manifestation of truth.

For us, however, the liturgy must chiefly be regarded from the standpoint of salvation. We should steadfastly endeavour to convince ourselves of its truth and its importance in our lives. When we recite the prayers and psalms of the liturgy, we are to praise God, nothing more. When we assist at Holy Mass, we must know that we are close to the fount of all grace. When we are present at an ordination, the significance of the proceedings must lie for us in the fact that the grace of God has taken possession of a fragment of human life. We are not concerned here with the question of powerfully symbolic gestures, as if we were in a spiritual theatre, but we have to see that our real souls should approach a little nearer to the real God, for the sake of all our most personal, profoundly serious affairs.

For it is only thus that perception of liturgical beauty will be vouchsafed to us. It is only when we participate in liturgical action with the earnestness begotten of deep personal interest that we become aware why, and in what perfection, this vital essence is revealed. It is only when we premise the truth of the liturgy that our eyes are opened to its beauty.

The degree of perception varies, according to our æsthetic sensitiveness. Perhaps it will merely be a pleasant feeling of which we are not even particularly conscious, of the profound appropriateness of both language and actions for the expression of spiritual realities, a sensation of quiet spontaneity, a consciousness that everything is right and exactly as it should be. Then perhaps an offertory suddenly flashes in upon us, so that it gleams before us like a jewel. Or bit by bit the whole sweep of the Mass is revealed, just as from out the vanishing mist the peaks and summits and slopes of a mountain chain stand out in relief, shining and clear, so that we imagine we are looking at them for the first time. Or it may be that in the midst of prayer the soul will be pervaded by that gentle, blithe gladness which rises into sheer rapture. Or else the book will sink from our hands, while penetrated with awe, we taste the meaning of utter and blissful tranquillity, conscious that the final and eternal verities which satisfy all longing have here found their perfect expression.

But these moments are fleeting, and we must be content to accept them as they come or are sent.

On the whole, however, and as far as everyday life is concerned, this precept holds good, 'Seek first the kingdom of God and His justice, and all else shall be added to you'—all else, even the glorious experience of beauty.

CHAPTER VII

THE PRIMACY OF THE LOGOS OVER THE ETHOS

The liturgy exhibits one peculiarity which strikes as very odd those natures in particular which are generously endowed with moral energy and earnestness—and that is its singular attitude towards the moral order.

People of the type instanced above chiefly regret one thing in the liturgy, that its moral system has few direct relations with everyday life. It does not offer any easily transposable motives, or ideas realisable at first hand, for the benefit of our daily conflicts and struggles. A certain isolation, a certain remoteness from actual life characterise it; it is celebrated in the somewhat sequestered sphere of spiritual things. A contrast exists between the study, the factory, and the laboratory of to-day, between the arena of public and social life and the Holy Places of solemn, divine worship, between the intensely practical tendency of our time, which is opposed to life by its wholly material force and acrid harshness, and the lofty, measured domain of liturgical conceptions and determination, with its clearness and elevation of form.

From this it follows that we cannot directly translate into action that which the liturgy offers us. There will always be a constant need, then, for methods of devotion which have their origin in a close connection with modern life, and for the popular devotions by which the Church meets the special demands and requirements of actual existence, and which, since they directly affect the soul, are immediately productive of practical results. The liturgy, on the contrary, is primarily occupied in forming the fundamental Christian temper. By it man is to be induced to determine correctly his essential relation to God, and to put himself right in regard to reverence for God, love and faith, atonement and the desire for sacrifice. As a result of this spiritual disposition, it follows that when action is required of him he will do what is right.

The question, however, goes yet deeper. What is the position of the liturgy generally to the moral order? What is the quality of the relation in it of the will to knowledge, as of the value of truth to the value of goodness? Or, to put it in two words, what is the relation in it of the Logos to the Ethos? It will be necessary to go back somewhat in order to find the answer.

It is safe to affirm that the Middle Ages, in philosophy at least, answered the question as to the relation between these two fundamental principles by decisively ranking knowledge before will and the activity attendant upon the functioning of the latter. They gave the Logos precedence over the Ethos. That is proved by the way in which certain frequently discussed questions are answered, and by the absolute priority which was assigned to the contemplative life over the active; this stands out as the fundamental attitude of the Middle Ages, which took the Hereafter as the constant and exclusive goal of all earthly striving.

Modern times brought about a great change. The great objective institutions of the Middle Ages—class solidarity, the municipalities, the Empire—broke up. The power of the Church was no longer, as formerly, absolute and temporal. In every direction individualism became more strongly pronounced and independent. This development was chiefly responsible for the growth of scientific criticism, and in a special manner the criticism of knowledge itself. The inquiry into the essence of knowledge, which formally followed a constructive method, now assumes, as a result of the profound spiritual changes which have taken place, its characteristic critical form. Knowledge itself becomes questionable, and as a result the centre of gravity and the fulcrum of the spiritual life gradually shifts from knowledge to the will. The actions of the independent individual become increasingly important. In this way active life forces its way before the contemplative, the will before knowledge.

Even in science, which after all is essentially dependent upon knowledge, a peculiar significance is assigned to the will. In place of the former penetration of guaranteed truth, of tranquil assimilation and discussion, there now develops a restless investigation of obscure, questionable truth. Instead of explanation and assimilation, education tends increasingly towards independent investigation. The entire scientific sphere exhibits an enterprising and aggressive tendency. It develops into a powerful, restlessly productive, labouring community.

This importance of the will has been scientifically formulated in the most conclusive manner by Kant. He recognised, side by side with the order of perception, of the world of things, in which the understanding alone is competent, the order of practicality, of freedom, in which the will functions. Arising out of the postulations of the will he admits the growth of a third order, the order of faith, as opposed to knowledge, the world of God and the soul. While the understanding is of itself incapable of asserting anything on these latter matters, because it is unable to verify them by the senses, it receives belief in their reality, and thus the final shaping of its conception of the world, from the postulations of the will which cannot exist and function without these highest data from which to proceed. This established the 'primacy of the will.' The will, together with the scale of moral values peculiar to it, has taken precedence of knowledge with its corresponding scale of values; the Ethos has obtained the primacy over the Logos.

The ice having been broken, there now follows the entire course of philosophic development which sets, in the place of the pure will logically conceived by Kant, the psychological will, constituting the latter, the unique rule of life—a development due to Fichte, Schopenhauer, and von Hartmann—until it finds its clearest expression in Nietzsche. He proclaims the 'will to power.' For him, truth is that which makes life sound and noble, leading humanity further towards the goal of the 'Superman.'

Such is the origin of pragmatism, by which truth is no longer viewed as an independent value in the case of a conception of the universe or in spiritual matters, but as the expression of the fact that a principle or a system benefits life and actual affairs, and elevates the character and stability of the will. Truth is fundamentally, if not entirely—though here we overstep the field marked out for our consideration—a moral, though hardly a vital fact.

This predominance of the will and of the idea of its value gives the present day its peculiar character. It is the reason for its restless pressing forward, the stringent limiting of its hours of labour, the precipitancy of its enjoyment; hence, too, the worship of success, of strength, of action; hence the striving after power, and generally the exaggerated opinion of the value of time, and the compulsion to exhaust oneself by activity till the end. This is the reason, too, why spiritual organisations such as the old contemplative orders, which formerly were automatically accepted by spiritual life everywhere and which were the darlings of the orthodox world, are not infrequently misunderstood even by Catholics, and have to be defended by their friends against the reproach of idle trifling. And if it is true that this attitude of mind has already become firmly established in Europe, whose culture is rooted in the distant past, it is doubly true where the New World is concerned. There it comes to light unconcealed and unalloyed. The practical will is everywhere the decisive factor, and the Ethos has complete precedence over the Logos, the active side of life over the contemplative.

What is the position of Catholicism in relation to this development? It must be premised that the best elements of every period and of every type of mind can and will find their fulfilment in this Religion, which is truly capable of being all things to all men. So it has been possible to adapt the tremendous development of power during the last five centuries in

Catholic life, and to summon ever fresh aspects from its inexhaustible store. A long investigation would be needed if we were to point out how many highly valuable personalities, tendencies, activities and views have been called forth from Catholic life as a result of this responsiveness to the needs of all ages. But it must be pointed out that an extensive, biased, and lasting predominance of the will over knowledge is profoundly at variance with the Catholic spirit.

Protestantism presents, its various forms, ranging from the strong tendency to the extreme of free speculation, the more or less Christian version of this spirit, and Kant has rightly been called its philosopher. It is a spirit which has step by step abandoned objective religious truth, and has increasingly tended to make conviction a matter of personal judgment, feeling, and experience. In this way truth has fallen from the objective plane to the level of a relative and fluctuating value. As a result, the will has been obliged to assume the leadership. When the believer no longer possesses any fundamental principles, but only an experience of faith as it affects him personally, the one solid and recognisable fact is no longer a body of dogma which can be handed on in tradition, but the right action as a proof of the right spirit. In this connection there can be no talk of spiritual metaphysics in the real sense of the word. And when knowledge has nothing ultimately to seek in the Above, the roots of the will and of feeling are in their turn loosened from their adherence to knowledge. The relation with the super-temporal and eternal order is thereby broken. The believer no longer stands in eternity, but in time, and eternity is merely connected with time through the medium of conviction, but not in a direct manner. Religion becomes increasingly turned towards the world, and cheerfully secular. It develops more and more into a consecration of temporal human existence in its various aspects, into a sanctification of earthly activity, of vocational labour, of communal and family life, and so on.

Everyone, however, who has debated these matters at any considerable length clearly perceives the unwholesomeness of such a conception of spiritual life, and the flagrance of its contradiction of all fundamental spiritual principles. It is untrue, and therefore contrary to Nature in the deepest sense of the word. Here is the real source of the terrible misery of our day. It has perverted the sacred order of Nature. It was Goethe who really shook the latter when he made the doubting Faust write, not 'In the beginning was the Word,' but 'In the beginning was the Deed.'

While life's centre of gravity was shifting from the Logos to the Ethos, life itself was growing increasingly unrestrained. Man's will was required to be responsible for him. Only one Will can do this, and that is creative in the absolute sense of the word, *i.e.*, it is the Divine Will. Man, then, was endowed with a quality which presumes that he is God. And since he is not, he develops a spiritual cramp, a kind of weak fit of violence, which takes effect often in a tragic, and sometimes (in the case of lesser minds) even a ludicrous manner. This presumption is guilty of having put modern man into the position of a blind person groping his way in the dark, because the fundamental force upon which it has based life—the will—is blind. The will can function and produce, but cannot see. From this is derived the restlessness which nowhere finds tranquillity. Nothing is left, nothing stands firm, everything alters, life is in continual flux; it is a constant struggle, search, and wandering.

Catholicism opposes this attitude with all its strength. The Church forgives everything more readily than an attack on truth. She knows that if a man falls, but leaves truth unimpaired, he will find his way back again. But if he attacks the vital principle, then the sacred order of life is demolished. Moreover, the Church has constantly viewed with the deepest distrust every ethical conception of truth and of dogma. Any attempt to base the truth of a dogma merely on its practical value is essentially un-Catholic. The Church represents truth—dogma—as an absolute fact, based upon itself, independent of all confirmation from the moral or even from the practical sphere. Truth is truth because it is truth. The attitude of the will to it, and its action towards it, is of itself a matter of indifference to truth. The will is not required to prove truth, nor is the latter obliged to give an account of itself to the will, but the will has to acknowledge itself as perfectly incompetent before truth. It does not create the latter, but it finds it. The will has to admit that it is blind and needs the light, the leadership, and the organising formative power of truth. It must admit as a fundamental principle the primacy of knowledge over the will, of the Logos over the Ethos.

This 'primacy' has been misunderstood. It is not a question of a priority of value or of merit. Nor is there any suggestion that knowledge is more important than action in human life. Still less does a desire exist to direct people as to the advisability of setting about their affairs with prayer or with action. The one is just as valuable and meritorious as the other. It is partly a question of disposition; the tone of a man's life will accentuate either knowledge or action; and the one type of disposition is worth as much as the other. The 'Primacy' is far rather a matter of culture–philosophy, and indeed it consists of the question as to which value in the whole of culture and of human life the leadership will be assigned, and which therefore will determine the decisive tendency; it is a precedence of order, therefore, of leadership, not of merit, significance, or even of frequency.

But if we concern ourselves further with the question, the idea occurs that the conception of the Primacy of the Logos over the Ethos could not be the final one. Perhaps it should be put thus: in life as a whole, precedence does not belong to action, but to existence. What ultimately matters is not activity, but development. The roots of and the perfection of everything lie, not in time, but in eternity. Finally, not the moral, but the metaphysical conception of the world is binding, not the worth-judgment, but the import-judgment, not struggle, but worship.

These trains of thought, however, trespass beyond the limits of this little book. The further question–if a final precedence must not be allotted to love–seems to be linked with a different chain of thought. Its solution perhaps lies within the possibilities we have already discussed. When one knows, for instance, that for a time truth is the decisive standard, it is still not quite established whether truth insists upon love or upon frigid majesty; the Ethos can be an obligation of the law, as with Kant, or the obligation of creative love. And even face to face with existence it is still an open question whether this obligation is a final rigid inevitability, or if it is love transcending all measure, in which the impossible itself becomes possible, to which hope can appeal against all hope. That is what is meant by the question whether love is not the greatest of these. Indeed, it is. Nothing less than this was announced by the 'good tidings.'

In this sense, too, as far as the primacy of truth—but 'truth in love'—is concerned, the present question is to be resolved.

As soon as this is done the foundation of spiritual health is established. For the soul needs absolutely firm ground on which to stand. It needs a support by which it can raise itself, a sure external point beyond itself, and that can only be supplied by truth. The knowledge of pure truth is the fundamental factor of spiritual emancipation. 'The truth shall make you free.' The soul needs that spiritual relaxation in which the convulsions of the will are stilled, the restlessness of struggle quietened, and the shrieking of desire silenced; and that is fundamentally and primarily the act of intention by which thought perceives truth, and the spirit is silent before its splendid majesty.

In dogma, the fact of absolute truth, inflexible and eternal, entirely independent of a basis of practicality, we possess something which is inexpressibly great. When the soul becomes aware of it, it is overcome by a sensation as of having touched the mystic guarantee of universal sanity; it perceives dogma as the guardian of all existence, actually and really the rock upon which the universe rests. 'In the beginning was the Word'—the Logos. . . .

For this reason the basis of all genuine and healthy life is a contemplative one. No matter how great the energy of the volition and action and striving may be, it must rest on the tranquil contemplation of eternal, unchangeable truth. This attitude is rooted in eternity. It is peaceful, it has that interior restraint which is a victory over life. It is not in a hurry, but has time. It can afford to wait and to develop.

This spiritual attitude is really Catholic. And if it is also a fact, as some maintain, that Catholicism is in many aspects, as compared with the other denominations, 'backward,' by all means let it be. Catholicism could not join in the furious pursuit of the unchained will, torn from its fixed and eternal order. But it has in exchange preserved something that is irreplaceably precious, for which, if it were to recognise it, the non-Catholic spiritual world would willingly exchange all that it has; and this is the primacy of the Logos over the Ethos, and by this, harmony with the established and immutable laws of all existence.

Although as yet the liturgy has not been specifically mentioned, everything which has been said applies to it. In the liturgy the Logos has been assigned its fitting precedence over the will. Hence the wonderful power of relaxation proper to the liturgy, and its deep reposefulness. Hence its apparent consummation entirely in the contemplation, adoration and glorification of Divine Truth. This is also the explanation of the fact that the liturgy is apparently so little disturbed by the petty troubles and needs of everyday life. It also accounts for the comparative rareness of its attempts at direct teaching and direct inculcation of virtue. The liturgy has something in itself reminiscent of the stars, of their eternally fixed and even course, of their inflexible order, of their profound silence, and of the infinite space in which they are poised. It is only in appearance, however, that the liturgy is so detached and untroubled by the actions and strivings and moral position of men. For in reality it knows that those who live by it will be true and spiritually sound, and at peace to the depths of their being; and that when they leave its sacred confines to enter life they will be men of courage.

Odo Casel
1886-1948

Odo Casel was born near Koblenz, Germany, and became a Benedictine monk in 1905. He studied at Maria Laach, Rome, and Bonn, earning doctoral degrees in both theology and philology. He served as spiritual director for the Benedictine sisters at Herstelle from 1922 to 1948, when he died during the celebration of the Easter Vigil.

Casel played an unusual role in the liturgical renewal. As editor of the Jahrbuch für Liturgiewissenschaft *in the two decades between the World Wars, he gradually set forth his dynamic conception of the liturgy as something more than the external observance of rubrics and rites. He drew upon his studies of the history of religions, especially the the Hellenistic mystery cults, as well as his extensive familiarity with the Fathers. The crucial element in his theology was the notion of "mystery," to which he constantly returned to explain the uniqueness of the liturgy. The most developed statement of his thought appeared in 1932, entitled* The Mystery of Christian Worship, *which did not appear in English until 30 years later, on the very eve of Vatican II.*

Casel was convinced that the salvific acts of Christ were not only represented but actually made present in the liturgy for all to share in. This "presence in mystery" (Mysteriengegenwart) was a teaching that caused more theological ferment than any other single idea of the time, resulting in more profound discussion of the theology of the liturgy than would ever have taken place otherwise. One can trace a direct line from the thought of Casel in the 1920s to that of Schillebeeckx in the 1970s, and important participants along the way included Monden, Bouyer, Daniélou and Journet.

That some aspects of Casel's theory were exaggerated is generally conceded today. Any real influence of the pagan mystery cults on early Christian worship is yet to be demonstrated, and many passages where the Fathers use the word "mystery" probably cannot bear the weight Casel tried to make them carry. But that should not blind one to his extraordinary contribution. The enriched theology of the liturgy endorsed by Pius XII in Mediator Dei *the year before Casel's death was closer to his thought than to that of many of his critics.*

The material in The Mystery of Christian Worship *had appeared earlier in article form for the most part. The selection which follows, chapter 5, was in the first edition of* Die Betende Kirche *in 1924. It sketches "The Church's Sacred Day" and thus conveys a sense of the depth of Casel's approach, his talent for combining spirituality and scholarship, the real roots of the renewal in which he has played such a role in the intervening half-century.*

THE MYSTERY OF CHRISTIAN WORSHIP

PART I

CHAPTER 5

THE CHURCH'S SACRED DAY

As the year is an image of the life of man and of mankind and thus of sacred history, each day too, with its rising of light and life, its growth to zenith and descent to sleep, forms an image which can serve as framework and symbol of the mystery of Christ. As Christ's sacrificial death is the climax of the world's history, mass is the climax of the day. In the church's year the *Logos* explains and expands the paschal mystery; in a single day the office clothes and comments on the mass: the office is the prayer which the Church puts round about the sacrifice.

The highest acts of every religion are prayer and sacrifice. The more spiritual a religion, the higher and more spiritual its concept and vision of these things. The exterior material sacrifices of Jews and pagans had an external, ritual prayer: the more pure, deep and inward, the more spiritual this prayer, the higher the notion of sacrifice which will accompany it. The more man sought to approach God in prayer with a real submission of mind, the less that prayer was lip-service and external form; it became a real call to God from the soul's depths, or a conversation with him. To the extent that this took place, the accompanying sacrifice became a full and selfless gift to God and the community. Thus prayer came more and more to correspond to its ideal, while on the other hand sacrifice, 'gift made to God', fulfilled its task of expressing the inner devotion of the will to God; the two drew near and were formed into one: sacrifice became, in a deeper sense than had been known before the high-point of the life of prayer.

The spiritualising of the notion of sacrifice brought a danger with it. If the essence of sacrifice is the inward adherence to

God, perhaps it would be better to do away with all external and exterior acts, and have only the pure devotion of the mind in prayer. This conclusion was drawn by many circles of pious pagans at the time Christianity was growing, in late antiquity, and by many Jews, too; all external, visible worship was to fall away, or be confined to common prayer, which themselves could be just as well or better performed by the individual recollected, undisturbed by the world about him. The danger came that the whole of worship would go inside man, that all religion would end as unbridled individualism and subjectivism, revolving round men rather than God.

In this as in everything else, Christianity gave its approval to all the excellence which the ages before Christ had discovered; still it remained infinitely superior to any non-Christian religion. It recognised of course that the external, material rites of pagan and Jewish ages were to be done away with in the new covenant. Now there was to be only a 'sacrifice in Spirit': an expression which is still preserved by the *oblatio rationabilis*, the *λογικὴ θυσία* of the Oriental liturgy. Yet this spiritual sacrifice is equated with the sacrifice of the mass, that is, with an external, liturgical celebration carried out by priest and people in concert and bound up with the rite of bread and wine. In spite of that, there is nothing external or material mixed up in it. For behind the visible, objective action is a wholly spiritual reality: the person of Christ, the Word incarnate, who, under the veil of mystical figures, presents his loving act of devotion to the Father in dying. The community joins with his sacrifice, its self and consciousness filled with the Spirit of God, and inspired by it, and completes with him a wholly spiritual sacrifice to God. Objectivity and personal sharing are joined in a loving unity: objectivity is made spiritual and inward; subjectivity finds a firm and changeless hold on the divine action of Christ which raises a man's action to himself and first gives it power and meaning. The vine gives the sap of life to the shoots; in this strength they can bring out rich fruit.

The act of Christ in the Christian sacrifice consists in his presenting once more his act of sacrifice and redemption beneath the veil of symbols; the share of the faithful expresses itself in the co-sacrifice, especially in the prayer which surrounds the sacrifice; therefore the *eucharistia* plays so important a role in the mass, particularly in the Canon, a greater one than prayer otherwise had in the sacrifice of the ancients; the relationship between sacrifice and prayer in Christianity is given deep and telling expression. Both elements are intimately joined, so much so that the elements themselves have kept the name of the prayer of thanks said over them, and are called 'the eucharist'. The objective act of Christ and the concomitant act of the congregation sharing in his experience, his thanks, his praise and his sacrifice form together the Christian eucharist, the prayer of sacrifice, the high-point of Christian worship.

All about this climax, in smaller and greater circles group the other prayers, like smaller peaks on the slopes of the highest one. First of all come the prayers of the mass with the chants, and in some measure the lessons as well. Then there is the whole day office of the church, which we are to treat in this Chapter, the gold setting for the jewel of the sacrifice. Its first business, of course, is to give countenance and place to this sacrifice; but it is also lovely and valuable of itself. Another example from art will make the relationship even clearer. There are paintings which present simple landscape and atmosphere with such an intensity that some tiny figures are required to give the moving eyes a place of rest, or perhaps they serve simply to give the painting a name and make it more amenable to the public. In other pictures the action depicted so dominates the whole that the background seems to have no weight at all. Still other works have figures and background completely in harmony; the surrounding puts the figure into a proper frame, while the figures give the whole composition greater value: the line which starts up in the actors continues, so to speak, in the trees, buildings, and other natural features, and comes to rest in them; they for their part find completion in the main persons of the picture. Undoubtedly this last is a good solution of the artistic problem, and the church has constructed mass and office on this plan. The vast and monumental ideas which are hidden and silent in the sacrificial action, and which the canon seeks to express, continue in the office and are, so to speak, resolved into the spectral colours. Much that could only be hinted at in the centre shows itself in various places, and is submitted to loving contemplation. The course of salvation's advance in the old alliance, the preparations for the appearance of the Saviour, the incarnate Christ, his teaching, suffering, death and resurrection, his mystical continuance in the church, the sufferings and glory of the martyrs and other saints, the march forward of the saving work in church and individual–in brief, the mysteries of God's saving design and grace–are all depicted lovingly and presented in daily prayers, and these again find their crown and finish in the sacramental mystery of the altar; all the rich, varied lines converge upon the sacrifice and broken colours go back to a splendid shining unity.

So the office moves, as it were, about a firm pole, the presence and display in ritual of the great event which is the heart of the Christian thing: redemption through incarnation, death and resurrection. The prayer of the office shares in the sacramental value of the act of sacrifice, and is raised to the latter's objective worth. All the church's prayer and all the prayer of each man becomes the prayer of Christ. Christ's Spirit, the Holy Spirit, carries up the congregation's prayer on strong wings and gives it a divine worth which it would never have of itself. It becomes a real prayer 'in the name of Jesus', to which the Lord himself has promised sure fulfilment. 'The man who abides in me as I do in him shall bear much fruit; without me you can do nothing. . . . If you remain in me and my words in you, you can ask what you will: it shall be done for you.'

This truth, that the church's prayer is not, however exalted, merely the prayer of an isolated soul, but prayer with Christ, as intimate as the bride's conversation with the bridegroom, as the body's connection with its head, must be taken as a firm principle, if we would really understand the character and meaning of the office. The church prays; but in her the Spirit prays with unspeakable groaning. The church makes petition, thinks and grows in consciousness, from the Spirit of Christ; it creates not merely human thoughts and feelings, or rather it brings them forth purified in the blood of Christ, glorified with the splendour of Christ. Of this prayer, too, St. Paul's saying holds good: 'I live, no, no longer I, but Christ lives in me.' All her words carry the mark of Christ her saviour, and are fashioned after him; all have passed through the atmosphere of his Spirit, and have a divine odour about them. All, therefore, have a meaning and a breadth which ranges high beyond every human meaning.

Upon this teaching rests a method of both practice and selection in liturgical prayer which is of very great importance, that of spiritual interpretation. The method is well-known; our Lord employed it, after his resurrection, after his exaltation to *Kyrios* and *Pneuma*. He 'interpreted the sense of scripture concerning himself'. It was expanded by the apostles and fathers of the church. But it has a perhaps even more important place in the liturgy; of course biblical and liturgical allegory are often in harmony, as to method and object; their great principle is the same. But the liturgy, by selection and placing, and giving a point of view to the texts, gives new and special material to the allegory: it lends it new bloom, freshness and variety.

Allegory (ἀλληγοαίρ) comes from the verb ἀλληγορεῖν (ἄλλος and ἀγορευειν). It means to say something other than what is directly expressed; a second meaning is there beside the plain sense of the words, and must be attended to. Allegory in religion rests on the view that the divinely inspired author, or the inspirer himself, spoke in this hidden way, partly in consideration for human weakness and lack of development, partly because of the impossibility of expressing the things of God in human language; in this way more is shown to deep vision than a superficial view would indicate. The spiritual sense towers above the literal one; its high places are not open to everybody. Only gradually does the light of later events and revelations bring this sense into view; but when this happens, the words gain a royal splendour, and point to the peaks where God's thoughts are. The Old Testament in particular was the object of this allegorical interpretation. The fathers, with the light of faith to guide them, saw everywhere—in the law, the prophets, the acts of Old Testament kings and saints here more clearly, there less—the figure of Jesus, glowing in the half-darkness, until it emerges in the gospel's brightness. What the ancients gradually and wearily came to was as clear as noon-day when the world's own light shone: the keys to all mysteries were in Christ; when this unfailing instrument, the key of David, is put to the explaining of scripture, the whole beauty, depth and clarity of Christian allegory is seen for what it really is in the liturgy. Its heart is the redeeming work of Christ and everything we read and pray in these texts points to that. All of them open their deepest secrets; all become a hymn to Christ which the church sings. As the bride speaks of her lover, sometimes openly, sometimes in hidden approaches to meaning, the church sings, and the soul with her, of the bridegroom from heaven; at one time she uses the clear words of dogmatic formulae, at another mysterious images and poetry, the speech of love, which show only their depth and beauty to the initiate. The fate of mankind, the sacred history of the Old Testament as it is delivered in the lessons, gain its full meaning because the Son of God, mediator between God and man, appears as its centre, high point and end; in him the world and time find fulfilment. So Christ reveals himself in the liturgy as the Lord of all time, ruler of the earth, 'King of kings, Lord of lords', as the leader of the people of God to everlasting salvation: he is God-man; only God-man could do all this.

Christ and the church: this is the content of the liturgy throughout, and so the content of the church's office—Christ, the God-man, the Saviour who showed himself to be the end and purpose with the words, 'I am the way, the truth and the life'. The church, not the casual sum of Christians now alive, but the sacred communion of all who go to the Father through Christ, all who bear within themselves the Holy Spirit, and whom grace makes perfect like our Father in heaven: one sacred body, unified and enlivened by the breath of life, the *pneuma*; one supernatural dwelling house of stones, chosen for variety and beauty, and joined together, the stones dependent one upon another, make up a work of art. This church is not only content, but subject of the liturgy: it is the church which prays in the office.

This gives us the deepest ground for the 'giveness', the objectivity of liturgy we have so often spoken of before. When the bride, filled with the Holy Spirit, prays with Christ, her head and bridegroom, this is no prayer of individuals casually come together, but a prayer in the spirit of God and therefore in the spirit of truth received; it is the prayer in which the communion of all Christ's members join. That all of this aids the deepest and most personal conscious life rather than hindering it, is obvious; we shall come back to the consideration of this fact.

Considered in this way, the church not only stretches far beyond all national boundaries of one age, but from the beginning of the world to the end, from penitent Adam the just man, to the last saint at the world's end. All pray and work in the building of our liturgy. There are times when it grows in a lively fashion, springs up, when life in the Spirit of Christ and the body is so strong that it creates a forceful artistic expression for itself; the first centuries particularly were an age of this kind. There are other ages which have been less fresh, less rich; they keep the truth and goodness they have inherited, cultivate and hand them on. In no case is it 'historicism' on the church's part when she holds fast to the ancient and traditional fashion of her worship; rather, this love of what she has received comes from her very nature, from the timeless personality which we have seen, belongs to her; in a fashion she shares God's everlastingness. The church does not belong to yesterday; she need not be always producing novelties; she has treasures which never grow old. Therefore she is happy with tradition. Men, creatures of a single day, can come and go, with no joy in antiquity; the church can wait. Other generations will come to be grateful for her conservatism.

When, therefore, the church of our time makes her celebration one of rigid pattern this follows from her loyalty to tradition and a love for real value which rests upon her everlastingness. The deepest realism, however, rests not on a mere adherence to traditional forms, but in the mind of Christ and the church, which reaches beyond all individuals. The discipline of the church, of course, prefers to hold fast to the rites and texts which were created in Christian antiquity, and does so in the belief that those ancient times created what they did with a peculiarly high awareness of the church's mind. Realism and a sense of form here protect not merely inner reality: exterior discipline serves inward order and proceeds from it.

It is characteristic of the church that every individual group, a part of the body, and under the one head forms in its own time and place the image of the whole church; the whole church is in that place, by virtue of the small group's presence. St. Cyprian writes in his *de Unitate Ecclesiae*, 'the office of bishop is one; individuals have such a share in it that each possesses the whole'. There are, then, many bishops in the Catholic church, yet their office has the mark of unity; their number brings no diversity into the church. So it is too, with the whole community. Where one congregation is united to its bishop, there is the church; there the church acts. Hence the ancients spoke of the 'church which is at Corinth', or just, 'the church at Corinth'.

We said earlier that the liturgy is the church's prayer: in practice this means a given community celebrating its office under the leadership of the priesthood. The community as such is therefore the subject of the liturgy; it enters this service as a community under discipline. Everyone takes his part in his own place: the bishop has one task, the priests another, the deacons another still, also the other clerics, virgins, and lay people. All together form a whole which praises God with one mouth.

From this it follows self-evidently that the office is to be celebrated in common, and, as far as the leaders of the congregation are concerned, in public. It will naturally be oral, then, audible and solemn as well. A common silence like the silent worship of the Quakers is no liturgy, although Catholic worship too has periods of pause and silence.

Thus Catholic worship has strongly objective lines: they are expressed in its form. Nothing subjective or arbitrary, no personal enthusiasm, momentary ecstasy or expressionism are to mark it; what it seeks are clarity beyond the limits of any single person, roots for a content that is divine and everlasting, a sober peaceful and measured expression of what belongs to it, in forms which give direction to the over-flow of thought and emotion, which put nature and passion within bonds. In this the liturgy shows herself the heiress of the ancient world for which the highest law of life and art was *σοφρόσυνη*, the observance of bounds; it revered order and measure as a reflection of the divine number and idea. Not lawlessness, lack of bounds, but things formed and measured, whatever their greatness and their depth, was divinity for the Greeks. The Book of Wisdom teaches that God has 'ordered all things according to measure, number and weight'. Not chaos but cosmos is the work of the creating spirit. All the struggling powers are brought to their end and their harmony in him. The liturgy, too, knows how to moderate and bring to order the terrible struggles which, for example, run through the psalms.

The musical setting of the office is to be judged according to the same standard; it proceeds from the very heart of worship. The filling of men with the Holy Spirit, 'enthusiasm', must needs show itself in a song of the Spirit, as St. Paul taught us; 'be filled with the Spirit, speak to one another in the Spirit's psalms, hymns and canticles, sing and chant the psalms in your hearts to the Lord'. If every kind of music rises on the one hand from deep emotion, away from the triviality of daily life and mere calculating reason in the open spaces of the mind, on the other hand it possesses a deep vision of harmony and beauty in rhythm and number. The plenitude of God's power and the upraising of the mind bring us into his freedom and order and lead to music, and music in pure, classical form. 'A lover sings,' says St. Augustine. The church says of love of God, 'he has set my love in order'. So, too, her song is put in order: it is made an image of God's rest and of rest in God. No peace of the grave but movement, lasting flow, movement with purpose and rhythm, and, for this reason, restful. The music of the Latin Church, called Gregorian after Pope St. Gregory who arranged it, is full of such peaceful movement and lively order. While there is often trouble and storm in the words, the music prepares the rainbow of peace, points to the harmony with no end. Sometimes the psalm melodies—usually those for the office—spread a sort of epic restfulness over the lyrical excitement of what the texts give us to sing. More mobile, yet with a steady measure, are the antiphons and hymns. Their task is to express the mood and words proper to each of the church's feasts, but they know better than to allow those moods a tone of excess or unrestraint. Fullness within limits, lively action in measure are the marks of liturgical form.

Language belongs to the very essence of liturgy. It is not the speech of every day, not the formal language of a single people, but a ritual language which age, tradition and history have made venerable: in the Western Church, Latin. A special characteristic of the language is that it transcends the national boundaries of the modern age, and gives recognition to a culture and religion which are universal. It takes us back into the Middle Ages, where the life of the nations was certainly vigorous, yet there was a real oneness in European culture as well, above and beyond their boundaries. The one Latin language gave the church in the West opportunity to display an *Imperium Romanum*, and in fact the use of the church's language depended on the continuance of the Roman Empire. In the Orient, where the Romans came up against a surface of hellenistic culture, the church keeps up Greek, Syriac and Coptic. But in these places, too, it is not a living language but an older, changeless form used specially in worship. This worship which turns to God, honours him and aims to lead men from all nations to him, prefers to use precise forms exalted above the language of every day, and thereby redolent of mystery, casting shadows of God's life. The mystery cannot stand in the crude light of day; it must show its supernatural worth in rare and precious vessels. *Cotidiana vilescunt*: 'the things of every day grow base', is an old and true saying. At the same time, the foreignness of the language makes for greater peace in the liturgy. What might have a harsh and importunate effect in one's own language becomes more moderate, takes quieter and nobler shape in the splendour cast by ancient and holy words. So, then, liturgical language also performs a task which belongs to worship: it speaks to man of God, not in order to delude him about his pain and suffering, but to enable him interiorly, to overcome them and give him a taste of the glory of heaven, its happiness and harmony, as the sun at evening gives heat to the places of men's daily trouble and pain, brings them colour, clarity, and splendour.

The content of the office gives voice to the whole relationship between the Church and her members on the one hand and God on the other through the mediation of Christ; better, its content is the mystery of Christ and the church. We shall say something on this very broad subject later on.

Externally the office is made up in great part of texts from the Old and New Testaments. It is obvious that in her prayer the church should use the books which God himself has given her at the hands of inspired men. No one can speak better of all that passes between God and the church or her individual member than the Spirit of God and the man filled with God. Fundamentally the church did not simply acquire the sacred writings but bore them under the breath and guidance of the Spirit. Throughout thousands of years she has set down her experiences in them. It is no wonder that she is glad to fall back upon them in her worship; the inspired writings in the strict sense, those of which it can be said in a special sense that they are written by the Spirit of God and the church, end with the apostles. But the Spirit has not left his church; again and again he moves her to write songs of love and of wisdom; men and women sing and pray. What they have said has been both the deepest expression of their own hearts and at the same time something coming from the mind of Christ and the Christian community: it thus became everyone's possession; and as such it was taken into the cult of the church. Hymns, antiphons, lessons from the Fathers and teachers came into the liturgy along with the scripture: the bishops and other leaders of worship created, from their contemplation, the solemn prayers and prefaces: even the use of Scripture became an act of recreation to the whole; music gave the final completion and consecration, bubbling up 'as the Holy Spirit dug in the hearts of holy men'. Human things and godly things are joined in unbreakable conjunction.

This bond between God and man, between grace and nature, is, throughout, the essential mark of the Christian life of prayer. Until now we have emphasised its givenness, because the whole age of modernity, resting as it does upon man's self-rule and self-created experience has need above all to learn submission to the given, divine norm. The individualist consciousness of modern man 'emancipates' the personality and isolates it: in so doing it reduces society to atoms and clears the way to collectivism; it sacrifices the person to the mass. The objective consciousness of community which the church possesses, submits the individual to a higher, God-given norm and gives it definite place; thereby it protects the personality, develops it and assures its status: place which belongs to it alone. The modern kind of order is a casual stone heap whose parts have no relationship to one another; they are pushed about, increased or diminished at will, and the picture they yield is one of immense confusion. The Christian thing is like an ancient temple which can be only as it is; in it every stone, every pillar, every beam and every statue has its place and displays its own beauty; together all the parts form a single work of art from which no part may be removed without injury to the whole. In this way liturgical prayer unites strong norms and respect for law with free movement and meaning for individual life. Even within the liturgy there are degrees of freedom. Just as ancient art, particularly Egyptian, Greek and ancient Christian painting and sculpture used the strictest forms for the greatest and most divine things, and then accepted freer movement as they came to human ones, yet avoided naturalism throughout, the church's prayer gives recognition to more volatile human feeling outside her solemn liturgical acts, and knows well how to express them.

It is neither possible nor necessary to depict all this in detail; some brief notes will suffice. We shall make them on the psalms, which are the heart of the office. In them no sort of religious experience is lacking; from deepest misery and sorrow, to abandonment and the full joy of oneness with God, from the feeling of oneness with the Lord's great congregation to the most intimate and personal experience of God; from the knowledge of God's dread majesty to enjoyment of his love: adoration, praise, thanks, the child's asking are all present. If, in addition, we take the allegorical interpretation regarding Christ and his church, the saving work of the new covenant, the changing lights which the festival, season or day have cast upon the psalm give us some shadowy glimpse of the inexhaustible riches of liturgical prayer. Usually the church tells us what use she is making of a psalm on a particular day and the mood she wants to express through it, by employing a particular antiphon as background or accompaniment. There are many of these refrains, or repeated verses; originally they were put in by the people after each verse or each three; now they frame the psalm, and come from it; their effect is, therefore, to make emphatic a particular theme of the psalm. Later, longer and more elaborate antiphons were created, to stand in looser connexion with the psalm, and lend it definite colour on a given day. The choral music, too, which is sung to the psalm, changes according to the musical tone of antiphon. One can see how simple and yet great are the means which the church uses here; the alleluia, for example, brings an Easter note to all the psalms it accompanies, even the serious *miserere*, and to the whole office an exalted and joyful aura.

Like the songs which David and the other God-inspired singers sang on their harps, the whole Scripture of the Old and New Testament, containing as it does an immense and inexhaustible sea of teaching, prayer, poetry and wisdom for living, is tuned into liturgy, and receives back from it a new and extraordinarily diverse life. Everyone knows how the prophecies, songs and sayings, the epistles and gospels are read, and begin to live, sparkle and send out new life. In addition the creators of the old liturgy who lived completely absorbed in the scriptures: men like Justin martyr, Origen, St. Ambrose, Gregory the Great and many others. They applied these texts to the sacred mysteries of Christ and the church, and brought out gold to mint from the scriptures' rich mines. They did not proceed with the exactitude of a modern philologist, but with an artist's freedom, as ancient man loved to do; yet they did not become fantastic. Their vision went to the great things, to the whole picture. For this reason they opened up the mysteries of those inspired books. Their work is not a scientific reference work, but a free composition on God's word. Here is revealed how God's truth can become man's real possession. Cassian requires of monks, that they should pray them as if they had written them. Christ is the first model of this; he prayed the words of a psalm, as he cried out to his Father in the depths of agony on the cross; so, too, the liturgy knows how to choose the right word from scripture for the right time, and to bring light from the other hemisphere into all the by-ways of this life of ours.

To inspired sources, then, are added the church's own creations, those of her saints, artists, teachers. The whole is a wonderful treasure. Different ages, peoples and ways of living, men and women, learned men, contemplatives have done their share in fashioning the garment which the liturgy has assumed to do God honour. How well the hymns, for example, give their own tone to each feast and season, so that a few words from one of them will call up before the mind's eye thoughts of the whole of it. How majestic is the Hymn for Christmas: 'Christ, redeemer of the world, the Father's only Son; thou wast born in ways beyond all speaking, before time ever was. . . .' Or the Hymn for Vespers of Easter, fragrant and intimate, binding together the mystery of Easter and the Eucharist, the true sacrament of Easter first food of the baptised: 'prepared for the banquet of the Lamb, clothed in white, the Red Sea past, we will sing to Christ, our Prince. His sacred body, his rose-coloured blood, his body, made ready on the Cross we taste, and live for God. We are protected from the angel of vengeance in the paschal night, set free from the hard yoke of Pharaoh. Our pasch is Christ now; he was sacrificed, as a lamb; as pure bread with no leaven his flesh was sacrificed.' A mixture of joy, love and longing marks the Hymn for Vespers of Ascension: 'Jesus, our salvation, love, our longing, God the creator, man at end of ages—how could goodness stretch to bring thee to bear our sins, suffer a terrible death, to set us free from all death. . . . Be thou our joy, as thou shalt one day be our prize. . . .' And on Pentecost the song is of the Spirit who moves the winds, full of power, like the rush of a great bird's wings yet gentle as a dove's song: 'Come, Creator Spirit, come: visit the minds which are thy own; fill with godly grace the hearts of thy own making. Thou art called the advocate, gift of the most high, living spring, tongue of fire, fire of love, oil of anointing. Thou art seven-fold in thy gifts finger of God's right hand, his promise, giver of tongues to speak. Light the flame within our spirits, pour thy love into our hearts, stiffen weak bodies with staying strength of thine. . . .'

Let us look briefly at the variety of lessons from the writings of the Fathers which form so pleasant an alternation to liturgical prayer. Each Father mirrors the light of Christianity in his own fashion; the writings of each differ in point of view, mood, content and form. There is sober exegesis, and then suddenly a burst of allegory; there is theological depth and practical wisdom, then mystical fires rise. But always it is a voice of deepest culture, and the most profound grasp of Christianity; often there is high and classical form as well.

Responding to measured variety of content are the vast and lively differences in carrying out the office, the result of which is that it is never monotonous, never tiring, but keeps the mind always fresh. The psalms rise and fall at a gentle pace; the melody is simple and pleasant, and for all its liveliness and constant exchange between the two choirs, spreads an epic peace over the whole. On the other hand the melodies are not lacking in lively variety. Each of the eight tones in which the antiphons are composed and according to which the psalms are sung has its own character: by its choice of tone, the church gives each new song its own proper colouring. The second, for example, is full of longing, the fourth more mystical, the seventh festive; the fifth full of deep emotion, the eighth strong and masculine. Still more precisely fitted to this varying content are the antiphons, which with their short, clear lines of direction, their freshness and buoyancy are miniature works of art, moments of Greek movement beside the oriental stillness of the psalms. When the mind is weary of the psalms' prayer and the burden of soul-searching they contain, the versicle brings up a shout at the end, like a blast of trumpets, breaking the monotone of the peaceful line, and passing on to something new: reading, petition, or the high points of the office, the Magnificat or Benedictus. These last in turn are sung in a specially solemn psalm tone, the eighth, for example, which recalls a royal march. The lessons have a simple tone of their own, which takes away all personal rhetoric, but leaves clear the divisions of meaning. Responsories follow the lessons; they are marked by a rich, solemn, slow-moving melody, and by the repetition of parts, as one choir answers the other. Thus they give shape to the moment of after-thought and contemplativeness which revolves deep, slow thoughts, and considers them now on one side, now on another, returning with alacrity to old sayings that can never be wrung out. The so-called long responses *responsoria prolixa* usually come in matins which have a particularly contemplative character, and join the lessons, with their stimuli to new thoughts. The short responses are usually found in Lauds and Vespers; one such may show how deep is the grasp which these forms of prayer have for the working of men's minds and prayer, and how finely they express the simple things they have to say:

V. From the lion's mouth, Lord, deliver me
R. From the lion's mouth, Lord, deliver me

V. Lord, deliver me
R. From the lion's mouth
V. Lord, deliver me

We can see and hear in the text and melody how this prayerful cry first springs up and forms itself in the soul of an individual or a few devoted persons, and then passes over to the whole community; a second, stronger cry is added; the choir stays with its first petition; the whole comes to rest in slow stages, and ends in a repetition of the first phrase by all which at the same time means that it has been heard. The hymns run more quickly in the same direction; their charm and liveliness is Greek. The church was very long in taking them into the office; only the activity of St. Ambrose brought them gradually closer to the church's seriousness. Then their light, impressionable, characteristic tone began to set the mood for the different feasts, and to give a stronger feeling to the individual days; as creations of the West they represented action as against the Oriental psalms, even more than the antiphons, of which we have already spoken.

In the last section we spoke frequently of the psychological basis for liturgical prayer and told how it became stylized in liturgical form. The structure of the office, too, both of individual hours and the day as a whole, is a psychological masterpiece. We shall give a view of the whole day office at the end of the chapter; here we want only to remark how some of the hours develop, Terce for example. After a moment for recollection, a cry of petition goes up to God, by which the leader also, so to speak, rouses the group: 'O God come to my assistance'; then the community answer, 'O Lord make speed to save me'. The *Gloria Patri* and alleluia which follow bring rest into this stormy cry, and at the same time mark the aim of the hour and its joyful character; then comes the freshness of the hymn, expressing briefly and clearly its meaning. At least one antiphon is struck up, to bring in the themes of the day or feast. The three psalms follow which make up the heart and high point of the hours: the antiphon is said. All of this brings the soul into the deep world of contemplation. But it cannot stay there forever; it grows tired, needs new stimuli; these come from the short lesson. From contemplation the soul passes at the versicle to petition, and so up to the intentions of the church, man, and the day: Lord have mercy; Our Father, then the special prayer of the day. With the verse of praise, *Benedicamus Domino* the brief, rich office closes; here was contemplation of divine truth, praise, thanks, adoration, petition: all drawn into one, every kind of prayer in its proper place.

The psychology of Vespers is even more striking. More psalms, given character and thrown up into a particular light by their antiphons, make up the contemplative element. Here too the weary mind is refreshed by a short reading from the scriptures, and then, in the Responsory, returns to the contemplative prayer we have mentioned before. The meditative response is followed by the melodic hymn, strongly connected with the day, its effect a fresh and lively one. After a versicle to lead the way, comes a particularly well-constructed antiphon for the Magnificat, which usually summarises clearly a feast's themes, and then carries its effect through the praise hymn of the Holy Virgin, enhancing its beauty. The Magnificat itself sinks deep into contemplation of the deep things of God and makes the offering of a humble mind to God's infinite love: it is the high point of the feast. When we go beyond it, it is to the *Our Father* and the prayer of the day; the latter, of course, is wholly caught up in the great mystical mood of the Magnificat. The structure of the morning and night services which belong closely together, is also quite remarkable. Three times we sing, 'O Lord open thou my lips,' 'and my heart shall declare thy praise'; dulled minds are called out to the joy of God's life. The prayerful psalm three puts the hindrances to prayer out of the way, so to speak. Then begins the invitatory, the great invitation, through which an antiphon runs, like an encouraging promise of all the feast's thinking, in the shortest possible space. In Psalm 94 the happy encouragement to be glad in God's presence stands side by side with earnest warnings, even threats, to the careless and the hard of heart. When the hymn is over, the mind is sufficiently awake and prepared. Now we come to the real purpose of night worship, contemplation. Vast, mysterious, difficult psalms pass before the soul's eye; the mysteries of God make themselves known in hard phrases. The soul wrestles with God for salvation, for knowledge of him. It joins its voice to the words Christ speaks in the psalm; it lives the life and suffering of the Lord with it; with him it hates sin and turns to the divine light; sees the miracle of God's mystical city, goes out in longing beyond the confusion and darkness of the world into God's freedom and clarity; it longs to go over out of the confusion and darkness of this world into God's freedom and clarity; it mourns loneliness and abandonment in this world, the faithlessness of men and is happy with the one true friend, God. Still, who could exhaust in words all the depths of contemplative prayer in the psalms? When the soul is weary of this pilgrimage on the high places, it goes down to the fresh waters of scripture; in the responsories it carries on its contemplation. Again a series of psalms and a refreshing group of lessons there follows. In the third nocturn come the shorter, brighter Cantica, songs from the prophets or wisdom writings; a homily from the Fathers goes with the gospel, interrupted and slowed down by responsories preparing for the appearance of Christ in whom all the difficulties of inner life find their solution. Yet before Christ himself appears in the gospel, the confident hope of the church breaks out in the majestic, powerful hymn *Te Deum*, which praises the Trinity and the Saviour, and at the end passes over to humble petition. Now the light of the world himself appears, and spreads his light over all the difficulties and confusion of church. Man's longing is fulfilled, the high-point of the office is here: the Lord speaks. So with a short word of praise and the prayer, Matins ends, and the mind gives itself to that jubilation which already sounded in the *Te Deum*: it grows stronger as Lauds progresses and reaches its far highest point in the *Benedictus*, the wonderful song of praise for the redemption in Christ. Throughout the whole of this as of every office, the church shows herself mistress of the deepest psychology, the psychology of prayer.

Before considering the psychological and artistic strength of the Day office, we should refer to a very important matter: the relationship of liturgy to nature. The polytheism of the heathen made the powers of nature divine, and submitted man to them; this 'service to the elements' often has great sensible joy, but ends in evil and in terror of the terrible power of nature which takes a man up and, after brief sport, destroys him. Pantheism makes man feel his oneness with the whole web of the cosmos; but this daemonic feeling, too, leads to the enslavement of the spiritual in man, to the tyranny of sense, and to panic before the predatory beasts which lurk in unredeemed nature. More or less pantheistic, restless and full of muddy emotion, and 'sentimental', is the feeling which the Romantics had for nature. The gnostic overestimates the evil of nature, treats her like something evil, is full of fear before her, runs from her; he is 'full of the sorrow for things'. The Christian too, knows that nature groans under sin, along with man; it longs for redemption, which will come to it when it comes to the children of God. But he also knows that nature is a work of God's; because it is, he can love it, see in it the print of God's passing. Yet he stands over it; nature is tool and image of the spiritual. The liturgy, therefore, from the very beginning, from the time when the Lord made bread and wine the elements of the mass, has given nature its part to play. The church was not afraid to take over natural symbols which the heathen had used in their worship and, by putting them into proper place, to give them their true value. By doing so she has made them holy, just as through the sacraments and sacred gestures, she made the human body; in fact the church has given to nature the first fruits of glory, the gifts of the children of God. For our theme the symbolism of light is of particular importance, connected as it is in the first place with the sun. This phenomenon in nature is much more striking to a Mediterranean than to us, because in that region its forms are so vivid and definite. The sun really stands in the heaven like a dread king, spreading terror and blessings: *sol invictus* as the ancients called him, the author of the 18th psalm among them. Terrible majesty glows, burns from heaven; it wakes life and kills it, giving life and blinding the eye that is too keen. It is no surprise that first orientals and then dwellers of the Mediterranean region should have honoured the sun-king as their high God. Even the philosophers gave it honour: Plato regarded the sun as a symbol of the good which was the sun in the kingdom of spirits. But in later neo-Platonism and the heathen religions of the first Christian centuries the invincible sun god was the centre of worship; this was expressed in many prayers. The morning light above all was revered as something divine. In Northern Europe and America one is fonder of broken colours, light and dark patches, where fantasy and emotion can be lost in muddy clouds. The typical man of antiquity had a sense for clarity and truth, for the genuine and the whole; he valued above all the dawn light with its unlimited fullness, 'glorious as on the first of days, as it streamed out of the hand of God over land lying dark and still a little while before; it streams up and gives things back their colour and brightness; it awakens life and joy. The East, therefore, a symbol of God, became itself divine; men turned to it when they sought God in prayer. Evening like morning was especially a time for prayer; yet the other phases of the sun's course all had their meaning in worship too.

The church has nurtured these ideas insofar as they are true, but purified them of their limitations, of their enslavement to the elements. For her the visible sun is not the godhead; it is, as Plato has already glimpsed, a symbol of the Spirit-son, Jesus Christ the incarnate Logos, who in the life of nature as in the world beyond wakens life and spreads it, as he himself says, 'I am the light of the world'. So the church has set up her office according to its changing course, and thereby given it new depth and beauty. 'Grace builds upon nature': it is fitting that man should fashion his daily life of prayer on the great image of nature, and give back its beauty, spiritualized, to the creator.

Still another point for brief consideration is the warning of Christ and the Apostles, 'pray always'. How does the church fulfil this command? In mind she is always with the Lord, as the Lord is always with her. This cannot be carried out literally, in external worship, but she nonetheless fulfils it. For in accordance with the ancient view there is a kind of earthly eternity in like, regular recurrence in time. As time renews itself in the regular movement of the years and moons, and by this continual re-birth becomes in a sense eternal, so an event becomes celebrated 'eternally' by being celebrated every month or year. The *sollemnitas*, yearly feast, becomes *aeternitas*, everlastingness. The celebration of the church year, especially the sundays, rest on this principle. Always the mysteries of salvation are carried out in the same rhythm; they become eternally real, until the solemnity in heaven passes into eternal reality in every sense of the word. The exhortation to pray always has been carried out by the church's praying each day at the same appointed times. These hours (*horae*), are laid down according to the sun's course; as we have said, the sun is a symbol of Christ. Historical occurrences from the life of Jesus yield symbolic meaning, or fall in with such meanings. Thus the sun's rising is the most striking image of the Saviour rising from the dead, and in fact the hour of his rising; Sext, the time he was nailed to the cross, but according to ancient tradition the hour of his ascensions as well, the high noon of his life; None was the hour at which he died on the cross. At the third hour of day, Terce recalls the out-pouring of the Holy Spirit.

Thus prepared we can consider the course and construction of the daily office. It begins on the previous evening, with 'first vespers'. For the ancients the day did not begin at midnight, a point which can only be determined by mechanical means or a mechanical clock; it ended when the sun went down, and the new one began. The service of worship held at the hour of dusk in the evening light (vesperus, ἑσπέρα, evening) belongs in time to the day before, but leads over to the day following. Hence at least the second part, and on great feasts the whole vespers, belongs liturgically to the feast of the following day. The mind is led into the ante-chamber of the feast's circle of ideas, and receives a first taste of its content. This is especially well expressed in the first vespers of Christmas.

As soon as the sun has disappeared behind the horizon, a new day begins in the night. Out of the night day rises; this deep consideration of ancient man which only children seem to have kept until now (they often reckon in nights) is the measure for the liturgy. The construction of the day office has its firm foundation in the night service.

The night gives darkness and silence; in it we see far out into the stars, feel comfort and dread, know the smallness of man and the greatness of his spirit: night is the time of great yet single vision. For Christians it has lost the terrors which pursued unredeemed mankind, but kept its sweetness, recollection and gentle dread. So it became the proper time for prayer, for raising the mind up to God. The work of ordinary day is over, consciousness less disturbed by the outside world, the ear enjoys valued stillness, and the stars give light. A shadow of eternity rests on the night; time seems brought to a point. For this reason the Romans called the night *intempesta*, timeless. The heathen had already shown preference for night in their deeper and more moving rites; the mysteries in which they hoped to be conjoined to God were celebrated at night, with no light but flickering torches, until the moment came when the light of the mysteries flamed up and told that the God was at hand. The church also celebrates her greatest mysteries, the incarnation, the resurrection, as they occurred, in the dead of night. The greater feasts are begun with night watches, vigils. Like the Greeks with their *παννυχίς*, the ancient church watched the whole night through before a principal feast, with prayer, song and reading. Holiest of all was the night of Easter, in which the splendour and glory of the risen Christ came streaming out of the passion's deep darkness, and brought the sunrise in high heaven to man who sat in the shadow of death. In the night these Christians of the early church waited for Christ to return: 'this is the night which shall be celebrated with watches for the coming (adventus, *παρουσία*) of our God and King. Its essence is twofold; after his suffering he returned in it to life, and later he will enjoy in it the lordship of the wide world.' There is a note of mystical expectation lying on all vigils:

This is the very time
when, as the gospel tells,
the bridegroom shall come one day
the Lord of everlasting heavens.
The holy virgins run to him,
run out as he will come
They bear their lamps along
and have their fill of joy.

Monks kept such a vigil every night, and because it was not possible always to watch through the whole night they took certain hours of it. This night celebration (called Matins, because held in the early morning) is all devoted to contemplation. The mind moves contemplatively, praying, loving the infinite thoughts of God; it struggles with the spirit of God, as Jacob once fought with the angel until dawn, and finally won God's blessing and the name Israel—who wrestles with God. Thus strengthened the soul can enter into the great mystic actions of the holy mass, carry them out with understanding and worth.

The night is over, the light comes in the first brightness of morning: the stars grow faint; only the pale morning star shines on. The church begins her morning service of praise: *Laudes*. The soul comes out of its deeper contemplation, and passes on to acts of praise and thanks. It can never be content with its praise; it must call up all creatures to help it in this work. Christ is already near, the sun of justice, the church's healing. The dawn of morning which precedes him is rosy: the Ambrosian hymn speaks of it: 'dawn goes up her path; let the Son, true dawn come all in the Father, as the Father is in him'. The mind looks in longing to that 'last morning' when it will see the divine light which will never be extinguished. Then at last, the sun comes like the victorious hero Christ after his long night of pain, blazing from the tomb to blind the watchers. This is the moment for the schola to begin the hymn of praise to redemption in Christ:

> Blessed be the Lord, the God of Israel
> He has visited his people
> and wrought their redemption . . .
> Salvation from our enemies, and
> from the hand of those that hate us . . .
> passing all our days in holiness,
> and approved in his sight . . .
> Such is the merciful kindness
> which has bidden him come to
> us, like a dawning from on high,
> to give light to those who live
> in darkness, in the shadow of
> death, and to guide our feet
> in the way of peace.

The sun goes higher; light calls to work, to the burden and heat of the day. It is the first hour, Prime. Before going out to work the Christian puts on the armour of prayer—plain, simple prayer, full of thoughts for the weariness, the earnestness of work, of petitions for help against difficulties which can come from both evil spirits and men. All the 'little hours' carry this strong character of petition, particularly Prime; the depth and exuberance of the night and dawn service has not gone out, but come to rest in the heart. Now is the time for work. The sun has lost the bright freshness of early morning and gone up into the heaven.

We think about this ripening power of God's living warmth, at the third hour, Terce, as we celebrate the descent of the divine *pneuma*, the *calor verbi* and sing of it in our hymn: Holy Ghost, one with the Father and the Son. Pour thyself out into our hearts and fill them. Mouth, tongue, unconscious and conscious mind, all life's powers are to sing praise of God, let its love spring up in full fire, its glow light the neighbour.' But the psalms tell of the misery of exile, of longing for the home country, of looking out to the eternal mountains of salvation and the Lord's city, Jerusalem.

Sext is prayed at the heat of mid-day when the mid-day demon goes about to bring harm to body and soul; it begs for cooling to the heats that do harm, soothing of contrary strife, health and harmony of soul and body. All that is what it hopes for from the Lord, to whom alone it looks, as the servant to his master.

The ninth hour, None, brings relief to the heat. Rest is at hand. The petition is for a bright evening, a holy death, and eternal glory after a life of weariness. The soul sees itself already free from imprisonment happy to gather the sheaves and bind them and enjoy rest with those it loves now rest is done.

Now the sun goes west, and descends. The marvellous play of colour at evening, the glory which spreads itself over the tired earth gives men a certain sight of the other, better kingdom; evening is ready to bring sorrowful longing for peace, harmony and unity to the heart of man. The ancients thought that the kingdom of the dead and the islands of the blessed are found in the West, where the sun goes into the sea. The Christian, too, is glad to think at evening of a happy departure from this world's weariness, to the light that stays. When St. Ignatius of Antioch takes up the word sunset in his epistle to the Romans, he thinks immediately of another setting, and writes, 'It is good to go down from this world and rise in God'. In this mood the church sings second vespers; after the psalms, responsories and hymns in which she has buried herself in the feast, she intones the *Magnificat*, the high song of the virgin of virgins which, so different from the strong, masculine freshness of the *Benedictus*, is deep, tender, as it were feminine. In it man thanks the Lord for the overflow of happiness he has experienced, for all the Lord, ever true to his promises, has done for him. Union with God, the great aim of all prayer and all worship finds its clearest expression in the *Magnificat* at the end of the day office. All the joy of liturgical prayer leads to oneness with God, and flows out of him again: 'And my spirit rejoiced in God my Saviour.'

Compline ends the day as a quiet night prayer with no special meaning.

If now we look back once more on the many questions with which the church's office confronted us, and the answers we gave, brief and hesitant though they were, it remains clear that the liturgy is as broad and as deep as the life of Christ and His church, the life they have in the Father. The liturgy is a hymn of love; at one time the bride praises the bridegroom, and then the order is reversed; at others it is they two who praise the Father. God's truth plays in the liturgy like sunlight in water; for liturgy is founded upon the words of Scripture and the fathers, upon an infallible, dogmatic faith. But it is in itself a stream flowing from God's great goodness; it does not merely teach, it leads to love. In it the word becomes a song of love; and where truth and goodness stand together beauty will not be lacking. In the liturgy God's truth is given form and shape, and so becomes a work of art, not through isolated aestheticism or dilettantism but of its own weight.

No other prayer can challenge with the liturgy's right, to hold God's truth, God's goodness, and God's beauty, and to send forth their splendours; no other is so near to the heart of Christ and of his whole church. In the last centuries has not the office become too much a mere duty while more intimate piety has passed over to the so-called devotions? It is our business to give back to the office its proper place, to make it once more what it is and has a right to be for us. God's honour and men's salvation cannot be separated: both proceed from the one great sacrifice. So too the office brings both glory to God and healing to men. 'The sacrifice of praise does me honour; it is the way on which I shall reveal salvation' (Psalms 49).

Anscar Vonier
1875-1938

Vonier was born in Ringschnait, Germany in 1875, and was baptized Martin. His family moved soon afterwards to Rissegg where he spent his early boyhood and first learned from the parish priest of the recent foundation of a Benedictine monastery at Buckfast by a group of exiled French monks. In 1888 he went to the College of the Holy Ghost Fathers in Beauvais, but in less than a year he entered the alumnate at Buckfast. In 1893 he took the habit and the religious name of Anscar. In 1898 he was ordained a priest.

The young Benedictine was sent to Rome to study philosophy, and completed his doctorate at Sant' Anselmo in one year. By 1900 he was back in Buckfast, which in 1902 was raised to the status of an Abbey with Dom Boniface Natter as its first abbot. Vonier had not been forgotten in Rome, however, and in 1905 he was called back to Sant' Anselmo to teach philosophy.

At the end of his first year of teaching in Rome, Vonier was requested by Abbot Natter to meet him in Spain to accompany him on a visitation to a South American monastery. The two sailed from Barcelona on August 3, 1906, and on the first day at sea suffered shipwreck. Three hundred people died, including Abbot Natter. Vonier survived and two months later was elected the second abbot of Buckfast. Convinced that his life had been spared for some special purpose, he immediately began rebuilding the abbey church on its ancient foundations. This massive task, done entirely by the monks, occupied him for the next 32 years.

Vonier somehow found time to write during these busy years. He had a gift for expressing difficult questions in simple language, and his mastery of English was noteworthy. In his day he stood out as one of the few theologians writing in English who had something to say and said it well. One index of this was the fact that his writings were still enough in demand nearly fifteen years after his death to warrant the publication of the three-volumes of his Collected Works *(1952).*

The three works that more or less established his reputation were The Human Soul *(1913),* The Personality of Christ *(1915), and* The Christian Mind *(1921). But the one that became a classic in its day and has kept the name of Vonier alive in later literature was* A Key to the Doctrine of the Eucharist *(1925), from which the following selection is taken.*

Vonier represents the advent of a new spirit in Catholic theological writing. As he puts it in the foreword to his work, his aim is "neither apologetic nor speculative, nor do I intend to write a book of devotion . . . An intense wish to instruct will be the only undisputed merit of this book . . . all I hope to do is to reproduce faithfully the mental attitude of the great theological age of which S. Thomas Aquinas is the king." The reception which was accorded the book demonstrated how ready Catholics at large were for this more positive approach.

One must keep in mind that this work was written forty years before the renewal of Vatican II, when the liturgical movement was in its infancy. Vonier's search for deeper foundations provided a doctrinal basis that exercised a beneficial influence on the entire development.

A KEY TO THE DOCTRINE OF THE EUCHARIST

CHAPTER I

FAITH

The Catholic doctrine of the Eucharist is a particular instance of the more universal problem of the mode of our union with Christ. We take for granted the Incarnation and the Atonement on the Cross; we take for granted, too, that the Son of God through his death has redeemed mankind in general and has satisfied for sin; we know that in Christ there is plentiful redemption; such things are for us unchallengeable and universal articles of belief which may be called God's side of the problem, that aspect of truth which is turned heavenward. The universal truths thus enunciated leave untouched that other problem of our own individual share in the treasures of redemption—how do individual men come into contact with that great Christ who is redemption personified? There is evidently in the Christian doctrine of redemption an element so absolute that it stands by itself, quite independent of man's benefit in it. Before it is at all possible to think of man's enrichment through the grace of Christ's redemption we have to assume that much greater result of Christ's sacrifice on the Cross which is aptly stated in the term "atonement," by which is meant, not directly the benefit of man, but the benefit of God: that full restoration of the thing lost to God through man's sin, his honour and glory. Christ's act on the Cross has given back to God all that was ever taken away from God by man, and the divine rights have been fully restored.

It is not an absurd hypothesis to think of Christ's great act of atonement as having an exclusively divine side—that is to say, Christ could have died on the cross with the exclusive purpose of giving back to the Father all the glory which the Father had lost through man's transgression, without the human race being in any way the better for it. But this is merely an hypothesis, though a perfectly rational one. Catholic doctrine says that Christ's sacrifice, besides being an atonement, was also a salvation,–in other words, a buying back into spiritual liberty of the human race which had become the slave of Evil. But even this aspect of Christ's divine act, though a perfectly human aspect, is still a universal aspect; salvation is primarily for mankind as a species; the entry of the individual into the redemptive plan remains still to be effected. How am I to be linked up effectively with that great mystery of Christ's death? When shall I know that Christ is not only Redeemer, but also my Redeemer? Mere membership with the human race does not link me up with Christ, though it be true that Christ died for the whole race. This membership is indeed a remote condition–*sine qua non*–of my becoming one day a member of Christ, but a member of Christ I shall not become unless some new realities be brought into play.

The new realities which make the link between me and Christ are, in the words of S Thomas, faith and the sacraments: "The power of Christ's passion is linked up with us through faith and through the sacraments. This, however, in different ways: for the linking up which is by faith takes place through an act of the soul, whilst the linking up which is by the sacraments takes place through the use of external things." This passage is of such paramount importance to the subject that I may be justified in presenting the reader with the Latin text: "Virtus passionis Christi copulatur nobis per fidem, et sacramenta: differenter tamen; nam continuatio, quae est per fidem, fit per actum animae: continuatio autem, quae est per sacramenta, fit per usum exteriorum rerum."

This is a favourite idea of S Thomas, that faith is truly a contact with Christ, a real, psychological contact which, if once established, may lead man into the innermost glories of Christ's life. Without this contact of faith we are dead unto Christ, the stream of his life passes us by without entering into us, as a rock in the midst of a river remains unaffected in the most turbulent rush of waters.

This contact of faith makes man susceptible to the influences of Christ; under normal conditions it will develop into the broader contact of hope and charity; but it is the first grafting of man on Christ which underlies all other fruitfulness. Till the contact of faith be established the great redemption has not become our redemption; the things of Christ are not ours in any true sense; we are members of the human race, but we are not members of Christ.

This contact of faith is, indeed, the most potent supernatural reality. It does not belong to my subject to enter into a discussion as to the reasons why one man has faith whilst another is without faith; nor do I propose to state that minimum of faith which is indispensable in order to establish true contact between the soul and Christ. It is sufficient unto our purpose to know that a man who has faith has laid his hand on the salvation of Christ. It is the most universal way of coming into touch with the redemption of the Cross; it is an approach which is possible from every direction, from the past as well as from the present. Mary, the Mother of God, through her faith, entered into Christ's passion in the very moment of time when it took place; Adam, in his very fall, plunged into it headlong; and it will be present to the last human generation through that wonderful act of the soul of which S Thomas speaks in the above text. Whether we say that Christ will suffer–*passarus est,* or whether we say that Christ has suffered–*passus est,* is quite immaterial to the immediateness of contact by faith. "As the ancient Fathers were saved through faith of the coming Christ, so are we also saved through faith of the Christ who has already been born and has suffered" ("Sicut antiqui Patres salvati sunt per fidem Christi venturi; ita et nos salvamur per fidem Christi jam nati, et passi").

I feel that we are less habituated in our times to think of faith as a kind of psychic link between the soul and Christ; yet such is the traditional concept of that wonderful gift. Anyone who has faith is in the supernatural state, and therefore is directly in touch with Christ's life, though he be otherwise in a state of mortal sin. The Council of Trent has taken great trouble to make clear this point of Catholic ethics. A man ceases to be Christ's solely through the sin of infidelity; he does not cease to be Christ's through any other sin, however heinous. As long as his faith is a true faith he remains a member of Christ's mystical Body, though there be grievous sores of mortal sins in him. Through that faith, which nothing can kill except the formal sin of infidelity, he keeps so near to the mystery of Christ's death on the Cross that his recovery from the snare of sin, even grievous sin, is a normal process of supernatural life, not a miraculous one. It is true that the faith of the believing Christian in the state of mortal sin is a *fides informis*, a faith devoid of the higher vitalities of charity, yet it is a real faith. Unless we grasp that function of faith as the psychic link between Christ and the soul, Catholicism becomes unintelligible. The Church would become, as it did in Lutheran theology, an adventitious gathering of the elect. The Church is constituted primarily through faith, and her powers are for those who possess that responsiveness of soul called faith. If we believe the Church to possess might enough to wipe away sin, we suppose, *ipso facto*, that sin is compatible with the mystical membership.

Actual incorporation with Christ, according to S Thomas, has a threefold degree; the first is through faith, the second is through the charity of life, the third is through the possession of heaven.

It is true that the whole tendency of faith is towards charity, that faith without charity cannot save us ultimately; none the less, charity cannot exist in man without faith, whilst there may be true faith in man without actual charity. All this goes to demonstrate that there is in faith an instrumental side, enabling man to open unto himself the door that leads to perfect union with Christ. There is no such instrumental side in charity, as charity is not a means towards the possession of God, but is, on the contrary, actual possession of God. S Thomas calls faith an indispensable endowment of the soul, because it is the beginning or principle of spiritual life: "Fides est necessaria tanquam principium spiritualis vitae."

This peculiar position of faith in the spiritual order as a kind of tool of supreme excellence will be seen in a more complete light when we shall come to ask ourselves the question whether there be another such set of means for man to get at Christ's redemptive life. Once more let it be emphasised that through the possession of charity we do not only get at Christ, but that we are actually in Christ. Charity is not an instrument, whilst faith has an instrumental role.

The sacraments are truly another set of means for that final object, to be united with Christ in charity. The sacraments complete and render more efficacious that instrumentality of faith just spoken of: they do not supersede the instrumentality of faith, but they render such instrumentality more real, if possible, and certainly more infallible in its effect. The relative position of faith and sacraments in bringing about man's justification through charity is an interesting theological question of which we shall have more to say by-and-by. The sacraments are essentially sacraments of the faith, *sacramenta fidei*, as S Thomas invariably calls them; both faith and sacraments have that power of divine instrumentality which will open to man the treasure-house of Christ's redemption.

I cannot end this chapter without translating from S Thomas a beautiful passage in which he describes God's action, which he calls grace, keeping faith alive in the soul of even the sinner: "Grace produces faith not only when faith begins to exist in the soul for the first time, but also whilst it abides in the soul permanently . . . God works the justification of man in the way in which the sun produces light in the air. Grace, therefore, when it strikes with its rays the one who is already a faithful believer is not less efficacious than when it comes for the first time to the unbeliever, because in both it is its proper effect to produce faith: in one case strengthening it and giving it increase, in the other case creating it as an entirely new thing."

The sun of divine grace once above the horizon sends forth the ray of faith into the minds of men, and nothing can resist it except blind obstinacy and infidelity.

CHAPTER II

SACRAMENTS

There is an excellent definition of the nature of the sacraments in the sixty-first Question of the third Part of the *Summa* of S Thomas, fourth Article: "Sacraments are certain signs protesting that faith through which man is justified" ("Sunt autem sacramenta quaedam signa protestantia fidem, qua justificatur homo"). Such a definition makes the transition from the role of faith to the role of the sacraments a very natural and easy one. The power of the sacraments could never be dissociated from the power of faith; the two supernatural agencies move forward hand in hand. A sacrament is always an external sign that is a most real witness of that more recondite quality of the soul, the faith that justifies man by bringing him into contact with Christ.

Two questions become paramount here: Firstly, why should there be such external witnessing to or protestation of the faith? Secondly, to what extent shall we give to those signs literalness in their efficacy of signification? The second point as it is settled either in one way or the other makes all the difference between Catholicism and Protestantism, or, it may even be said, between Judaism and Christianity. In one way or another this will be the main burden of this work; but, for the moment, let us dwell on that other aspect of the matter, the radical oneness of the Catholic theory concerning the means of justification. Faith and sacraments are indissolubly united, though faith may be called the vaster, the older, the more universal reality. The sacramental system is grafted on faith; it is essentially the executive of our faith; it is, shall we say, the reward of faith. Because of her faith the Church is granted those further powers of reaching Christ which make Christ not only the object of mental apprehension, but of physical possession; the sacramental thing is granted to those who have faith; such as the sequel of Christ's teaching in the sixth Chapter of S John's Gospel. He who does the work of God by believing in him whom the Father has sent is the one to whom Christ will give his Flesh to eat and his Blood to drink. We may apply here that general principle concerning spiritual goodness which Christ enunciates more than once: "To every one that hath shall be given, and he shall abound, but from him that hath not, that also which he seemeth to have shall be taken away." Because of her abundant faith the Church is given the further riches of her sacraments. At no time are faith and the sacraments dissociated; what might appear at first sight to be the exception to the rule is only a more profound application of it, I mean Baptism bestowed on infants. S Thomas, following S Augustine, falls back on the faith of the Church herself in order to keep intact the union between faith and the sacraments of faith. "In the Church of the Saviour the little ones believe through others, as through others they contract those sins which are washed out in Baptism"; these are words of S Augustine quoted by S Thomas in Question lxviii, Article ix ad 2m, and the medieval Doctor completes the theology of the earlier Father with the following pregnant words: "The faith of the whole Church is of profit to the little one through the operation of the Holy Ghost, who makes the Church into one and makes the one share the goods of the other" ("Fides autem unius, immo totius Ecclesiae, parvulo prodest per operationem Spiritus Sancti, qui unit Ecclesiam, et bona unius alteri communicat"). There could hardly be a more incongruous reproach brought against the Catholic Church than the accusation that through her great insistence on the sacramental life she diminishes the power of faith.

It is properly the Puritan, not the Protestant, who is the enemy of the sacramental system taken in the wider aspect of that Thomistic definition with which we opened this chapter. For the Puritan, faith is not in need of any help or any adjuncts. The reasons given by the Catholic theologians for the presence in the Christian dispensation of these external signs of the internal faith are chiefly psychological; they contend that man's nature being what it is, sacraments are indispensable to a full life of faith. S Thomas has a threefold reason for the institution of the sacraments: "Sacramenta sunt necessaria ad humanam salutem, *triplici ratione*." But this threefold reason is really one reason, fallen man's psychology: firstly, the condition of man's nature, being a composite of spirit and sense; secondly, man's estate, which is slavedom to material things and which is to be remedied by the spiritual power inside the material thing; thirdly, man's activities, so prone to go astray in external interests, finding in the sacraments a true bodily exercise which works out for salvation.

Nothing would be easier than to develop this subject with all the fascination of human psychology coming into play; the sacramental life of the Church is truly a perfect understanding of man's needs. Sacraments are, through their very nature, an extension of the Incarnation, a variant of that mystery expressed in the words: "And the Word was made flesh and dwelt among us." Is not the Son of God made man the Sacrament *par excellence*, the *magnum sacramentum*, the invisible made visible? "And evidently great is the mystery of godliness, which was manifested in the flesh, was justified in the spirit, appeared unto angels, hath been preached unto the Gentiles, is believed in the world, is taken up in glory."

The definition of the sacrament quoted above, that it is a protestation of the faith which is in us, is not the whole definition of the Christian sacrament, though it may be considered as a complete definition of the sacrament in its widest meaning. S Thomas never hesitates in giving to some of the major rites of the Old Law the name of sacrament, always making it quite clear that the power of these ancient sacraments never went beyond signifying the things of the patriarchal faith, whilst the Christian sacrament has a much higher degree of signification, a signification that has effectiveness associated with it. It would be quite unwise and very ungenerous not to grant to the ancient rites instituted by God sacramental dignity of at least an inferior degree; they all were external signs of the faith in the coming redemption. They were tremendous helps to that faith, though they were not direct causations of grace.

S Thomas divides the life of mankind into four seasons—the state of innocence before the fall, the state of sin before Christ, the state of sin after Christ, and the state of bliss in heaven. No sacraments are necessary in the first and in the last state; sacraments are necessary to man in the two middle states. But it is in the "state of sin after Christ" that sacraments reach their perfection; the seven sacraments of the Christian dispensation are sacraments in the highest sense, because, besides signifying the grace which is the inheritance of faith, they also contain that grace and cause it: "Nostra autem sacramenta gratiam continent, et causant."

An objector seems to find fault with the theory that God has given to man different sacraments before Christ and different sacraments after Christ. Does this not argue mutability in the divine will? The answer of S Thomas is quaint, but it is a perfect synthesis of that vaster view of the sacramental system which makes of the sacrament a thing as old as the world: "To the third objection let us answer: that the father of the family is not said to be of changeable disposition because he gives different orders to his household according to the variety of seasons, and does not command the same work to be done in summer and in winter; thus there is not mutability in God's doings because he institutes one set of sacraments after the coming of Christ and another set of sacraments in the time of the Old Law; for these latter were fitting as prefigurements of grace, whilst the former are calculated to show forth grace already present amongst us."

CHAPTER III

THE POWER OF SACRAMENTAL SIGNIFICATION

It is the very essence of a sacrament to be a sign; it is its proper definition. "We speak now specifically of sacraments as far as they imply a relationship of sign" ("Specialiter autem nunc loquimur de sacramentis, secundum quod important habitudinem signi"). Let us never deprive a sacrament, even the most excellent sacrament, of this constitutional property of relationship of sign. The greatest realist in the Catholic theology of the sacraments, if he be at all orthodox, proclaims boldly his faith, I do not say in the symbolical nature of the sacrament, but in the demonstrative nature of the sacrament as a sign, or, if we like the word better, in the representative nature of the sacrament as a sign. As we shall see by-and-by, this power of signification inside the one and the same sacrament is not simple but multiple, the sacramental element signifying in various ways and also signifying various things; yet there is a certain definiteness, a clearly outlined circle of signification, which has been traced by the hand of God. It is the divine institution which is responsible directly for the selection of those signs which, again in the words of S Thomas, are given us for a more explicit signification of Christ's grace, through which the human race is sanctified: "Ad expressiorem significationem gratiae Christi, per quam humanum genus sanctificatur." The angelic Doctor adds, with that true liberality of mind so specially his own, that this clear circumscribing of the sacramental signs does not in any way narrow down the road of salvation, because the things which are of indispensable use in the sacraments are commonly to be had, or may be procured, with very little trouble. Sacraments, then, are true signs from heaven. In no other sphere of human reality does the external thing become such a messenger of the internal thing. There is in Question lx, Article iii, a passage of S Thomas which may be called truly classical as stating the power of signification proper to the sacraments; its importance justifies me in giving the Latin first, in spite of its length, to be followed by a translation: "Respondeo dicendum, quod, sicut dictum est (*art. praec.*,) sacramentum proprie dicitur quod ordinatur ad significandam nostram sanctificationem, in qua *tria* possunt considerari: videlicet ipsa *causa* sanctificationis nostrae, quae est passio Christi; et *forma* nostrae sanctificationis, quae consistit in gratia, et virtutibus; et ultimus *finis* sanctificationis nostrae, qui est vita aeterna. Et haec omnia per sacramenta significantur; unde sacramentum est et signum rememorativum ejus quod praecessit, scilicet passionis Christi, et demonstrativum ejus quod in nobis efficitur per Christi passionem, scilicet gratiae, et prognosticum, idest praenuntiativum futurae gloriae." ("My answer is, as has been already said, that the sacrament, properly so-called, is the thing ordained to the purpose of signifying our sanctification; in this *three* phases may be taken into consideration, namely—the *cause* of our sanctification, which is the passion of Christ; the *essence* of our sanctification, which consists in grace and virtue; and then the ultimate *goal* of our sanctification, which is eternal life. Now these three things are signified by the sacraments; therefore a sacrament is a commemorative sign of what has gone before, I mean the passion of Christ, and a demonstrative sign of what is being brought about in us through the passion of Christ, that is grace, and a prognostic, that is a prophetic sign, of the future glory.")

Every sacrament, then, announces something; it brings back the past, it is the voice of the present, it reveals the future. If the sacrament did no longer proclaim as a sign something which is not seen, it would not be a sacrament; in every sacrament there is a past, a present, and a future; the death of Christ is its past; supernatural transformation is its present; eternal glory is its future. It can embrace heaven and earth, time and eternity, because it is a sign; were it only a grace it would be no more than the gift of the present hour; but being a sign the whole history of the spiritual world is reflected in it: "For as often as you shall eat this bread and drink the chalice, you shall show the death of the Lord, until he come." What S Paul says of the Eucharist about its showing forth a past event is true in other ways of every other sacrament. The text we have transcribed from S Thomas is applied by him to every one of the seven sacraments.

Let us make a comparison in order to elucidate more completely this all-important role of the sacraments as being signs of God. If my heart be touched by God's grace, such a spiritual phenomenon, excellent and wonderful as it may be, is not a sign of anything else; it is essentially a thing of the present, and ends, as it were, in itself. It has no relationship of significance with anything either past, present, or future. Such is not the case with the sacraments; through them it has become possible to condense far distant things in one point; through them historic acts of centuries ago are renewed for us with great reality, and we anticipate the future in a very definite way. All this is possible through the power of the sign, which power, shall we say, becoming most modern, "films" the distant thing, and brings it before us at the present hour.

"O sacrum convivium, in quo Christus sumitur; recolitur memoria passionis ejus: mens impletur gratia, et futurae gloriae nobis pignus datur" ("O sacred Banquet, wherein Christ is received, the memory of his passion is kept, the mind is filled with grace, and there is given unto us a pledge of the coming glory"). This verse from the Office of the Blessed Sacrament, when compared with the above text of the *Summa*, betrays at once its Thomistic origin. But though the Eucharist does that function of cosmic representation in the spiritual order in a more excellent degree, all the other sacraments do it in their several ways. All the sacraments give us the blessed power of stepping outside the present. Much confusion of thought in the doctrine of the sacraments, and particularly in the doctrine of the Eucharist, would be spared us if we never let go of that elemental definition of the sacrament, that it is a relationship of signification. Whatever reality there is in a sacrament is deeply modified by this rule of signification. Baptism, to quote only one sacrament, is not any kind of cleansing of the soul, but it is a cleansing of the soul which is a burial with Christ and which is a resurrection with Christ. Baptism is not only the present, but also the past and the future. "Know you not that all we who are baptised in Christ Jesus are baptised in his death? For we are buried together with him by baptism into death: that, as Christ is risen from the dead by the glory of the Father, so we also may walk in newness of life. For if we have been planted together in the likeness of his death, we shall be also in the likeness of his resurrection."

The current definition of the sacrament as an external sign of an internal grace would certainly be too narrow a definition for S Thomas if by internal grace we meant nothing but the actual transformation of the soul. This would only be one-third of the sacramental function. But if by internal grace we also mean the cause of grace—*i.e.*, Christ's passion—and the goal of grace—*i.e.*, eternal life—then the definition may be considered as complete. But to limit the power of significance of the sacrament to the present moment only, to the transformation of the soul at the time when the sacrament is applied to man, would be an unwarranted minimising of the sacramental doctrine, and would make much of the scriptural language unintelligible. How, for instance, could the Eucharist be a memory of Christ if it were merely a supernatural feeding of the soul at the present moment? When Christ said: "Do this for a commemoration of me," he gave the Eucharist an historic import which is not to be found in a mere spiritual raising up of the individual soul. A commemoration is essentially a sign, a monument, something related to a definite act or person of the past.

S Thomas lays down as an axiom that a sacrament is always a thing of the senses. A merely spiritual thing, an act of our intellect or will, could never fulfil that role of sign which is so essential to the sacrament; the sign, on the contrary, is an external manifestation of the intellectual process of thought and volition: "Effectus autem intelligibiles non habent rationem signi." In the same passage S Thomas quotes from S Augustine a very succinct definition of what a sign is: "A sign is that which, besides the impression it makes on the senses, puts one in mind of something else." When I see the baptismal water poured on the head of the catechumen, and when I hear the words of the priest who does the christening, if I am a man of faith, my mind, roused by these external rites and signs, travels a long way. I go back to the Jordan, where Christ is being baptised; I go back to Calvary, where blood and water issue from the side of Christ; my mind leaps forward to that people who stand before the Throne of God in white robes which have been washed in the Blood of the Lamb; and, more audacious still, my mind gazes right into the innermost soul of the catechumen and distinguishes that soul from all other non-baptised souls, through that spiritual seal which makes it a member of Christ. The sacramental sign is pregnant with all that spiritual vision of my faith.

When we speak of signs, we mean, of course, words as well as things; the words are often necessary to complete the signification of the thing. "A repetition of words, when words are added to the visible things in sacraments, is not superfluous, because one receives determination through the other."

In a text already quoted S Thomas makes the clear-cut distinction between the two roads which lie before us, and which lead directly to the passion of Christ—an act of the soul, and the use of external things, "actus animae, usus exteriorum rerum." The former is faith, the latter is the sacrament. Let us give this distinction its full value. The "external things" are as solid a road to Christ as the "act of the soul." The sacramental signs, which are the external things alluded to by the Thomistic distinction, have become, in God's providence, a distinct supernatural world, as real as the supernatural world of the graces given to the souls of men; at the same time, those blessed signs differ radically from the acts of man's soul done under the inspiration of the Holy Ghost. They are things, visible, palpable realities, not breathings of the Spirit in the hearts of men. They are not mere aids to man's memory; they are not only opportune reminders of the invisible. "If anyone say that sacraments have been instituted solely for the purpose of fostering faith, let him be anathema." External things have been taken hold of by God as directly as men's souls have been taken hold of by him. Like this visible planet of ours, the supernatural world of salvation is divided into land and water. The graces of the Holy Ghost are the water; the external things, the sacraments, are the land.

CHAPTER XII

THE ESSENCE OF THE EUCHARISTIC SACRIFICE

Keenness for divine things and love of objective truth have oftentimes led Catholic divines to the very threshold of the unknown. In this matter of the Eucharistic sacrifice they have tried to find out whether there is, or there is not, something that happens in Christ's own self so as to establish him in the state of Victim on our altars. The more extreme spirits among them have looked for the essence of the Eucharistic sacrifice in Christ's own self, not in the sacrament. Their sense of reality seems to remain unsatisfied until Christ's own self be directly touched by the knife of immolation. In their controversy with the Protestant symbolists they have become extreme realists, perhaps ultra-realists, and they end by explaining the sacrifice of Mass in terms of Person, no longer in terms of sacrament. It is as if they conceived the *processus* of the Eucharistic sacrifice to be something in the following order. The glorious Person of Christ is produced on the altar through the power of consecration; under the sacramental veil, no doubt, yet directly in its totality; and, once produced, it is immolated and offered up as the perfect sacrifice, in some mysterious, indefinable manner. They would call it, perhaps, sacramental manner, though by an abuse of words, but their commonest term is the word "mystical." In other words, they put Christ's self first, the sacrifice and the sacrament after. This is, I think, a fair description of much theological and devotional phraseology inside the liberal tolerance of Catholic dogma.

At first sight it may seem an easier, and even more helpful, concept of the Eucharistic sacrifice, to think of Christ's glorious Person as being in a mysterious way on the altar, as dying mystically, and as being offered up mystically; yet when we come to strict theology, and when we have to state the Eucharist in terms which will make it possible for us to defend it against all enemies, we can no longer express the nature of the Catholic sacrifice in the way just indicated. Shall we say that no one need be disturbed if, for the practical working of his devotion, he adopts the *processus* of thought I have described? The contents of the Eucharistic mystery are so great that whosoever holds faithfully to Transubstantiation and the Real Presence cannot err substantially ever after. At the same time there is a need for clear thinking in this sublime matter as in everything else, if sentiment, even pious sentiment, is to be kept within the bounds of the objective realities.

It is evident that S Thomas, who represents so much of Catholic thought and tradition, is far from that view of the Eucharistic sacrifice which I have given above. At no time does S Thomas feel the need of asking himself whether anything wonderful happens within Christ's own self when Mass is offered up; in fact, it is a cardinal point of his theology to deny every kind of change in Christ's own Person in the whole Eucharistic *processus*. S Thomas is too keen and too clear-headed a sacramentalist ever to become an ultra-realist; even when he says that Christ is immolated in the sacrament, his whole mode of thinking is sacramental, as his words imply, not natural, in the sense in which in a former chapter we opposed the sacrament to nature.

A long study of the Eucharistic doctrine of S Thomas fills one with admiration for his power of grasping a truth and never swerving from it. When one sees how constant has been the tendency of pious men to slip from sacramental thought into natural thought one cannot help admiring S Thomas, who does not show one single instance of such a lapse.

The essence, then, of the sacrifice of Mass ought to be completely stated before we reach Christ in the personal aspect; that is to say, the Eucharistic sacrifice is not directly a mystery of Christ's Person, but it is directly a mystery of Christ's Body and Blood. Christ's Body is offered up, Christ's Blood is offered up; these are the inward kernel of the external sign in the sacrificial rite; and beyond these—the Body and the Blood—the sacrament, as sacrament, does not go. No conclusion could be more certain. If the Eucharist is to remain a sacrament in our theology, the Body of Christ and the Blood of Christ must be that divine prolongation of our sacramental *actio* at Mass, otherwise the sacrament would not signify the truth. Body and Blood must be the inward kernel of the external signification. In this we must find the whole essence of the sacrifice; I might almost say we must rest content with this and not go beyond, as we have no authority to go beyond.

When we offer up the great sacrifice we say that we are acting Christ's death sacramentally. Now, Christ's death is Body and Blood separated; we do neither more nor less when we sacrifice at the altar. We do not enter directly into the mystery of Christ's Person; we enter into the mystery of Christ's Body and Blood. In the mystery of Christ's Body and Blood we must find the essence of the Eucharistic sacrifice.

The sacrifice of Mass, then, is this, that we have a separation between Christ's Body and Christ's Blood brought about, not by a fiat of God's omnipotence, irrespective of any precedent or human connections, but as a prolongation, as the inward kernel of reality, of the whole commemorative rite which historically, and as an unbroken chain of remembrance, is linked up with the dead Christ on the cross. Separation of Body and Blood on the altar in itself, absolutely considered, would not make a sacrifice; nor would a figurative rite make a true sacrifice; but the two together, one as the human act of commemoration, and the other as the divine prolongation, the infinitely real inwardness, of that same act, make the Eucharistic sacrifice. Were we to admit that in the sacrifice of Mass there is some mysterious change in the state of Christ's self, this change could not be anywhere else than in his Body and in his Blood, as the words of consecration do not signify anything sacramentally beyond Body and Blood. Suppose, for the sake of argument, that the immolation of Christ on the altar really affected the Person of Christ, it could not affect him except in his Body and in his Blood. It is the Body that is offered up, it is the Blood that is poured out in virtue of the consecration words. By all the laws of sacramental reality we ought not to look for the essence of the sacrifice to any other portions of Christ than his Body and his Blood, supposing even that an internal change in Christ were necessary in order to make Mass a real and actual sacrifice. But S Thomas has succeeded in giving to Mass the highest degree of sacrificial reality, nay, even of immolation, without the necessity of any change whatever in Christ's own self.

It is the misfortune of anyone who undertakes to expound these high matters that he has constantly to promise further explanations, as he feels, as by instinct, the reader's temporary bewilderment. Here I have to promise a chapter to be written on the nature of Eucharistic concomitance, where it will be shown how the whole Person of Christ, with all the adjuncts of a complete life, may be in the Eucharist, though the concept of the Eucharistic sacrifice discards everything except the Body and Blood of Christ.

The Council of Trent insists emphatically on the distinction of role between sacrament and concomitance, copying, almost word for word, the language of S Thomas himself. But it is no exaggeration to say that for the purpose of explaining the sacrifice of Mass we need not remember anything else except Christ's Body and Christ's Blood. To such an extent is this accurate that if Mass had been celebrated by one of the Apostles directly after Christ's death on the cross, when Body and Blood were separated, and Christ's Soul was in limbo, there would have been as complete and as true a sacrifice as on any Christian altar to-day. The principal portion of Christ's Person, his Soul, would not have been united to that Body and that Blood; but this could make no difference in the sacramental sacrifice as the sacramental signification terminates directly and exclusively in Christ's Body and Christ's Blood.

This hypothesis is made much of by S Thomas and the other medieval theologians. "The soul of Christ is in the sacrament through real concomitance, because it is not without the body; but it is not in the sacrament through the power of consecration, and therefore if this sacrament had been consecrated or celebrated at the time when the soul was really separated from the body, the soul of Christ would not have been under the sacrament." And again: "If at the time of Christ's passion when the blood was really separated from the body of Christ this sacrament had been consecrated, under the appearance of bread there would only have been the body, and under the appearance of wine there would only have been the blood."

It is evident from the very nature of the hypothesis here made by S Thomas that the reality of the Eucharistic sacrifice could never depend on an intrinsic change, either in Christ's Person or in Christ's Body and Blood at the moment of the sacrificial immolation on the Christian altar. May we not say that the Eucharistic immolation by its very nature is supposed to take Christ's Body and Christ's Blood such as it finds them, in the state in which they happen to be? The immolation itself never causes a new state, either in Christ's Person or in Christ's Body and Blood. If Christ, considered in his natural existence, be a mortal man like ourselves, as he was at the Last Supper, the Eucharistic immolation is accomplished in the mortal Body and Blood; if Christ, in his natural existence, be in the glorious state as he is now in heaven, the Eucharistic immolation is accomplished in an immortal Body and Blood; if Christ be really dead, the Eucharistic immolation is accomplished in a Body and Blood which are not inhabited by the Soul which give life. In other words, the Eucharistic immolation is above the states either of Christ's Person or of Christ's Body and Blood; it does not cause any state. Such varieties of state are caused by Christ's natural mode of existence at the time. This projection, as we might call it, of either the passing or the permanent state of Christ, as considered in his natural existence, into the Eucharistic existence is thus stated by S Thomas: "Whatever belongs to Christ as considered in himself (*i.e.*, what is intrinsic to Christ) may be attributed to him both in his natural existence and in his sacramental existence, such as to live, to die, to suffer pain, to be animate or inanimate, and other such attributes. But whatever concerns Christ in connection with external bodies (*i.e.*, what is extrinsic to Christ), can be attributed to him in his natural existence only, and not in his sacramental existence, such as to be mocked, to be spat upon, to be crucified, to be scourged, and other such things."

The meaning of S Thomas is clear and extremely important. Variety of state in the sacrament only comes from variety of state in Christ's natural existence; sacramental immolation, as such, does not cause a new variety of state. As a further and even bolder hypothesis S Thomas takes it for granted that if an Apostle had consecrated actually at the moment of Christ's dying, or if the consecrated elements had been preserved during the whole drama of Christ's agony on the cross, there would have been real suffering and real death in the blessed sacrament then, though there would not have been in the sacrament the external violence done to Christ's Body by the executioners. This S Thomas expresses thus: "And therefore Christ as he is under the sacrament cannot suffer (*i.e.*, external violence), but he can die" ("Et ideo Christus, secundum quod est sub hoc sacramento, pati non potest, potest tamen mori"). This, of course, refers to the hypothetical sacramental presence at the moment of the crucifixion.

Suppositions like this are very instructive because they bring home to us the great truth that if there are changes in Christ's state under the Eucharistic form, such changes are not the result of the sacramental immolation, but they are anterior to it; we offer up at the altar the Body and Blood such as we find them, I say this again.

It may be described as a tendency of modern piety to read into the mystery of the Eucharistic sacrifice certain elements of a more drastic kind which seem to give greater reality to the Eucharistic immolation than is warranted by the strictly sacramental view. But let us remember over and over again that in the sacrament we are not dealing with the natural life of Christ; we are dealing with his representative life, representing the natural life. The Eucharistic Body and the Eucharistic Blood represent Christ's natural Body and Christ's natural Blood. The Protestant would go so far as to say that the Eucharistic bread and wine represent Christ's Body and Christ's Blood; the Catholic goes beyond that and says that Christ's Eucharistic Body under the appearance of bread, and Christ's Eucharistic Blood under the appearance of wine, represent Christ's natural Body and Christ's natural Blood as they were on Calvary. This is the true and final expression of sacramental representation; and such representation suffices by itself to constitute the sacrifice, because the representation is of that period of Christ's wonderful existence when he was nothing but sacrifice, as his Blood was separated from his Body.

Protestantism has denied the Eucharistic sacrifice on various grounds, into which we need not enter for the moment. The non-Catholic attitude which in a way is nearest to Catholicism is that frame of mind which admits all, or nearly all, of the

Catholic doctrine of the Real Presence, and yet denies the Eucharistic sacrifice. It is a belief in the Eucharist minus the sacrifice. The earlier periods of Protestantism, chiefly of Lutheranism, exhibited that attitude of an almost total faith in the Eucharistic realities combined with fierce denial of the Eucharistic sacrifice.

To meet this kind of unbelief the Church might have adopted two modes of defence; she might have said that the whole Eucharistic doctrine, as it stands, as the Scriptures reveal it, as those very Protestants of the meeker type hold it, with the dual consecration, must be a sacrifice if it has any meaning at all; that the Church, in her Eucharistic liturgy as handed down from the Apostles, is a sacrificant as well as a communicant, from the very nature of the case.

Or the Church might have appealed to another revelation, as if she had said that she knew through tradition that the Eucharistic rite contained a hidden element of sacrifice which is not evident in the rite itself, but which is known to the Church in virtue of her revelation *ad hoc*. The Church then would have made it her principal business to produce the authentic proofs of such revelation.

It is evident that the line of defence of the Church has been the former of the two alternatives. The Church has maintained that the Eucharistic rite, as she learned it from Christ and his Apostles, with the dual consecration and all the sacramental signification that surrounds it, is a true sacrifice. The Church does not appeal to a hidden element, to something recondite, not manifested in Eucharistic revelation such as it stands in the Scriptures. The Church says this: the Eucharist as we have learned it from the Son of God and his Apostles, as even those well-meaning Protestants hold it, is an evident sacrifice in the eyes of all those who have the clear vision of the things of Christ.

CHAPTER XVII

TRANSUBSTANTIATION

Nothing could give us a clearer insight into the Eucharistic doctrine than the position which Transubstantiation holds in the Eucharist. We have already quoted S Thomas (P. III, Q. lxxviii, Art. iv) telling us that the power which changes comes after the power of signification; in other words, the whole external sacramental action in words and deeds signifies one thing, and one thing only, the Body of Christ and the Blood of Christ. This is the oldest form under which we meet the Eucharist in Christian tradition. The Church has simply given a literal interpretation to the words of the Eucharistic rite. It was not said first that bread was being changed into Christ's Body and that wine was being changed into Christ's Blood; what was said first and is said at all times, is: "This is my Body, this is my Blood"; the additional concept of change may be truly called an after-thought.

The Church could not give the reason of her great sacramental utterances without giving for her explanation this mysterious change which is so near to the heart of the main mystery itself that it may truly be called a part of it. The substance of bread is changed into Christ's Body and the substance of wine is changed into Christ's Blood. Transubstantiation, then, is not so much the sacrament, as the divinely revealed explanation of the truth of the sacrament; Transubstantiation is not the Eucharistic sacrifice, but it is the hidden power that makes the sacrifice a reality, not a mere symbol.

An instance from another portion of Catholic theology makes this relative position of Transubstantiation in the Eucharistic mystery quite comprehensible.

Catholic theology holds that God creates directly every human soul, and unites it with the human embryo. Now this doctrine of God's direct creative act in producing the soul is not a doctrine that stands in the first rank of truths; but it is a doctrine which has to be brought in as the only satisfactory hypothesis in the explanation of man's nature. A doctrine that stands in the first rank of evidence is this, that man, as we know him, is endowed with an intellectual soul; this is the thing that matters to us, and which is evident to us in its own directness of proof. Yet when we come to ask the question, How is this intellectual principle found in man? the only answer is this: God creates it in every instance. So it is with Transubstantiation. The doctrine that stands in the first rank of evidence is the

Body and Blood of Christ given to us in the form of sacrifice. This is the mystery we approach at once; we enter into it directly; nothing prepares us for it except the authority of Christ and his Church. In matters of the Eucharist we truly enter at once *in medias res*; so to speak, we stumble without any preparation on the sacrament of Christ's Body and Christ's Blood. The holiest thing is the first thing we meet. We do not bring Christ down from heaven; we do not raise him up from the depths through the sacramental signification; he is in our hands and in our mouths before we know where we are. The sacrifice is consummated through the lightening power of the sacramental words that announce it. Overawed, as it were, by the might of the thing that has happened, we ask: How did it happen? The answer is, Transubstantiation. As in the case of the human personality shining in power of intellect, and showing forth a splendid soul, the unseen fiat of God in a mother's womb is the only satisfactory hypothesis at the root of that splendour of personality which meets me in the human being, perfect in mind and body, so is Transubstantiation at the root of the Eucharistic blessings.

Transubstantiation, then, is not, and could not be, the same thing as the Eucharist, both in its aspect of sacrifice and food; but it is at the root of the sacrament, deep down in the abyss of being, where God's omnipotence is supreme.

Theologians sometimes, more devout than learned, have given this visualising of the Eucharistic sacrifice. In every sacrifice, they said, the first thing is the bringing in of the victim; then there is the consecration of the victim; and thirdly there is its immolation. They thought that Transubstantiation could be made to answer exactly for the first stage of a sacrifice, the bringing in of a victim, as, through it, Christ's Body and Christ's Blood were brought to our altars. But who does not see how infelicitous a role Transubstantiation is thus given? It places it in the first rank of sacramental truth, instead of making it the explanation of sacramental truth. In such a theory Transubstantiation would be the sacrament itself, and we should have for sacrament, not a divine thing, but the act of God in itself, because Transubstantiation is the act of God. It is as if we made that act by which he creates every individual soul part and parcel of the individual nature of the men whom we meet. This, of course, would be an unpardonable confusion of thought. Let us say it once more, Transubstantiation is not the same thing as the sacrament of Christ's Body and Christ's Blood; those things we hold in virtue of sacramental formulas of consecration; but it is the hidden act of God, which is absolutely indispensable if the sacramental consecration be true.

There is a beautiful phrase of S Thomas in the seventy-fifth Question, Article two, *ad primum*. The article sets out to prove that the substance of bread and wine does not remain after the consecration: "God has yoked his divinity, that is to say, his divine power, to bread and wine, not so that they should remain in the sacrament, but so as to make from bread and wine, his body and his blood" ("Deus conjugavit divinitatem suam, idest divinam virtutem, pani et vino, non ut remaneant in hoc sacramento, sed ut faciat inde corpus et sanguinem suum").

The power we call Transubstantiation is a transient act, whilst the sacrament abides for a time, more or less prolonged. This power does not remain in the sacrament, but the Body and Blood of Christ remain. This consideration should be enough to make it clear to us what a difference there is between Transubstantiation and the sacrament properly so called; and to show what confusion would arise in our theological thinking if we made Transubstantiation at any time to stand for an element in the essence of the Eucharistic sacrifice.

After these considerations on the comparatively relative position of Transubstantiation in the Eucharistic doctrine, let us come now to a few aspects which will endear to us this divine thing, Transubstantiation, as being the most simple—nay, even the most beautiful explanation of all we know of the Eucharistic mystery. If it is not the sacrament itself, it is certainly the sweet and gracious mother of the sacrament. In its simplicity it has all the grace and charm of eternal wisdom.

The best way I know in order to make clear to the reader the glory of Transubstantiation is this assertion, that after Christ, the Son of God, had done the great deed of the first consecration at the Last Supper, the miracle was complete, and nothing new has happened since. The circumstance that thousands of priests consecrate to-day in all parts of the world is no new marvel. Transubstantiation contained it all from the beginning. Transubstantiation is the power of Christ to change bread into his Body and wine into his Blood. Now this is an absolute power, not limited in any way. If the thing can be done once, it can be done always, in every place, wherever bread and wine are found. There are no fresh, no new difficulties, because the power of Transubstantiation is concerned directly with the whole species of bread and wine. If you admit once that Christ has power to raise up the dead, or if he has raised up a dead man once, you are not surprised if he raises up a hundred or a thousand or a million dead men; it is all the same to him, if he has power over death. It would, indeed, be a childish attitude of mind to think that it is more difficult for God to heal ten lepers than to heal one leper, to raise up ten dead men than to raise up one dead man. So with this power of Transubstantiation: if one piece of bread, if one cup of wine may be changed by Christ into his Body and his Blood, why not a hundred breads or a hundred cups? The mystery is identical.

There is truly no more reason to be astonished at the number of Eucharistic sacrifices offered up than at the number of Baptisms administered in the world. If there is the power in the Church to regenerate into spiritual life one soul—and this power is a tremendous power, much greater than we think—every soul may be brought under the influence of Baptismal regeneration. If Christ, holding bread and the cup of wine, could declare them to be the same thing as the Body and the Blood that then were constituent elements of his living Personality, the same declaration may be repeated with the same truthfulness, because the underlying power remains unaltered, undiminished: this is Transubstantiation. Its wisdom, or, if you prefer, the wisdom of the Church, in declaring Transubstantiation to be the only explanation she has of her mystery of faith, may be seen more clearly if we compare Transubstantiation with another mode, a hypothetical one, of course, which has been excogitated by thinkers, more ardent, perhaps, than illumined, in order to have a satisfactory answer to the question how Christ is present on so many altars. They have recourse to metaphysical theories on the nature of space and place; they have said, in so many words, that the Body of Christ could come into every corner of the world simultaneously, as possessing a kind of multiplicity of presence. Such a theory, if it mean anything at all, would certainly imply this one element, that Christ, in his bodily nature, would be moving backward and forward in space with incredible rapidity so as to be present on every altar at the moment of consecration. This is a bewildering way of explaining the Real Presence, and the fact of its having been patronised by pious men does not make it less confusing. It would make of the Eucharist a thing of material mobility and velocity. Not so Transubstantiation. Wherever a priest, in the virtue of Christ, pronounces the sacramental consecration, the substance of the bread and the substance of the wine are changed into that one thing, the substance of Christ's Body and the substance of Christ's Blood. There is no bringing down from heaven of the Body and Blood of Christ; this is not the Eucharist; but Christ's Body and Christ's Blood are truly produced in an act of divine power, as grace is produced in the human soul at Baptism. The thing produced in the Eucharist is, of course, wonderfully greater than that produced in Baptism; but in both cases it is a production—nay, in both cases it is a change. In Baptism the soul is changed from sin unto grace; in the Eucharist the substance of bread and the substance of wine are changed into the substance of Christ's Body, into the substance of Christ's Blood.

It is not only a change into a greater thing than Baptism, but it is also a greater change, because the whole reality is changed, down to the very roots of being; yet, let us repeat it, in both cases, in Baptism and in the Eucharist, the sacrament is a changing.

Multiplicity of the sacramental act, both in time and space, adds nothing to the sacrament. In the words of S Thomas, we do not say, or ought not to say, that Christ is on many altars, as in so many places, but as in the sacrament: "The body of Christ is not in this sacrament in the manner in which a body is in a place, having its dimensions rounded off by the place; but he is present in a certain special manner, which belongs exclusively to this sacrament; so we say that the body of Christ is on many altars, not as in so many places, but as in the sacrament; by which we do not mean that Christ is there only in a sign, although the sacrament be of the genus sign; but we understand that the body is there . . . according to the manner proper to the sacrament" ("Corpus Christi non est eo modo in hoc sacramento, sicut corpus in loco, quod suis dimensionibus loco commensuratur, sed quodam speciali modo, qui est proprius huic sacramento: unde dicimus, quod corpus Christi est in diversis altaribus, non sicut in diversis locis, sed sicut in sacramento: per quod non intelligimus, quod Christus sit ibi solum sicut in signo, licet sacramentum sit in genere signi; sed intelligimus corpus Christi hic esse, sicut dictum est . . . secundum modum proprium huic sacramento").

The uninitiated may be startled when he hears S Thomas declare that the Body of Christ in the sacrament is not in a place, as he is in heaven in a place; yet such is the emphatic and unswerving teaching of S Thomas. For the great Doctor it is simply unthinkable—nay, it implies a metaphysical contradiction—that the Body of Christ should ever be considered as moving simultaneously from place to place, or as overcoming, in some miraculous manner, all spatial hindrances. Transubstantiation is infinitely simpler. Wherever bread is found, wherever wine is found, their hidden substance is transubstantiated into the hidden substance of Christ's Body and Blood, in the same way in which it was done at the Last Supper. This is what S Thomas means when he says that the Body of Christ is not in a place but in a sacrament. The thing, the Body of Christ, is not taken hold of, hurried through space and put into a definite place on a definite altar; this is not Eucharist at all; but the divine invocation, as the words of consecration are so often called by the Fathers, makes the substance of a definite bread and the substance of a definite cup of wine into a new thing, and what is that new thing? It is simply that thing which is in heaven, the Body and Blood of Christ, but which, not for one instant, has left heaven.

The usual term which makes the difference between the Catholic and the Protestant view of the Eucharist is "Real Presence." Christ's Body and Christ's Blood are really present—nay, the whole Christ is really present, as will be seen in a later chapter. But, confining ourselves to Body and Blood, they are present; yet we say with great attention to accuracy of thought that Christ is not on the altar as in a place. No doubt for most men to be present somewhere is the same thing as being placed there; there is, however, a vast difference. The bread and wine before the consecration are truly on the altar as in a place, they are put on the altar by the minister. What are called the accidents of bread and wine, the external appearances, remain on the altar during the sacrifice, even after the consecration. But there is a thing, an inward element of reality in that bread and wine which the sacramental consecration changes into a much greater reality, Christ's Body and Christ's Blood; and that change is the only reason why Christ is there.

Christ is on the altar as in a sacrament, according to the fine expression of S Thomas, in virtue of a hidden change within the nature of the bread and wine. Here we have the application in its sublimest form, that the sacrament produces the thing which it signifies; it signifies the Body and Blood of Christ, and it produces It.

As already insinuated, the difference between the Eucharist and the other sacraments is not one of kind, but one of degree. They are all of them powers of changing. In the other sacraments the change is in the soul of men, in this sacrament the change is in the very elements, bread and wine. Perhaps we think it a less difficult marvel, a lighter tax on our faith, that the soul of the infant, through Baptismal regeneration, should receive the life of God, the imprint of Christ, the likeness of the angels, than that bread and wine should be made into the holy thing that was on the cross, that was poured out on Calvary. But is it really a more incredible thing?

S Thomas speaks of the two marvels in the same breath, as if they were not essentially different, as if the one ought to prepare us for the other: "What the power of the Holy Ghost is with regard to the water of Baptism, this the true body of Christ is with regard to the appearances of bread and wine" ("Sicut autem se habet virtus Spiritus Sancti ad aquam baptismi, ita se habet corpus Christi verum ad speciem panis et vini"). Once we admit that God dwells in material things as a source of eternal life—and this is the very concept of the Christian sacrament—have we not admitted the Eucharistic mystery, the Real

Presence? The thing which is Christ's Body and Christ's Blood is under the material appearances of bread and wine.

The Christian sacraments are infinitely fertile things. The material, the external sign in the word and element becomes fruitful beyond calculation in the realm of grace. Is it not an ancient metaphor with the Fathers to call the baptismal waters a mother's womb? The Eucharistic sacrament is the most fertile of them, yet its fertility belongs to the same secret source of life.

The older mode of conceiving the Eucharist places itself exclusively at this angle of vision, the wonderful productiveness of power. Christ's Eucharistic Body is produced in the manner in which his divine hands produced bread when he multiplied the loaves. The older thinkers are not hampered by what might be called the spatial difficulty in the Eucharist; they saw no spatial difficulty, because there is none. The power of Christ to change bread and wine is the only thing they knew of, and their Eucharistic theology is, indeed, simple in the extreme, because they believed in the power of the sacrament to produce what it signifies.

Two simple metaphysical concepts of S Thomas may fitly conclude this chapter. There is in the metaphysical presentment of the Eucharist by S Thomas a wonderful calmness of outlook, and a complete avoidance of the worry of thought from which even good theologians have not always been able to escape. "Through the power of a finite agent no one form can be changed into another form, no one matter can be changed into another matter; but such a change can be effected through the power of an infinite agent, whose action extends over the whole realm of being. . . . What is being in one, the author of being may change into that which is being in another, by removing that which made the difference." When S Thomas says that God has power over the whole realm of being he has truly given us the last word in this matter; and yet how simple this last word is: "Habet actionem in totum ens."

Another such serene utterance is concerned with the cessation of the sacramental presence. When the appearances of bread and wine lose their identity, as they do very rapidly—for the Eucharist, being a sacrament, is essentially of a transient nature—the Body and Blood also cease to be present. How do Body and Blood cease to be there? How does It depart? "The body of Christ remains in the sacrament, not only for the day after the consecration, but even for a future time, as long as the sacramental appearances remain. If they cease to be what they are, then the body of Christ ceases to be under them, not because the body of Christ depends on them (for its existence), but simply because the relationship of Christ's body to those appearances is taken away. In this manner God ceases to be the Lord of a creature whose existence ceases" ("Corpus Christi remanet in hoc sacramento, non solum in crastino, sed etiam in futuro, quousque species sacramentales manent, quibus cessantibus, desinit esse corpus Christi sub eis, non quia ab eis dependeat, sed quia tollitur habitudo corporis Christi ad illas species: per quem modum Deus desinit esse dominus creaturae desinentis").

May it not be said that the Eucharistic mystery is really no exception to those laws of being, both finite and infinite, created and increate, which Catholic theology has studied and enunciated with success? But if, instead of metaphysics of being, we were to use sentiment and imagination in giving the account of our faith, should we not very soon find ourselves hopelessly entangled?

CHAPTER XXII

THE EUCHARISTIC BANQUET

We have come nearly to the end of our book, and perhaps more than one reader may be mildly shocked to find that a book could be written on the Eucharist with so little about Holy Communion. But let me assure my patient friend who has followed me so far that nothing is dearer to me than the Bread of Life. I could write him a whole book on the subject, and not say all I would love to say. But as this little effort bears the name of *A Key to the Doctrine of the Eucharist,* I am not so much a dispenser of the divine Bread as an opener of the mystical Bethlehem, the House of Bread. The Bread of Life, the Eucharist as the food of man, is not to be found anywhere and everywhere, but it is essentially a thing from the altar. "The chalice of benediction which we bless, is it not the communion of the blood of Christ? And the bread which we break, is it not the partaking of the body of the Lord? . . . Behold Israel according to the flesh. Are not they that eat of the sacrifice partakers of the altar?" At no time ought we to surrender this great Christian privilege that we are partakers of the altar of God. It is the glory of the Eucharistic bread that it is not ordinary divine bread, but a bread from the altar of God.

There ought not to be in classical Christianity a real division of spiritual attitude between Mass and Communion. Suppose, *per impossibile*, that there were an extreme multiplicity of private communions by the faithful, on the one hand, and an ever-dwindling attendance at the sacrifice of Mass on the other hand, it would indeed be the gravest spiritual disorder; it would falsify the Eucharistic setting; it would lower the sacrament through a misconception of its true role. The *usus sacramenti*, as S Thomas calls it constantly, the use of the sacrament, follows upon the sacrament according to that terse phrase on which we have already commented. The sacrament-sacrifice is followed by the sacrament-food. Such was the order at the institution of the Eucharist, when Christ himself partook, before giving to his Apostles, thus completing in his own Person the whole Eucharistic sacrament.

It is anything but service done to this greatest of the Catholic sacraments to describe Holy Communion in terms which many a pantheist might love. The union with God when we eat the Bread of Life takes hold of us in a very definite portion of our spiritual being; it brings us back, as all sacraments do bring us back, to the passion of Christ; we take and eat the holy Thing that is offered up, the Body; we drink the cup of the testament in the Blood of Christ. Communion is a sacramental thing, and in this it differs from those other visitations of the spirit which lead men to God, not sacramentally but personally.

Divine things are wonderfully ordered; they do not encroach on each other, their functions are not interchangeable. Not all the spiritual work is done by the sacrament; the Spirit himself bloweth where he listeth; Eucharistic Communion is not all communion with God; but it is a definite communion with the Christ who shed his Blood for us.

The sixth chapter of the Gospel of S John, where Christ announces the gift of the Bread of Life, is no mere promise of a new manna coming down from heaven without passing through the altar of sacrifice. "The bread of God is that which cometh down from heaven and giveth life to the world." Now that Bread of God, Christ himself, comes down from heaven, not merely as a thing falling gently to the ground, just to be gathered up by man, but it comes down from heaven with the set purpose of a sacrificial nature: "Because I came down from heaven not to do my own will, but the will of him that sent me." If he is the living Bread, a Bread that will give life to the world, it is because he first has given his Flesh for the life of the world. "This is the bread which cometh down from heaven: that if any man eat of it, he may not die. I am the living bread which came down from heaven. If any man eat of this bread he shall live for ever: and the bread that I will give is my flesh, for the life of the world." These last words, "And the bread I will give is my flesh, for the life of the world," have a clear sacrificial ring about them. Moreover, that emphatic distinction between flesh and blood, which is such a marked feature of Christ's discourse at Capharnaum, is clearly an allusion to the ever-recurring sacrifices of flesh and blood.

The Eucharistic banquet, then, is essentially a sacrificial banquet: as such it makes an impassable gulf between light and darkness, between the world and God, between Satan and Christ. "You cannot drink the chalice of the Lord and the chalice of devils: you cannot be partakers of the table of the Lord and the table of the devils." The chalice of the devils and the table of the devils in this text are not metaphorical, immaterial things as might appear to some who are always eager to give to the Eucharistic texts of the Scriptures merely symbolical meaning. St Paul means a very material thing, the meats that come from the altar before the idol in the heathen temples. "But the things which the heathens sacrifice, they sacrifice to devils and not to God. And I would not that you should be made partakers with devils."

Do any of my readers still remember the ancient theological distinction between the "sacrament," the "sacrament and thing," and the "thing" which I have explained in a former chapter? It is a favourite idea with S Thomas that the "thing" of the sacrament, or, if you like, the sacramental grace, is the mystical Body of Christ; Christ's sacramental Body makes Christ's mystical Body. The whole Eucharistic spirit is a spirit of charity, a spirit between the members of Christ. Here again S Paul says the trenchant word: "For we, being many, are one bread, one body: all that partake of one bread." The sacrament signifies this society of the elect, as it signifies the true Body of Christ. So much is S Thomas convinced of this membership with Christ's mystical Body being the essence of the Eucharistic grace in the soul of man that he sees there the reason why communion in mortal sin is not only a grievous offence, but is actually a sacrilege. "Whosoever, then, receives the sacrament, signifies by that very fact that he is united to Christ and incorporated into his members. Now this (union with Christ) takes place through faith fully informed (with charity) which no one can possess with the guilt of mortal sin. And therefore it is manifest that whosoever receives the sacrament with the guilt of mortal sin on him, commits a falsehood against this sacrament, and accordingly he incurs a sacrilege as one who violates the sacrament; and for this reason he sins mortally."

Membership with Christ and the whole mystical Body of Christ ought to be considered to be the specific Eucharistic grace, as distinguished from all other graces. "Qui manducat meam earnem et bibit meum sanguinem, in me manet, et ego in illo. Sicut misit me vivens Pater, et ego vivo propter Patrem: et qui manducat me, et ipse vivet propter me." To make this profession of divine membership in a state of mortal sin is a direct violation of the truth of things. S Thomas reasons out that heinous offence to its logical consequences; he calls it in the text quoted: "*Falsitatem in hoc sacramento*," a falseness in the very midst of the sacrament.

The Eucharistic sacrifice is profoundly a corporate act; it is the act of the Church herself; we are never isolated worshippers in the great rite, even when we are but a few gathered at the altar in some remote church, as we are in communion with the whole Catholic Church. But the eating of the divine offering is again invested with social significance. We become all members of one Body, eating one Bread: this is the classical, traditional concept of the Eucharistic assemblies of Christians. The society of the elect here on earth are gathered in love and brotherhood, performing such mysterious rites as will open the portals of heaven itself, and make Angels and men come together. It would be a disastrous day for the Christian cause if, in the minds of the faithful, the Eucharistic mystery were shorn of that all-important social character, if their frequent eating of the heavenly Bread meant to them nothing but individual spiritual satisfaction, without furthering the great cause of Christ's mystical Body, the society of the elect.

The world's salvation is in the Eucharist. This is not a hyperbolical phrase; it is a sober statement of spiritual reality. The world's salvation is its approximation to the redemptive mystery of Christ. If this mystery becomes the constant occupation of human society, its daily deed, its chief concern, its highest aspiration, then society is saved. Holy Mass is the difference between paganism and Christianity, let us be under no illusion. There is no charity possible as an institution, as a thing that is a world-power, outside the sacrament of Christ's mystical Body. The ideal world of which the saint dreams is a human society where there is practical knowledge of the meaning of the Eucharistic sacrifice, where men and women have a clear comprehension of the divine mysteries, and where purity and justice are cherished because without them men would be unfit for the Communion of the Body of God.